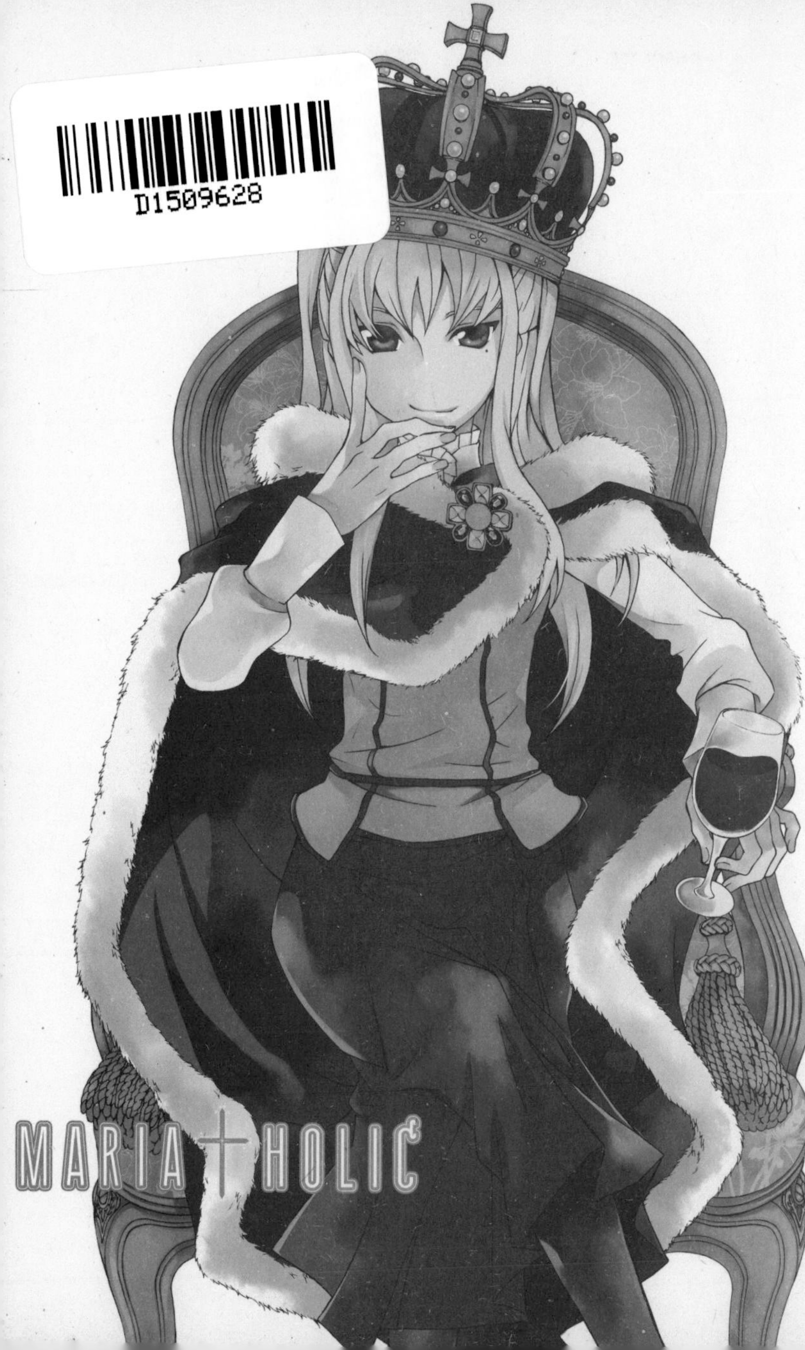
MARIA†HOLIC

MARIA
HOLIC

7

MARIA ✝ HOLIC

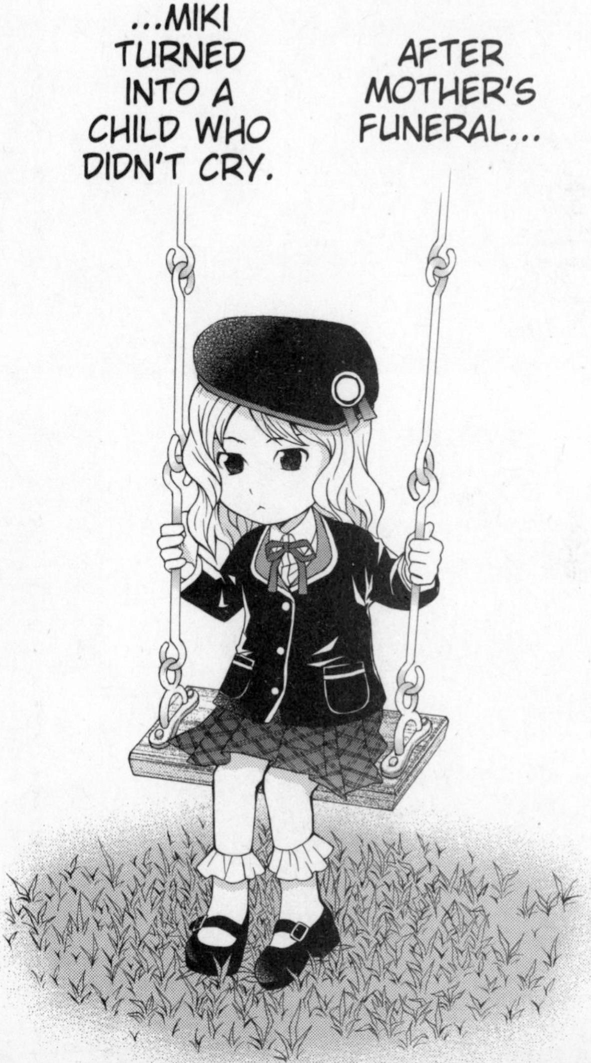
AFTER MOTHER'S FUNERAL...
...MIKI TURNED INTO A CHILD WHO DIDN'T CRY.

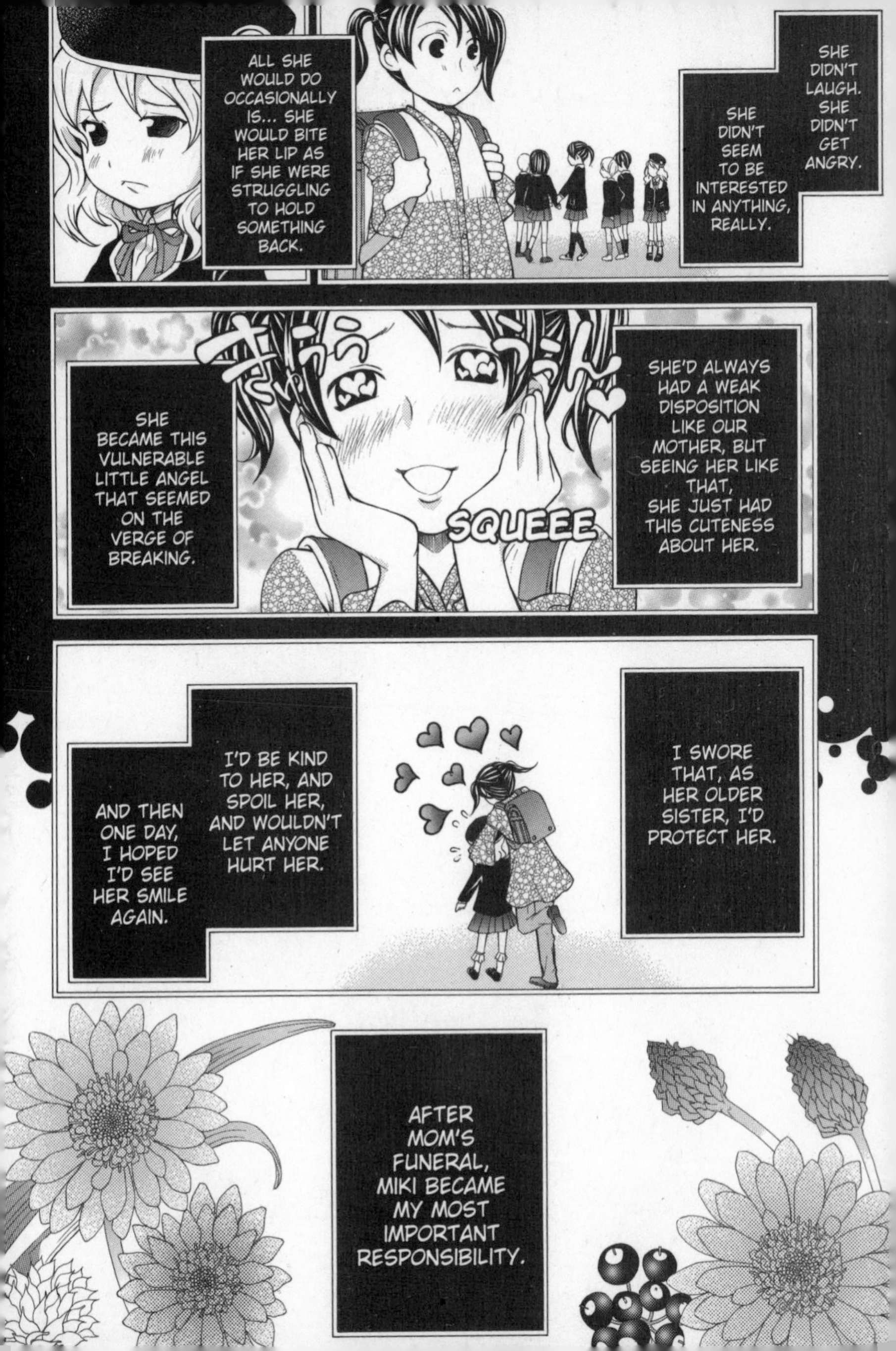
SHE DIDN'T LAUGH. SHE DIDN'T GET ANGRY.
SHE DIDN'T SEEM TO BE INTERESTED IN ANYTHING, REALLY.
ALL SHE WOULD DO OCCASIONALLY IS... SHE WOULD BITE HER LIP AS IF SHE WERE STRUGGLING TO HOLD SOMETHING BACK.
SHE'D ALWAYS HAD A WEAK DISPOSITION LIKE OUR MOTHER, BUT SEEING HER LIKE THAT, SHE JUST HAD THIS CUTENESS ABOUT HER.
SQUEEE
SHE BECAME THIS VULNERABLE LITTLE ANGEL THAT SEEMED ON THE VERGE OF BREAKING.
I SWORE THAT, AS HER OLDER SISTER, I'D PROTECT HER.
I'D BE KIND TO HER, AND SPOIL HER, AND WOULDN'T LET ANYONE HURT HER.
AND THEN ONE DAY, I HOPED I'D SEE HER SMILE AGAIN.
AFTER MOM'S FUNERAL, MIKI BECAME MY MOST IMPORTANT RESPONSIBILITY.

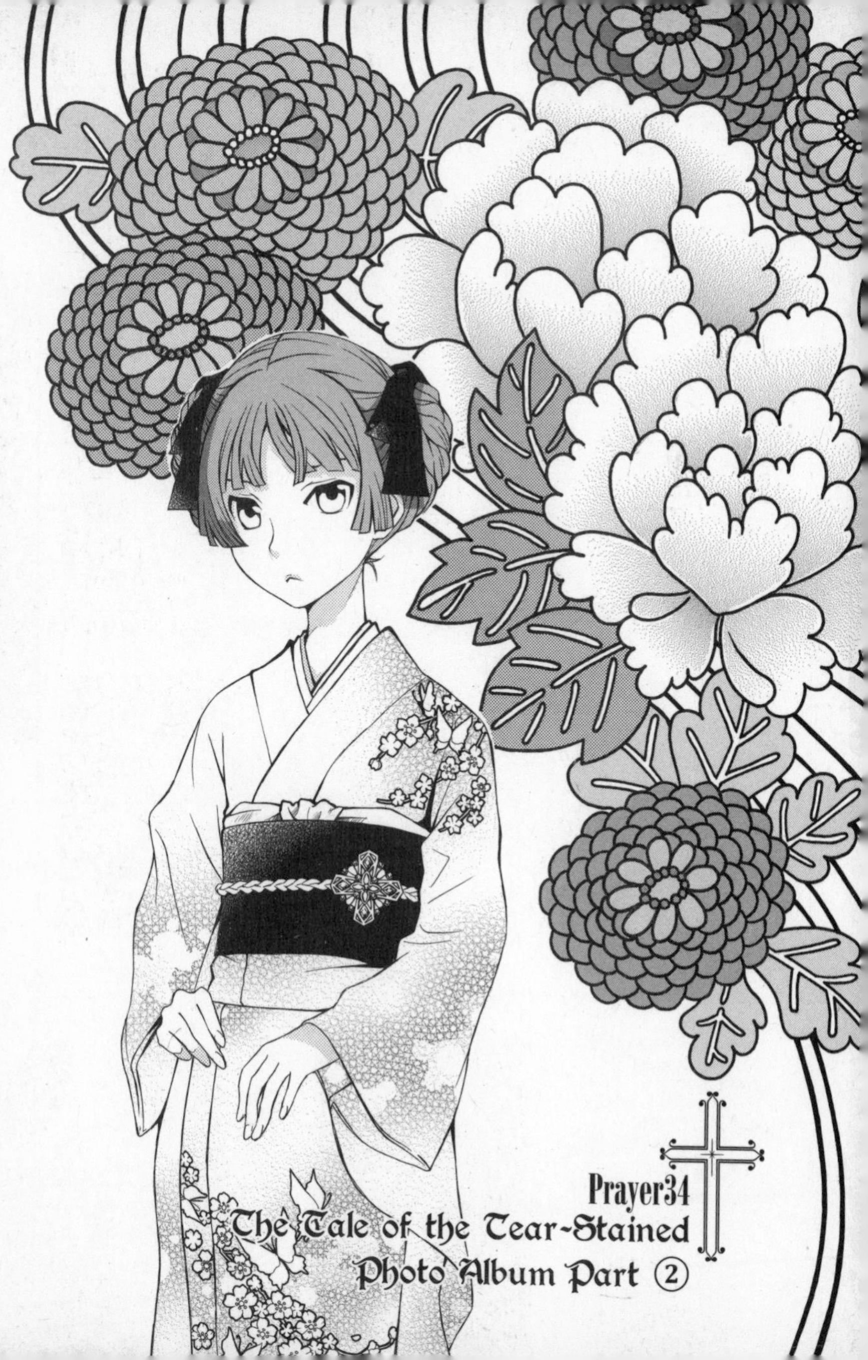

Prayer34
The Tale of the Tear-Stained Photo Album Part ②

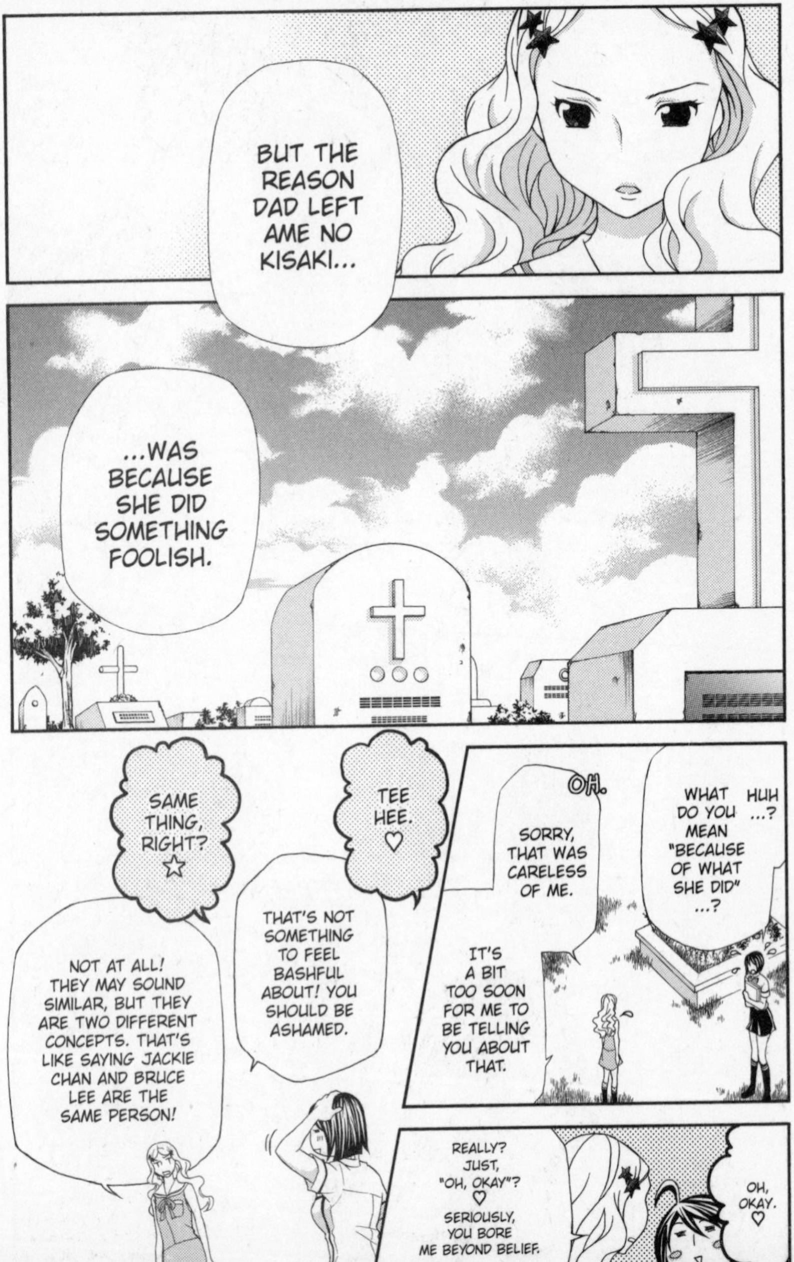

BUT THE REASON DAD LEFT AME NO KISAKI...
...WAS BECAUSE SHE DID SOMETHING FOOLISH.
HUH ...?
WHAT DO YOU MEAN "BECAUSE OF WHAT SHE DID" ...?
OH.
SORRY, THAT WAS CARELESS OF ME.
IT'S A BIT TOO SOON FOR ME TO BE TELLING YOU ABOUT THAT.
OH, OKAY. ♡
REALLY? JUST, "OH, OKAY"? ♡
SERIOUSLY, YOU BORE ME BEYOND BELIEF.
TEE HEE. ♡
SAME THING, RIGHT? ☆
THAT'S NOT SOMETHING TO FEEL BASHFUL ABOUT! YOU SHOULD BE ASHAMED.
NOT AT ALL! THEY MAY SOUND SIMILAR, BUT THEY ARE TWO DIFFERENT CONCEPTS. THAT'S LIKE SAYING JACKIE CHAN AND BRUCE LEE ARE THE SAME PERSON!

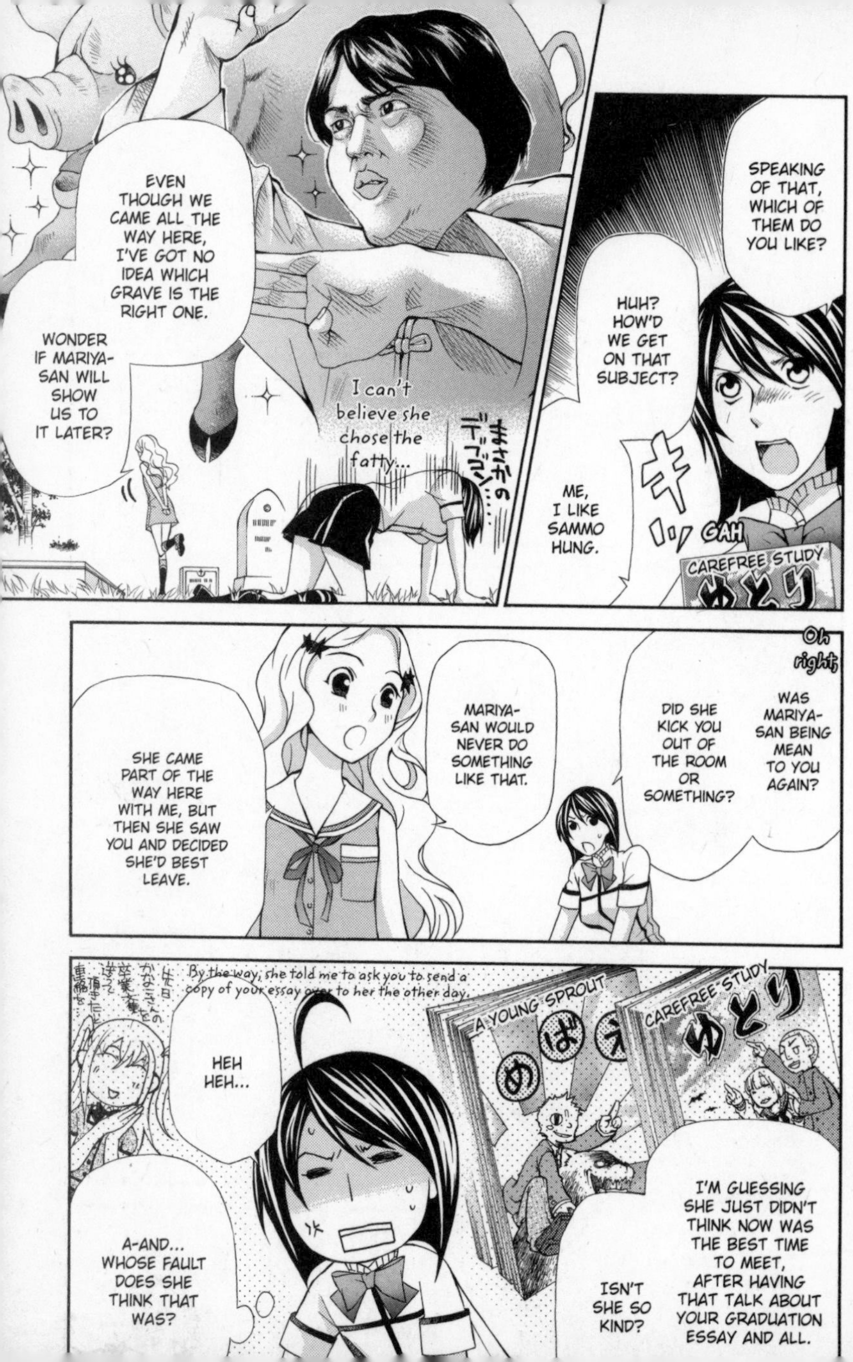
SPEAKING OF THAT, WHICH OF THEM DO YOU LIKE?
HUH? HOW'D WE GET ON THAT SUBJECT?
GAH
CAREFREE STUDY ゆとり
ME, I LIKE SAMMO HUNG.
EVEN THOUGH WE CAME ALL THE WAY HERE, I'VE GOT NO IDEA WHICH GRAVE IS THE RIGHT ONE.
WONDER IF MARIYA-SAN WILL SHOW US TO IT LATER?
まさかのデブゴン…
I can't believe she chose the fatty...
Oh right,
WAS MARIYA-SAN BEING MEAN TO YOU AGAIN?
DID SHE KICK YOU OUT OF THE ROOM OR SOMETHING?
MARIYA-SAN WOULD NEVER DO SOMETHING LIKE THAT.
SHE CAME PART OF THE WAY HERE WITH ME, BUT THEN SHE SAW YOU AND DECIDED SHE'D BEST LEAVE.
CAREFREE STUDY ゆとり
A YOUNG SPROUT めばえ
I'M GUESSING SHE JUST DIDN'T THINK NOW WAS THE BEST TIME TO MEET, AFTER HAVING THAT TALK ABOUT YOUR GRADUATION ESSAY AND ALL.
ISN'T SHE SO KIND?
HEH HEH...
A-AND... WHOSE FAULT DOES SHE THINK THAT WAS?
By the way, she told me to ask you to send a copy of your essay over to her the other day.
先日かなこさんの卒業文集を送って頂きたいと連絡を…

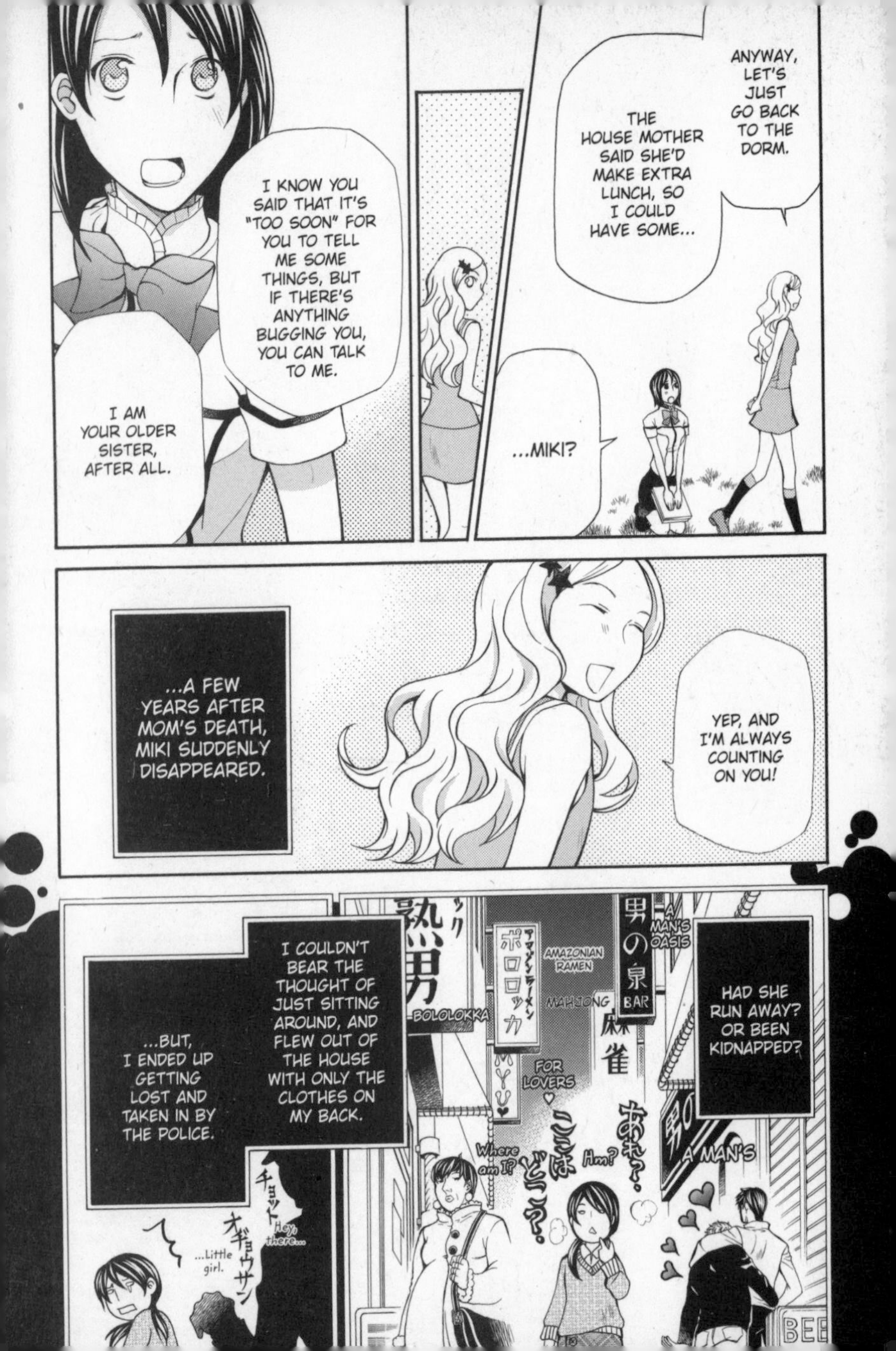
ANYWAY, LET'S JUST GO BACK TO THE DORM.
THE HOUSE MOTHER SAID SHE'D MAKE EXTRA LUNCH, SO I COULD HAVE SOME...
...MIKI?
I KNOW YOU SAID THAT IT'S "TOO SOON" FOR YOU TO TELL ME SOME THINGS, BUT IF THERE'S ANYTHING BUGGING YOU, YOU CAN TALK TO ME.
I AM YOUR OLDER SISTER, AFTER ALL.
YEP, AND I'M ALWAYS COUNTING ON YOU!
...A FEW YEARS AFTER MOM'S DEATH, MIKI SUDDENLY DISAPPEARED.
HAD SHE RUN AWAY? OR BEEN KIDNAPPED?
A MAN'S OASIS
BAR
AMAZONIAN RAMEN
MAHJONG
BOLOLOKKA
FOR LOVERS
A MAN'S
あれ？
Hm?
ここはどこ？
Where am I?
I COULDN'T BEAR THE THOUGHT OF JUST SITTING AROUND, AND FLEW OUT OF THE HOUSE WITH ONLY THE CLOTHES ON MY BACK.
...BUT, I ENDED UP GETTING LOST AND TAKEN IN BY THE POLICE.
Hey, there...
...Little girl.

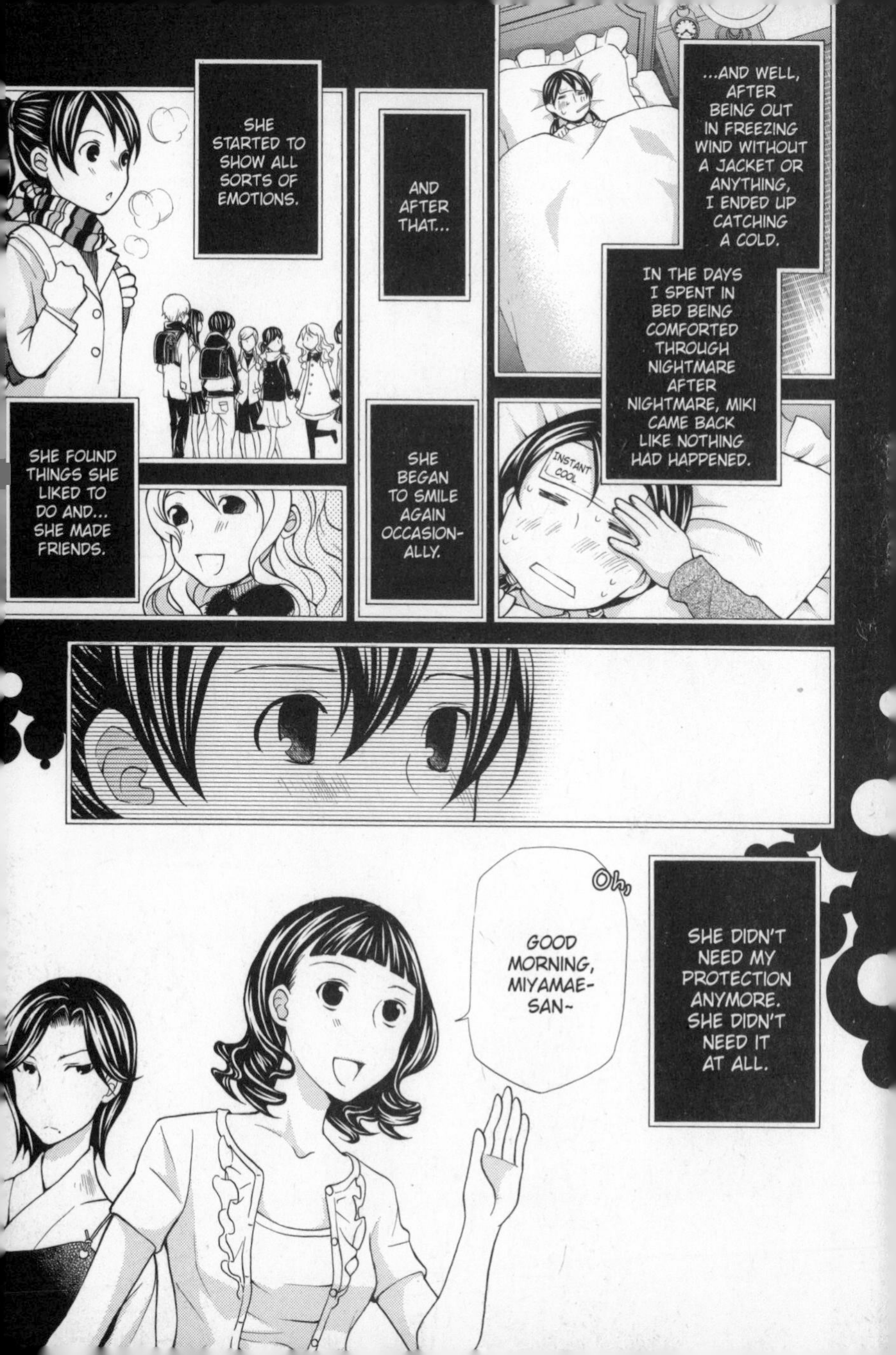
...AND WELL, AFTER BEING OUT IN FREEZING WIND WITHOUT A JACKET OR ANYTHING, I ENDED UP CATCHING A COLD.
IN THE DAYS I SPENT IN BED BEING COMFORTED THROUGH NIGHTMARE AFTER NIGHTMARE, MIKI CAME BACK LIKE NOTHING HAD HAPPENED.
INSTANT COOL
AND AFTER THAT...
SHE BEGAN TO SMILE AGAIN OCCASION-ALLY.
SHE STARTED TO SHOW ALL SORTS OF EMOTIONS.
SHE FOUND THINGS SHE LIKED TO DO AND... SHE MADE FRIENDS.
SHE DIDN'T NEED MY PROTECTION ANYMORE. SHE DIDN'T NEED IT AT ALL.
Oh,
GOOD MORNING, MIYAMAE-SAN~

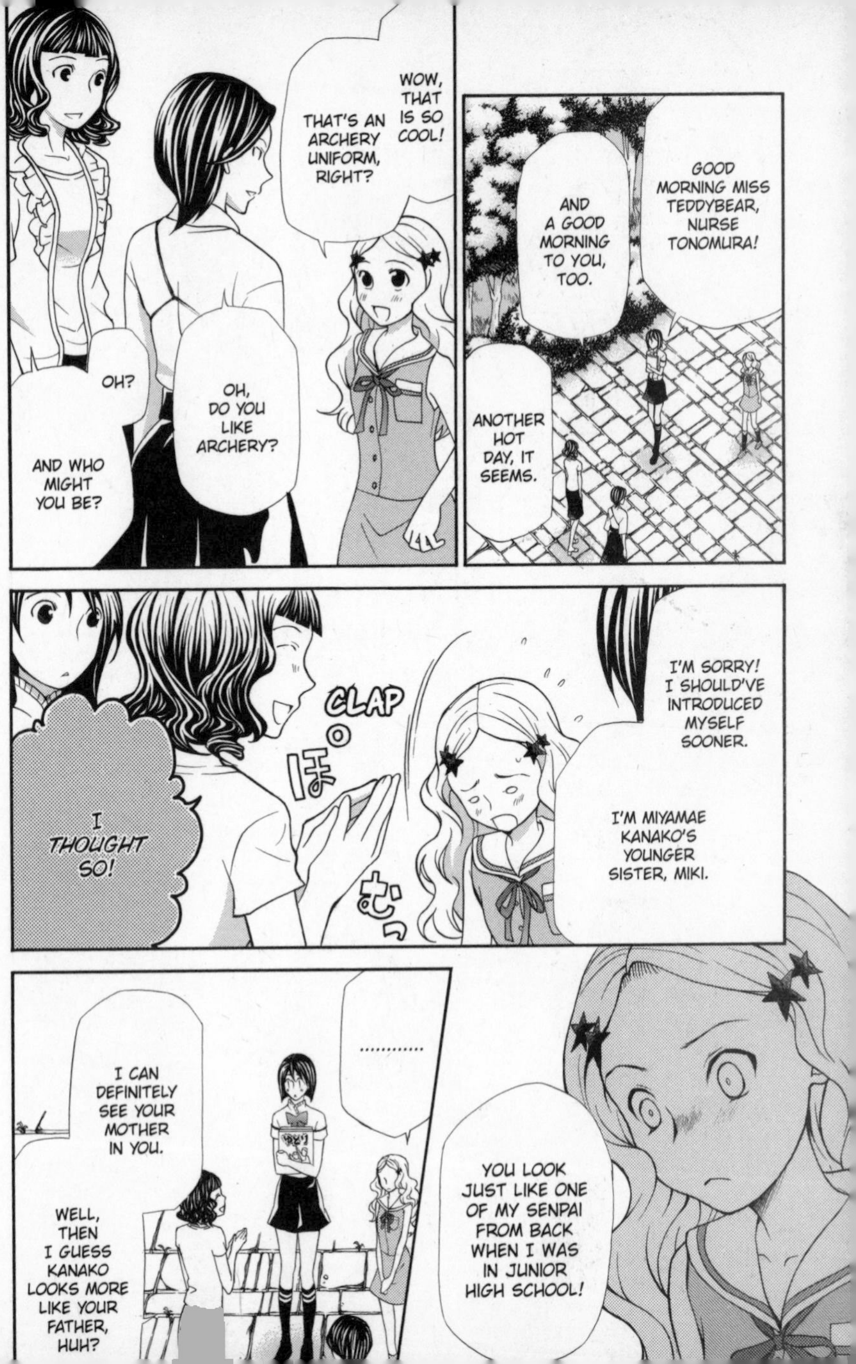
GOOD MORNING MISS TEDDYBEAR, NURSE TONOMURA!
AND A GOOD MORNING TO YOU, TOO.
ANOTHER HOT DAY, IT SEEMS.
WOW, THAT IS SO COOL!
THAT'S AN ARCHERY UNIFORM, RIGHT?
OH, DO YOU LIKE ARCHERY?
OH?
AND WHO MIGHT YOU BE?
I'M SORRY! I SHOULD'VE INTRODUCED MYSELF SOONER.
I'M MIYAMAE KANAKO'S YOUNGER SISTER, MIKI.
むっ
CLAP
ぽ
I THOUGHT SO!
YOU LOOK JUST LIKE ONE OF MY SENPAI FROM BACK WHEN I WAS IN JUNIOR HIGH SCHOOL!
....
I CAN DEFINITELY SEE YOUR MOTHER IN YOU.
WELL, THEN I GUESS KANAKO LOOKS MORE LIKE YOUR FATHER, HUH?

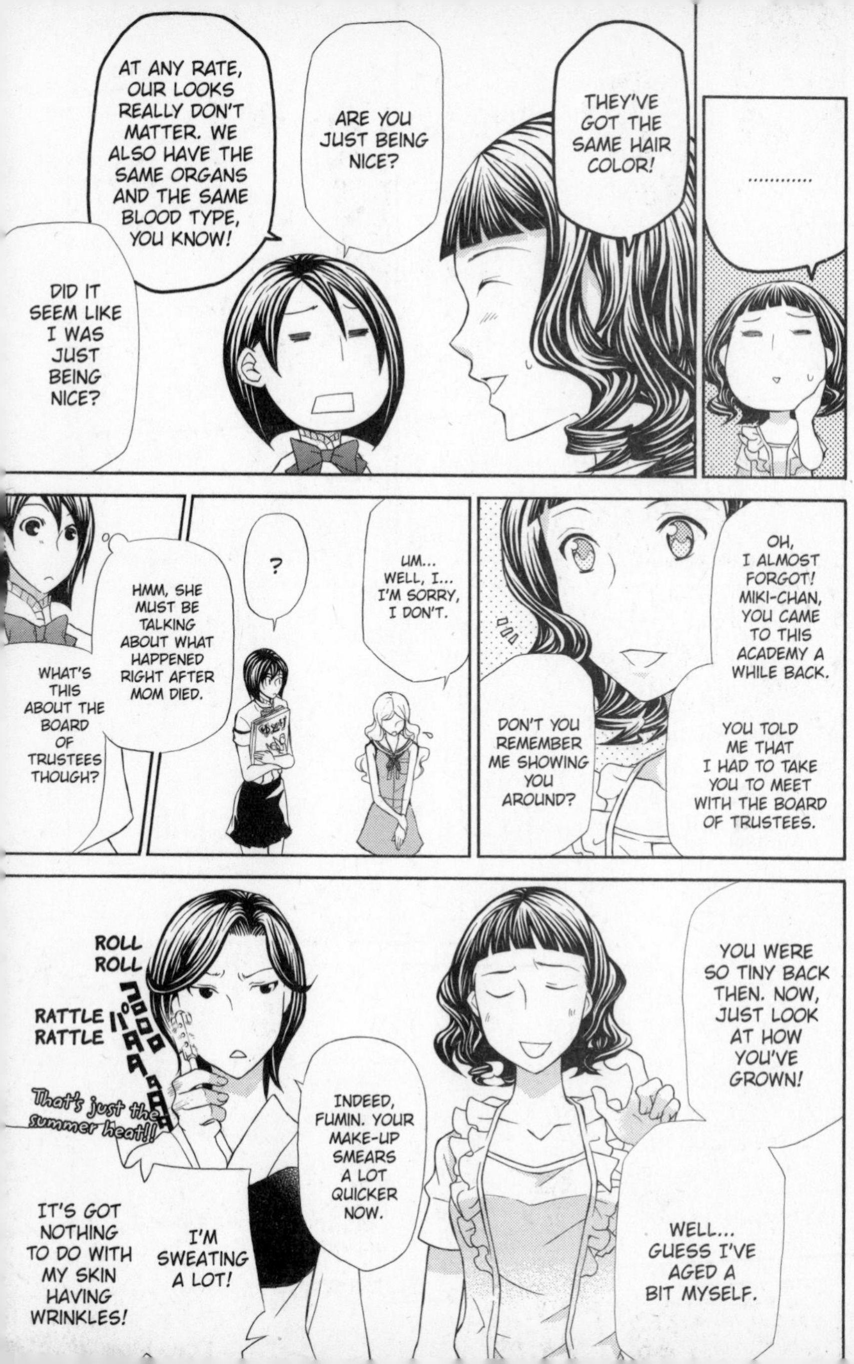
....
THEY'VE GOT THE SAME HAIR COLOR!
ARE YOU JUST BEING NICE?
AT ANY RATE, OUR LOOKS REALLY DON'T MATTER. WE ALSO HAVE THE SAME ORGANS AND THE SAME BLOOD TYPE, YOU KNOW!
DID IT SEEM LIKE I WAS JUST BEING NICE?
OH, I ALMOST FORGOT! MIKI-CHAN, YOU CAME TO THIS ACADEMY A WHILE BACK.
YOU TOLD ME THAT I HAD TO TAKE YOU TO MEET WITH THE BOARD OF TRUSTEES.
DON'T YOU REMEMBER ME SHOWING YOU AROUND?
UM... WELL, I... I'M SORRY, I DON'T.
?
HMM, SHE MUST BE TALKING ABOUT WHAT HAPPENED RIGHT AFTER MOM DIED.
WHAT'S THIS ABOUT THE BOARD OF TRUSTEES THOUGH?
YOU WERE SO TINY BACK THEN. NOW, JUST LOOK AT HOW YOU'VE GROWN!
WELL... GUESS I'VE AGED A BIT MYSELF.
INDEED, FUMIN. YOUR MAKE-UP SMEARS A LOT QUICKER NOW.
ROLL ROLL
RATTLE RATTLE
I'M SWEATING A LOT!
IT'S GOT NOTHING TO DO WITH MY SKIN HAVING WRINKLES!
That's just the summer heat!!

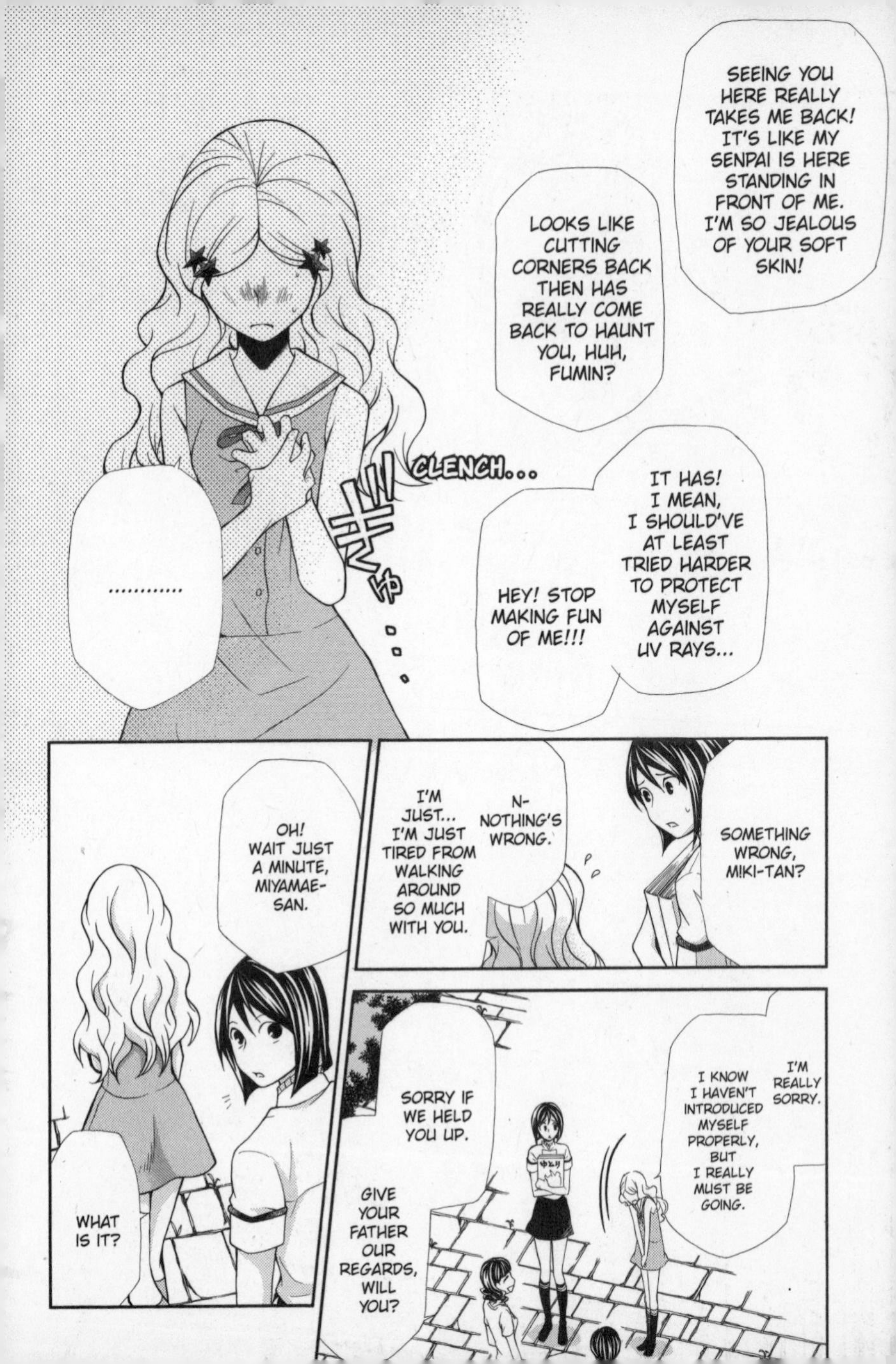
SEEING YOU HERE REALLY TAKES ME BACK! IT'S LIKE MY SENPAI IS HERE STANDING IN FRONT OF ME. I'M SO JEALOUS OF YOUR SOFT SKIN!
LOOKS LIKE CUTTING CORNERS BACK THEN HAS REALLY COME BACK TO HAUNT YOU, HUH, FUMIN?
IT HAS! I MEAN, I SHOULD'VE AT LEAST TRIED HARDER TO PROTECT MYSELF AGAINST UV RAYS...
HEY! STOP MAKING FUN OF ME!!!
CLENCH...
ぎゅ...
....
SOMETHING WRONG, MIKI-TAN?
N- NOTHING'S WRONG.
I'M JUST... I'M JUST TIRED FROM WALKING AROUND SO MUCH WITH YOU.
I'M REALLY SORRY.
I KNOW I HAVEN'T INTRODUCED MYSELF PROPERLY, BUT I REALLY MUST BE GOING.
SORRY IF WE HELD YOU UP.
GIVE YOUR FATHER OUR REGARDS, WILL YOU?
OH! WAIT JUST A MINUTE, MIYAMAE-SAN.
WHAT IS IT?

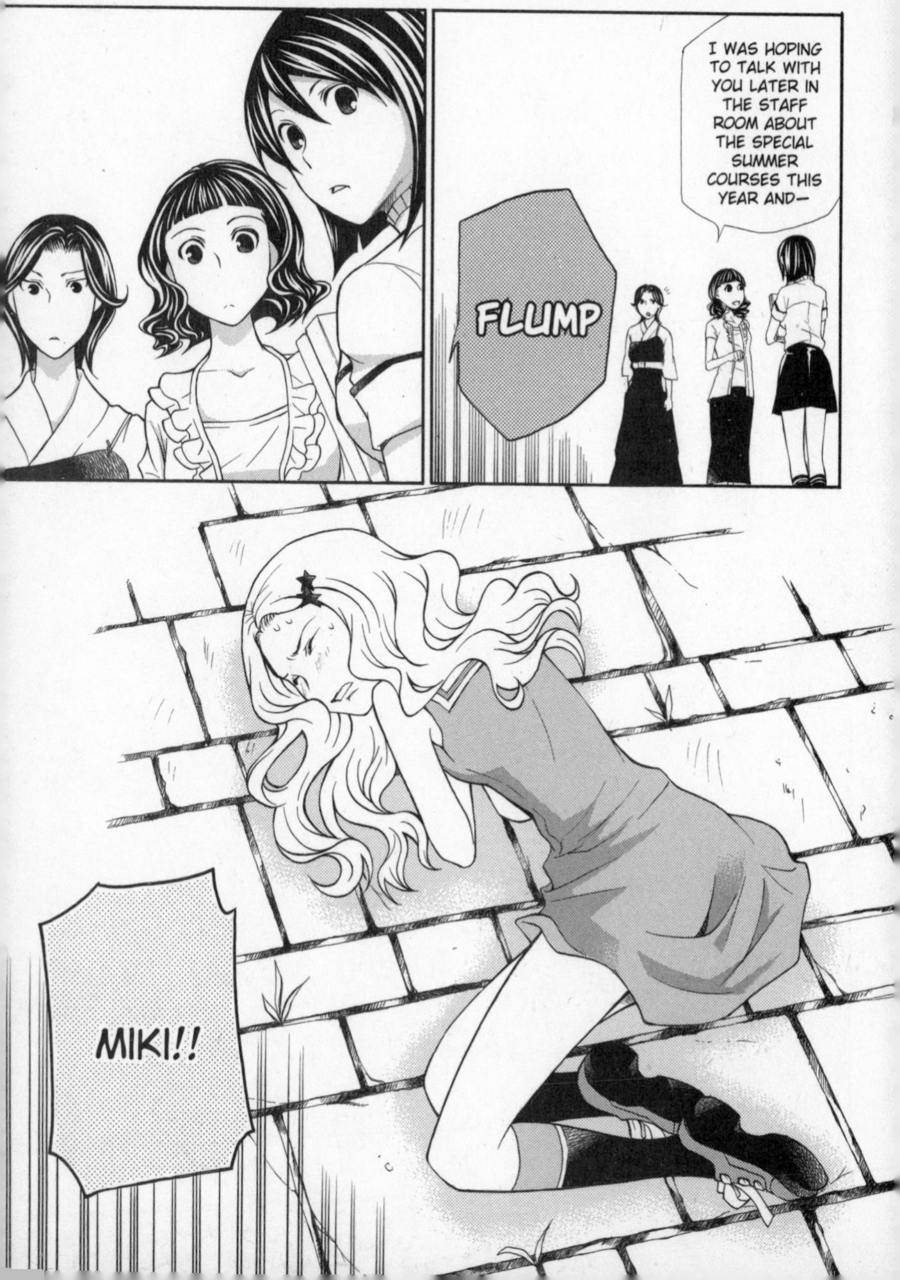
I WAS HOPING TO TALK WITH YOU LATER IN THE STAFF ROOM ABOUT THE SPECIAL SUMMER COURSES THIS YEAR AND—
FLUMP
MIKI!!

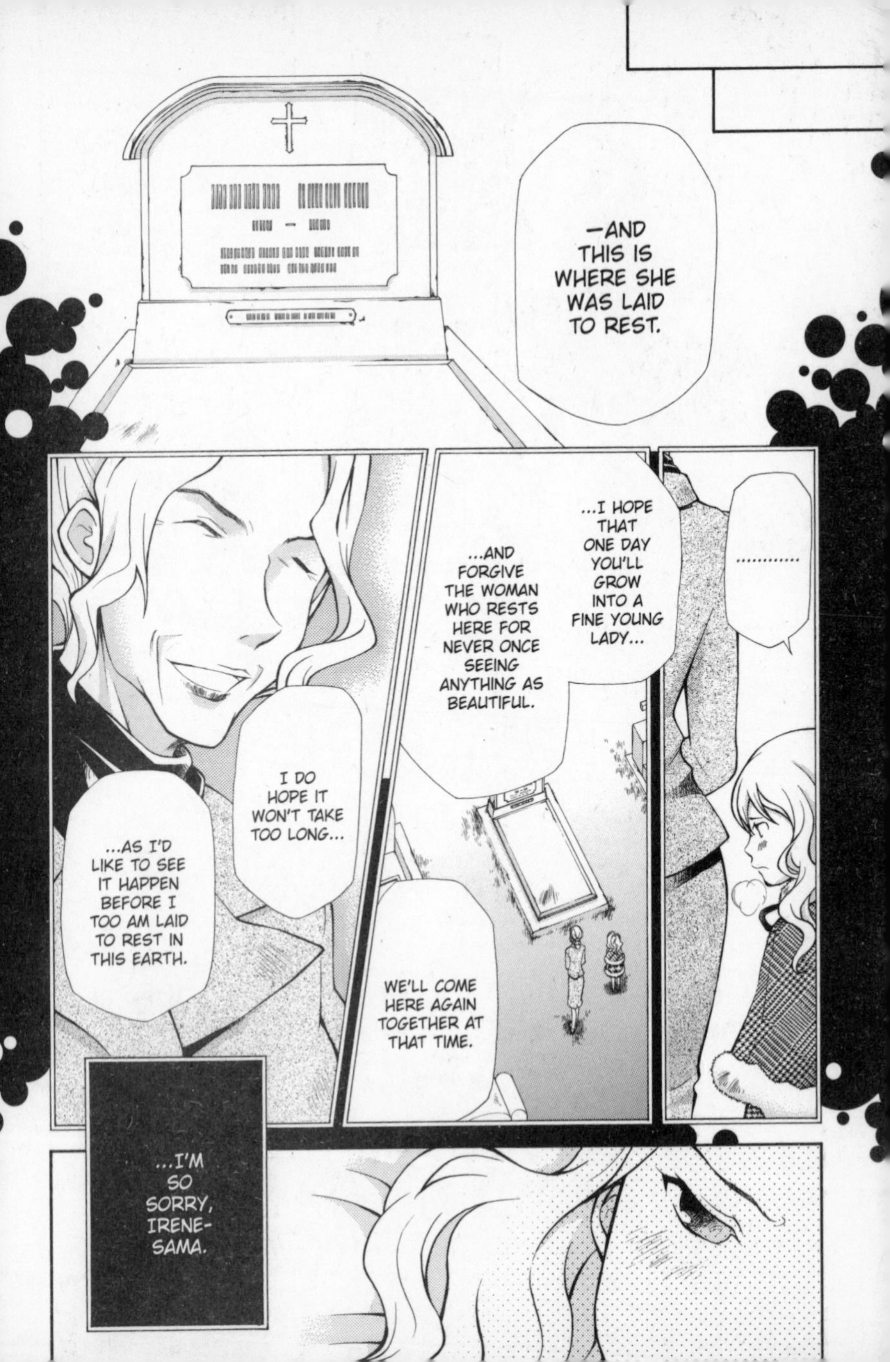
—AND THIS IS WHERE SHE WAS LAID TO REST.
....
...I HOPE THAT ONE DAY YOU'LL GROW INTO A FINE YOUNG LADY...
...AND FORGIVE THE WOMAN WHO RESTS HERE FOR NEVER ONCE SEEING ANYTHING AS BEAUTIFUL.
WE'LL COME HERE AGAIN TOGETHER AT THAT TIME.
I DO HOPE IT WON'T TAKE TOO LONG...
...AS I'D LIKE TO SEE IT HAPPEN BEFORE I TOO AM LAID TO REST IN THIS EARTH.
...I'M SO SORRY, IRENE-SAMA.

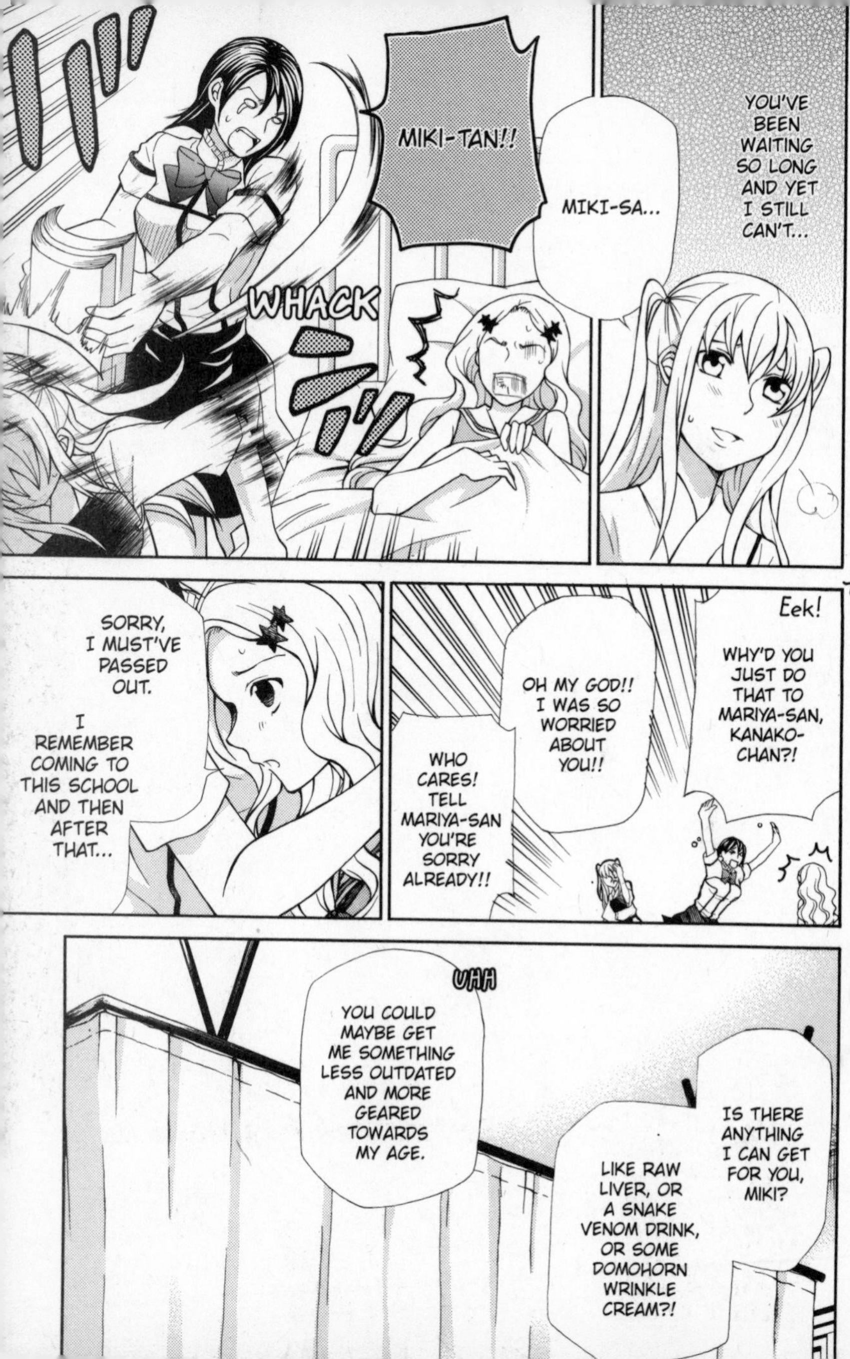
YOU'VE BEEN WAITING SO LONG AND YET I STILL CAN'T...
MIKI-SA...
MIKI-TAN!!
WHACK
Eek!
WHY'D YOU JUST DO THAT TO MARIYA-SAN, KANAKO-CHAN?!
OH MY GOD!! I WAS SO WORRIED ABOUT YOU!!
WHO CARES! TELL MARIYA-SAN YOU'RE SORRY ALREADY!!
SORRY, I MUST'VE PASSED OUT.
I REMEMBER COMING TO THIS SCHOOL AND THEN AFTER THAT...
IS THERE ANYTHING I CAN GET FOR YOU, MIKI?
LIKE RAW LIVER, OR A SNAKE VENOM DRINK, OR SOME DOMOHORN WRINKLE CREAM?!
UHH
YOU COULD MAYBE GET ME SOMETHING LESS OUTDATED AND MORE GEARED TOWARDS MY AGE.

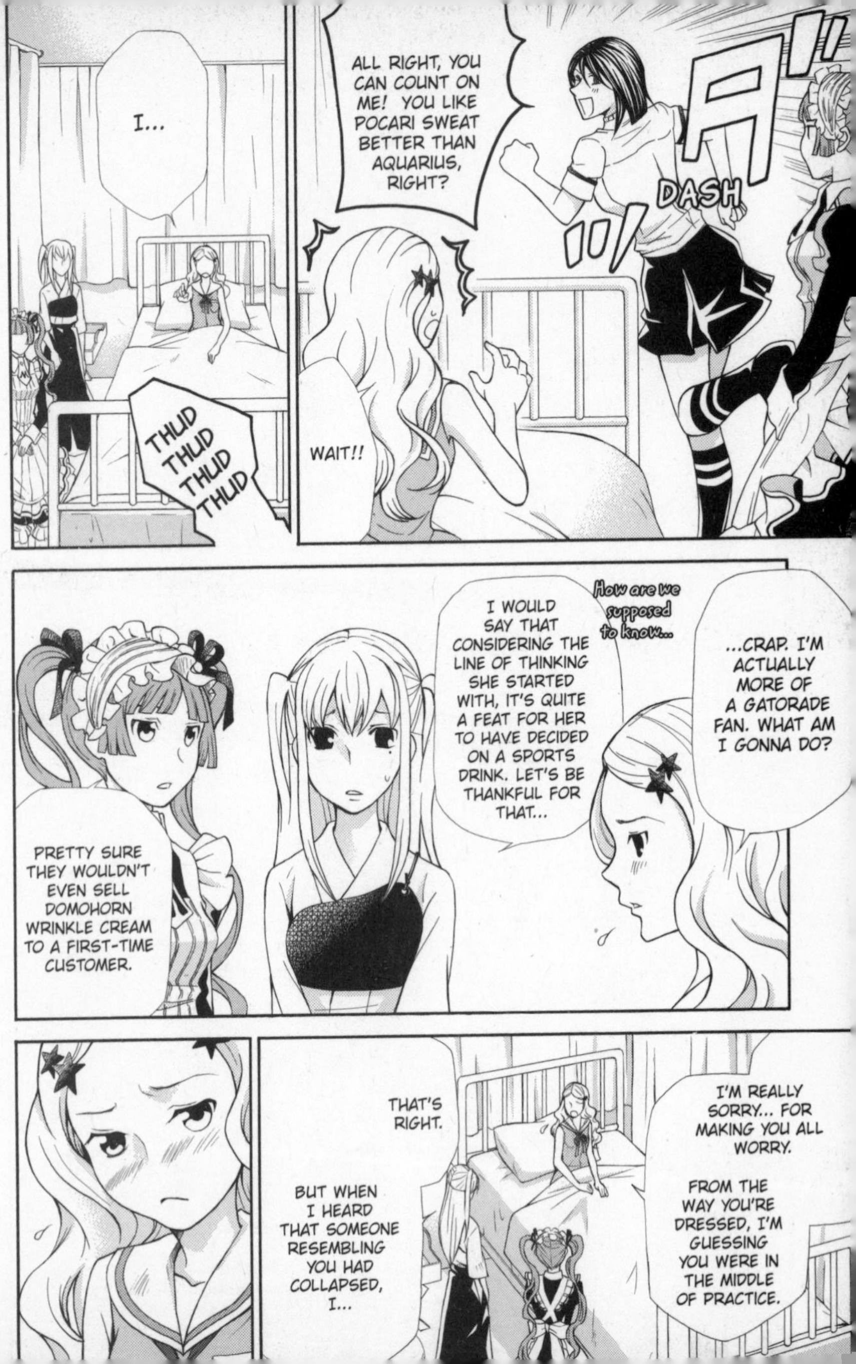
ALL RIGHT, YOU CAN COUNT ON ME! YOU LIKE POCARI SWEAT BETTER THAN AQUARIUS, RIGHT?
DASH
WAIT!!
I...
THUD THUD THUD THUD
...CRAP. I'M ACTUALLY MORE OF A GATORADE FAN. WHAT AM I GONNA DO?
How are we supposed to know...
I WOULD SAY THAT CONSIDERING THE LINE OF THINKING SHE STARTED WITH, IT'S QUITE A FEAT FOR HER TO HAVE DECIDED ON A SPORTS DRINK. LET'S BE THANKFUL FOR THAT...
PRETTY SURE THEY WOULDN'T EVEN SELL DOMOHORN WRINKLE CREAM TO A FIRST-TIME CUSTOMER.
I'M REALLY SORRY... FOR MAKING YOU ALL WORRY.
FROM THE WAY YOU'RE DRESSED, I'M GUESSING YOU WERE IN THE MIDDLE OF PRACTICE.
THAT'S RIGHT.
BUT WHEN I HEARD THAT SOMEONE RESEMBLING YOU HAD COLLAPSED, I...

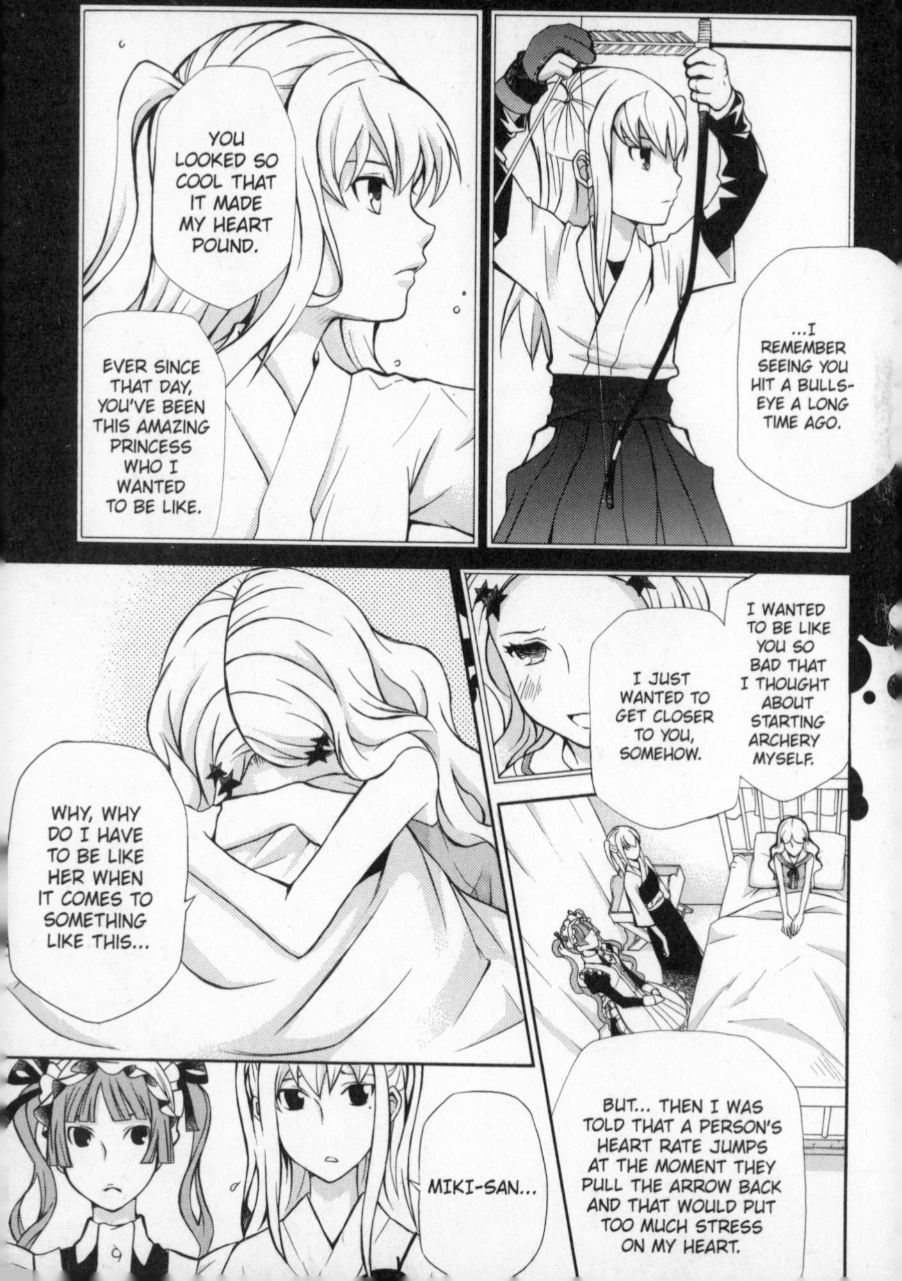
...I REMEMBER SEEING YOU HIT A BULLS-EYE A LONG TIME AGO.
YOU LOOKED SO COOL THAT IT MADE MY HEART POUND.
EVER SINCE THAT DAY, YOU'VE BEEN THIS AMAZING PRINCESS WHO I WANTED TO BE LIKE.
I WANTED TO BE LIKE YOU SO BAD THAT I THOUGHT ABOUT STARTING ARCHERY MYSELF.
I JUST WANTED TO GET CLOSER TO YOU, SOMEHOW.
BUT... THEN I WAS TOLD THAT A PERSON'S HEART RATE JUMPS AT THE MOMENT THEY PULL THE ARROW BACK AND THAT WOULD PUT TOO MUCH STRESS ON MY HEART.
WHY, WHY DO I HAVE TO BE LIKE HER WHEN IT COMES TO SOMETHING LIKE THIS...
MIKI-SAN...

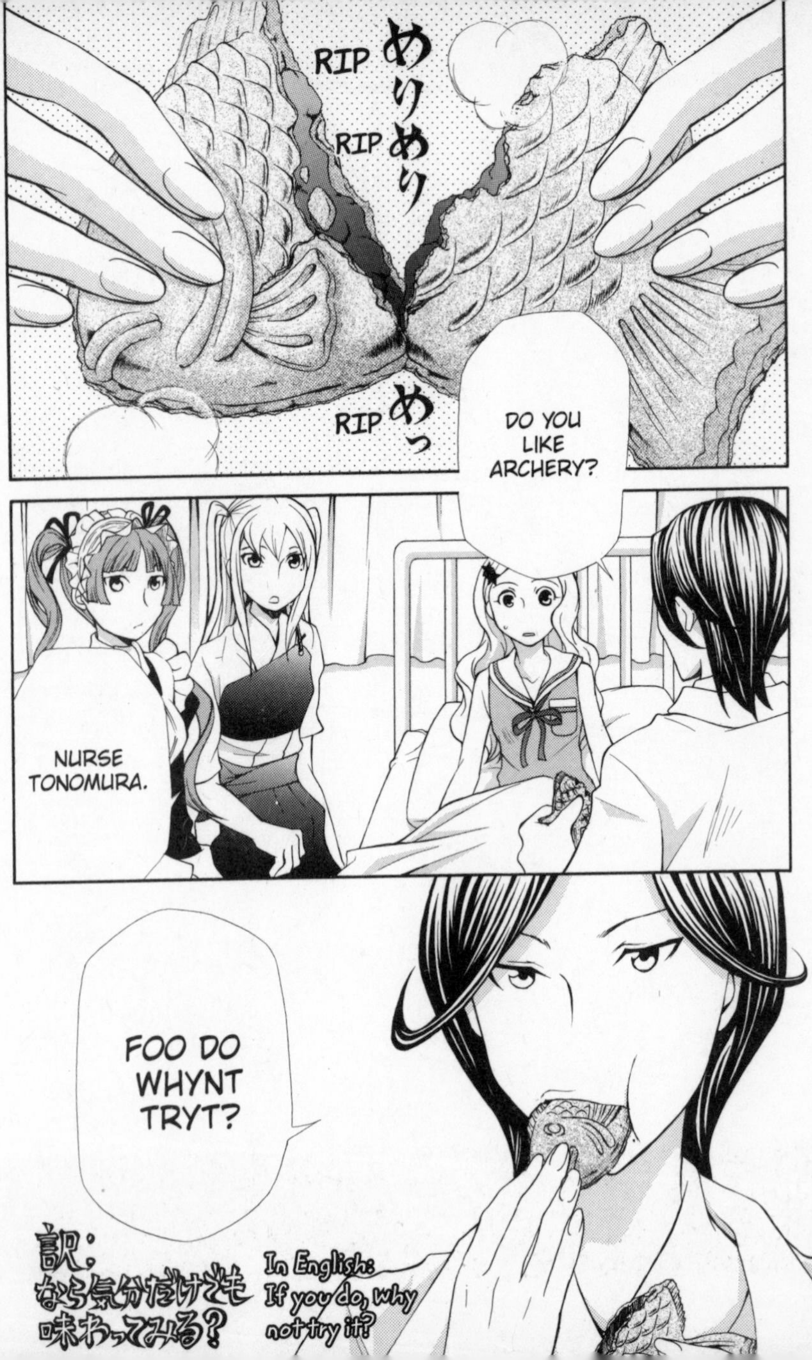
めりめり
RIP
RIP
めっ
RIP
DO YOU LIKE ARCHERY?
NURSE TONOMURA.
FOO DO WHYNT TRYT?
訳：
なら気分だけでも味わってみる？
In English:
If you do, why not try it?

M A R I A H O L I C

MARIA HOLIC

M A R I A H O L I C

MARIA†HOLIC

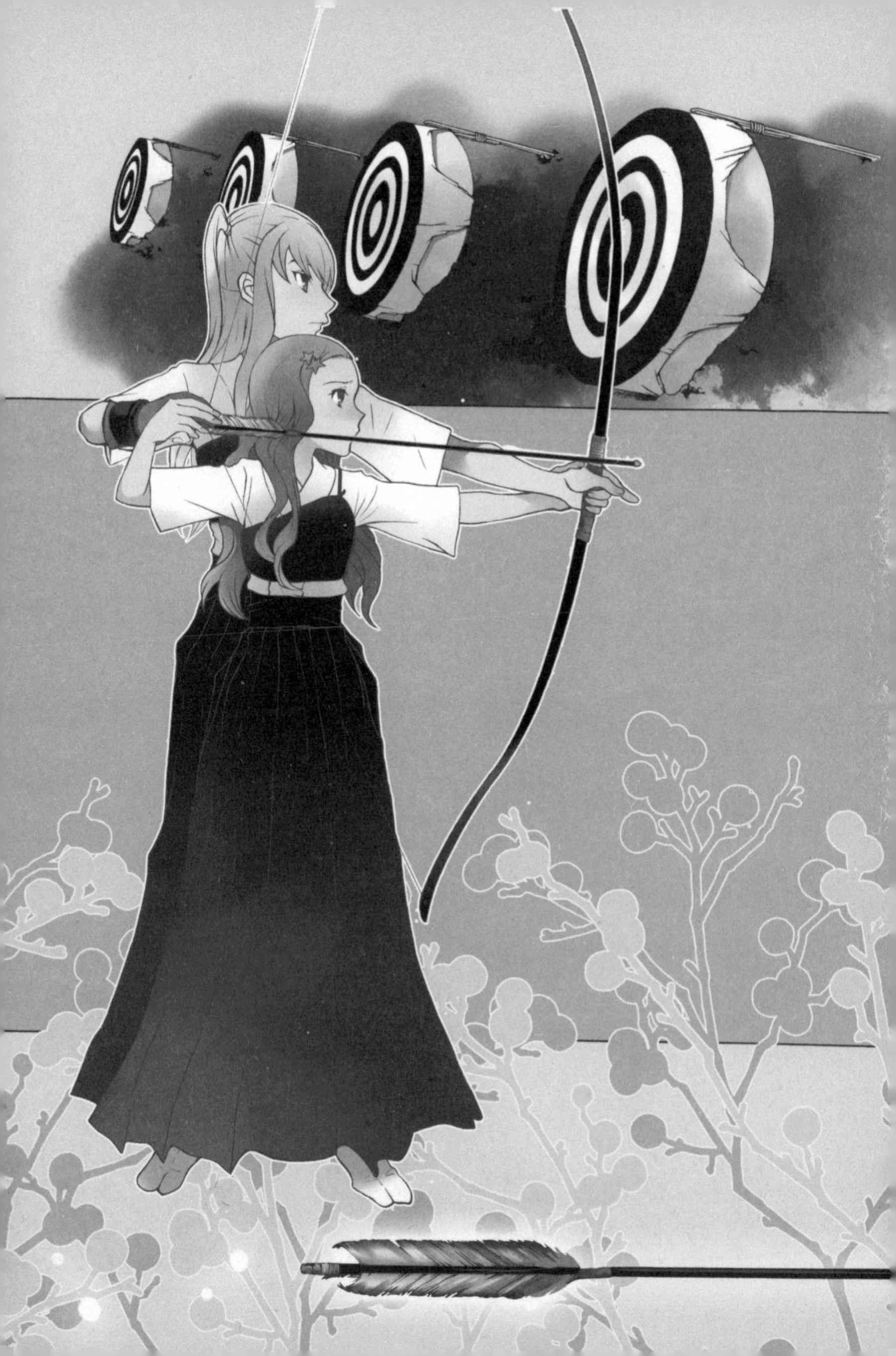

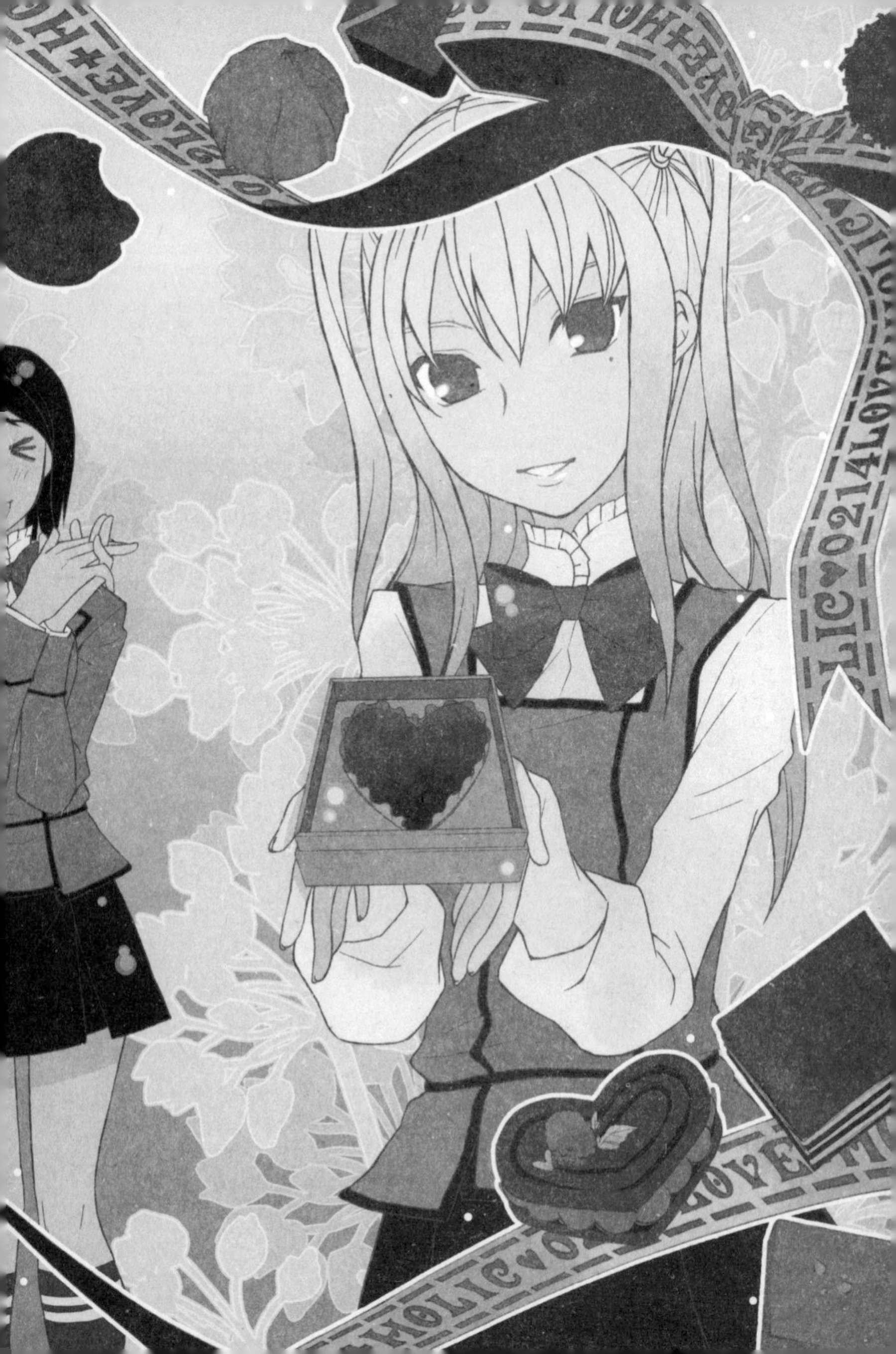
LIC♥0214LOVE
HOLIC♥O
LOVE

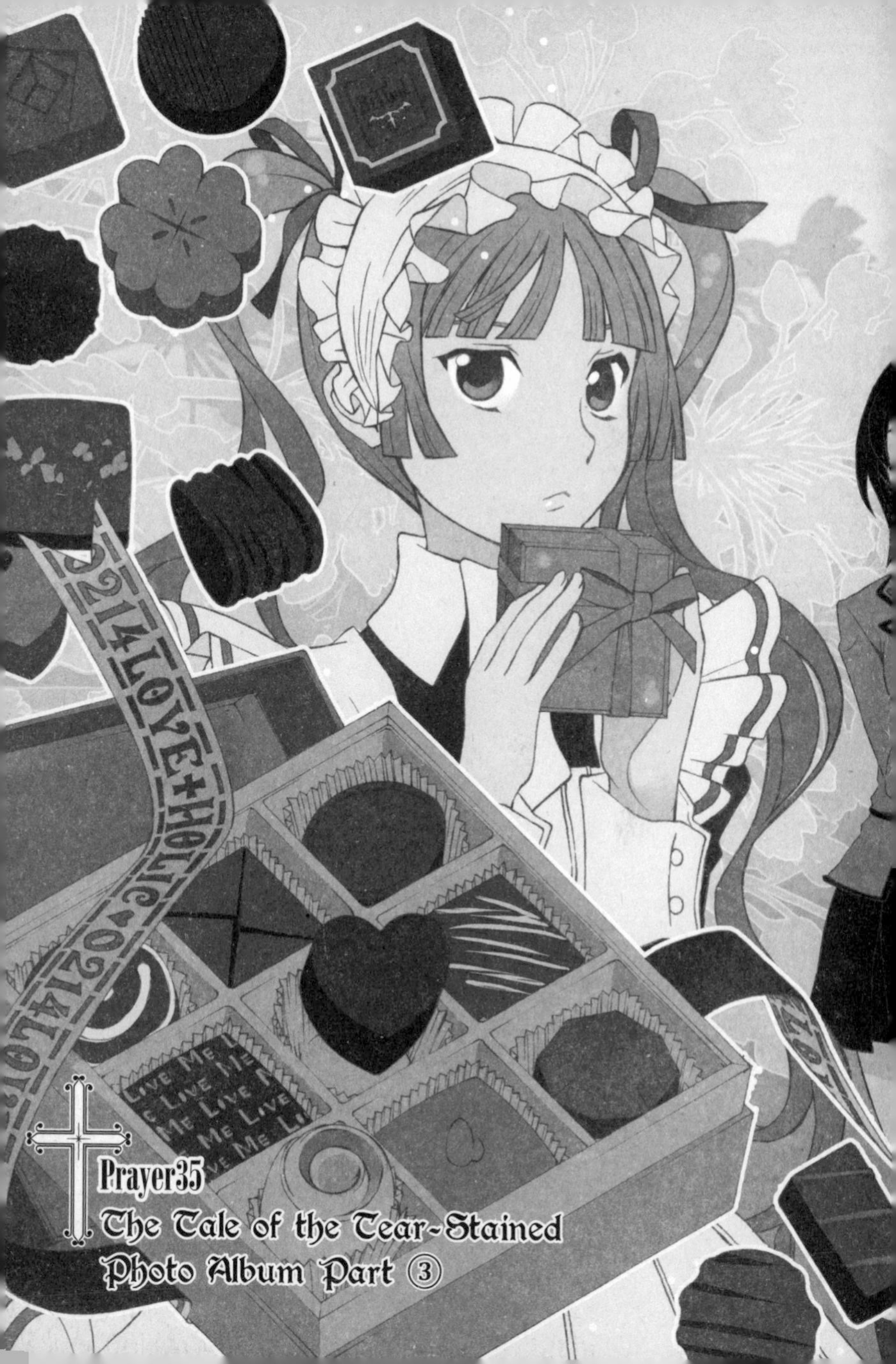
0214LOVE+HOLIC+0214LOVE
LIVE ME LIVE ME
Prayer35
The Tale of the Tear-Stained Photo Album Part ③

M A R I A H O L I C

MARIA†HOLIC

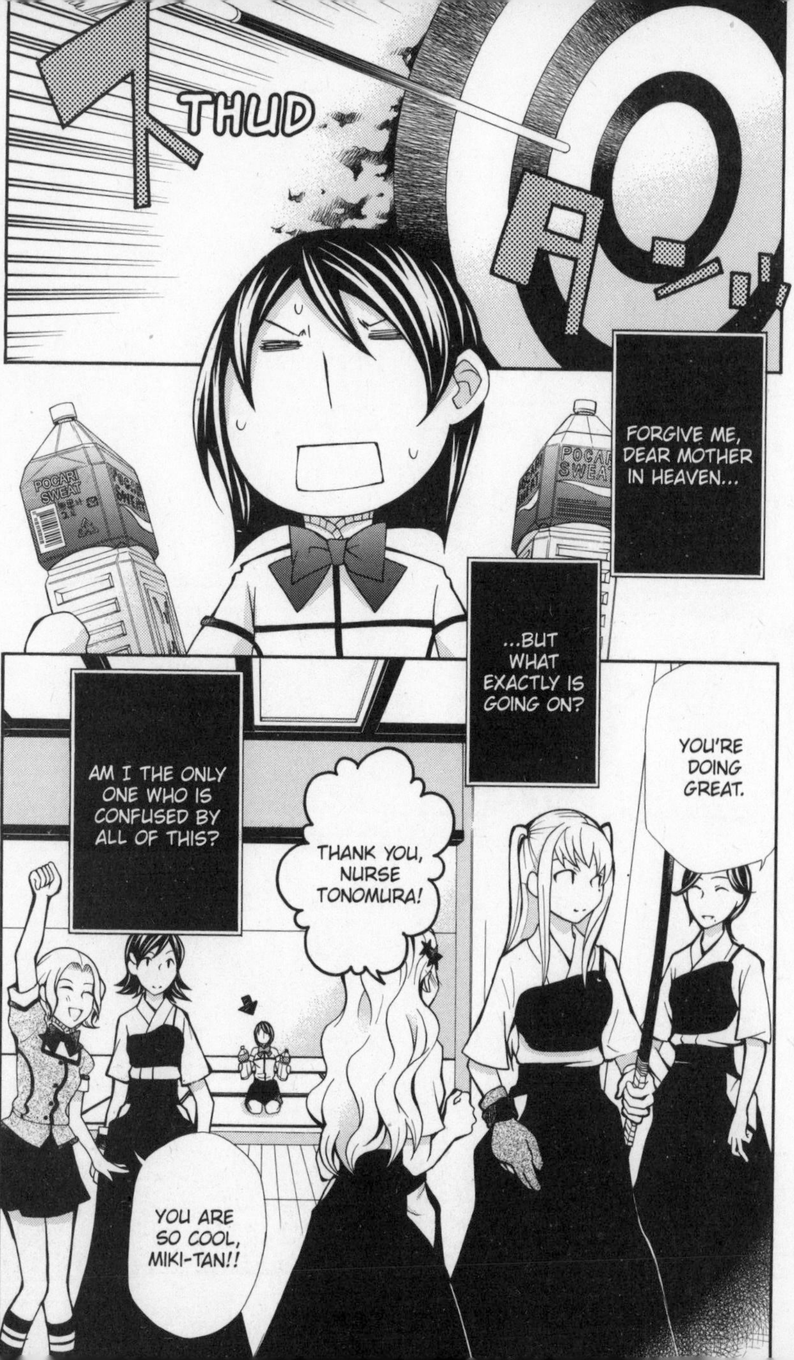
THUD
POCARI SWEAT
POCARI SWEAT
FORGIVE ME, DEAR MOTHER IN HEAVEN...
...BUT WHAT EXACTLY IS GOING ON?
YOU'RE DOING GREAT.
THANK YOU, NURSE TONOMURA!
AM I THE ONLY ONE WHO IS CONFUSED BY ALL OF THIS?
YOU ARE SO COOL, MIKI-TAN!!

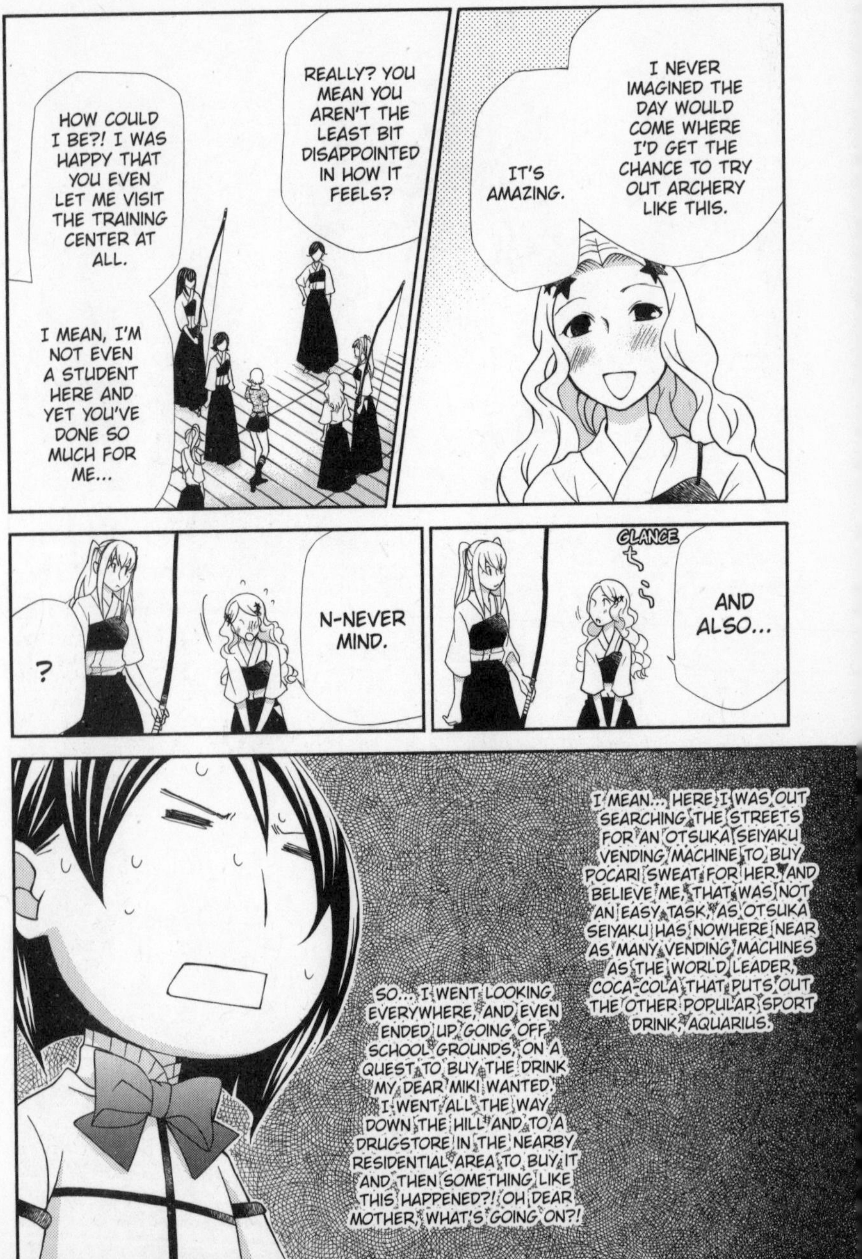
I NEVER IMAGINED THE DAY WOULD COME WHERE I'D GET THE CHANCE TO TRY OUT ARCHERY LIKE THIS.
IT'S AMAZING.
REALLY? YOU MEAN YOU AREN'T THE LEAST BIT DISAPPOINTED IN HOW IT FEELS?
HOW COULD I BE?! I WAS HAPPY THAT YOU EVEN LET ME VISIT THE TRAINING CENTER AT ALL.
I MEAN, I'M NOT EVEN A STUDENT HERE AND YET YOU'VE DONE SO MUCH FOR ME...
GLANCE
AND ALSO...
N-NEVER MIND.
?
I MEAN... HERE I WAS OUT SEARCHING THE STREETS FOR AN OTSUKA SEIYAKU VENDING MACHINE TO BUY POCARI SWEAT FOR HER. AND BELIEVE ME, THAT WAS NOT AN EASY TASK, AS OTSUKA SEIYAKU HAS NOWHERE NEAR AS MANY VENDING MACHINES AS THE WORLD LEADER, COCA-COLA THAT PUTS OUT THE OTHER POPULAR SPORT DRINK, AQUARIUS.
SO... I WENT LOOKING EVERYWHERE, AND EVEN ENDED UP GOING OFF SCHOOL GROUNDS, ON A QUEST TO BUY THE DRINK MY DEAR MIKI WANTED. I WENT ALL THE WAY DOWN THE HILL AND TO A DRUGSTORE IN THE NEARBY RESIDENTIAL AREA TO BUY IT AND THEN SOMETHING LIKE THIS HAPPENED?! OH DEAR MOTHER, WHAT'S GOING ON?!

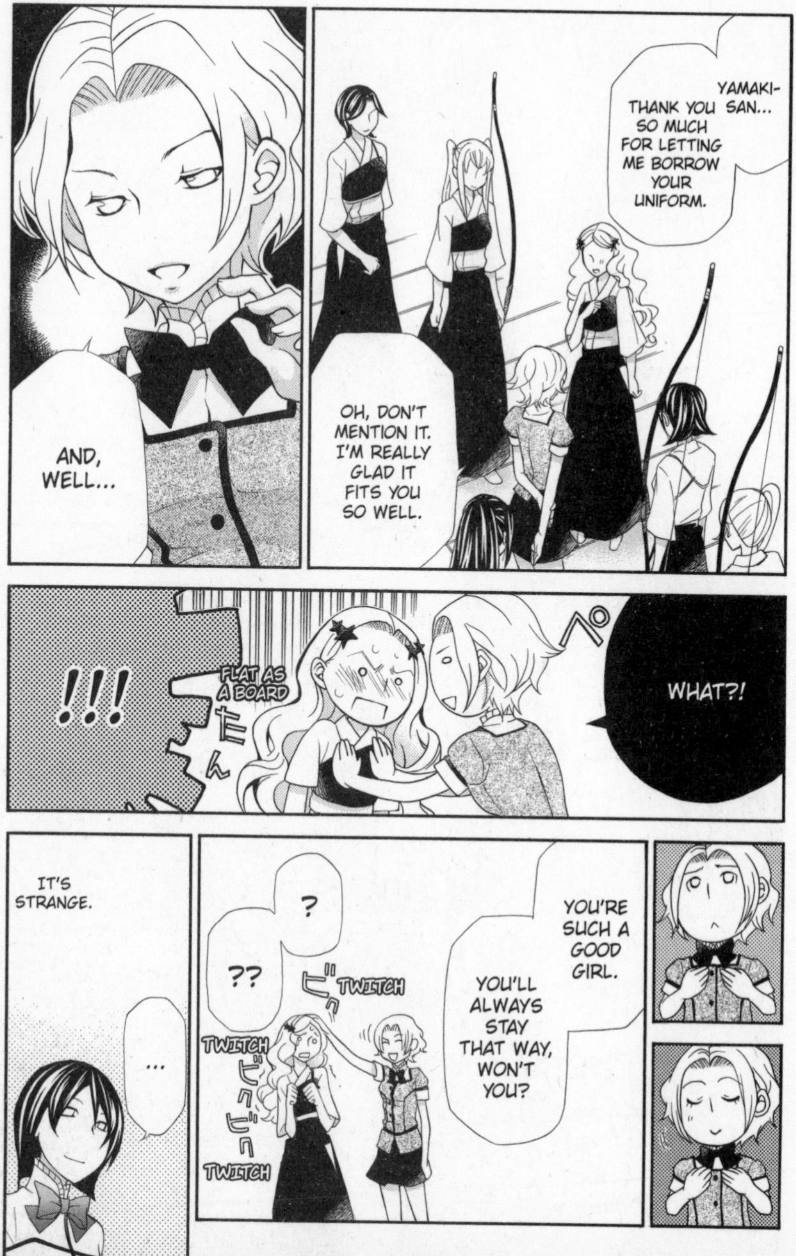
YAMAKI-SAN... THANK YOU SO MUCH FOR LETTING ME BORROW YOUR UNIFORM.
OH, DON'T MENTION IT. I'M REALLY GLAD IT FITS YOU SO WELL.
AND, WELL...
へ°
WHAT?!
FLAT AS A BOARD
たん
!!!
YOU'RE SUCH A GOOD GIRL.
YOU'LL ALWAYS STAY THAT WAY, WON'T YOU?
?
??
ビク
TWITCH
TWITCH
ビクビク
TWITCH
IT'S STRANGE.
...

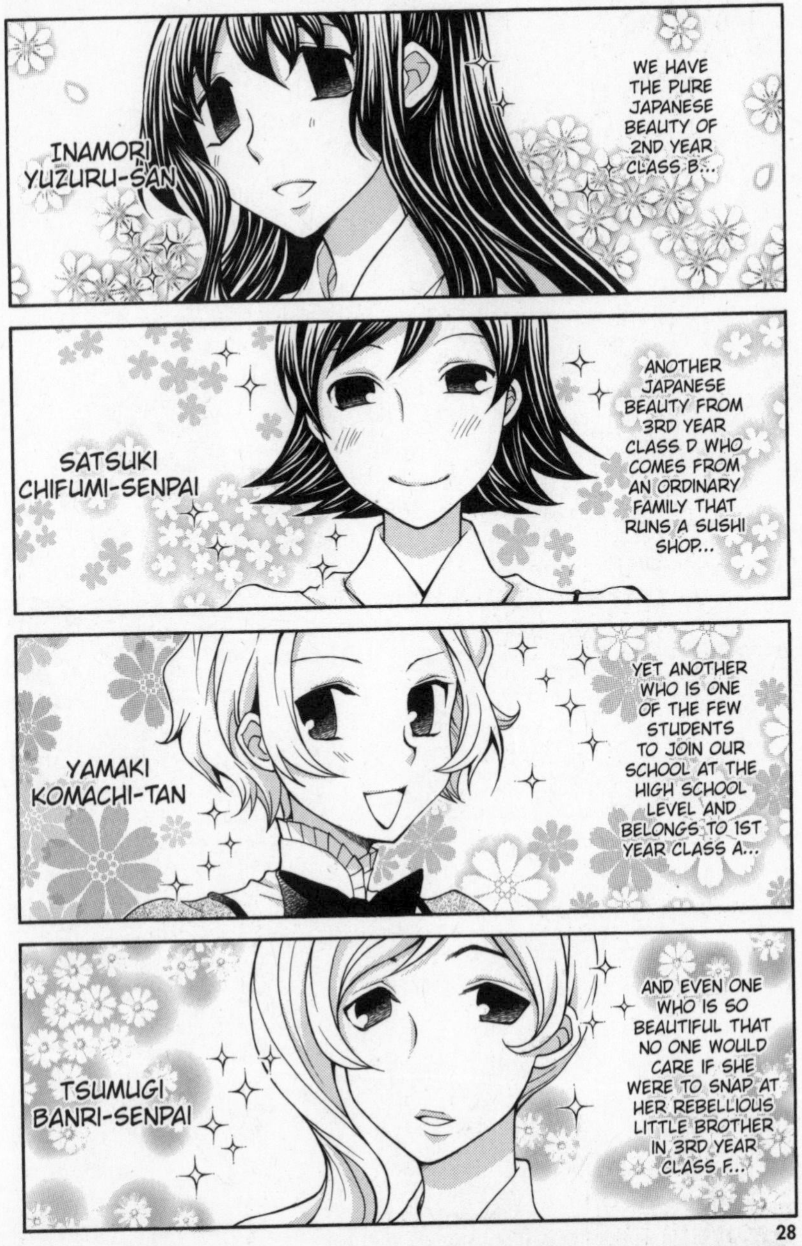

WE HAVE THE PURE JAPANESE BEAUTY OF 2ND YEAR CLASS B...
INAMORI YUZURU-SAN
ANOTHER JAPANESE BEAUTY FROM 3RD YEAR CLASS D WHO COMES FROM AN ORDINARY FAMILY THAT RUNS A SUSHI SHOP...
SATSUKI CHIFUMI-SENPAI
YET ANOTHER WHO IS ONE OF THE FEW STUDENTS TO JOIN OUR SCHOOL AT THE HIGH SCHOOL LEVEL AND BELONGS TO 1ST YEAR CLASS A...
YAMAKI KOMACHI-TAN
AND EVEN ONE WHO IS SO BEAUTIFUL THAT NO ONE WOULD CARE IF SHE WERE TO SNAP AT HER REBELLIOUS LITTLE BROTHER IN 3RD YEAR CLASS F...
TSUMUGI BANRI-SENPAI

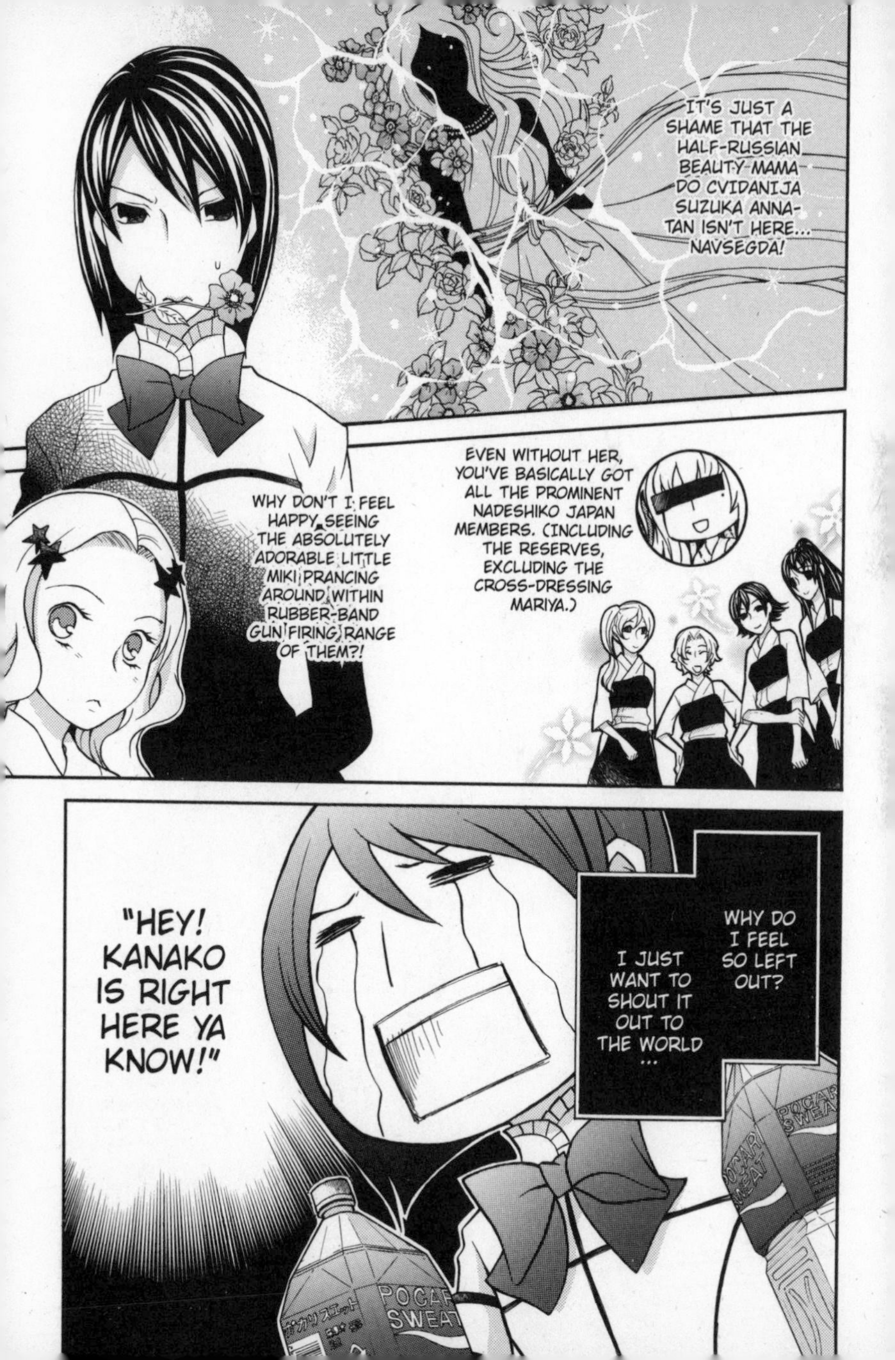
IT'S JUST A SHAME THAT THE HALF-RUSSIAN BEAUTY MAMA DO CVIDANIJA SUZUKA ANNA-TAN ISN'T HERE... NAVSEGDA!
EVEN WITHOUT HER, YOU'VE BASICALLY GOT ALL THE PROMINENT NADESHIKO JAPAN MEMBERS. (INCLUDING THE RESERVES, EXCLUDING THE CROSS-DRESSING MARIYA.)
WHY DON'T I FEEL HAPPY SEEING THE ABSOLUTELY ADORABLE LITTLE MIKI PRANCING AROUND WITHIN RUBBER-BAND GUN FIRING RANGE OF THEM?!
WHY DO I FEEL SO LEFT OUT?
I JUST WANT TO SHOUT IT OUT TO THE WORLD ...
"HEY! KANAKO IS RIGHT HERE YA KNOW!"

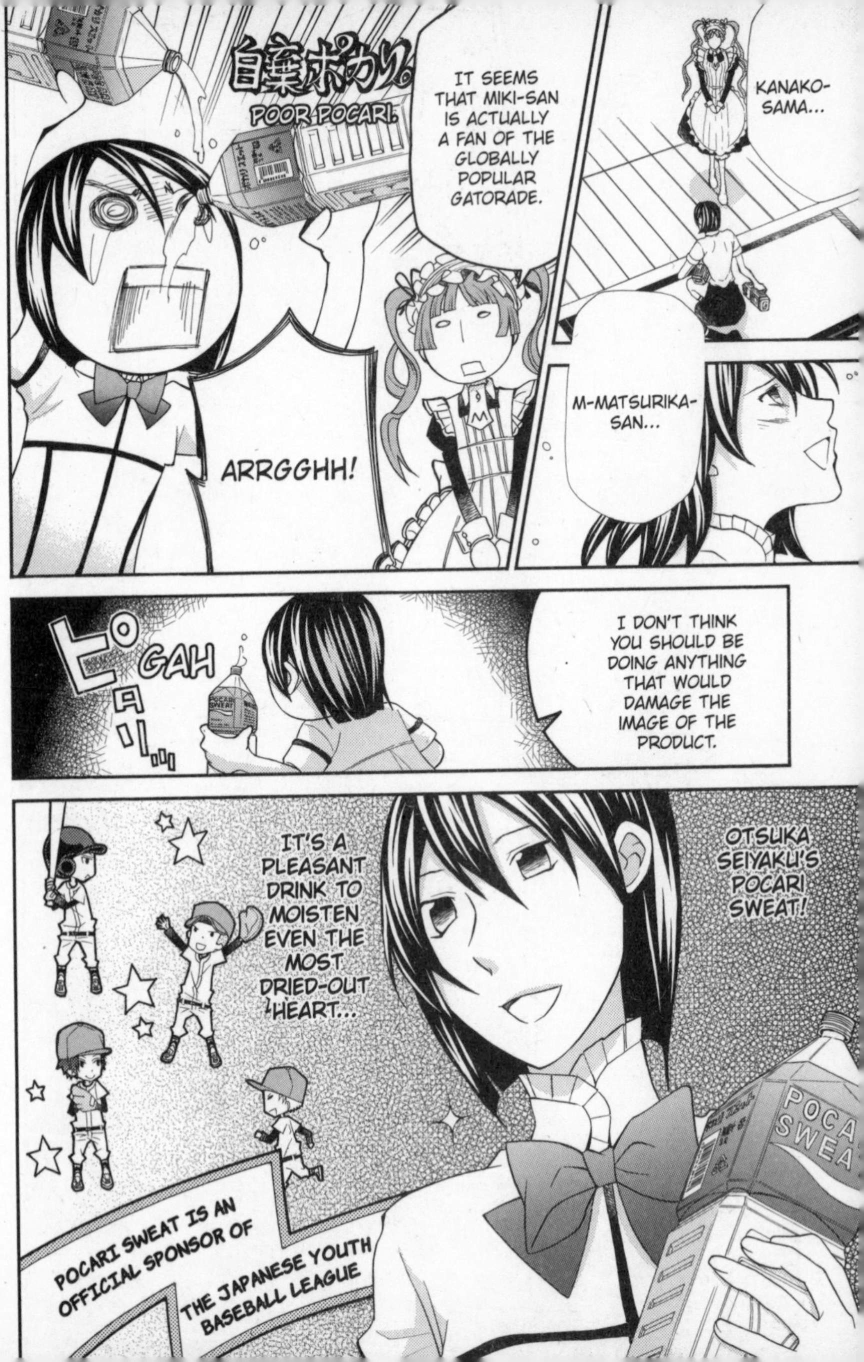
KANAKO-SAMA...
M-MATSURIKA-SAN...
IT SEEMS THAT MIKI-SAN IS ACTUALLY A FAN OF THE GLOBALLY POPULAR GATORADE.
自業ポカリ。
POOR POCARI.
ARRGGHH!
I DON'T THINK YOU SHOULD BE DOING ANYTHING THAT WOULD DAMAGE THE IMAGE OF THE PRODUCT.
GAH
OTSUKA SEIYAKU'S POCARI SWEAT!
IT'S A PLEASANT DRINK TO MOISTEN EVEN THE MOST DRIED-OUT HEART...
POCARI SWEAT IS AN OFFICIAL SPONSOR OF THE JAPANESE YOUTH BASEBALL LEAGUE

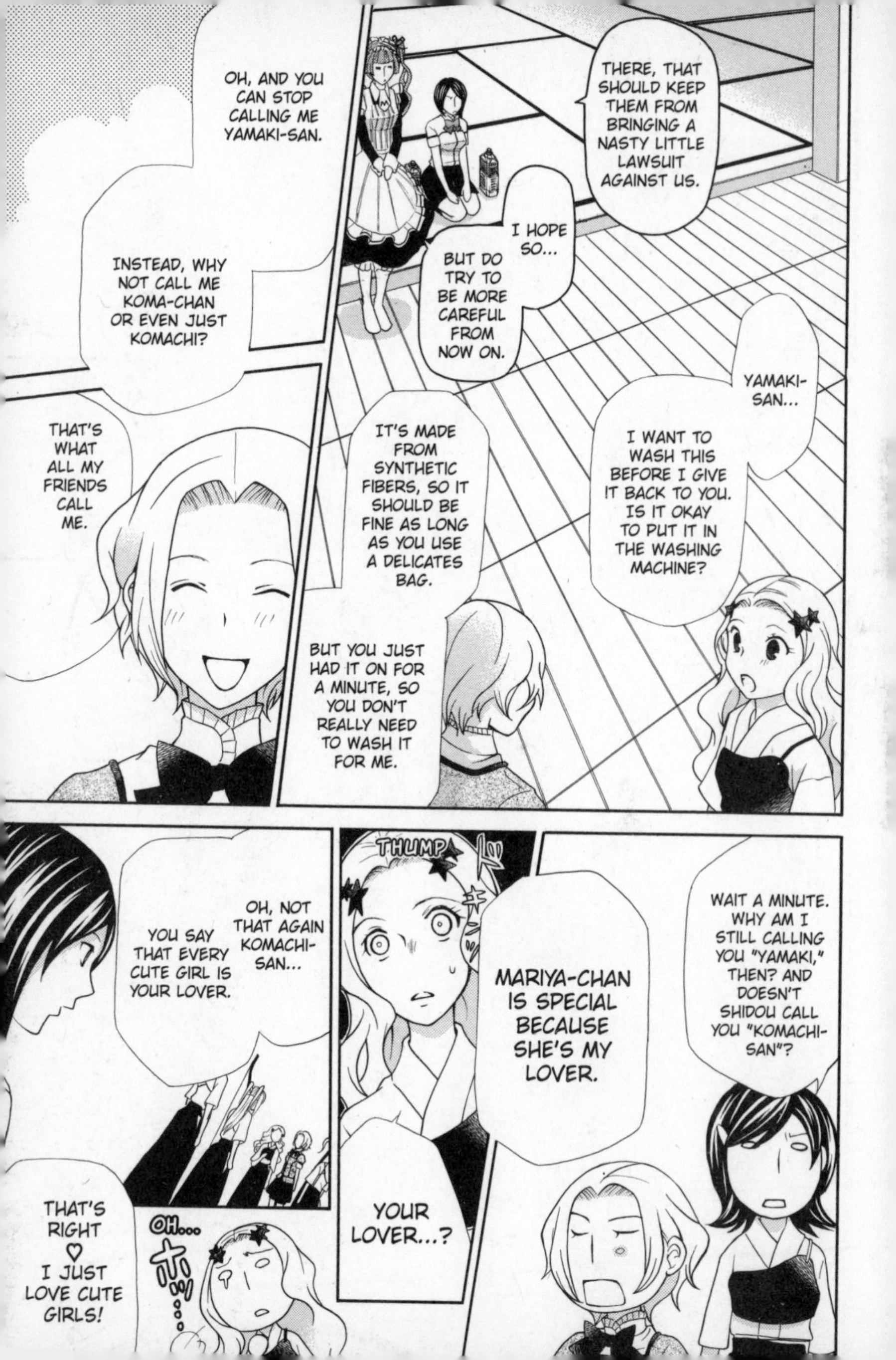
THERE, THAT SHOULD KEEP THEM FROM BRINGING A NASTY LITTLE LAWSUIT AGAINST US.
I HOPE SO...
BUT DO TRY TO BE MORE CAREFUL FROM NOW ON.
YAMAKI-SAN...
I WANT TO WASH THIS BEFORE I GIVE IT BACK TO YOU. IS IT OKAY TO PUT IT IN THE WASHING MACHINE?
IT'S MADE FROM SYNTHETIC FIBERS, SO IT SHOULD BE FINE AS LONG AS YOU USE A DELICATES BAG.
BUT YOU JUST HAD IT ON FOR A MINUTE, SO YOU DON'T REALLY NEED TO WASH IT FOR ME.
OH, AND YOU CAN STOP CALLING ME YAMAKI-SAN.
INSTEAD, WHY NOT CALL ME KOMA-CHAN OR EVEN JUST KOMACHI?
THAT'S WHAT ALL MY FRIENDS CALL ME.
WAIT A MINUTE. WHY AM I STILL CALLING YOU "YAMAKI," THEN? AND DOESN'T SHIDOU CALL YOU "KOMACHI-SAN"?
MARIYA-CHAN IS SPECIAL BECAUSE SHE'S MY LOVER.
YOUR LOVER...?
THUMP
OH, NOT THAT AGAIN KOMACHI-SAN...
YOU SAY THAT EVERY CUTE GIRL IS YOUR LOVER.
THAT'S RIGHT ♡ I JUST LOVE CUTE GIRLS!
OH...

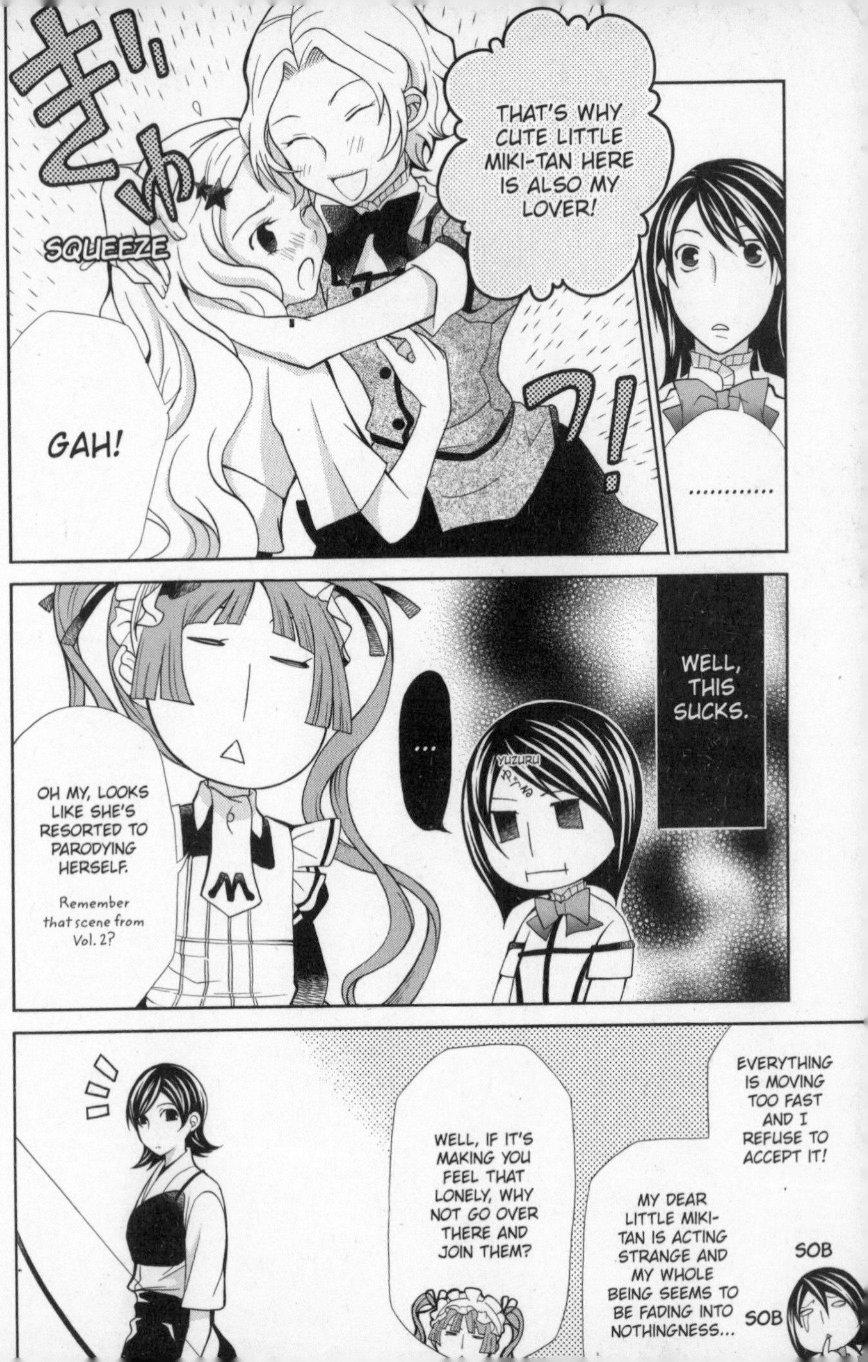
THAT'S WHY CUTE LITTLE MIKI-TAN HERE IS ALSO MY LOVER!
ぎゅ
SQUEEZE
GAH!
?!
....
WELL, THIS SUCKS.
...
YUZURU
OH MY, LOOKS LIKE SHE'S RESORTED TO PARODYING HERSELF.
Remember that scene from Vol. 2?
EVERYTHING IS MOVING TOO FAST AND I REFUSE TO ACCEPT IT!
MY DEAR LITTLE MIKI-TAN IS ACTING STRANGE AND MY WHOLE BEING SEEMS TO BE FADING INTO NOTHINGNESS...
SOB
SOB
WELL, IF IT'S MAKING YOU FEEL THAT LONELY, WHY NOT GO OVER THERE AND JOIN THEM?

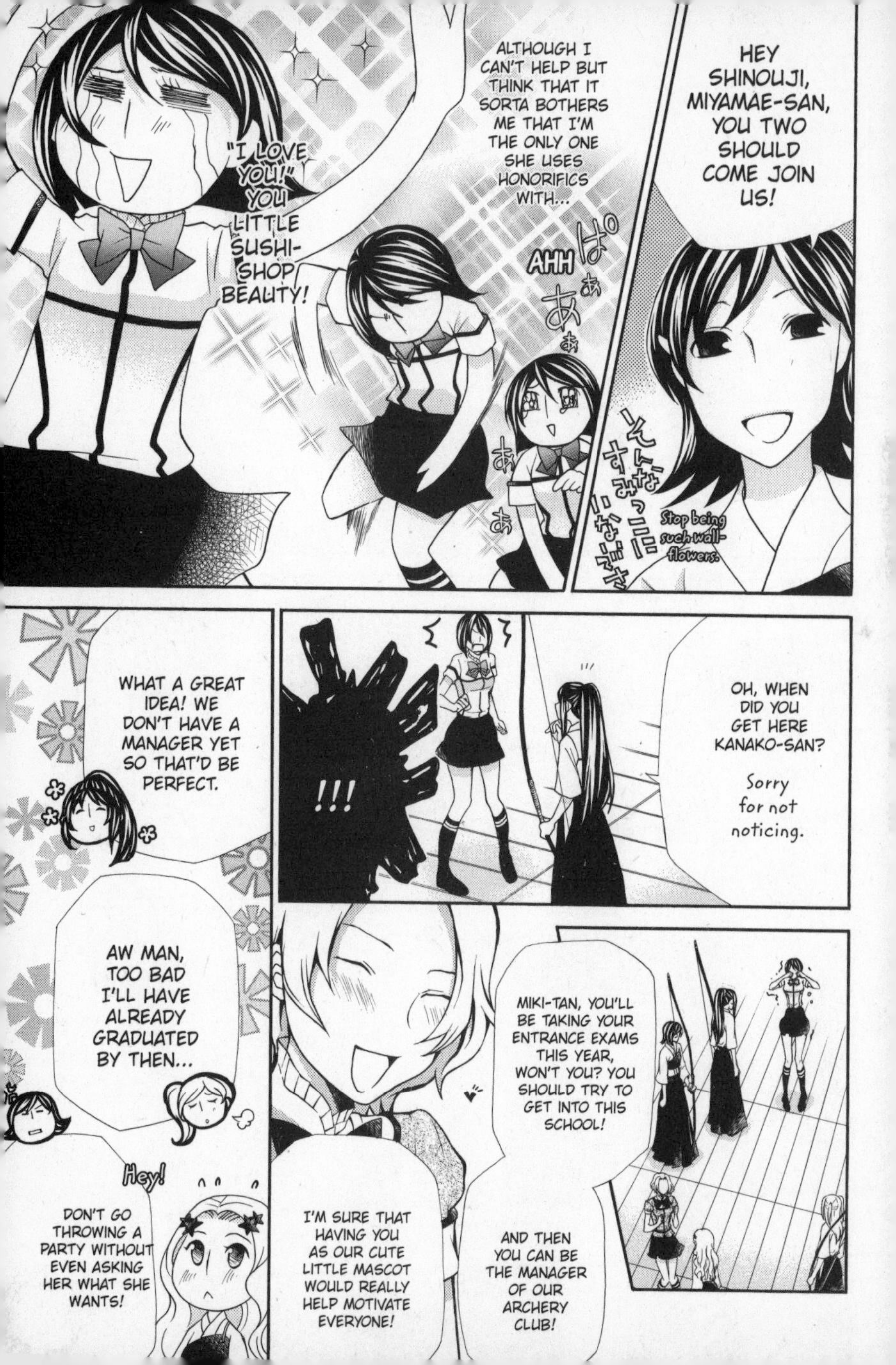
HEY SHINOUJI, MIYAMAE-SAN, YOU TWO SHOULD COME JOIN US!
Stop being such wall-flowers.
ALTHOUGH I CAN'T HELP BUT THINK THAT IT SORTA BOTHERS ME THAT I'M THE ONLY ONE SHE USES HONORIFICS WITH...
AHH
"I LOVE YOU!" YOU LITTLE SUSHI-SHOP BEAUTY!
OH, WHEN DID YOU GET HERE KANAKO-SAN?
Sorry for not noticing.
!!!
MIKI-TAN, YOU'LL BE TAKING YOUR ENTRANCE EXAMS THIS YEAR, WON'T YOU? YOU SHOULD TRY TO GET INTO THIS SCHOOL!
AND THEN YOU CAN BE THE MANAGER OF OUR ARCHERY CLUB!
I'M SURE THAT HAVING YOU AS OUR CUTE LITTLE MASCOT WOULD REALLY HELP MOTIVATE EVERYONE!
WHAT A GREAT IDEA! WE DON'T HAVE A MANAGER YET SO THAT'D BE PERFECT.
AW MAN, TOO BAD I'LL HAVE ALREADY GRADUATED BY THEN...
Hey!
DON'T GO THROWING A PARTY WITHOUT EVEN ASKING HER WHAT SHE WANTS!

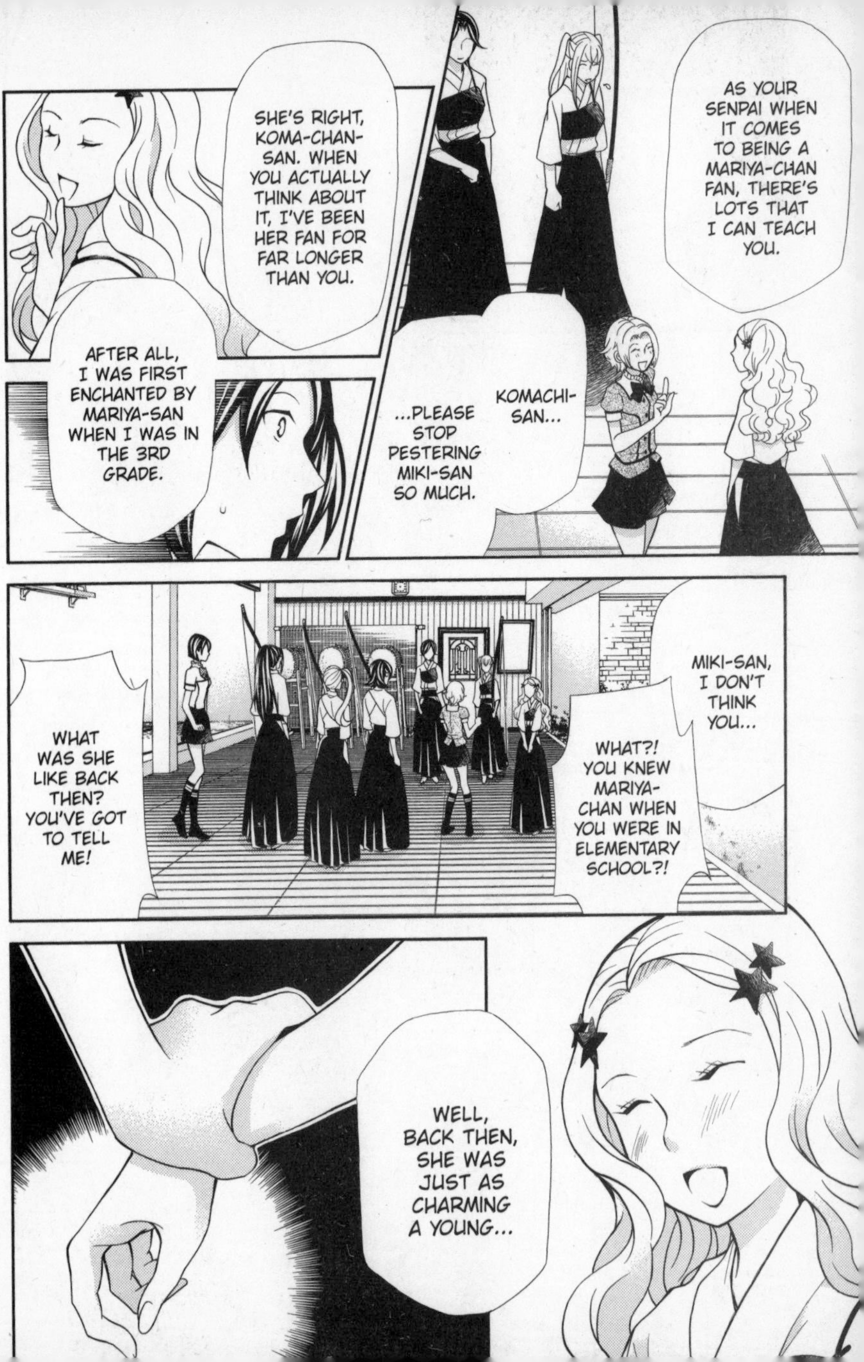
AS YOUR SENPAI WHEN IT COMES TO BEING A MARIYA-CHAN FAN, THERE'S LOTS THAT I CAN TEACH YOU.
KOMACHI-SAN...
...PLEASE STOP PESTERING MIKI-SAN SO MUCH.
SHE'S RIGHT, KOMA-CHAN-SAN. WHEN YOU ACTUALLY THINK ABOUT IT, I'VE BEEN HER FAN FOR FAR LONGER THAN YOU.
AFTER ALL, I WAS FIRST ENCHANTED BY MARIYA-SAN WHEN I WAS IN THE 3RD GRADE.
MIKI-SAN, I DON'T THINK YOU...
WHAT?! YOU KNEW MARIYA-CHAN WHEN YOU WERE IN ELEMENTARY SCHOOL?!
WHAT WAS SHE LIKE BACK THEN? YOU'VE GOT TO TELL ME!
WELL, BACK THEN, SHE WAS JUST AS CHARMING A YOUNG...

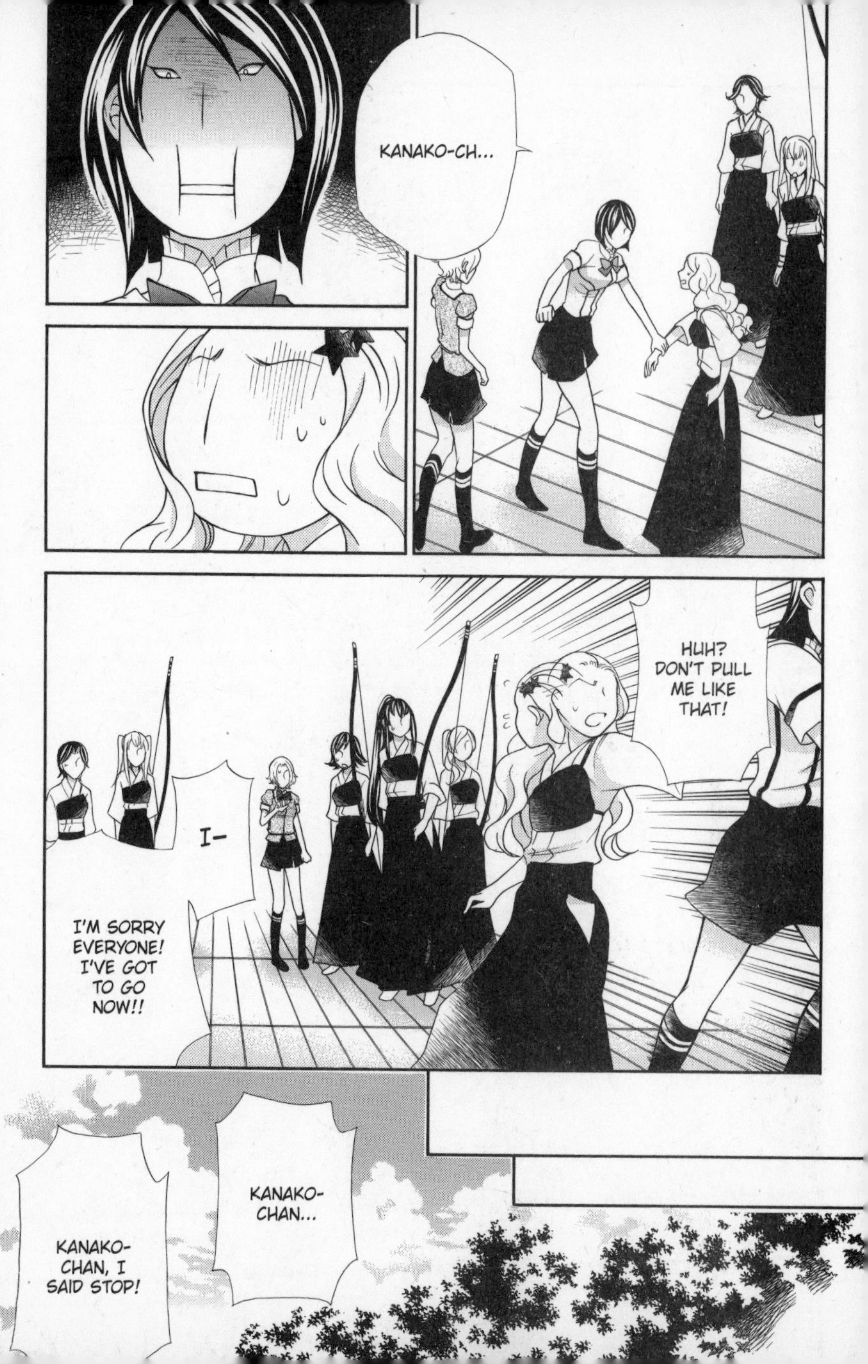
KANAKO-CH...
HUH? DON'T PULL ME LIKE THAT!
I-
I'M SORRY EVERYONE! I'VE GOT TO GO NOW!!
KANAKO-CHAN...
KANAKO-CHAN, I SAID STOP!

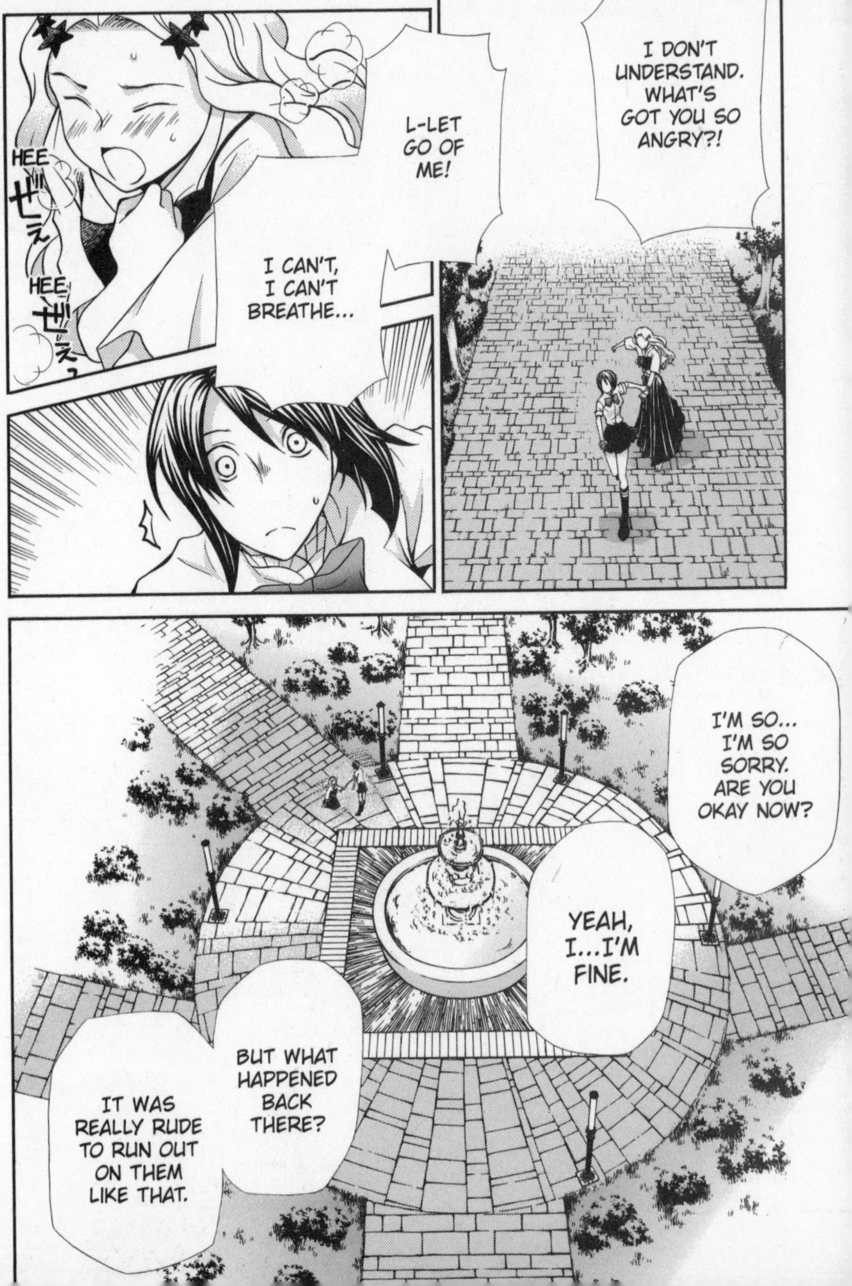
I DON'T UNDERSTAND. WHAT'S GOT YOU SO ANGRY?!
L-LET GO OF ME!
I CAN'T, I CAN'T BREATHE...
HEE ぜぇ
HEE ぜぇっ
I'M SO... I'M SO SORRY. ARE YOU OKAY NOW?
YEAH, I...I'M FINE.
BUT WHAT HAPPENED BACK THERE?
IT WAS REALLY RUDE TO RUN OUT ON THEM LIKE THAT.

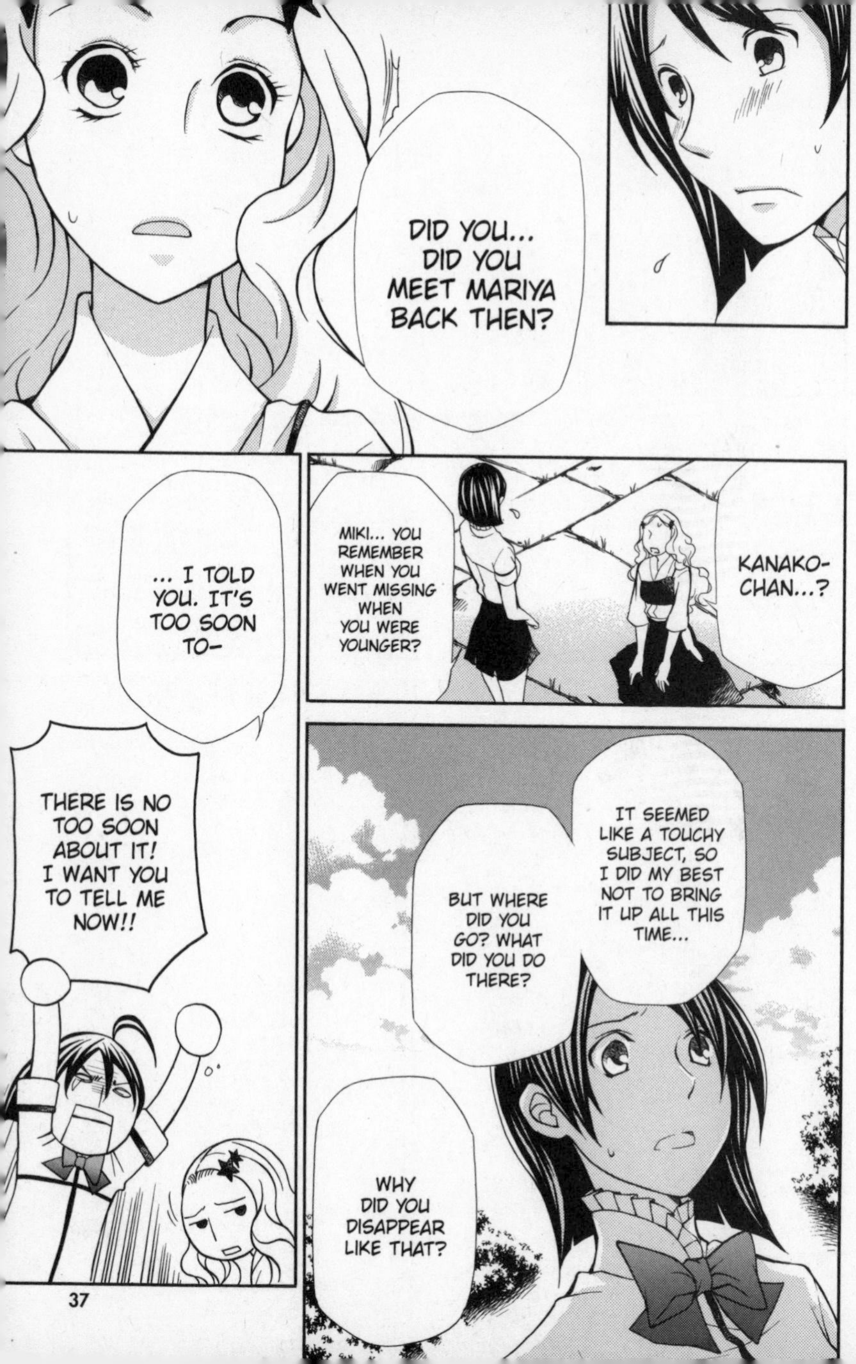
DID YOU... DID YOU MEET MARIYA BACK THEN?
KANAKO-CHAN...?
MIKI... YOU REMEMBER WHEN YOU WENT MISSING WHEN YOU WERE YOUNGER?
... I TOLD YOU. IT'S TOO SOON TO-
IT SEEMED LIKE A TOUCHY SUBJECT, SO I DID MY BEST NOT TO BRING IT UP ALL THIS TIME...
BUT WHERE DID YOU GO? WHAT DID YOU DO THERE?
WHY DID YOU DISAPPEAR LIKE THAT?
THERE IS NO TOO SOON ABOUT IT! I WANT YOU TO TELL ME NOW!!

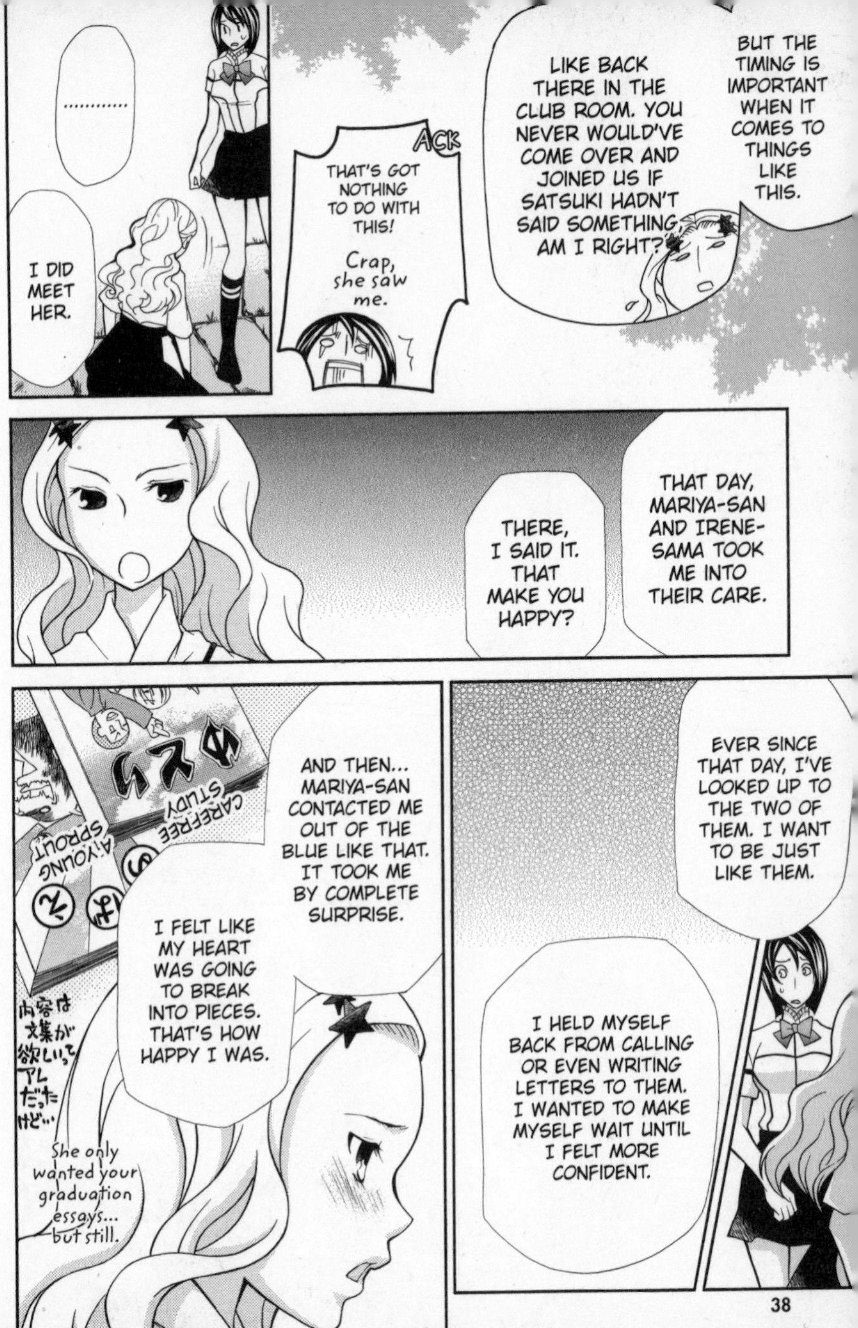
BUT THE TIMING IS IMPORTANT WHEN IT COMES TO THINGS LIKE THIS.
LIKE BACK THERE IN THE CLUB ROOM. YOU NEVER WOULD'VE COME OVER AND JOINED US IF SATSUKI HADN'T SAID SOMETHING, AM I RIGHT?
ACK
THAT'S GOT NOTHING TO DO WITH THIS!
Crap, she saw me.
....
I DID MEET HER.
THAT DAY, MARIYA-SAN AND IRENE-SAMA TOOK ME INTO THEIR CARE.
THERE, I SAID IT. THAT MAKE YOU HAPPY?
EVER SINCE THAT DAY, I'VE LOOKED UP TO THE TWO OF THEM. I WANT TO BE JUST LIKE THEM.
I HELD MYSELF BACK FROM CALLING OR EVEN WRITING LETTERS TO THEM. I WANTED TO MAKE MYSELF WAIT UNTIL I FELT MORE CONFIDENT.
AND THEN... MARIYA-SAN CONTACTED ME OUT OF THE BLUE LIKE THAT. IT TOOK ME BY COMPLETE SURPRISE.
CAREFREE STUDY
A YOUNG SPROUT
I FELT LIKE MY HEART WAS GOING TO BREAK INTO PIECES. THAT'S HOW HAPPY I WAS.
内容は文集が欲しいってアレだったけど…
She only wanted your graduation essays... but still.

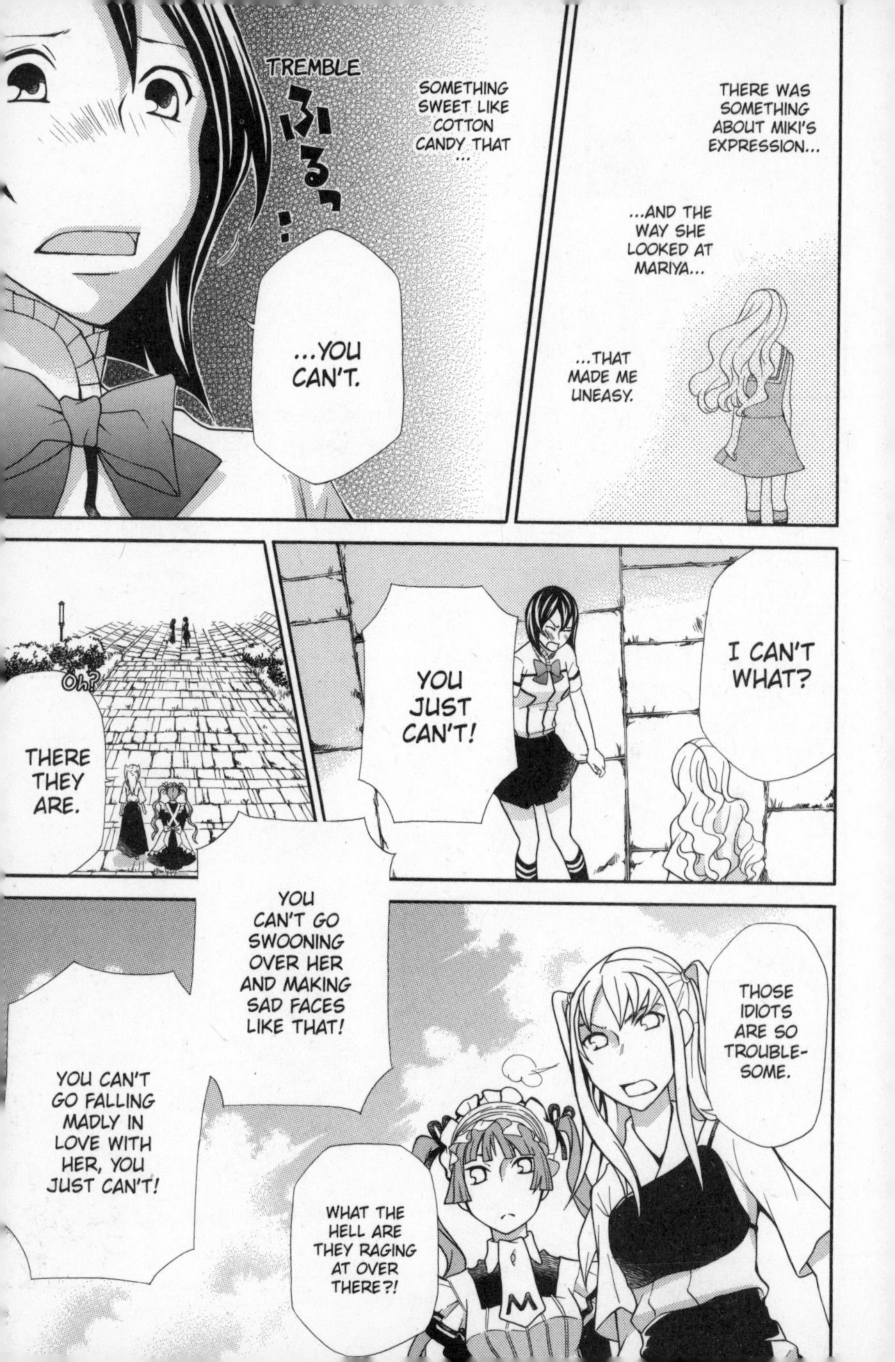
THERE WAS SOMETHING ABOUT MIKI'S EXPRESSION...
...AND THE WAY SHE LOOKED AT MARIYA...
...THAT MADE ME UNEASY.
SOMETHING SWEET LIKE COTTON CANDY THAT ...
TREMBLE
ふるっ
...YOU CAN'T.
I CAN'T WHAT?
YOU JUST CAN'T!
Oh?
THERE THEY ARE.
YOU CAN'T GO SWOONING OVER HER AND MAKING SAD FACES LIKE THAT!
THOSE IDIOTS ARE SO TROUBLE-SOME.
WHAT THE HELL ARE THEY RAGING AT OVER THERE?!
YOU CAN'T GO FALLING MADLY IN LOVE WITH HER, YOU JUST CAN'T!

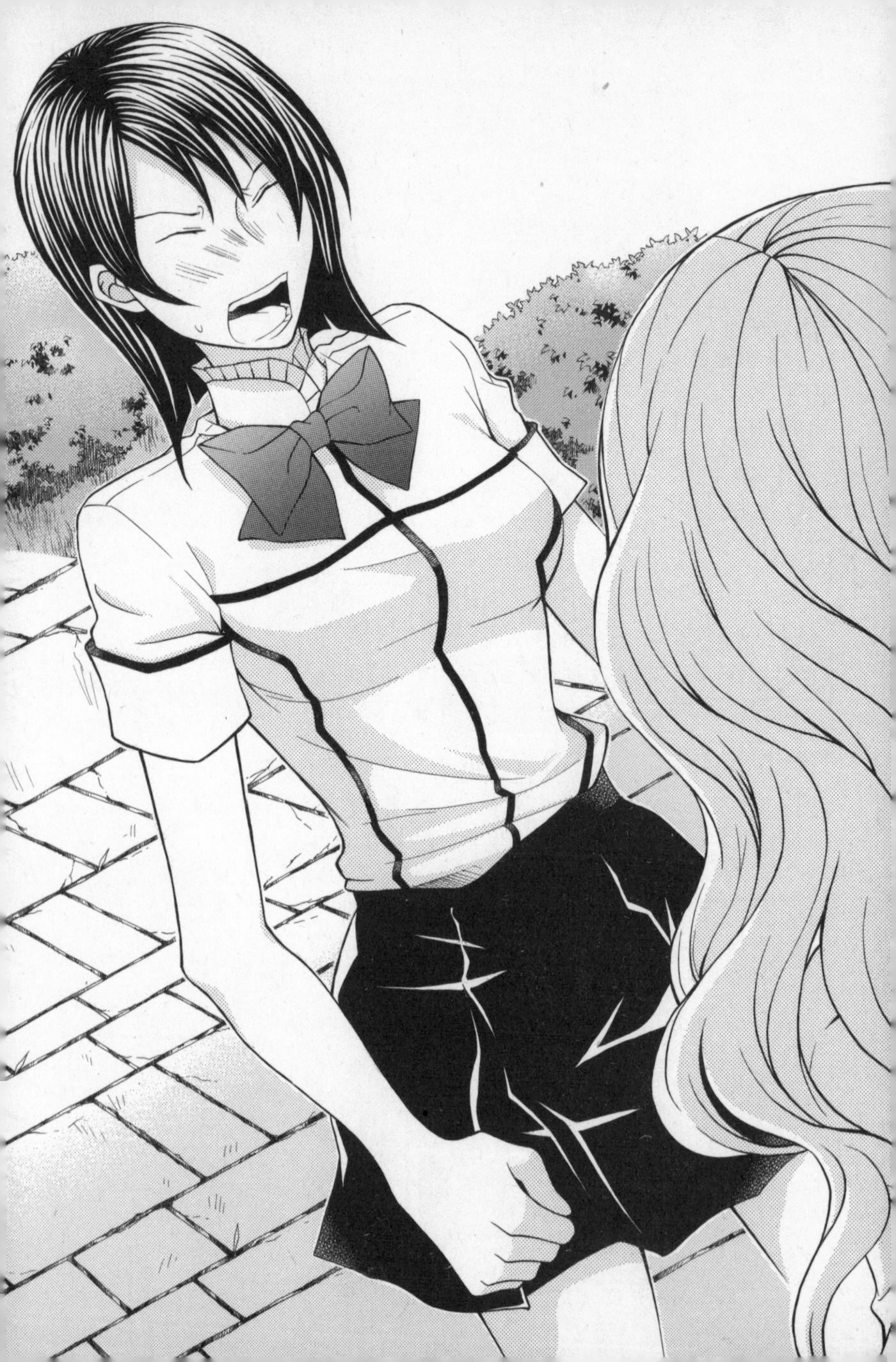

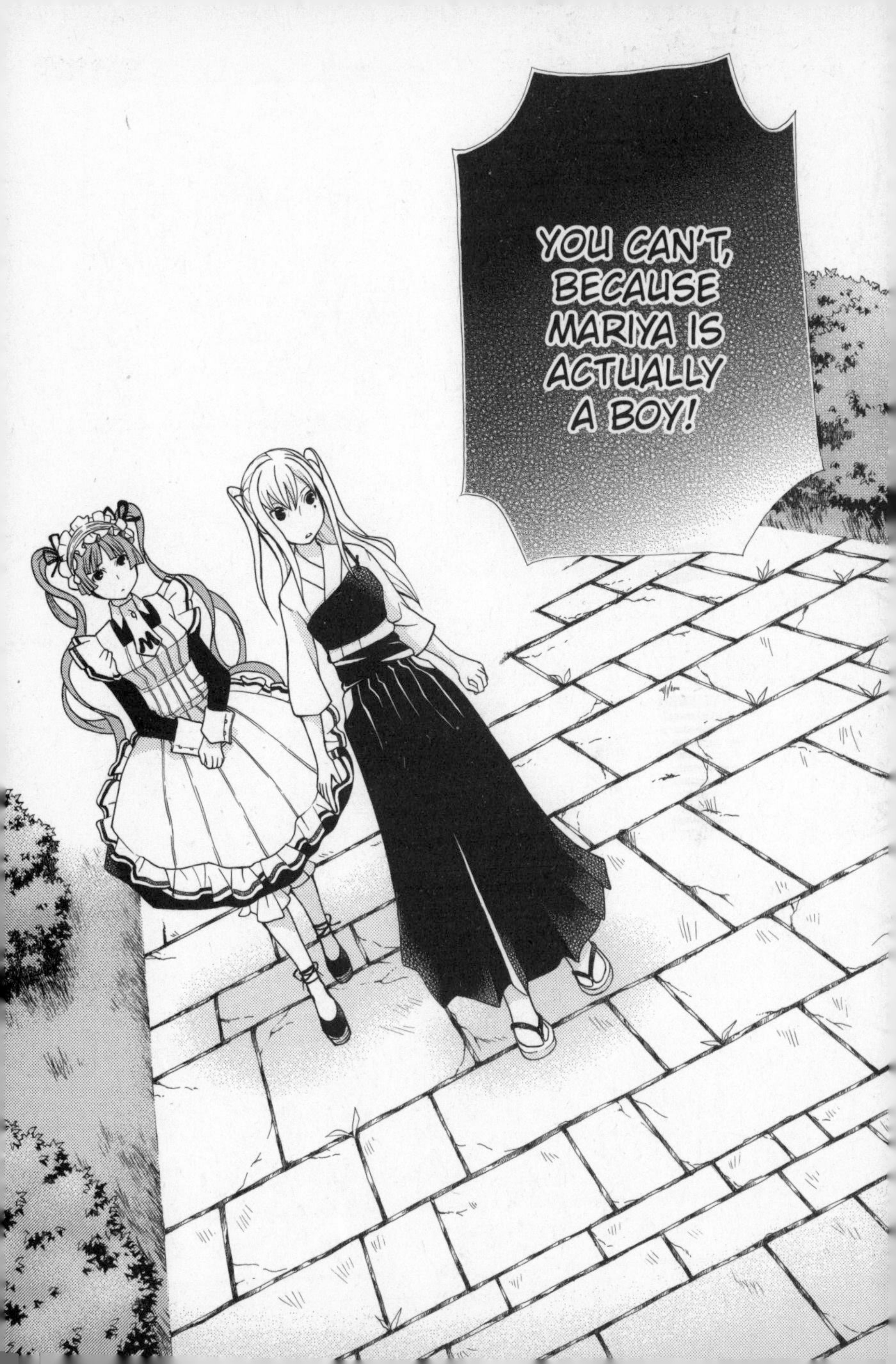
YOU CAN'T, BECAUSE MARIYA IS ACTUALLY A BOY!

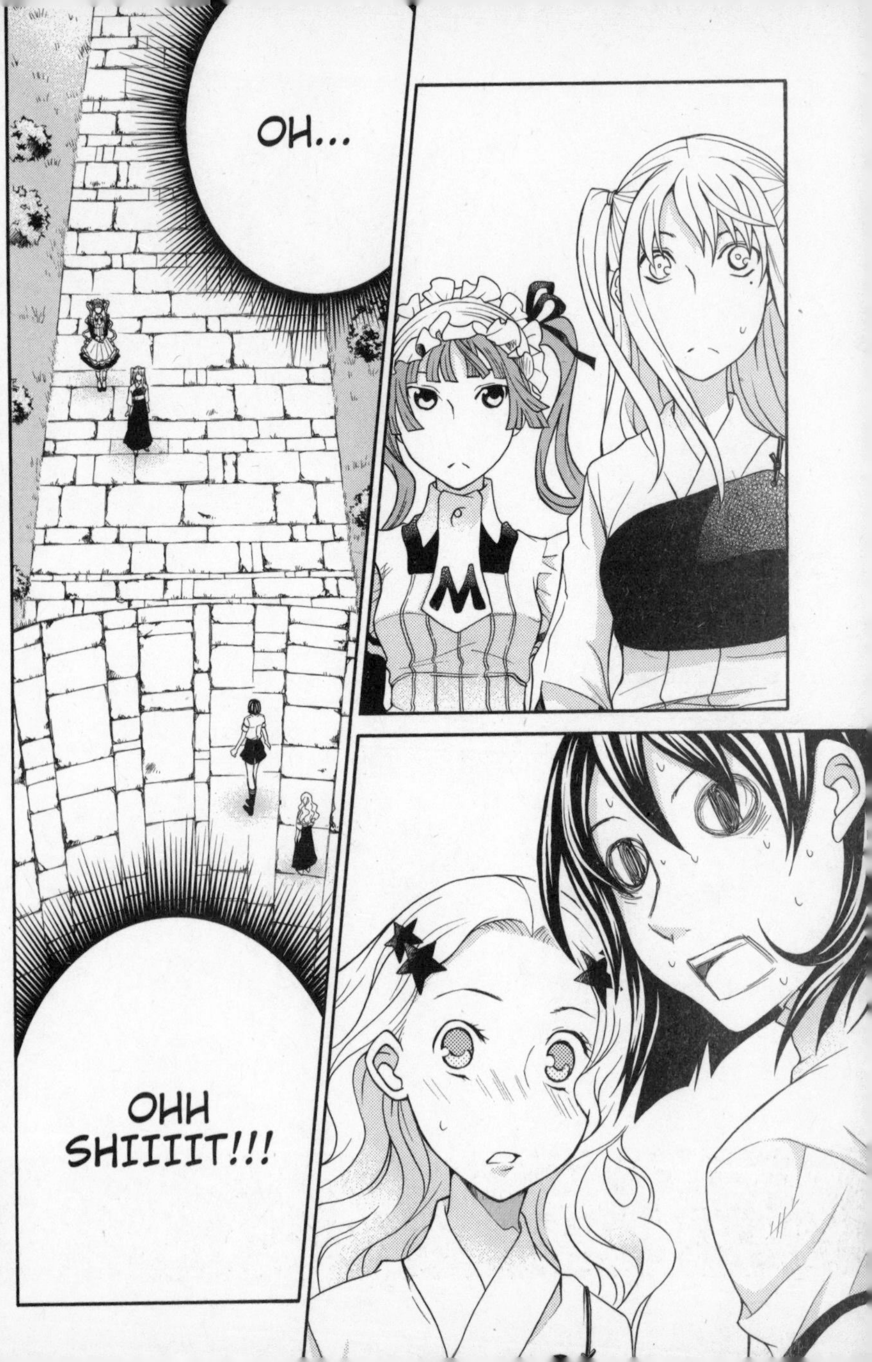
OH...
OHH SHIIIIT!!!

M A R I A H O L I C

MARIA HOLIC

M A R I A H O L I C

MARIA HOLIC

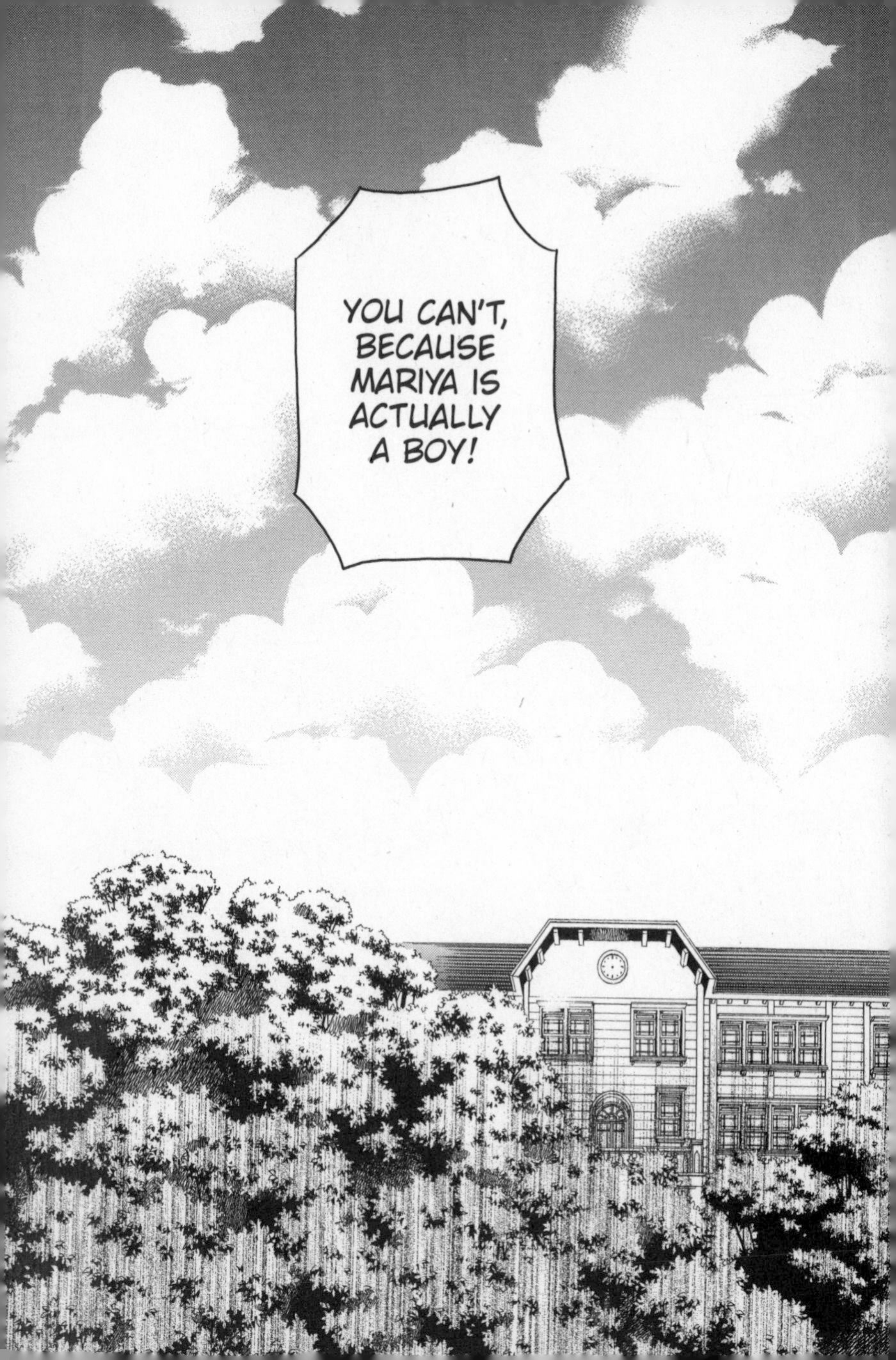
YOU CAN'T, BECAUSE MARIYA IS ACTUALLY A BOY!

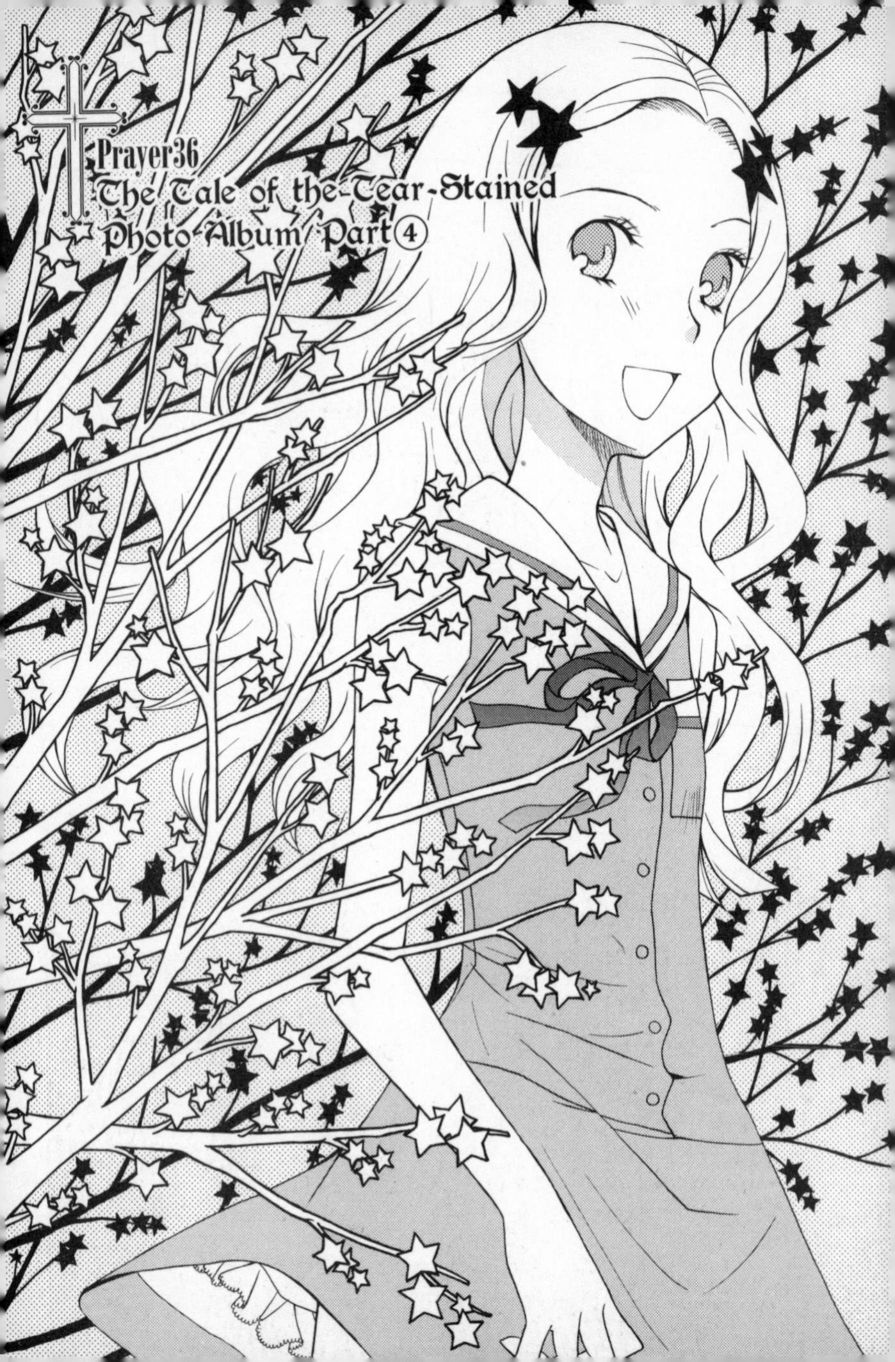
Prayer 36
The Tale of the Tear-Stained Photo Album Part 4

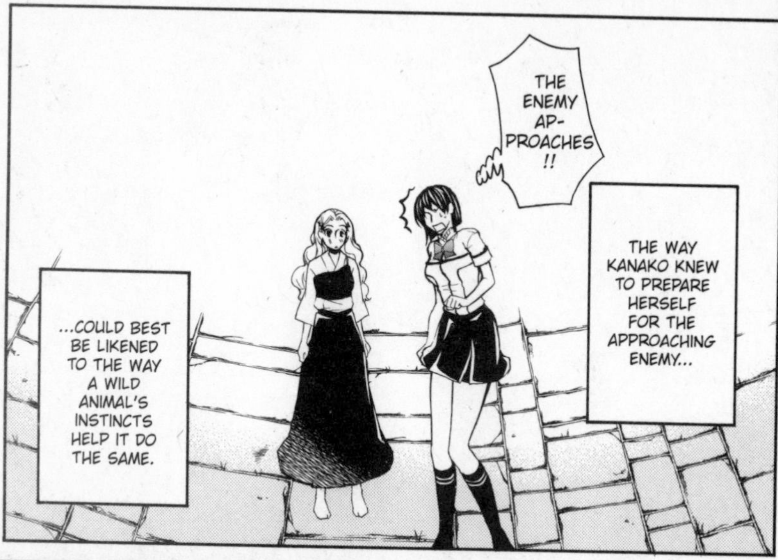
THE ENEMY AP- PROACHES !!
THE WAY KANAKO KNEW TO PREPARE HERSELF FOR THE APPROACHING ENEMY...
...COULD BEST BE LIKENED TO THE WAY A WILD ANIMAL'S INSTINCTS HELP IT DO THE SAME.
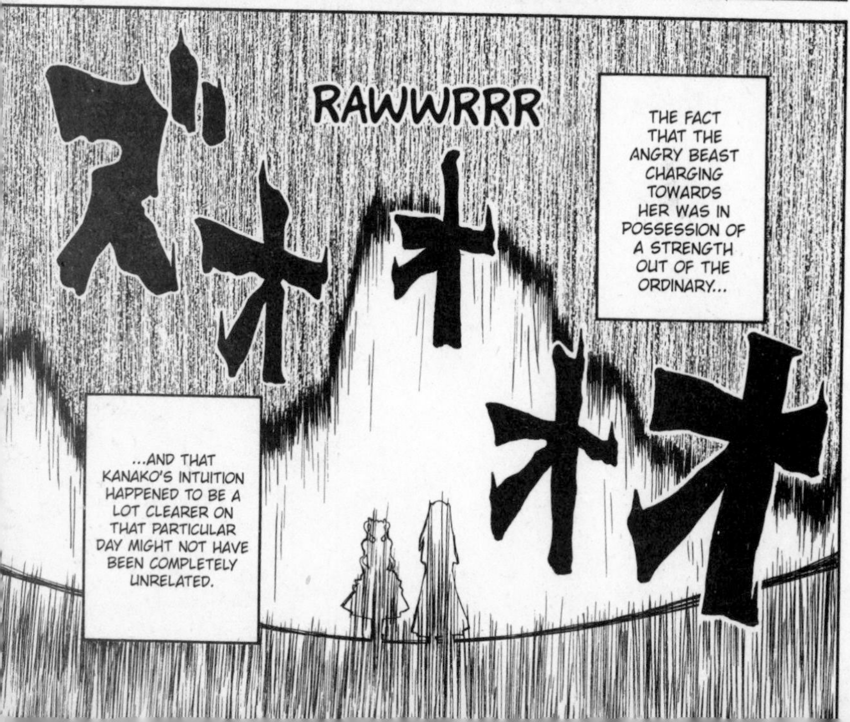
RAWWRRR
THE FACT THAT THE ANGRY BEAST CHARGING TOWARDS HER WAS IN POSSESSION OF A STRENGTH OUT OF THE ORDINARY...
...AND THAT KANAKO'S INTUITION HAPPENED TO BE A LOT CLEARER ON THAT PARTICULAR DAY MIGHT NOT HAVE BEEN COMPLETELY UNRELATED.

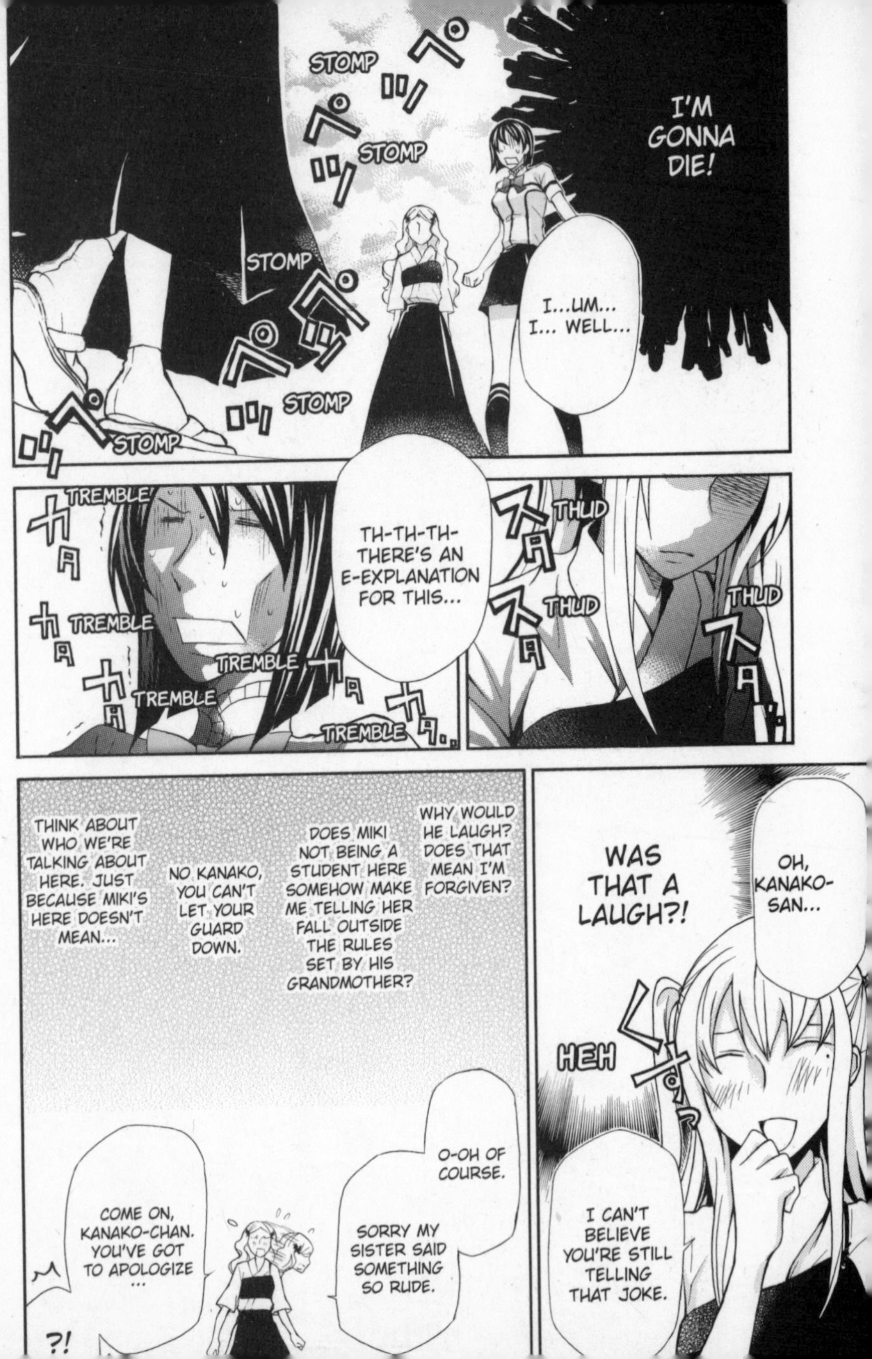
I'M GONNA DIE!
STOMP
STOMP
STOMP
STOMP
STOMP
I...UM... I... WELL...
THUD
THUD
THUD
TH-TH-TH- THERE'S AN E-EXPLANATION FOR THIS...
TREMBLE
TREMBLE
TREMBLE
TREMBLE
TREMBLE
OH, KANAKO-SAN...
WAS THAT A LAUGH?!
HEH
I CAN'T BELIEVE YOU'RE STILL TELLING THAT JOKE.
WHY WOULD HE LAUGH? DOES THAT MEAN I'M FORGIVEN?
DOES MIKI NOT BEING A STUDENT HERE SOMEHOW MAKE ME TELLING HER FALL OUTSIDE THE RULES SET BY HIS GRANDMOTHER?
NO KANAKO, YOU CAN'T LET YOUR GUARD DOWN.
THINK ABOUT WHO WE'RE TALKING ABOUT HERE. JUST BECAUSE MIKI'S HERE DOESN'T MEAN...
O-OH OF COURSE.
SORRY MY SISTER SAID SOMETHING SO RUDE.
COME ON, KANAKO-CHAN. YOU'VE GOT TO APOLOGIZE ...
?!

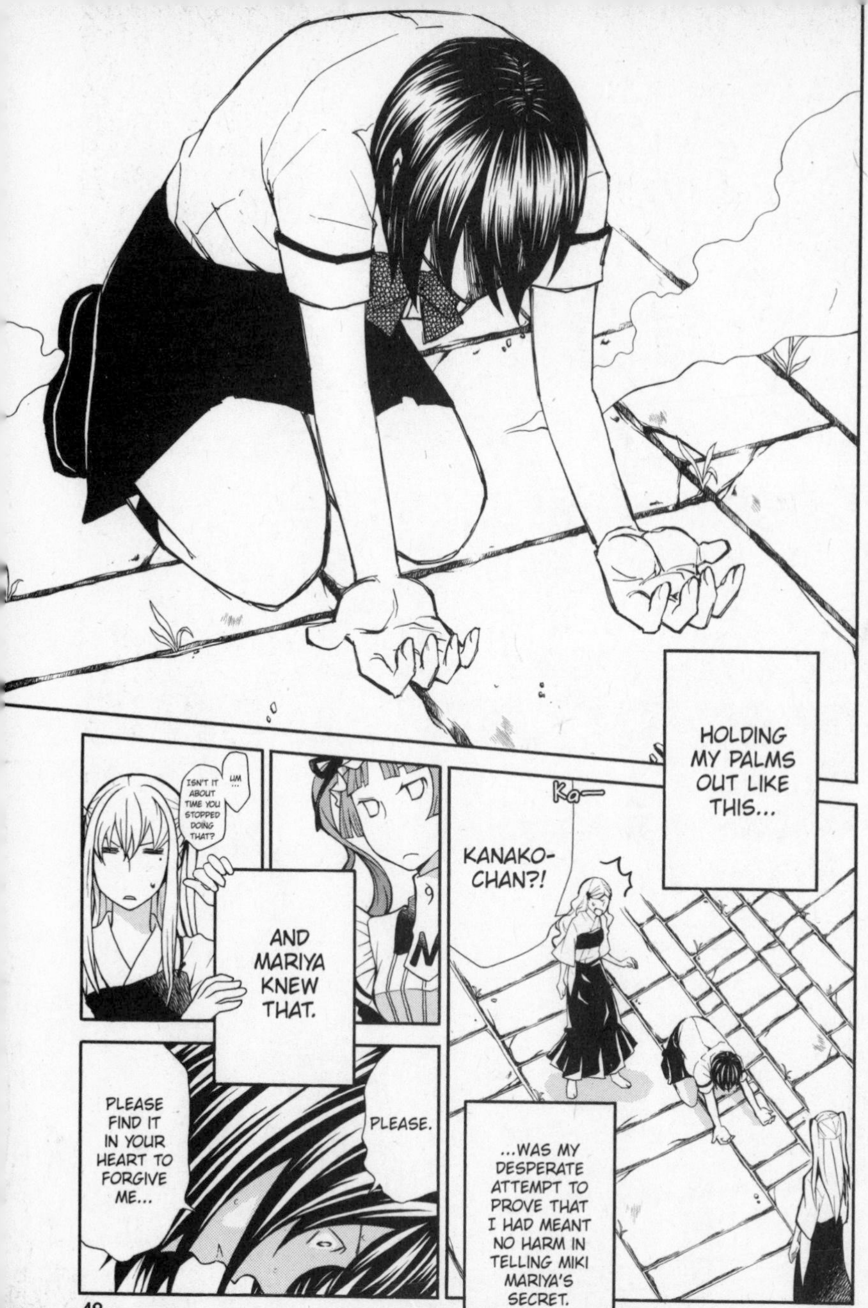
HOLDING MY PALMS OUT LIKE THIS...
Ka—
KANAKO-CHAN?!
...WAS MY DESPERATE ATTEMPT TO PROVE THAT I HAD MEANT NO HARM IN TELLING MIKI MARIYA'S SECRET.
UM ...
ISN'T IT ABOUT TIME YOU STOPPED DOING THAT?
AND MARIYA KNEW THAT.
PLEASE.
PLEASE FIND IT IN YOUR HEART TO FORGIVE ME...

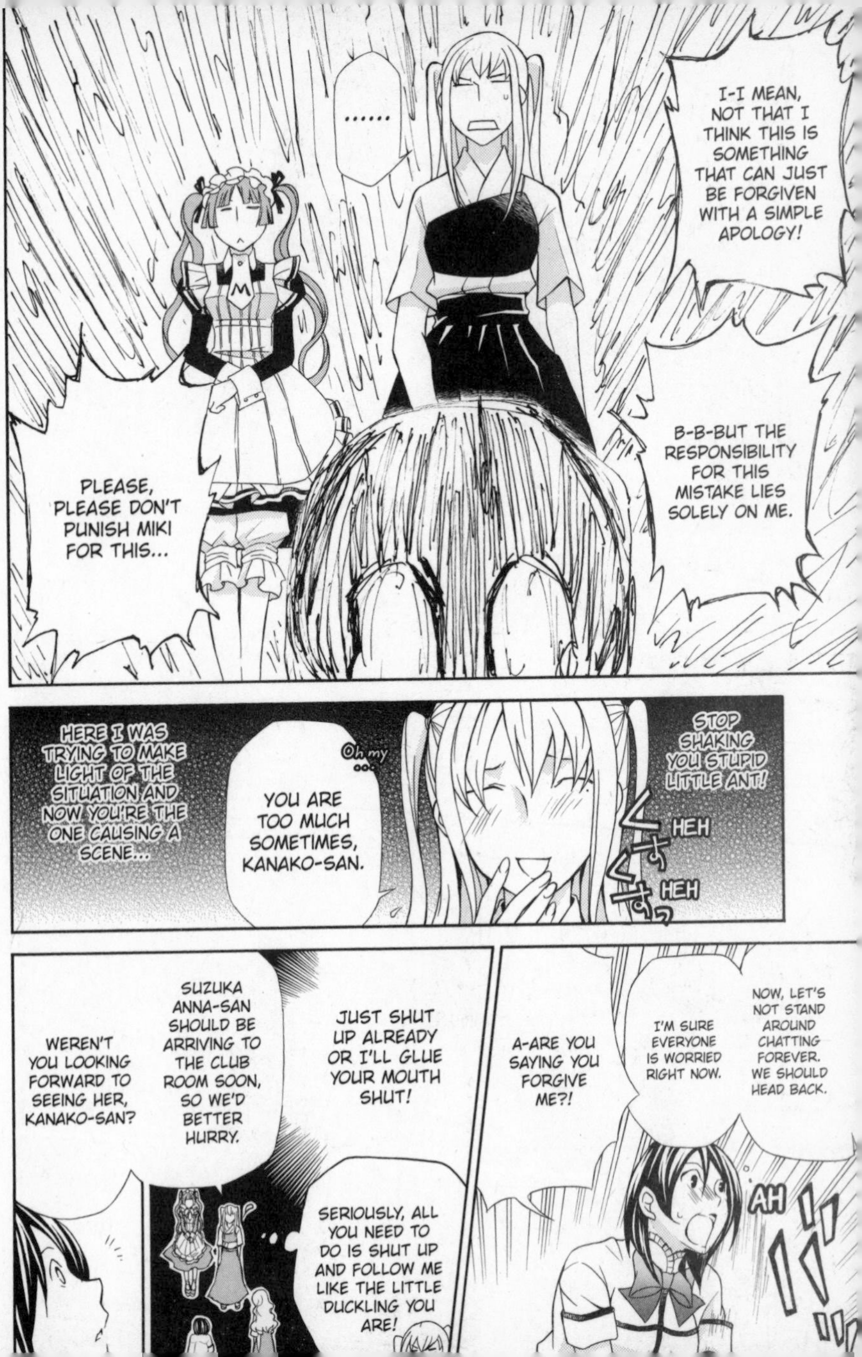
I-I MEAN, NOT THAT I THINK THIS IS SOMETHING THAT CAN JUST BE FORGIVEN WITH A SIMPLE APOLOGY!
......
B-B-BUT THE RESPONSIBILITY FOR THIS MISTAKE LIES SOLELY ON ME.
PLEASE, PLEASE DON'T PUNISH MIKI FOR THIS...
STOP SHAKING YOU STUPID LITTLE ANT!
HEH
HEH
Oh my ...
YOU ARE TOO MUCH SOMETIMES, KANAKO-SAN.
HERE I WAS TRYING TO MAKE LIGHT OF THE SITUATION AND NOW YOU'RE THE ONE CAUSING A SCENE...
NOW, LET'S NOT STAND AROUND CHATTING FOREVER. WE SHOULD HEAD BACK.
I'M SURE EVERYONE IS WORRIED RIGHT NOW.
A-ARE YOU SAYING YOU FORGIVE ME?!
AH
JUST SHUT UP ALREADY OR I'LL GLUE YOUR MOUTH SHUT!
SUZUKA ANNA-SAN SHOULD BE ARRIVING TO THE CLUB ROOM SOON, SO WE'D BETTER HURRY.
WEREN'T YOU LOOKING FORWARD TO SEEING HER, KANAKO-SAN?
SERIOUSLY, ALL YOU NEED TO DO IS SHUT UP AND FOLLOW ME LIKE THE LITTLE DUCKLING YOU ARE!

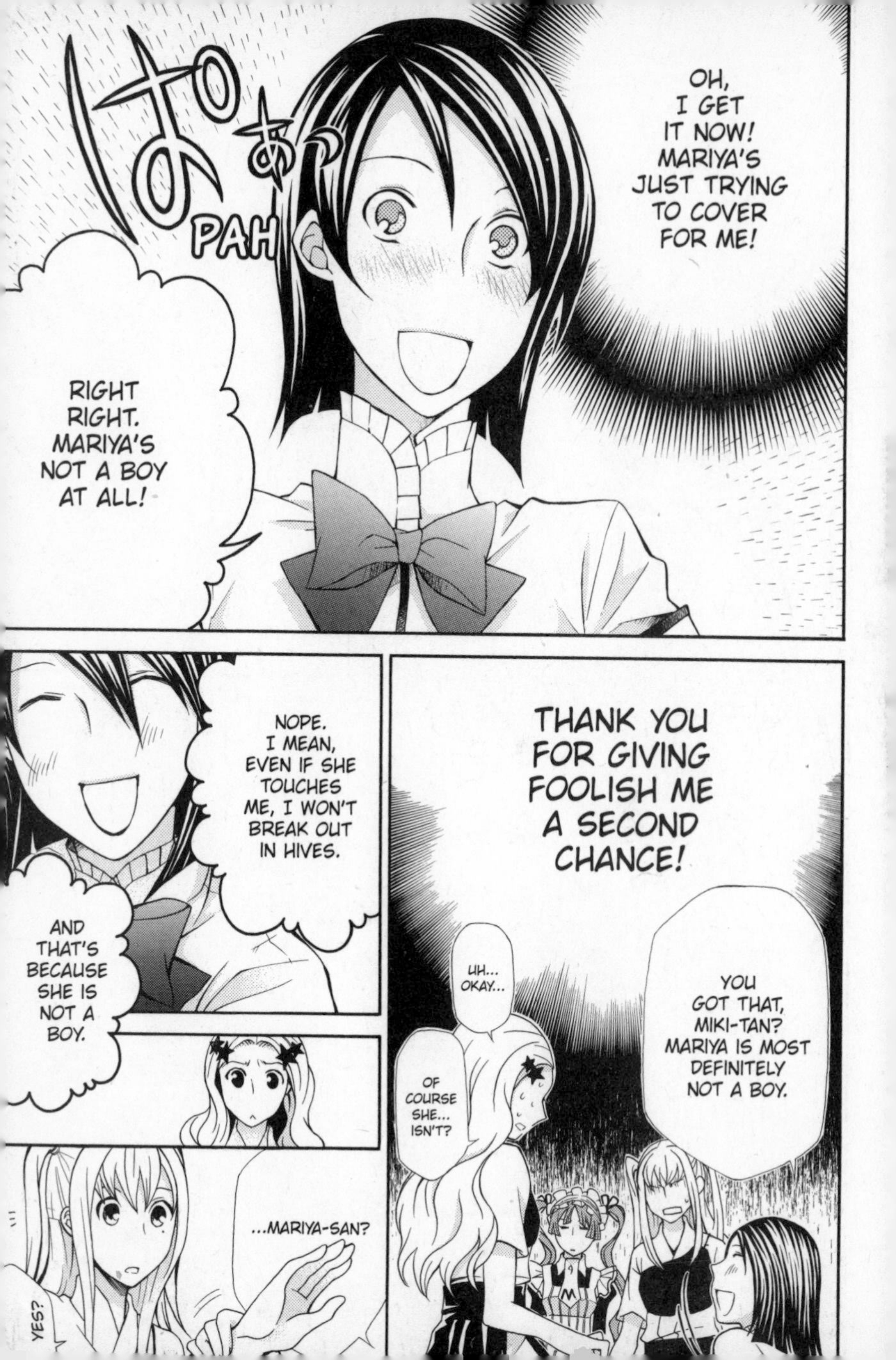
OH, I GET IT NOW! MARIYA'S JUST TRYING TO COVER FOR ME!
PAH
RIGHT RIGHT. MARIYA'S NOT A BOY AT ALL!
THANK YOU FOR GIVING FOOLISH ME A SECOND CHANCE!
YOU GOT THAT, MIKI-TAN? MARIYA IS MOST DEFINITELY NOT A BOY.
UH... OKAY...
OF COURSE SHE... ISN'T?
NOPE. I MEAN, EVEN IF SHE TOUCHES ME, I WON'T BREAK OUT IN HIVES.
AND THAT'S BECAUSE SHE IS NOT A BOY.
...MARIYA-SAN?
YES?

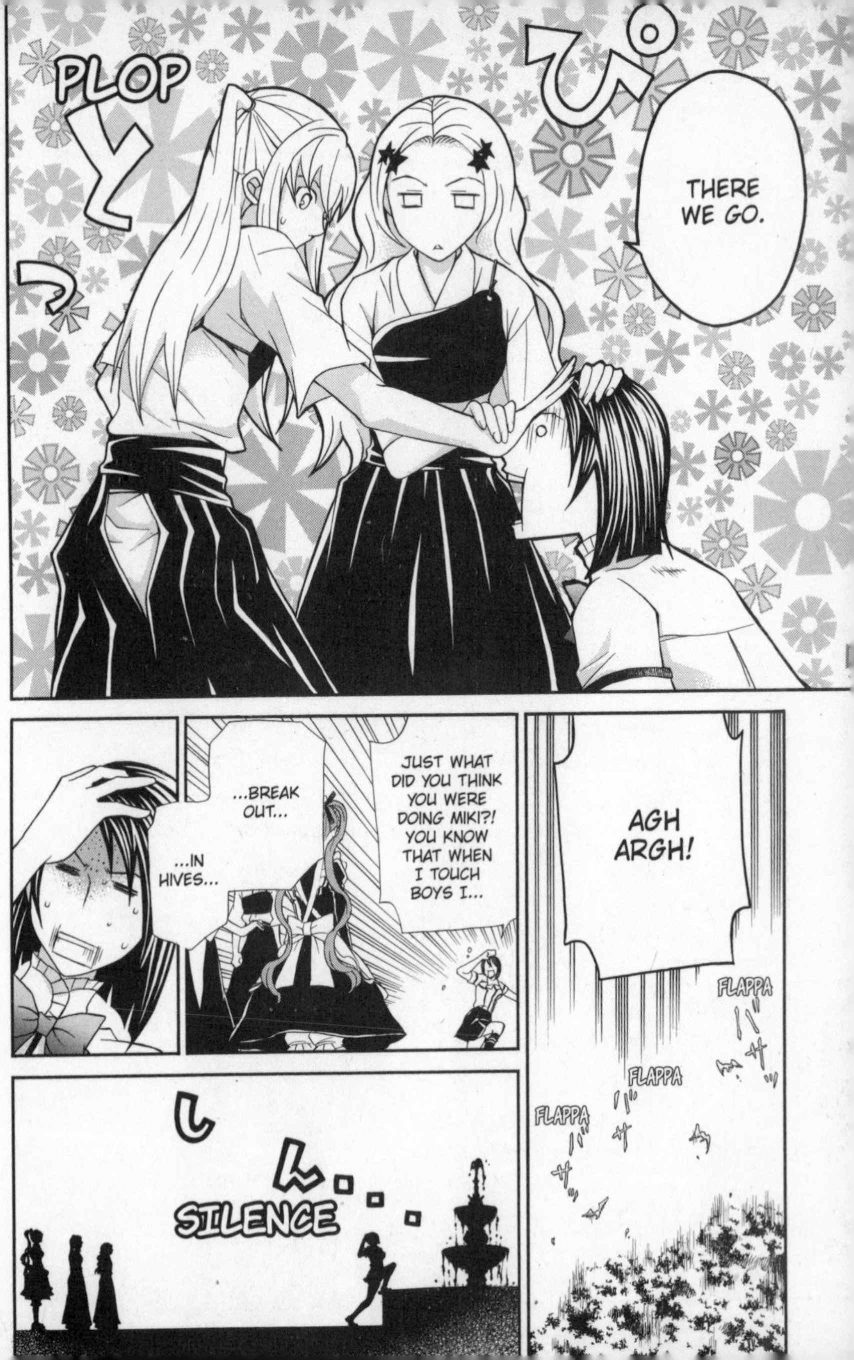
ぴ
THERE WE GO.
PLOP
とっ
AGH ARGH!
FLAPPA
FLAPPA
FLAPPA
JUST WHAT DID YOU THINK YOU WERE DOING MIKI?! YOU KNOW THAT WHEN I TOUCH BOYS I...
...BREAK OUT...
...IN HIVES...
しん...
SILENCE

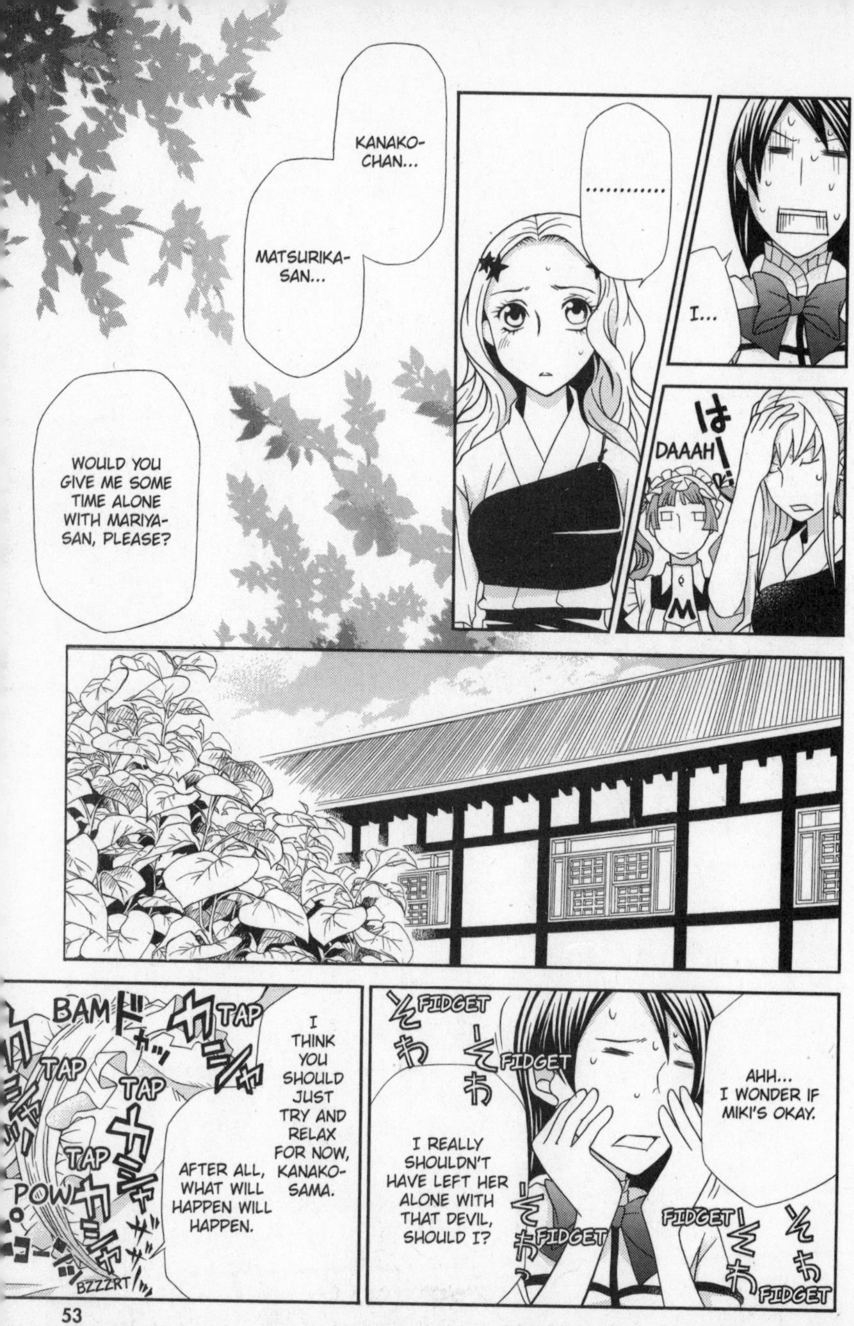
I...
DAAAH
....
KANAKO-CHAN...
MATSURIKA-SAN...
WOULD YOU GIVE ME SOME TIME ALONE WITH MARIYA-SAN, PLEASE?
AHH... I WONDER IF MIKI'S OKAY.
FIDGET
FIDGET
FIDGET
FIDGET
FIDGET
I REALLY SHOULDN'T HAVE LEFT HER ALONE WITH THAT DEVIL, SHOULD I?
I THINK YOU SHOULD JUST TRY AND RELAX FOR NOW, KANAKO-SAMA.
AFTER ALL, WHAT WILL HAPPEN WILL HAPPEN.
TAP
BAM
TAP
TAP
TAP
POW
BZZZRT

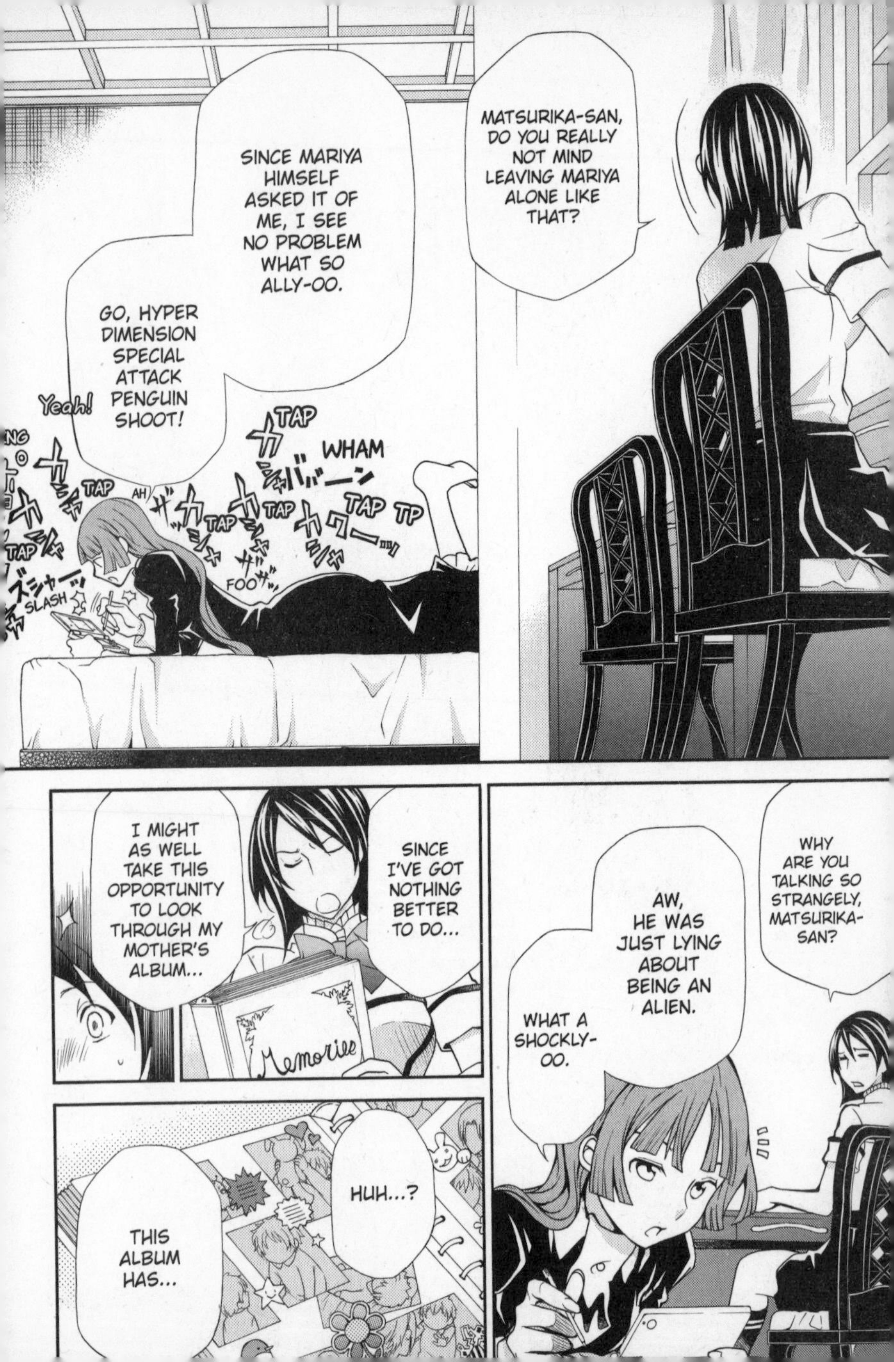
MATSURIKA-SAN, DO YOU REALLY NOT MIND LEAVING MARIYA ALONE LIKE THAT?
SINCE MARIYA HIMSELF ASKED IT OF ME, I SEE NO PROBLEM WHAT SO ALLY-OO.
GO, HYPER DIMENSION SPECIAL ATTACK PENGUIN SHOOT!
Yeah!
TAP
WHAM
TAP TP
TAP
TAP
AH
TAP
FOO
TAP
SLASH
WHY ARE YOU TALKING SO STRANGELY, MATSURIKA-SAN?
AW, HE WAS JUST LYING ABOUT BEING AN ALIEN.
WHAT A SHOCKLY-OO.
SINCE I'VE GOT NOTHING BETTER TO DO...
I MIGHT AS WELL TAKE THIS OPPORTUNITY TO LOOK THROUGH MY MOTHER'S ALBUM...
Memories
HUH...?
THIS ALBUM HAS...

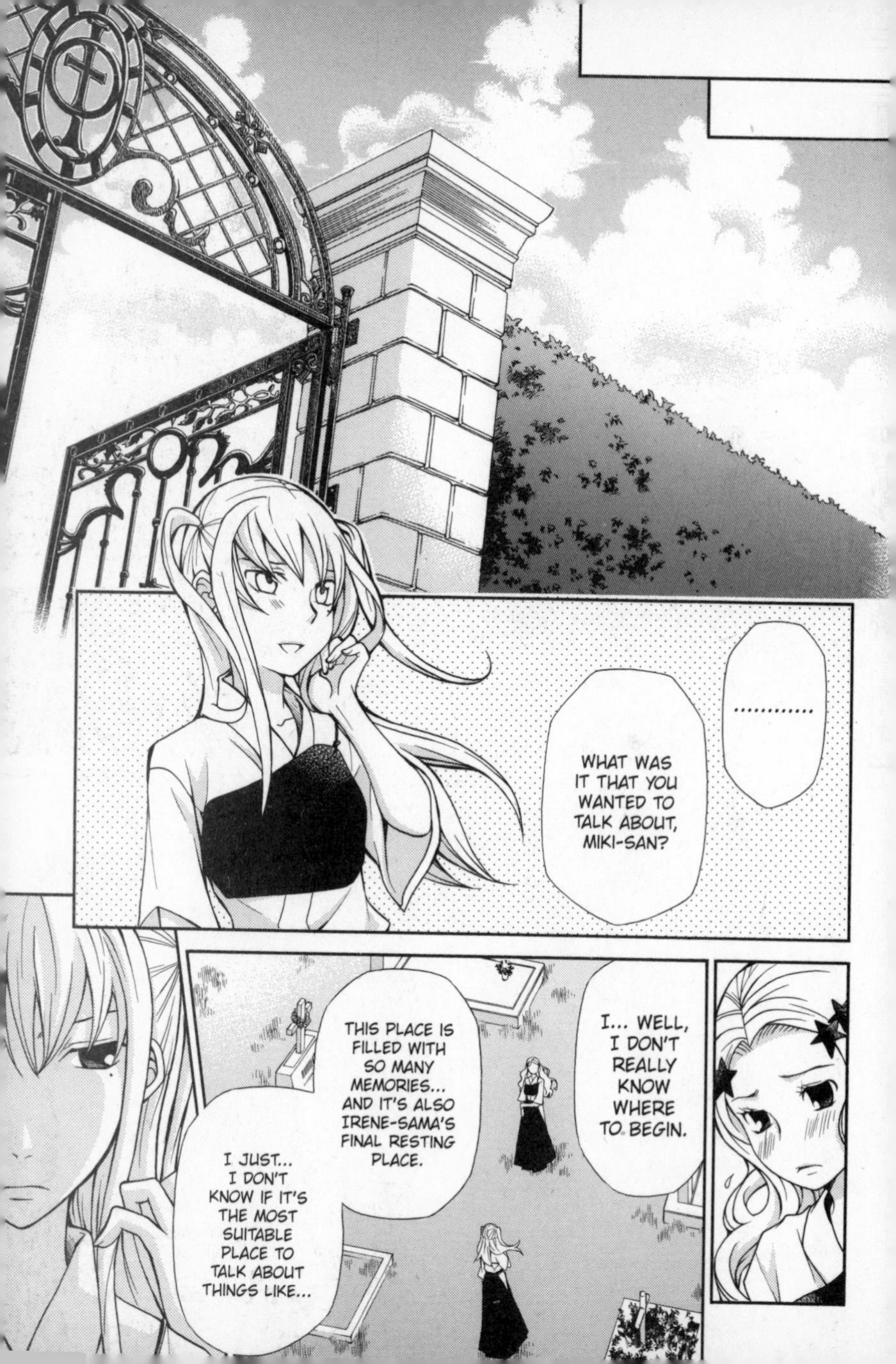
....
WHAT WAS IT THAT YOU WANTED TO TALK ABOUT, MIKI-SAN?
I... WELL, I DON'T REALLY KNOW WHERE TO BEGIN.
THIS PLACE IS FILLED WITH SO MANY MEMORIES... AND IT'S ALSO IRENE-SAMA'S FINAL RESTING PLACE.
I JUST... I DON'T KNOW IF IT'S THE MOST SUITABLE PLACE TO TALK ABOUT THINGS LIKE...

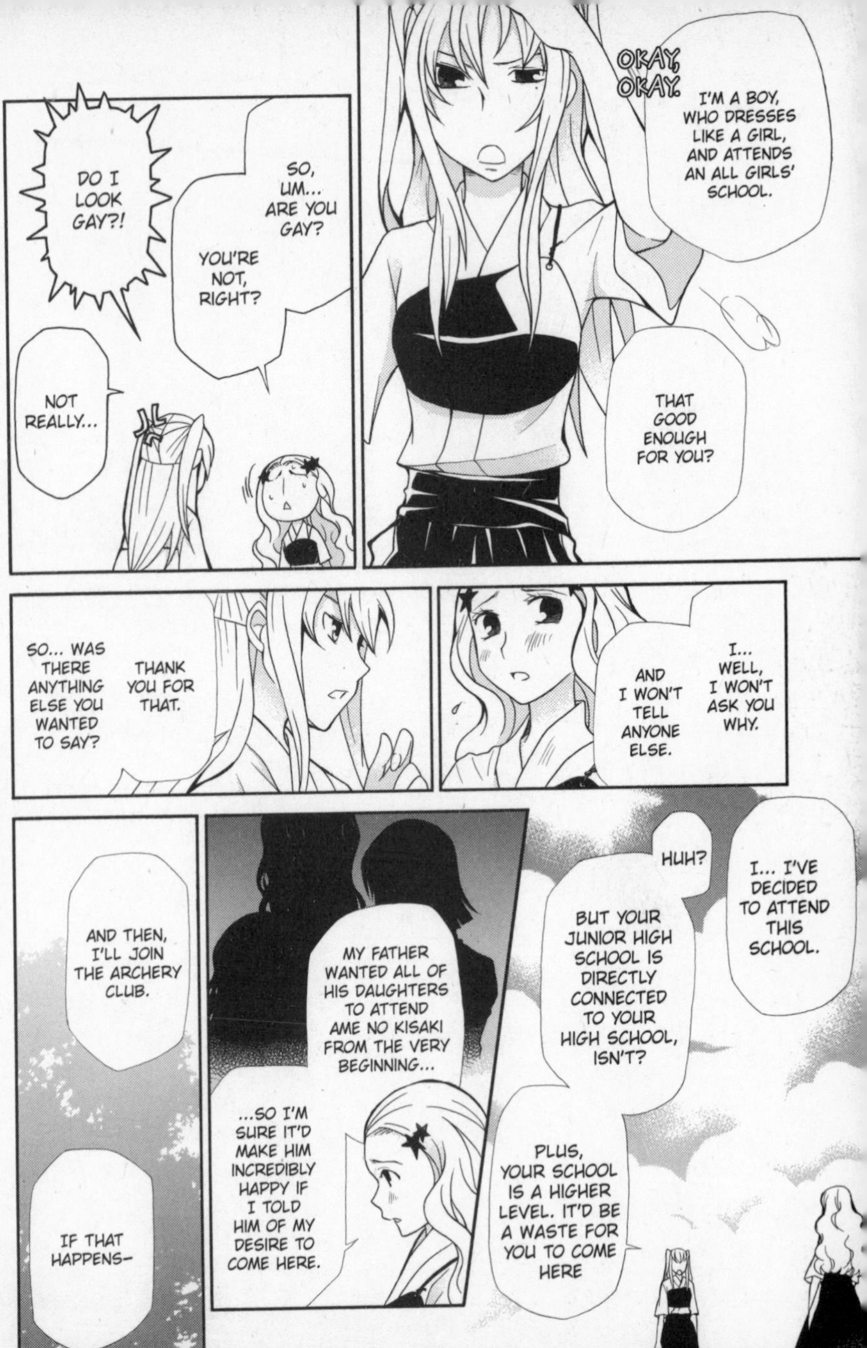
OKAY, OKAY.
I'M A BOY, WHO DRESSES LIKE A GIRL, AND ATTENDS AN ALL GIRLS' SCHOOL.
THAT GOOD ENOUGH FOR YOU?
SO, UM... ARE YOU GAY?
YOU'RE NOT, RIGHT?
DO I LOOK GAY?!
NOT REALLY...
I... WELL, I WON'T ASK YOU WHY.
AND I WON'T TELL ANYONE ELSE.
THANK YOU FOR THAT.
SO... WAS THERE ANYTHING ELSE YOU WANTED TO SAY?
I... I'VE DECIDED TO ATTEND THIS SCHOOL.
HUH?
BUT YOUR JUNIOR HIGH SCHOOL IS DIRECTLY CONNECTED TO YOUR HIGH SCHOOL, ISN'T?
PLUS, YOUR SCHOOL IS A HIGHER LEVEL. IT'D BE A WASTE FOR YOU TO COME HERE
MY FATHER WANTED ALL OF HIS DAUGHTERS TO ATTEND AME NO KISAKI FROM THE VERY BEGINNING...
...SO I'M SURE IT'D MAKE HIM INCREDIBLY HAPPY IF I TOLD HIM OF MY DESIRE TO COME HERE.
AND THEN, I'LL JOIN THE ARCHERY CLUB.
IF THAT HAPPENS-

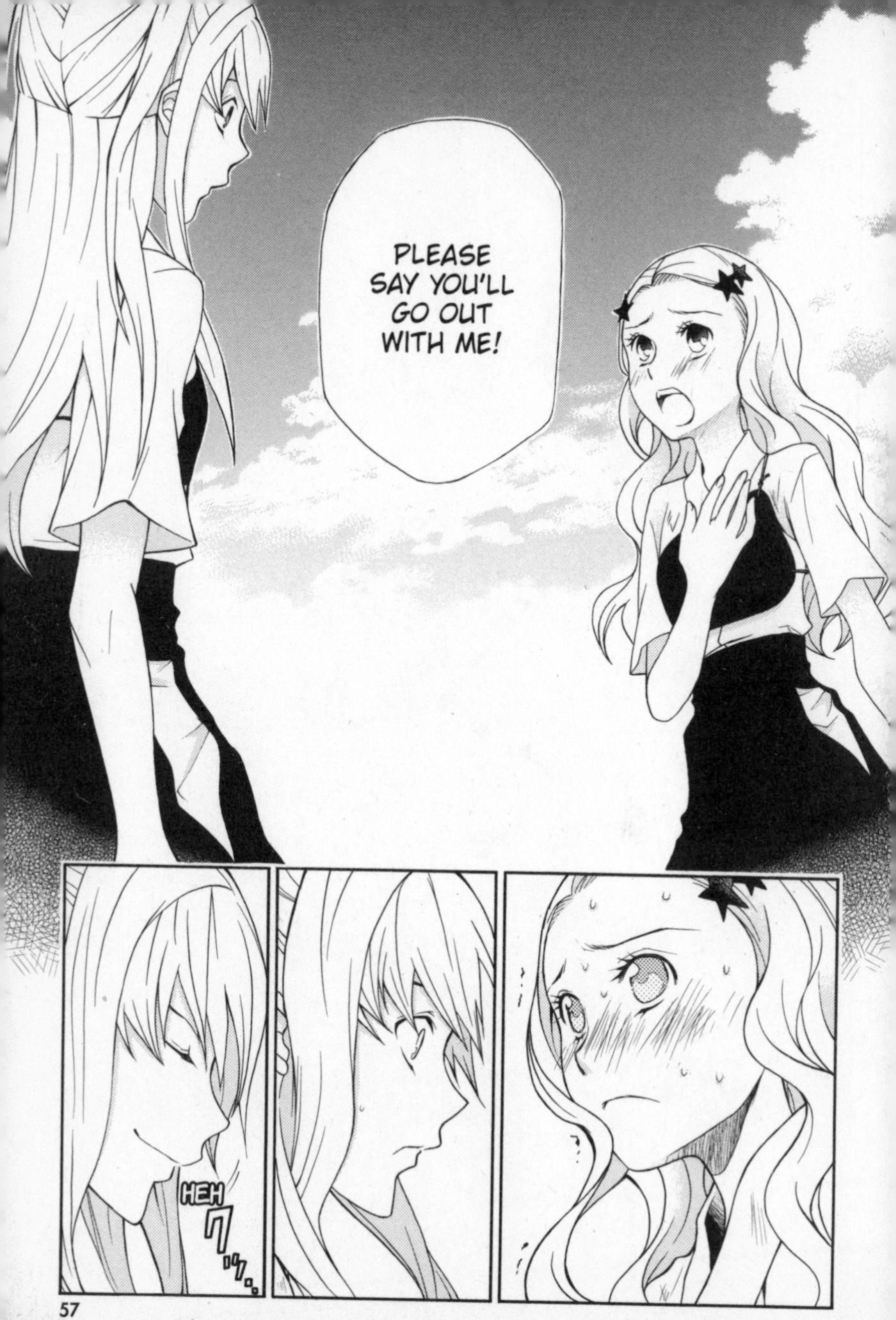
PLEASE SAY YOU'LL GO OUT WITH ME!
HEH

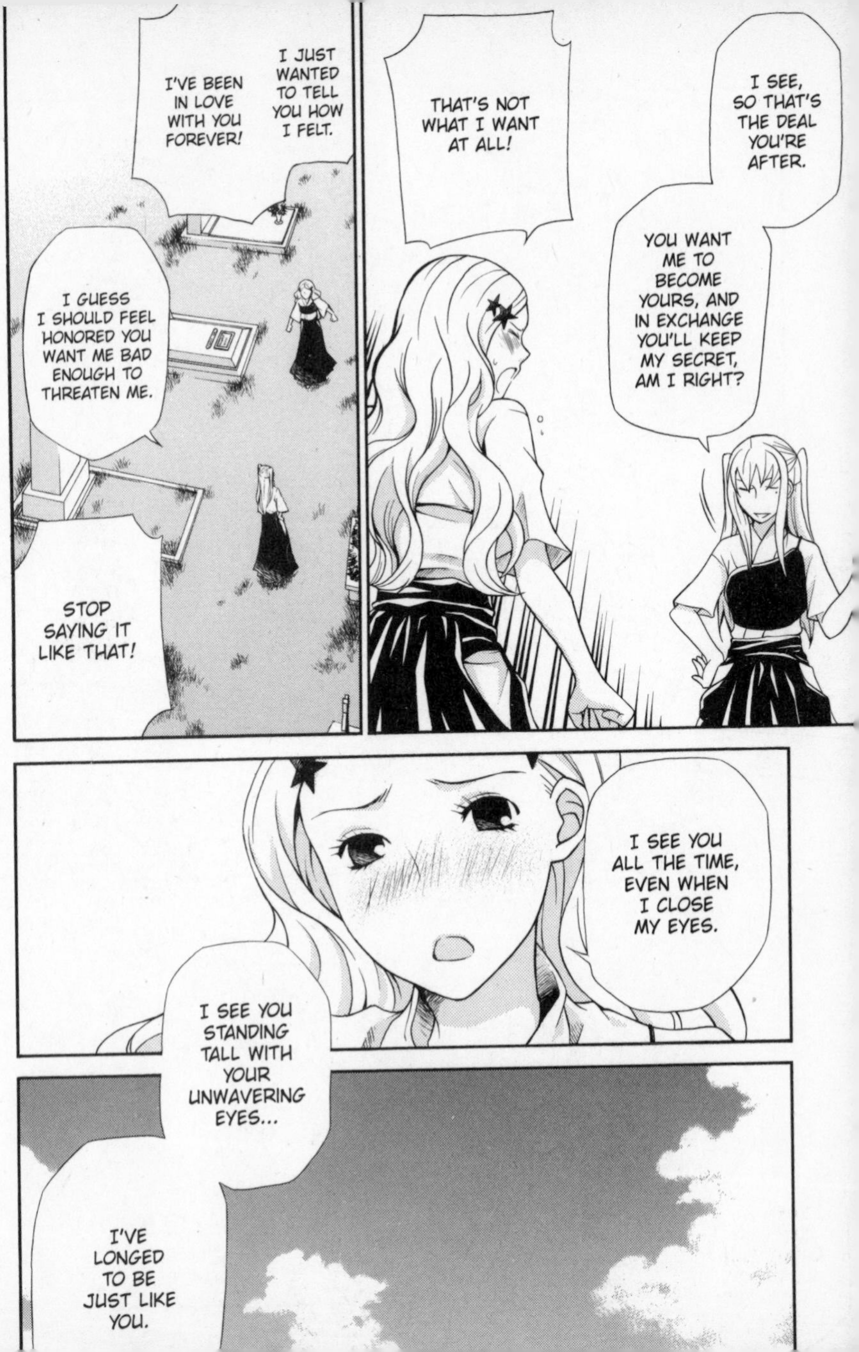
I SEE, SO THAT'S THE DEAL YOU'RE AFTER.
YOU WANT ME TO BECOME YOURS, AND IN EXCHANGE YOU'LL KEEP MY SECRET, AM I RIGHT?
THAT'S NOT WHAT I WANT AT ALL!
I JUST WANTED TO TELL YOU HOW I FELT.
I'VE BEEN IN LOVE WITH YOU FOREVER!
I GUESS I SHOULD FEEL HONORED YOU WANT ME BAD ENOUGH TO THREATEN ME.
STOP SAYING IT LIKE THAT!
I SEE YOU ALL THE TIME, EVEN WHEN I CLOSE MY EYES.
I SEE YOU STANDING TALL WITH YOUR UNWAVERING EYES...
I'VE LONGED TO BE JUST LIKE YOU.

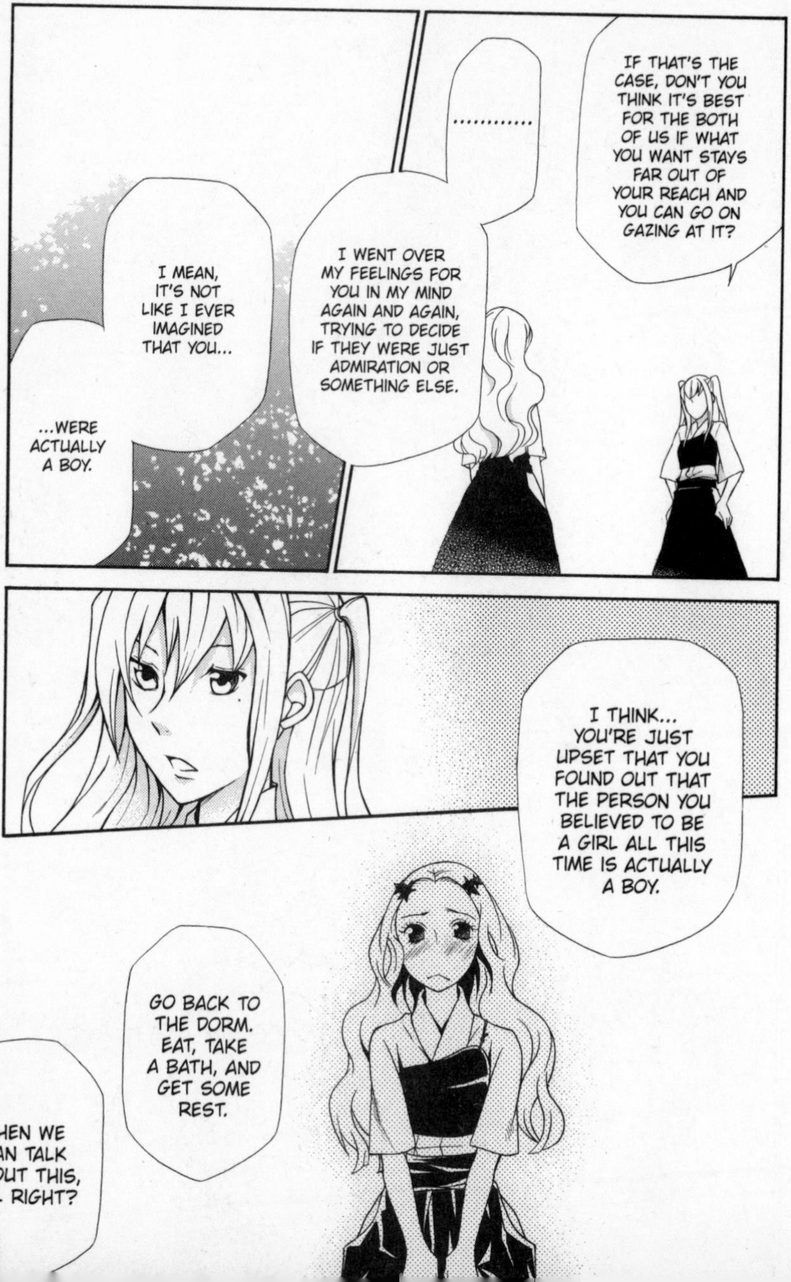

IF THAT'S THE CASE, DON'T YOU THINK IT'S BEST FOR THE BOTH OF US IF WHAT YOU WANT STAYS FAR OUT OF YOUR REACH AND YOU CAN GO ON GAZING AT IT?
....
I WENT OVER MY FEELINGS FOR YOU IN MY MIND AGAIN AND AGAIN, TRYING TO DECIDE IF THEY WERE JUST ADMIRATION OR SOMETHING ELSE.
I MEAN, IT'S NOT LIKE I EVER IMAGINED THAT YOU...
...WERE ACTUALLY A BOY.
I THINK... YOU'RE JUST UPSET THAT YOU FOUND OUT THAT THE PERSON YOU BELIEVED TO BE A GIRL ALL THIS TIME IS ACTUALLY A BOY.
GO BACK TO THE DORM. EAT, TAKE A BATH, AND GET SOME REST.
THEN WE CAN TALK ABOUT THIS, ALL RIGHT?

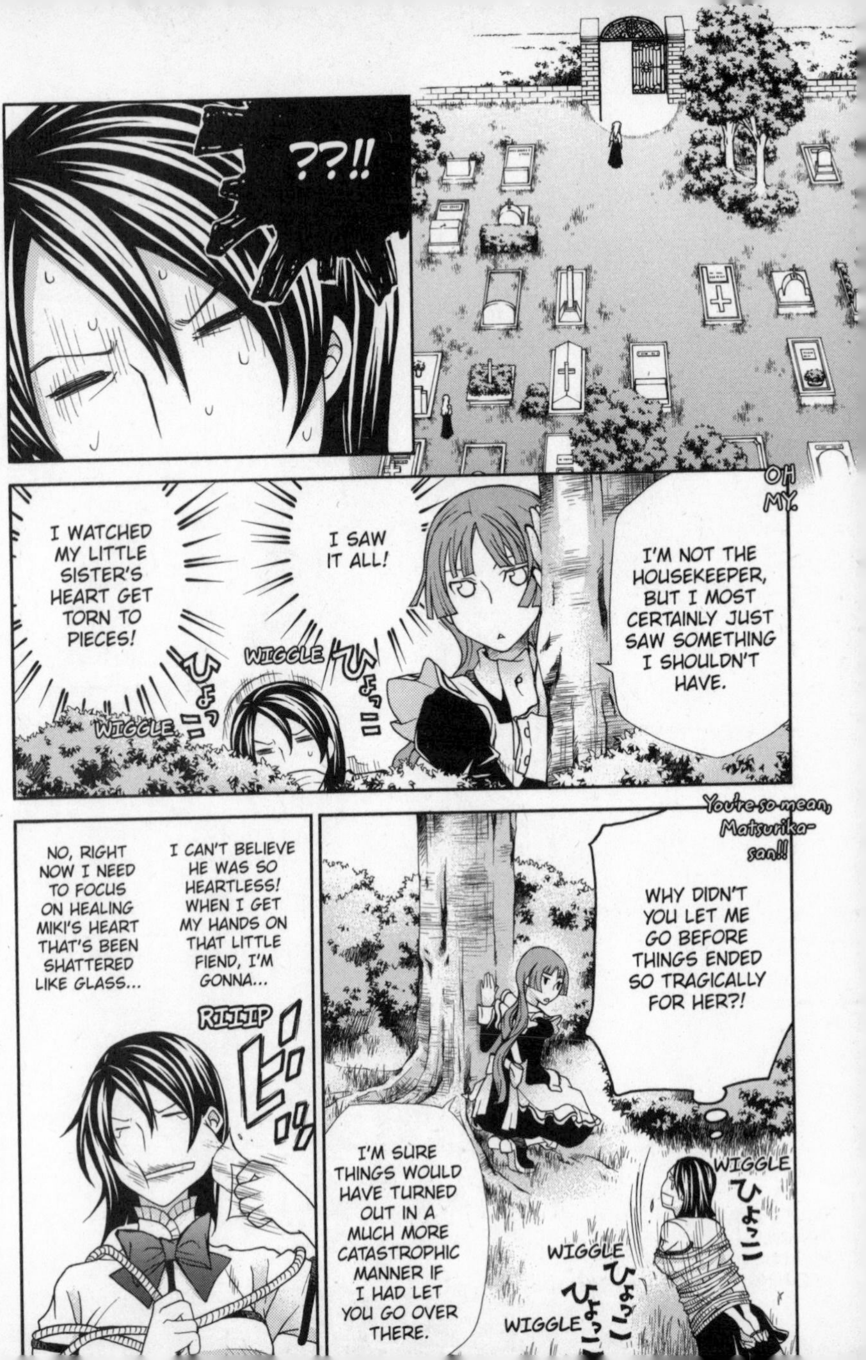
??!!
OH MY.
I'M NOT THE HOUSEKEEPER, BUT I MOST CERTAINLY JUST SAW SOMETHING I SHOULDN'T HAVE.
I SAW IT ALL!
I WATCHED MY LITTLE SISTER'S HEART GET TORN TO PIECES!
WIGGLE
WIGGLE
You're so mean, Matsurika-san!!
WHY DIDN'T YOU LET ME GO BEFORE THINGS ENDED SO TRAGICALLY FOR HER?!
I'M SURE THINGS WOULD HAVE TURNED OUT IN A MUCH MORE CATASTROPHIC MANNER IF I HAD LET YOU GO OVER THERE.
WIGGLE
WIGGLE
WIGGLE
I CAN'T BELIEVE HE WAS SO HEARTLESS! WHEN I GET MY HANDS ON THAT LITTLE FIEND, I'M GONNA...
NO, RIGHT NOW I NEED TO FOCUS ON HEALING MIKI'S HEART THAT'S BEEN SHATTERED LIKE GLASS...
RIIIP

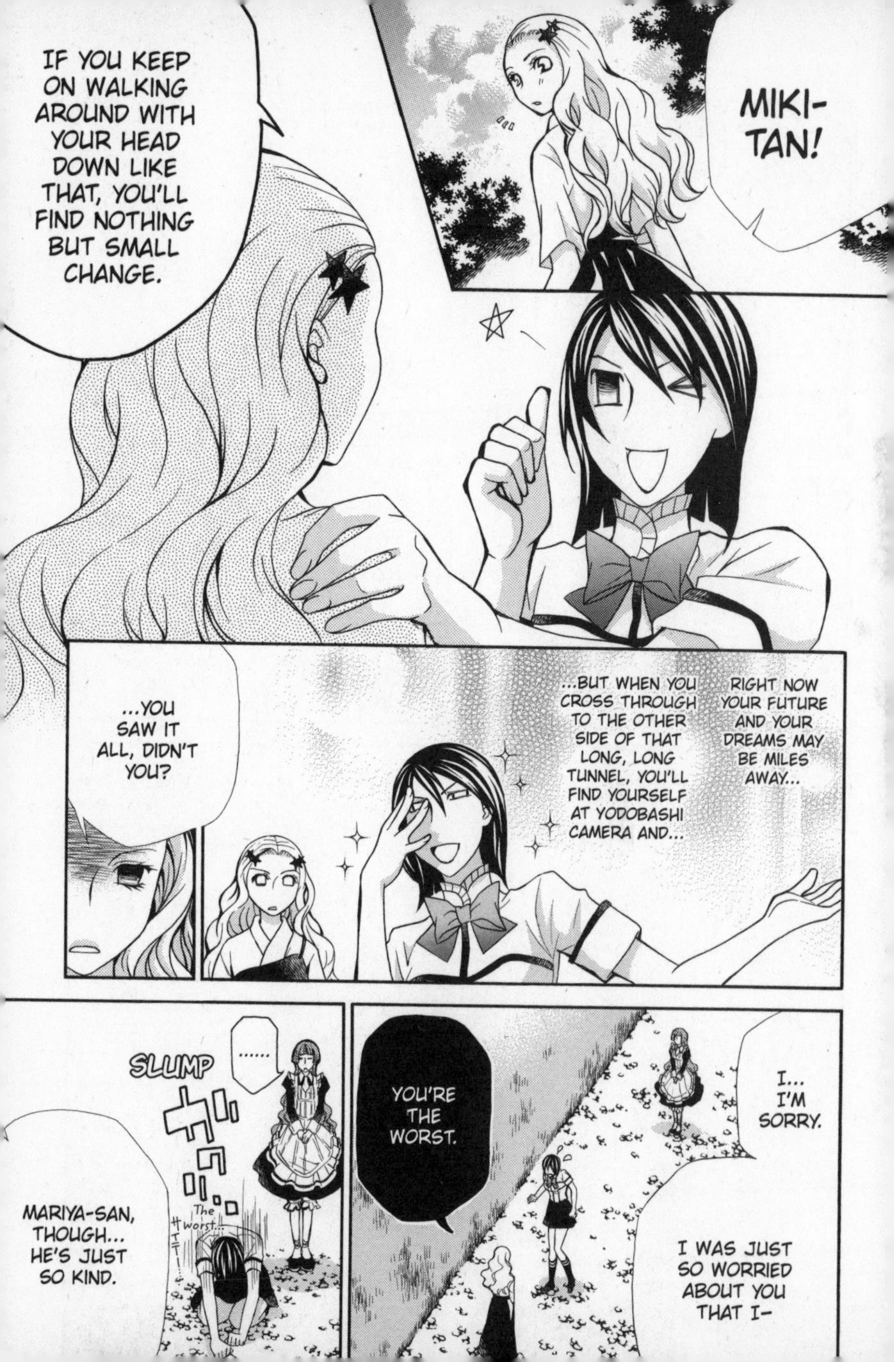
MIKI-TAN!
IF YOU KEEP ON WALKING AROUND WITH YOUR HEAD DOWN LIKE THAT, YOU'LL FIND NOTHING BUT SMALL CHANGE.
RIGHT NOW YOUR FUTURE AND YOUR DREAMS MAY BE MILES AWAY...
...BUT WHEN YOU CROSS THROUGH TO THE OTHER SIDE OF THAT LONG, LONG TUNNEL, YOU'LL FIND YOURSELF AT YODOBASHI CAMERA AND...
...YOU SAW IT ALL, DIDN'T YOU?
I... I'M SORRY.
I WAS JUST SO WORRIED ABOUT YOU THAT I-
YOU'RE THE WORST.
......
SLUMP
The worst...
MARIYA-SAN, THOUGH... HE'S JUST SO KIND.

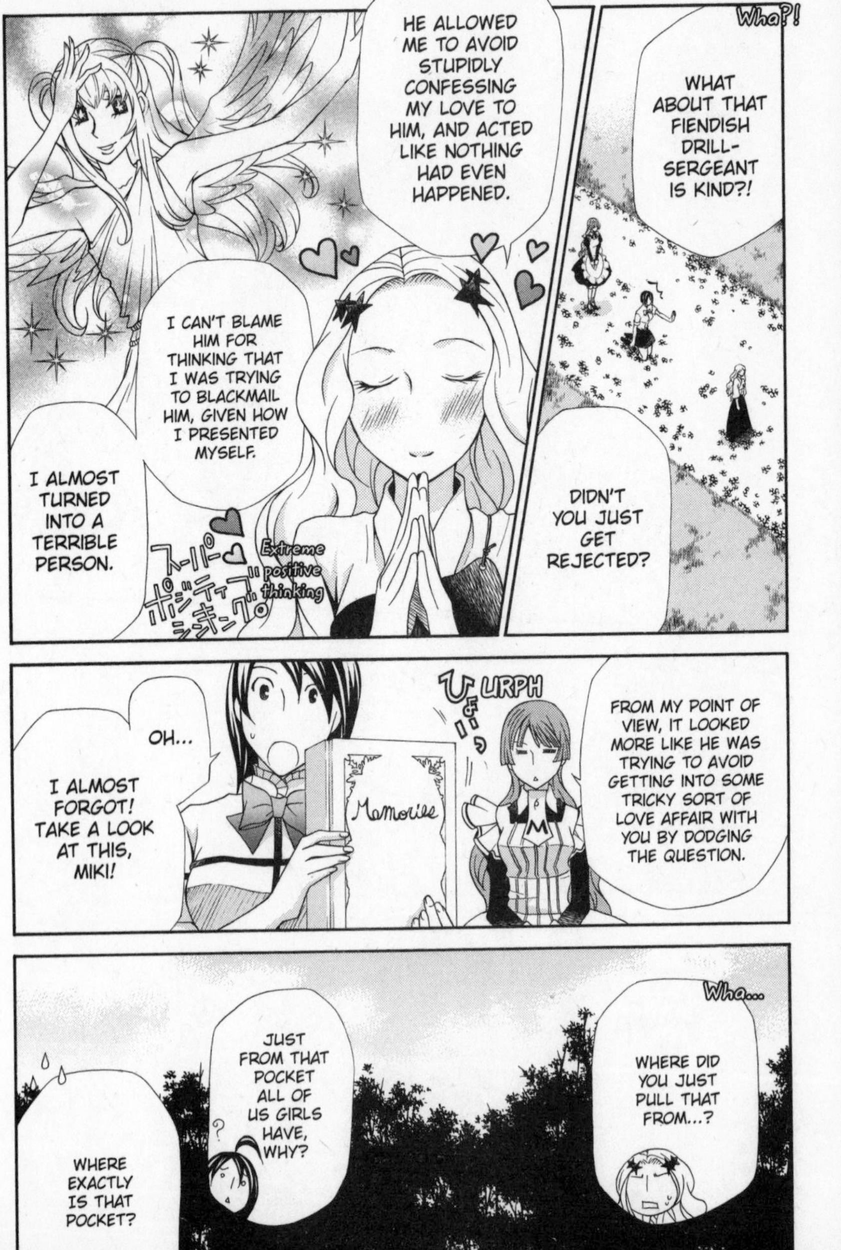
Wha?!
WHAT ABOUT THAT FIENDISH DRILL-SERGEANT IS KIND?!
DIDN'T YOU JUST GET REJECTED?
HE ALLOWED ME TO AVOID STUPIDLY CONFESSING MY LOVE TO HIM, AND ACTED LIKE NOTHING HAD EVEN HAPPENED.
I CAN'T BLAME HIM FOR THINKING THAT I WAS TRYING TO BLACKMAIL HIM, GIVEN HOW I PRESENTED MYSELF.
I ALMOST TURNED INTO A TERRIBLE PERSON.
スーパーポジティブシンキング
Extreme positive thinking
URPH
FROM MY POINT OF VIEW, IT LOOKED MORE LIKE HE WAS TRYING TO AVOID GETTING INTO SOME TRICKY SORT OF LOVE AFFAIR WITH YOU BY DODGING THE QUESTION.
OH...
I ALMOST FORGOT! TAKE A LOOK AT THIS, MIKI!
Memories
Wha...
WHERE DID YOU JUST PULL THAT FROM...?
JUST FROM THAT POCKET ALL OF US GIRLS HAVE, WHY?
WHERE EXACTLY IS THAT POCKET?

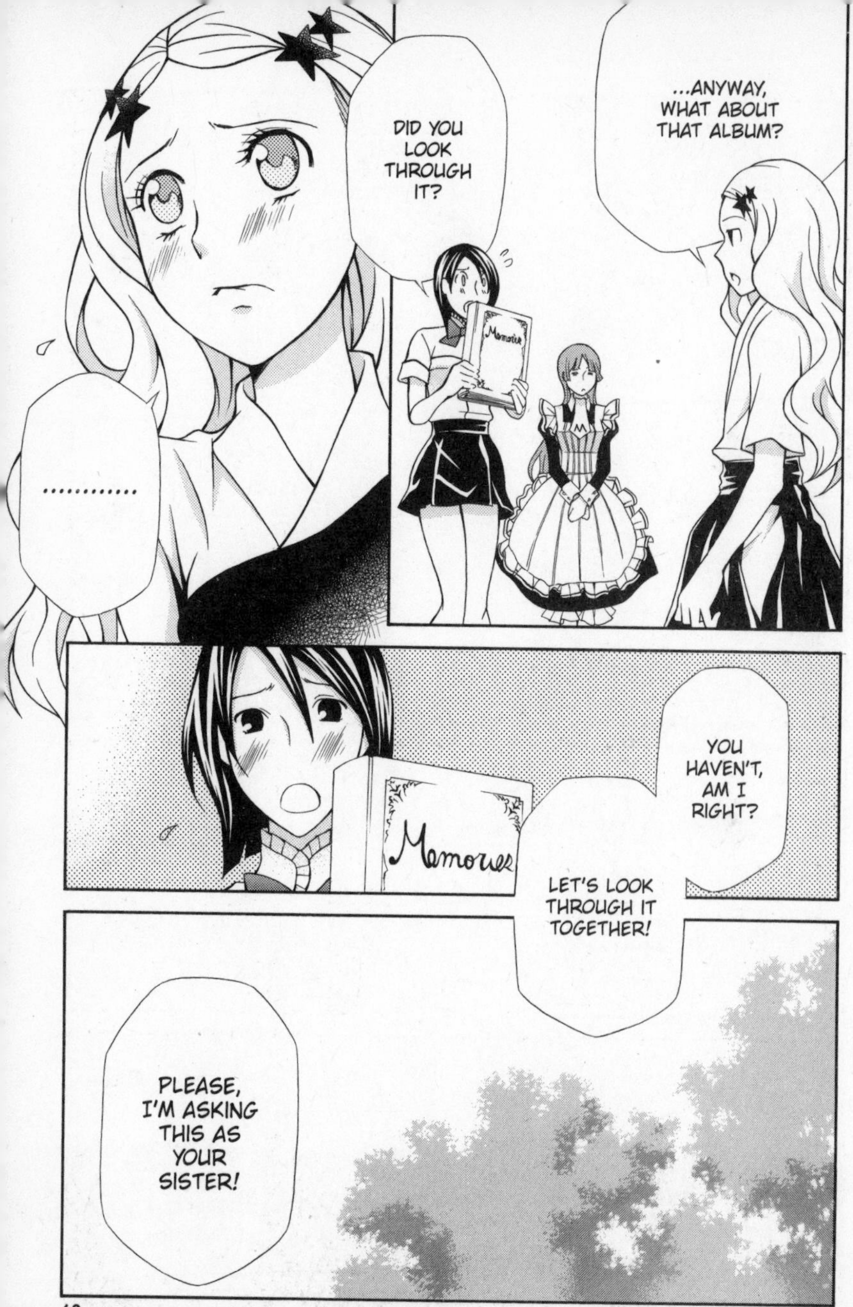
...ANYWAY, WHAT ABOUT THAT ALBUM?
DID YOU LOOK THROUGH IT?
....
YOU HAVEN'T, AM I RIGHT?
LET'S LOOK THROUGH IT TOGETHER!
PLEASE, I'M ASKING THIS AS YOUR SISTER!

M A R I A H O L I C

MARIA HOLIC

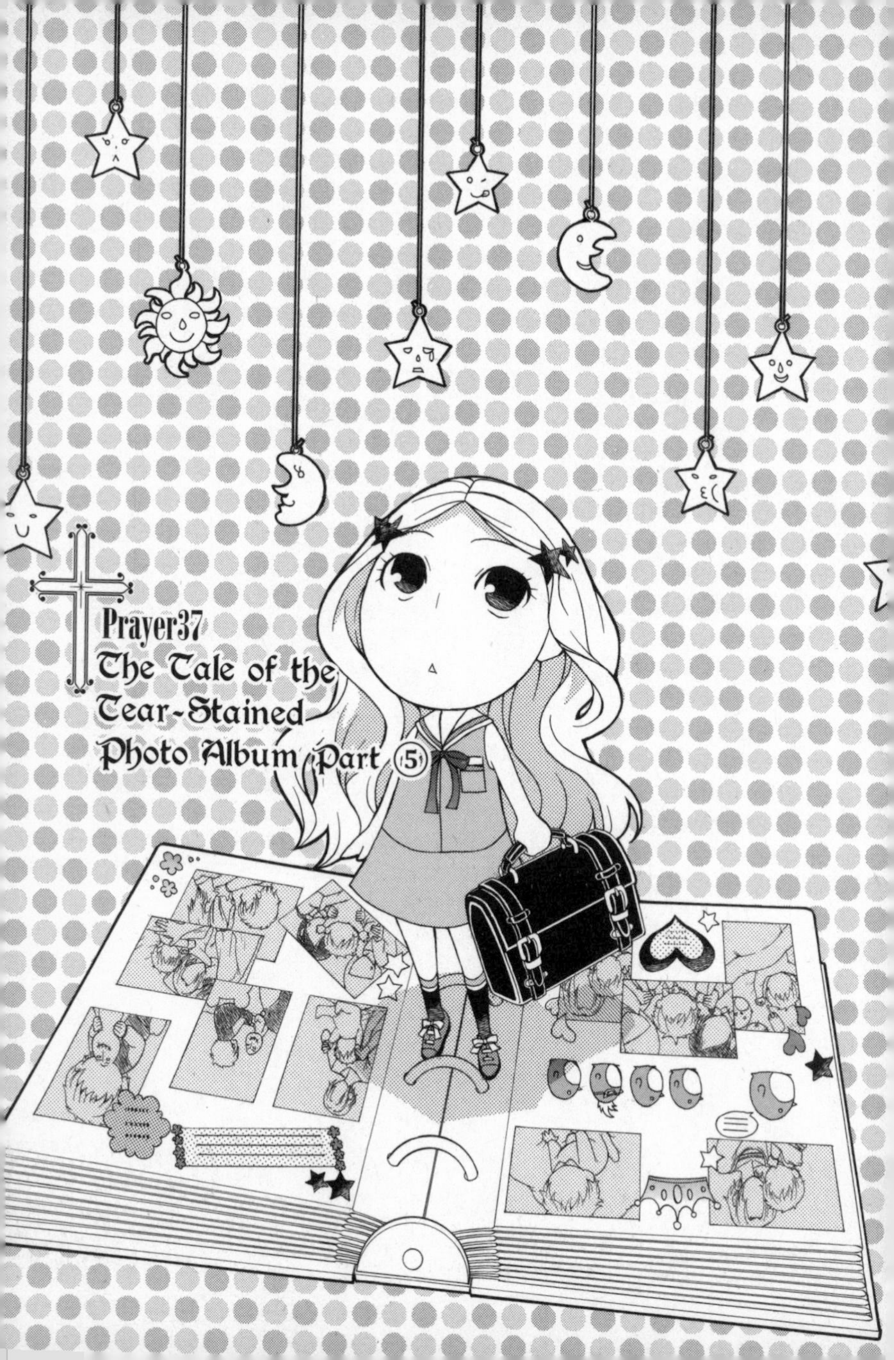
Prayer37
The Tale of the Tear-Stained Photo Album Part ⑤

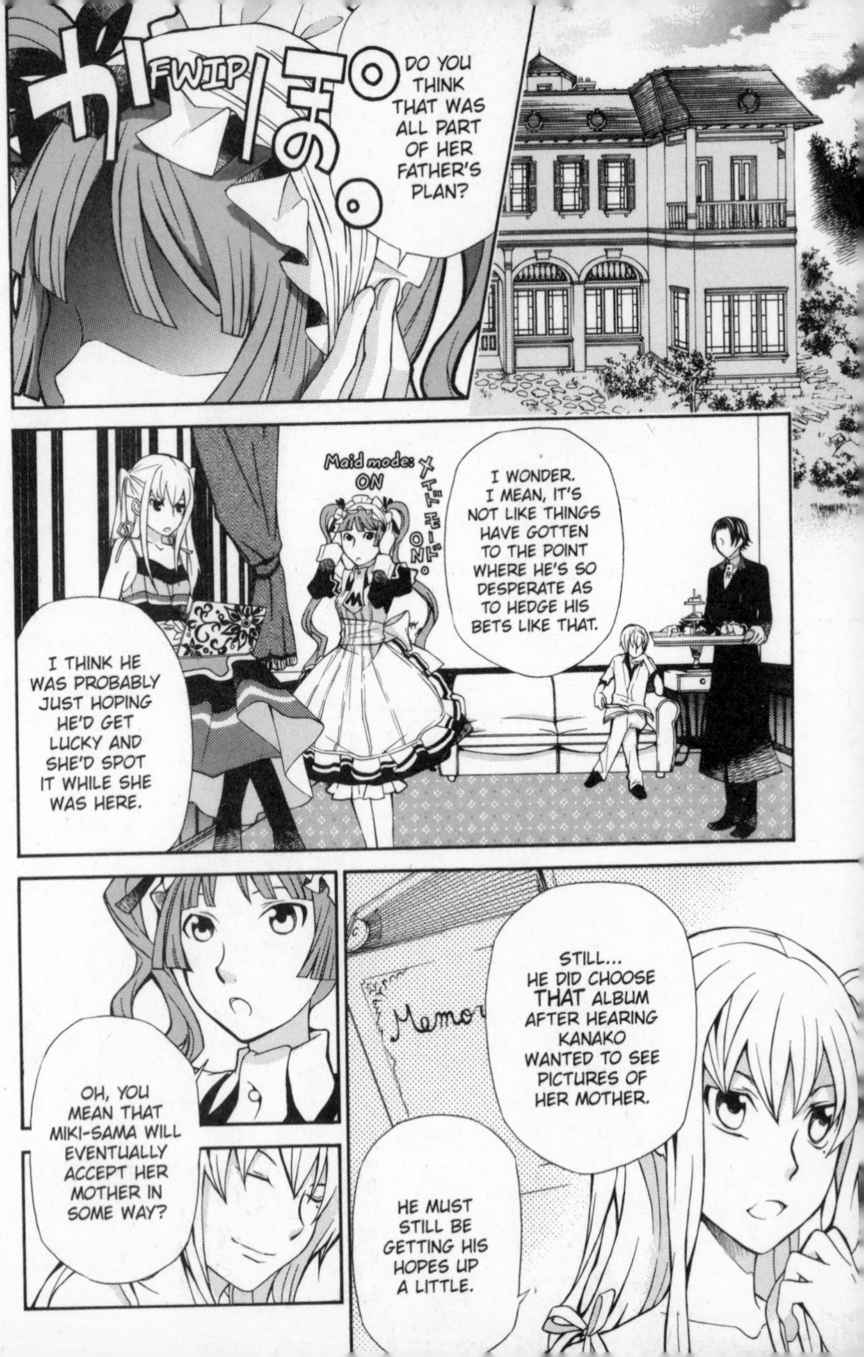
FWIP
DO YOU THINK THAT WAS ALL PART OF HER FATHER'S PLAN?
Maid mode: ON
I WONDER. I MEAN, IT'S NOT LIKE THINGS HAVE GOTTEN TO THE POINT WHERE HE'S SO DESPERATE AS TO HEDGE HIS BETS LIKE THAT.
I THINK HE WAS PROBABLY JUST HOPING HE'D GET LUCKY AND SHE'D SPOT IT WHILE SHE WAS HERE.
STILL... HE DID CHOOSE THAT ALBUM AFTER HEARING KANAKO WANTED TO SEE PICTURES OF HER MOTHER.
HE MUST STILL BE GETTING HIS HOPES UP A LITTLE.
OH, YOU MEAN THAT MIKI-SAMA WILL EVENTUALLY ACCEPT HER MOTHER IN SOME WAY?

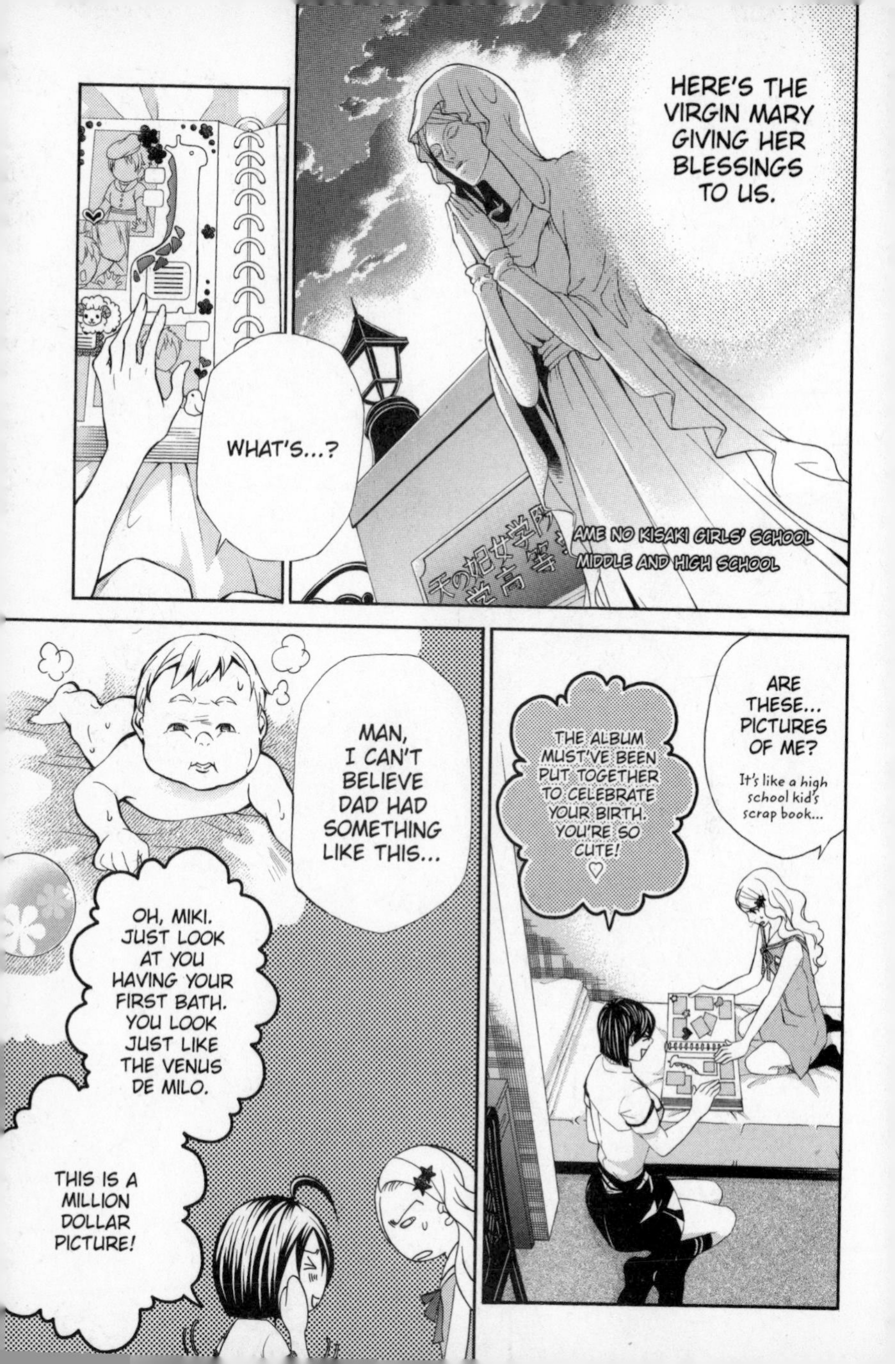
HERE'S THE VIRGIN MARY GIVING HER BLESSINGS TO US.
AME NO KISAKI GIRLS' SCHOOL MIDDLE AND HIGH SCHOOL
WHAT'S...?
ARE THESE... PICTURES OF ME?
It's like a high school kid's scrap book...
THE ALBUM MUST'VE BEEN PUT TOGETHER TO CELEBRATE YOUR BIRTH. YOU'RE SO CUTE! ♡
MAN, I CAN'T BELIEVE DAD HAD SOMETHING LIKE THIS...
OH, MIKI. JUST LOOK AT YOU HAVING YOUR FIRST BATH. YOU LOOK JUST LIKE THE VENUS DE MILO.
THIS IS A MILLION DOLLAR PICTURE!

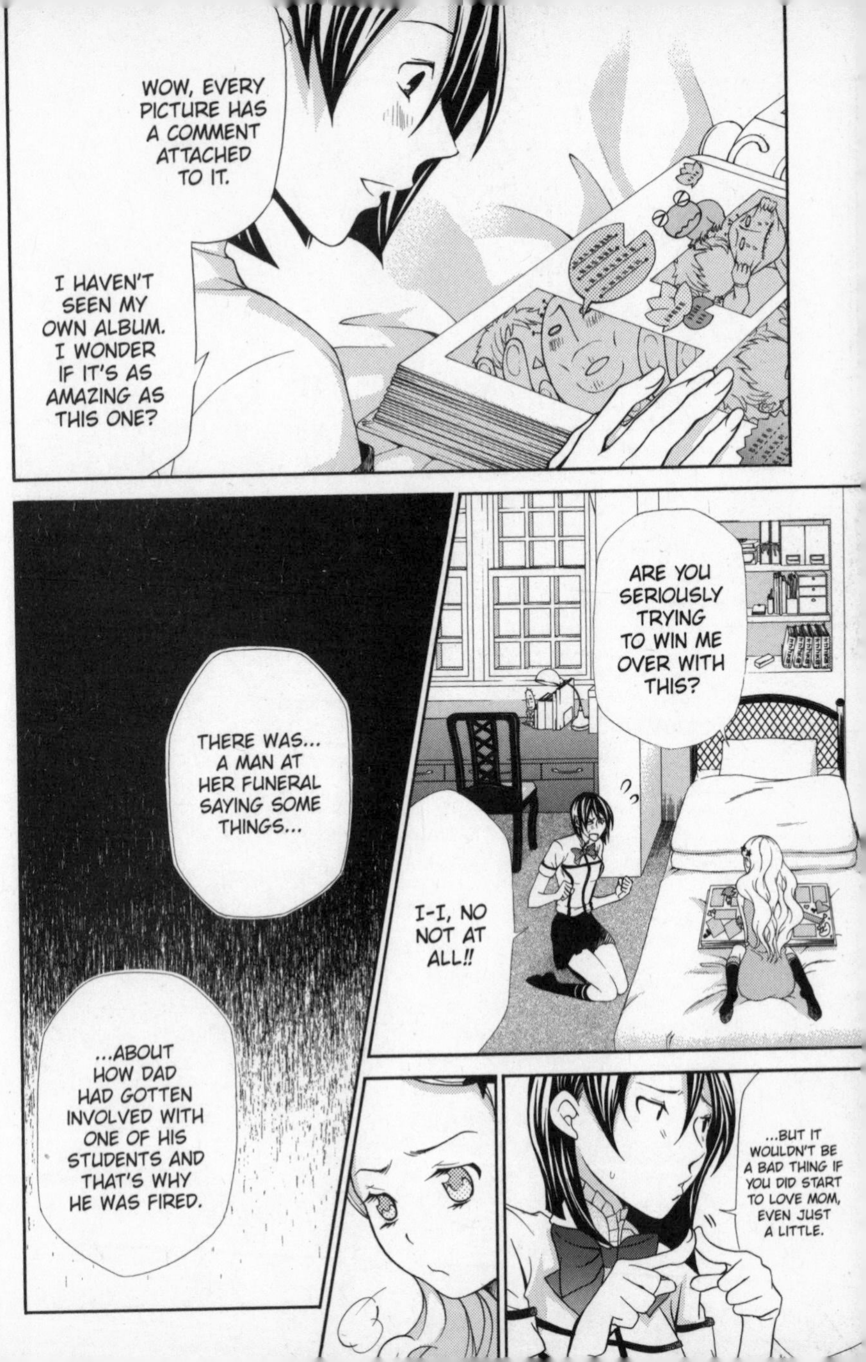
WOW, EVERY PICTURE HAS A COMMENT ATTACHED TO IT.
I HAVEN'T SEEN MY OWN ALBUM. I WONDER IF IT'S AS AMAZING AS THIS ONE?
ARE YOU SERIOUSLY TRYING TO WIN ME OVER WITH THIS?
I-I, NO NOT AT ALL!!
...BUT IT WOULDN'T BE A BAD THING IF YOU DID START TO LOVE MOM, EVEN JUST A LITTLE.
THERE WAS... A MAN AT HER FUNERAL SAYING SOME THINGS...
...ABOUT HOW DAD HAD GOTTEN INVOLVED WITH ONE OF HIS STUDENTS AND THAT'S WHY HE WAS FIRED.

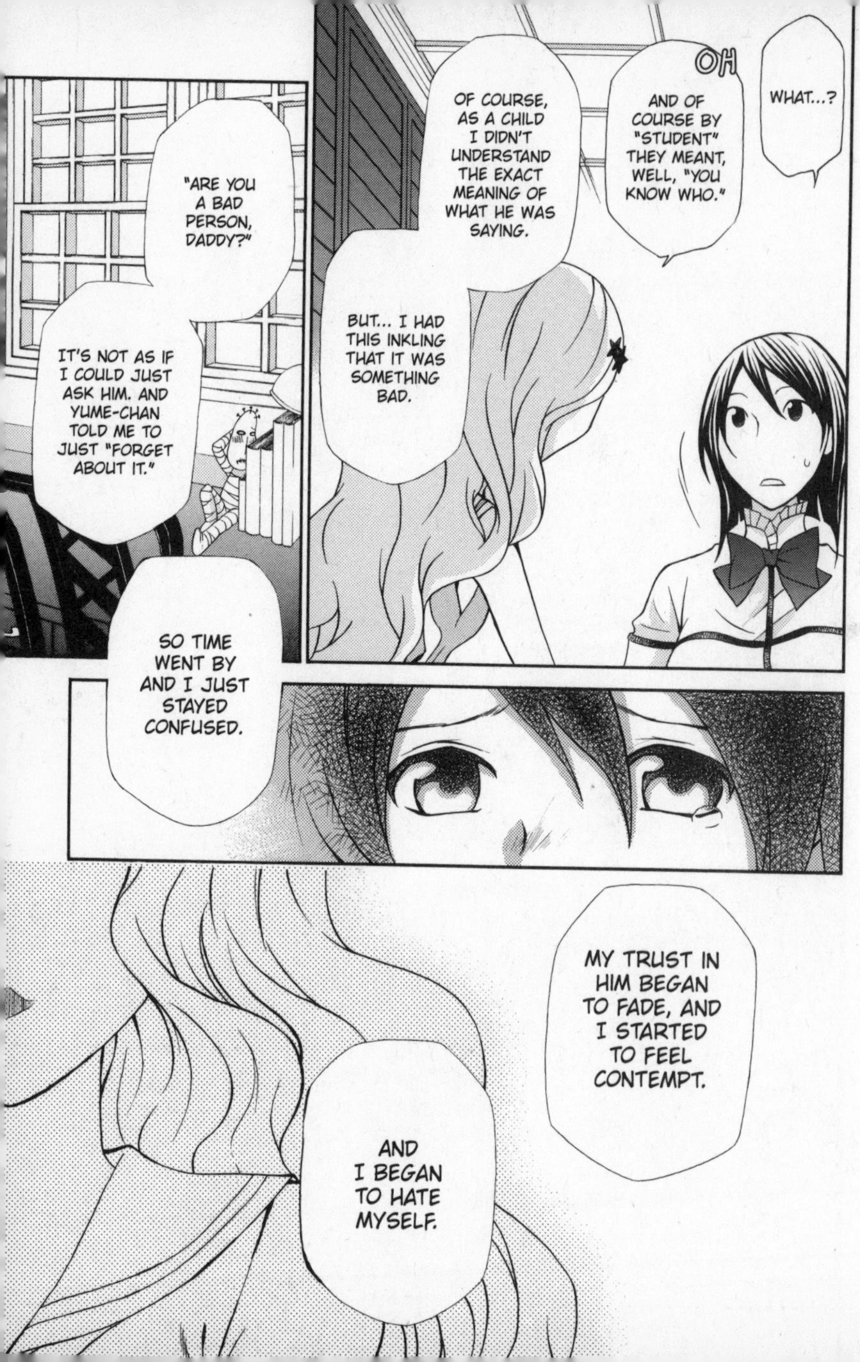
WHAT...?
OH
AND OF COURSE BY "STUDENT" THEY MEANT, WELL, "YOU KNOW WHO."
OF COURSE, AS A CHILD I DIDN'T UNDERSTAND THE EXACT MEANING OF WHAT HE WAS SAYING.
BUT... I HAD THIS INKLING THAT IT WAS SOMETHING BAD.
"ARE YOU A BAD PERSON, DADDY?"
IT'S NOT AS IF I COULD JUST ASK HIM. AND YUME-CHAN TOLD ME TO JUST "FORGET ABOUT IT."
SO TIME WENT BY AND I JUST STAYED CONFUSED.
MY TRUST IN HIM BEGAN TO FADE, AND I STARTED TO FEEL CONTEMPT.
AND I BEGAN TO HATE MYSELF.

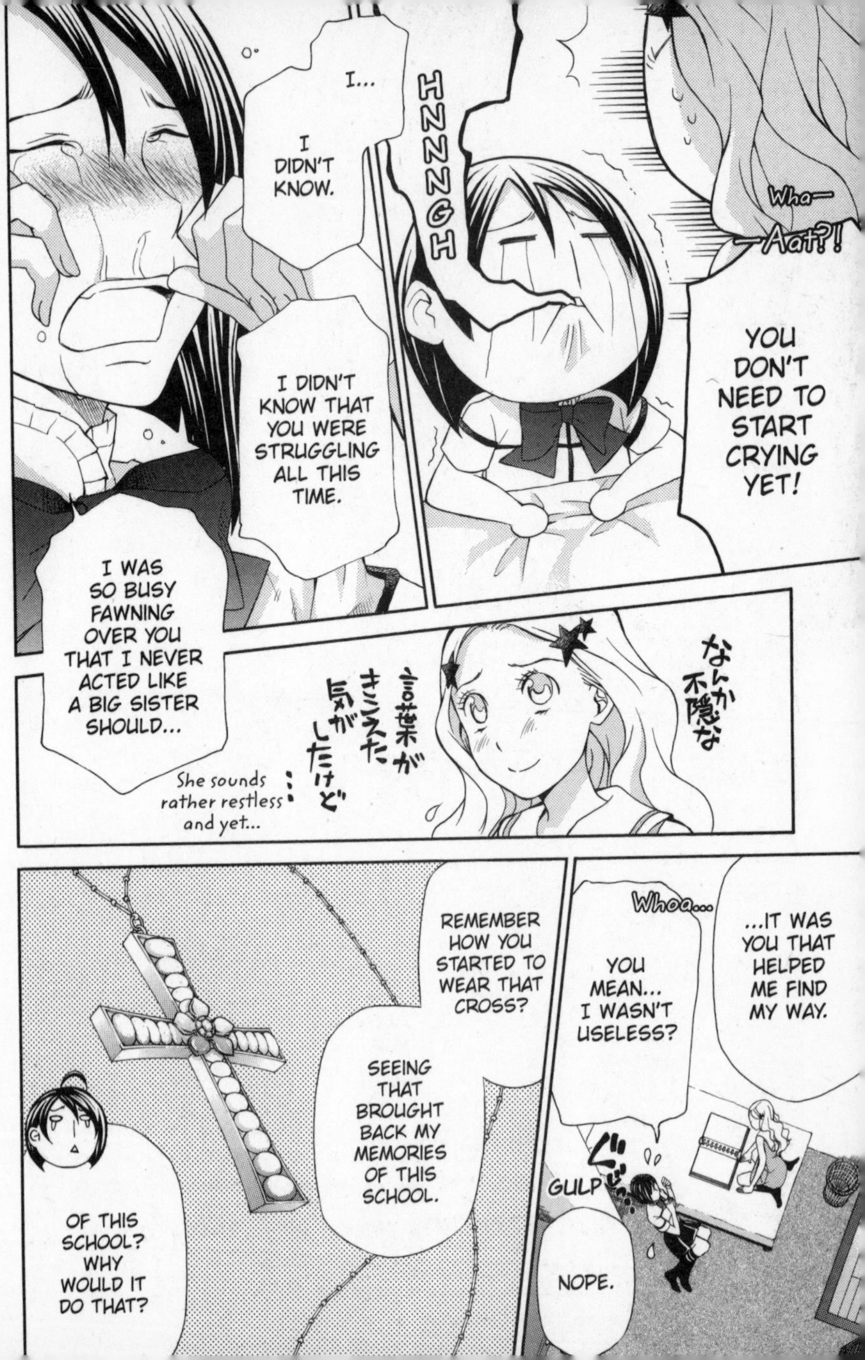
Wha—
—Aat?!
YOU DON'T NEED TO START CRYING YET!
HNNNNGH
I...
I DIDN'T KNOW.
I DIDN'T KNOW THAT YOU WERE STRUGGLING ALL THIS TIME.
I WAS SO BUSY FAWNING OVER YOU THAT I NEVER ACTED LIKE A BIG SISTER SHOULD...
なんか不隠な言葉がきこえた気がしたけど
She sounds rather restless and yet...
...IT WAS YOU THAT HELPED ME FIND MY WAY.
Whoa...
YOU MEAN... I WASN'T USELESS?
GULP
NOPE.
REMEMBER HOW YOU STARTED TO WEAR THAT CROSS?
SEEING THAT BROUGHT BACK MY MEMORIES OF THIS SCHOOL.
OF THIS SCHOOL? WHY WOULD IT DO THAT?

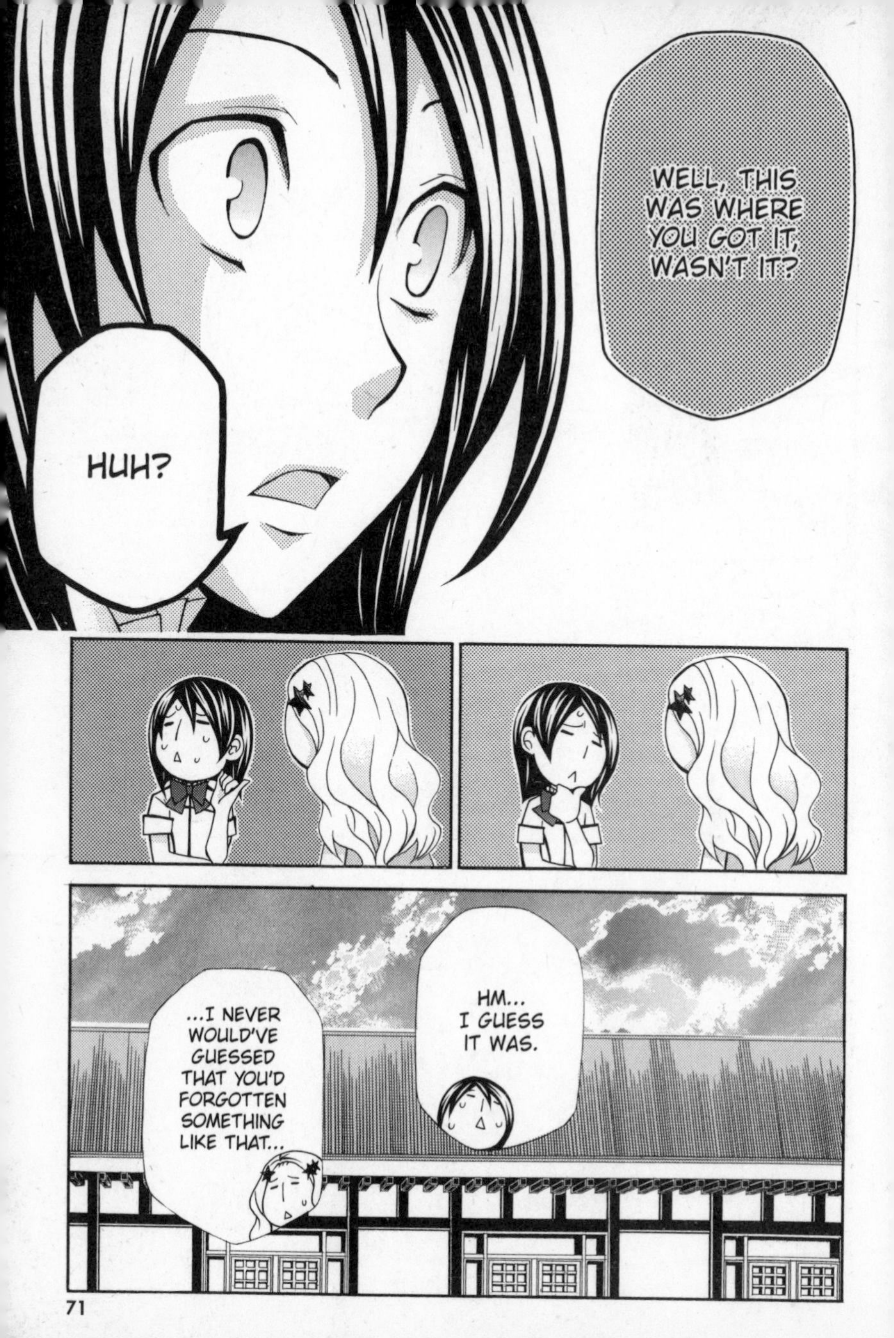
WELL, THIS WAS WHERE YOU GOT IT, WASN'T IT?
HUH?
HM... I GUESS IT WAS.
...I NEVER WOULD'VE GUESSED THAT YOU'D FORGOTTEN SOMETHING LIKE THAT...

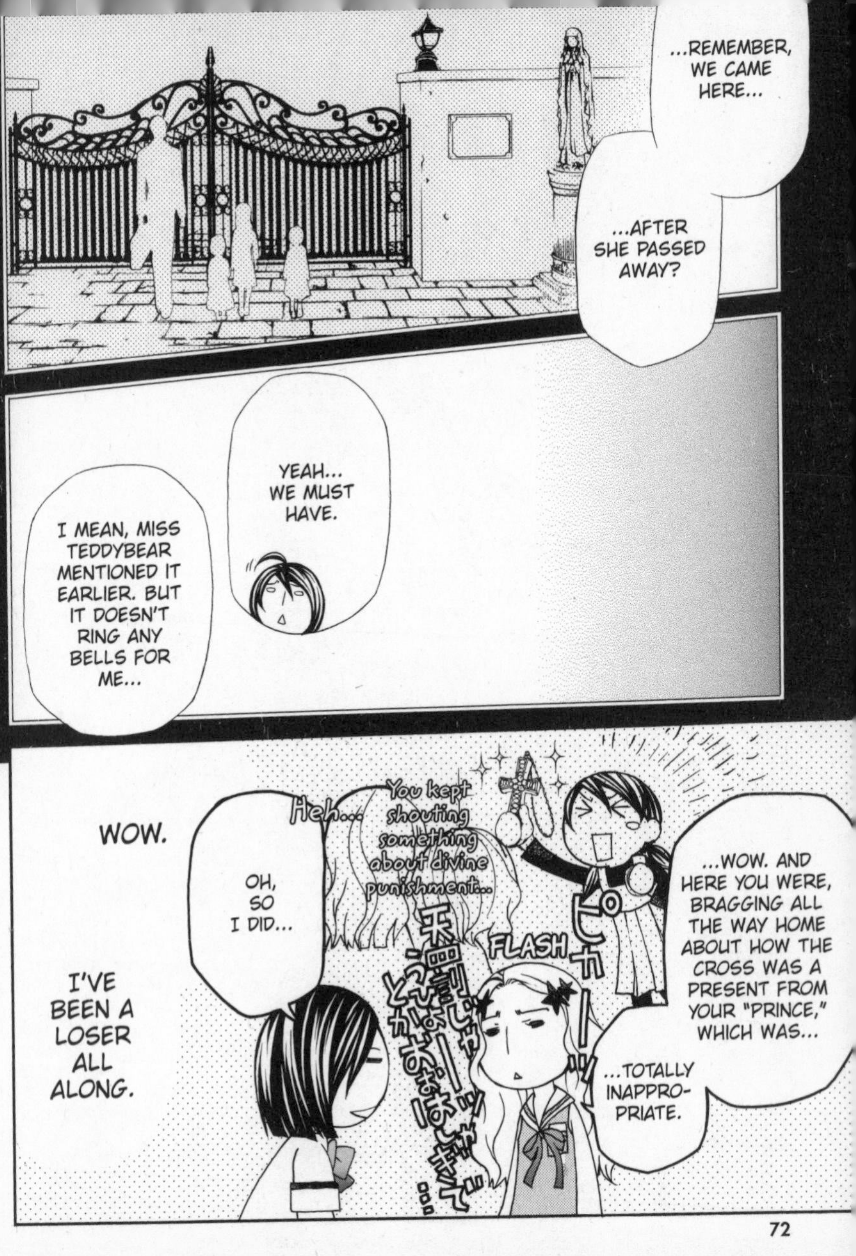

...REMEMBER, WE CAME HERE...
...AFTER SHE PASSED AWAY?
YEAH... WE MUST HAVE.
I MEAN, MISS TEDDYBEAR MENTIONED IT EARLIER. BUT IT DOESN'T RING ANY BELLS FOR ME...
...WOW. AND HERE YOU WERE, BRAGGING ALL THE WAY HOME ABOUT HOW THE CROSS WAS A PRESENT FROM YOUR "PRINCE," WHICH WAS...
...TOTALLY INAPPROPRIATE.
FLASH
You kept shouting something about divine punishment...
Heh...
OH, SO I DID...
WOW.
I'VE BEEN A LOSER ALL ALONG.

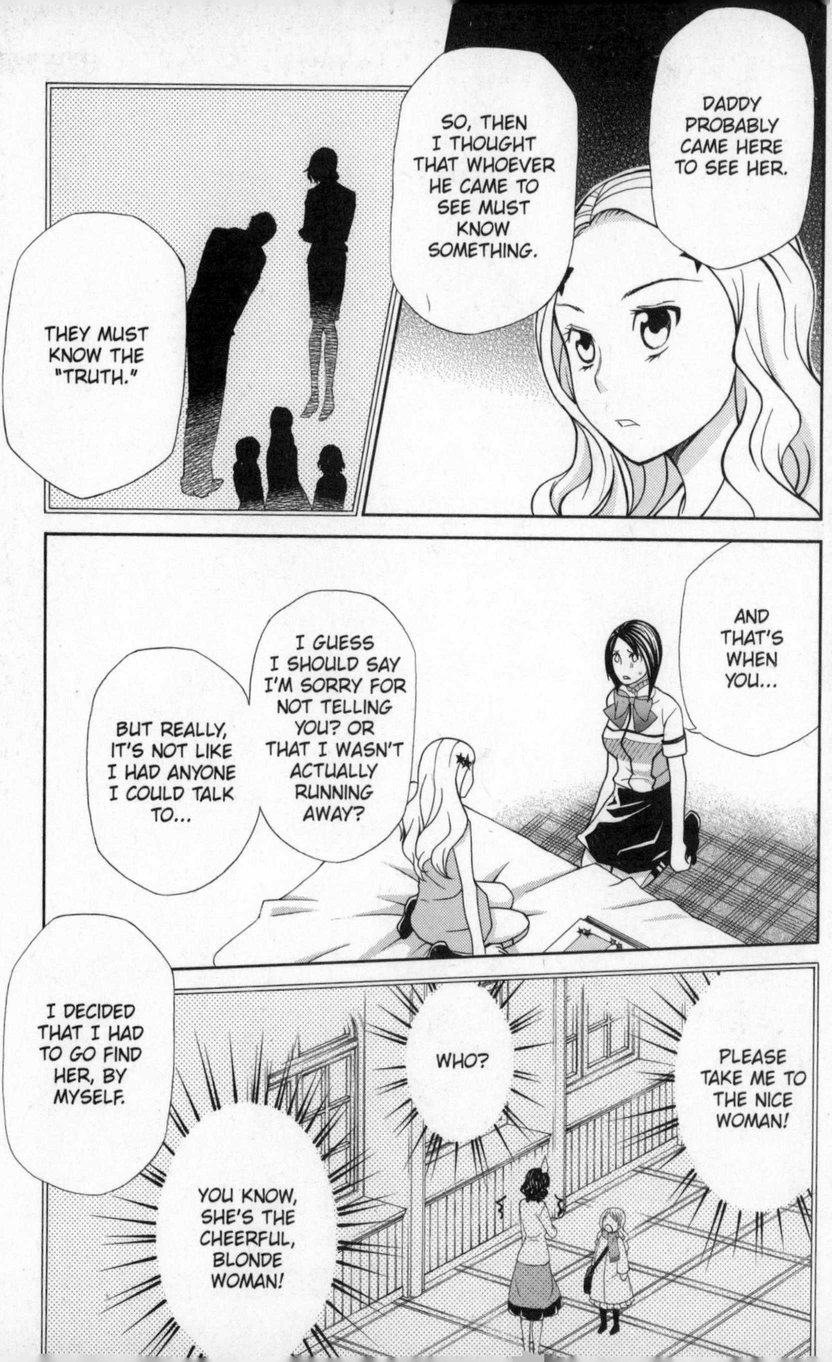
DADDY PROBABLY CAME HERE TO SEE HER.
SO, THEN I THOUGHT THAT WHOEVER HE CAME TO SEE MUST KNOW SOMETHING.
THEY MUST KNOW THE "TRUTH."
AND THAT'S WHEN YOU...
I GUESS I SHOULD SAY I'M SORRY FOR NOT TELLING YOU? OR THAT I WASN'T ACTUALLY RUNNING AWAY?
BUT REALLY, IT'S NOT LIKE I HAD ANYONE I COULD TALK TO...
I DECIDED THAT I HAD TO GO FIND HER, BY MYSELF.
PLEASE TAKE ME TO THE NICE WOMAN!
WHO?
YOU KNOW, SHE'S THE CHEERFUL, BLONDE WOMAN!

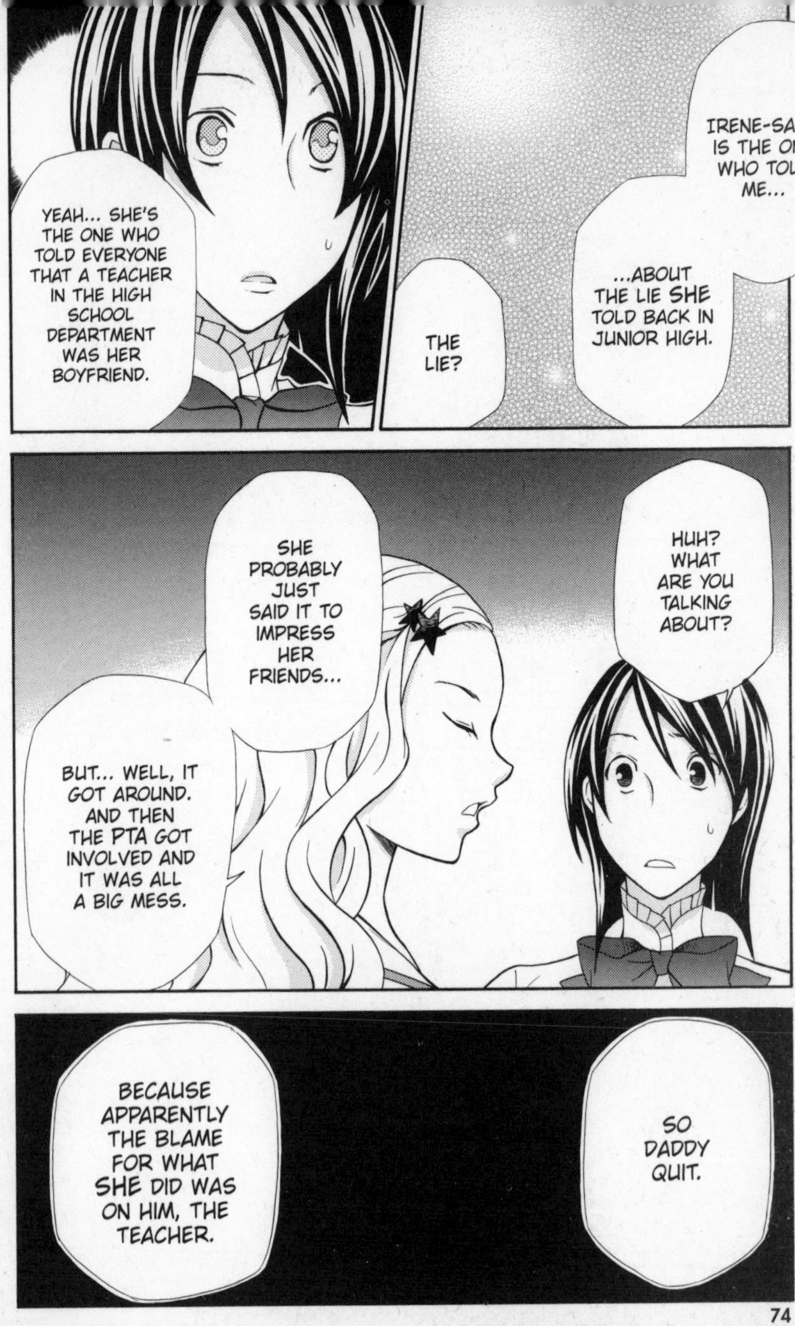
IRENE-SAMA IS THE ONE WHO TOLD ME...
...ABOUT THE LIE SHE TOLD BACK IN JUNIOR HIGH.
THE LIE?
YEAH... SHE'S THE ONE WHO TOLD EVERYONE THAT A TEACHER IN THE HIGH SCHOOL DEPARTMENT WAS HER BOYFRIEND.
HUH? WHAT ARE YOU TALKING ABOUT?
SHE PROBABLY JUST SAID IT TO IMPRESS HER FRIENDS...
BUT... WELL, IT GOT AROUND. AND THEN THE PTA GOT INVOLVED AND IT WAS ALL A BIG MESS.
SO DADDY QUIT.
BECAUSE APPARENTLY THE BLAME FOR WHAT SHE DID WAS ON HIM, THE TEACHER.

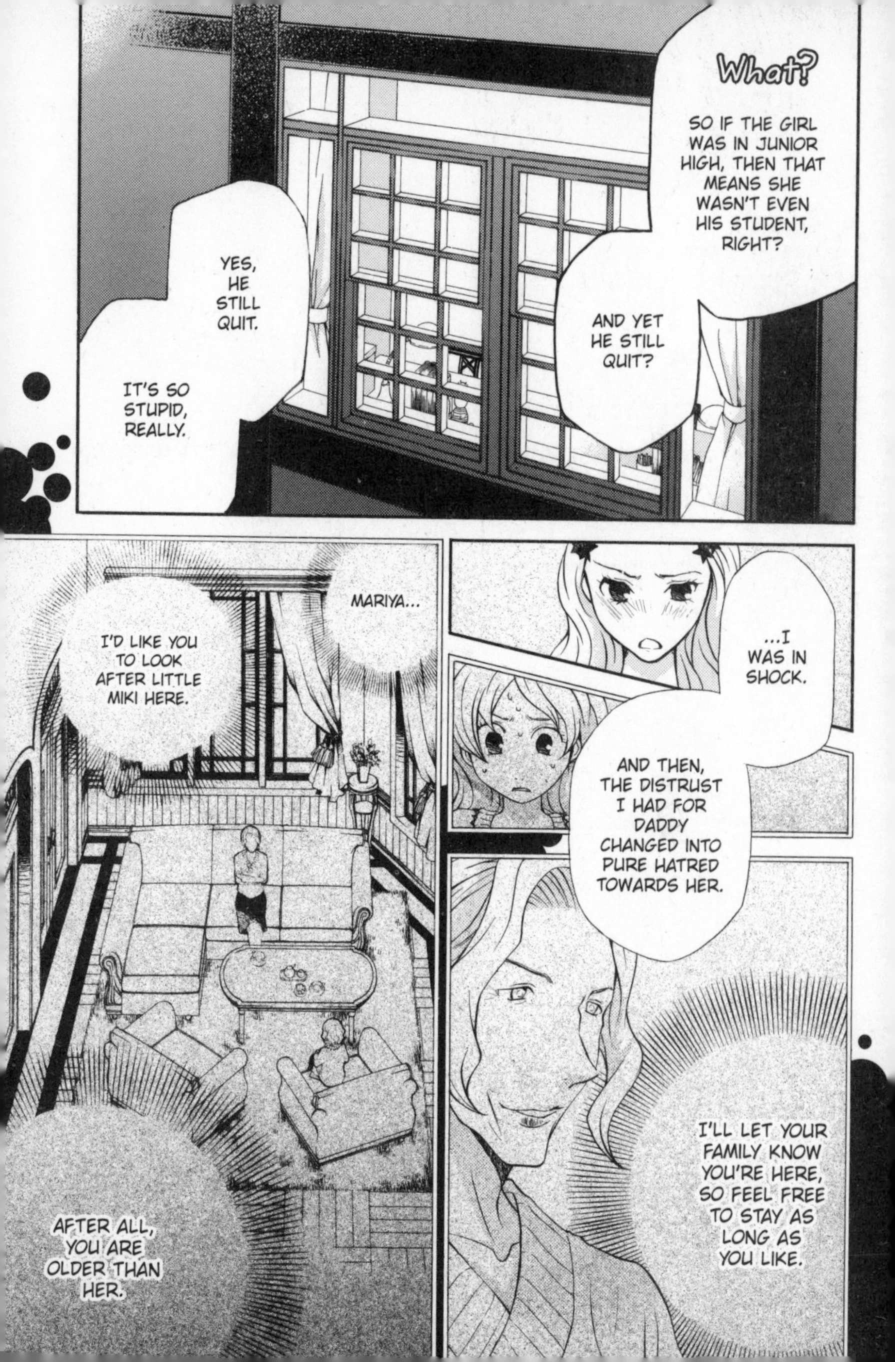
What?
SO IF THE GIRL WAS IN JUNIOR HIGH, THEN THAT MEANS SHE WASN'T EVEN HIS STUDENT, RIGHT?
AND YET HE STILL QUIT?
YES, HE STILL QUIT.
IT'S SO STUPID, REALLY.
...I WAS IN SHOCK.
AND THEN, THE DISTRUST I HAD FOR DADDY CHANGED INTO PURE HATRED TOWARDS HER.
I'LL LET YOUR FAMILY KNOW YOU'RE HERE, SO FEEL FREE TO STAY AS LONG AS YOU LIKE.
MARIYA...
I'D LIKE YOU TO LOOK AFTER LITTLE MIKI HERE.
AFTER ALL, YOU ARE OLDER THAN HER.

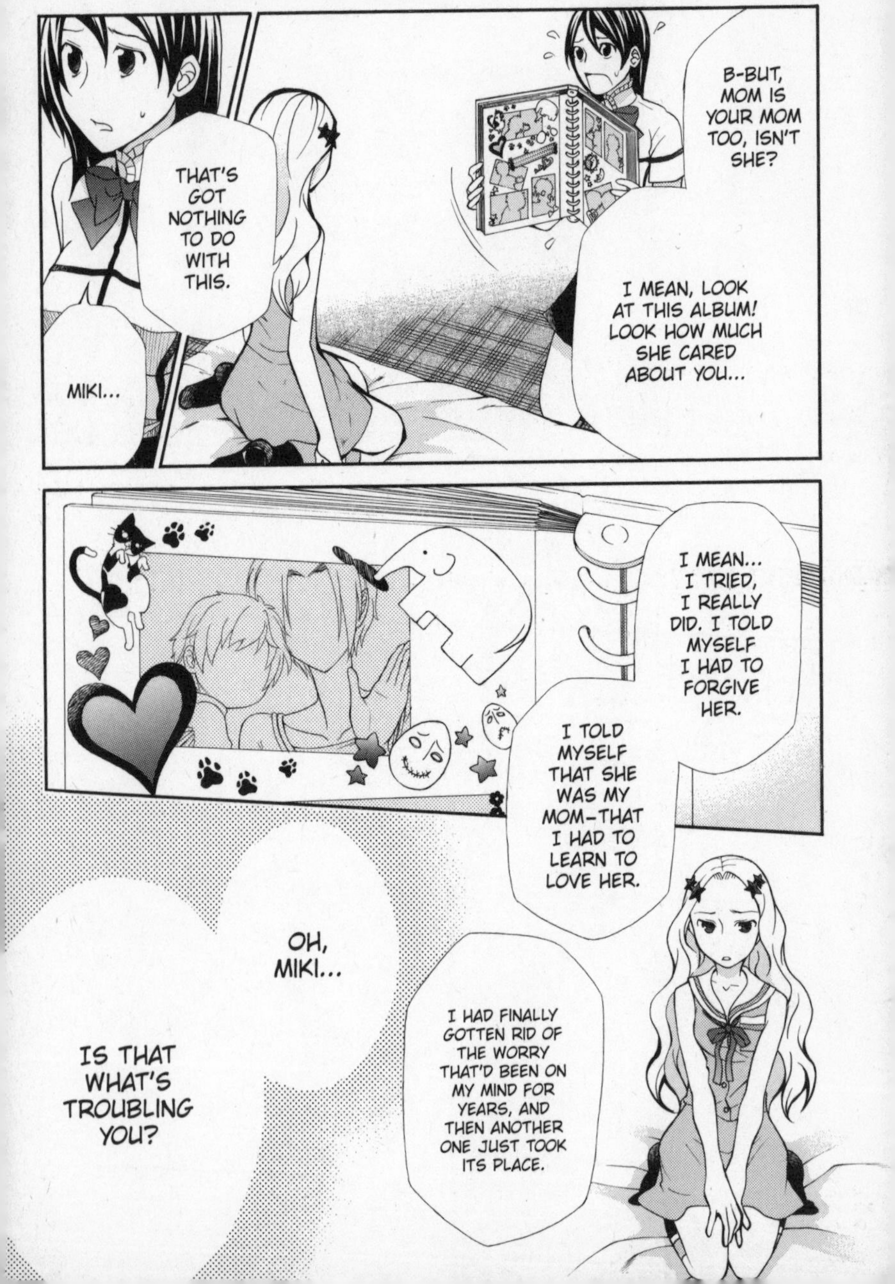
B-BUT, MOM IS YOUR MOM TOO, ISN'T SHE?
I MEAN, LOOK AT THIS ALBUM! LOOK HOW MUCH SHE CARED ABOUT YOU...
THAT'S GOT NOTHING TO DO WITH THIS.
MIKI...
I MEAN... I TRIED, I REALLY DID. I TOLD MYSELF I HAD TO FORGIVE HER.
I TOLD MYSELF THAT SHE WAS MY MOM—THAT I HAD TO LEARN TO LOVE HER.
I HAD FINALLY GOTTEN RID OF THE WORRY THAT'D BEEN ON MY MIND FOR YEARS, AND THEN ANOTHER ONE JUST TOOK ITS PLACE.
OH, MIKI...
IS THAT WHAT'S TROUBLING YOU?

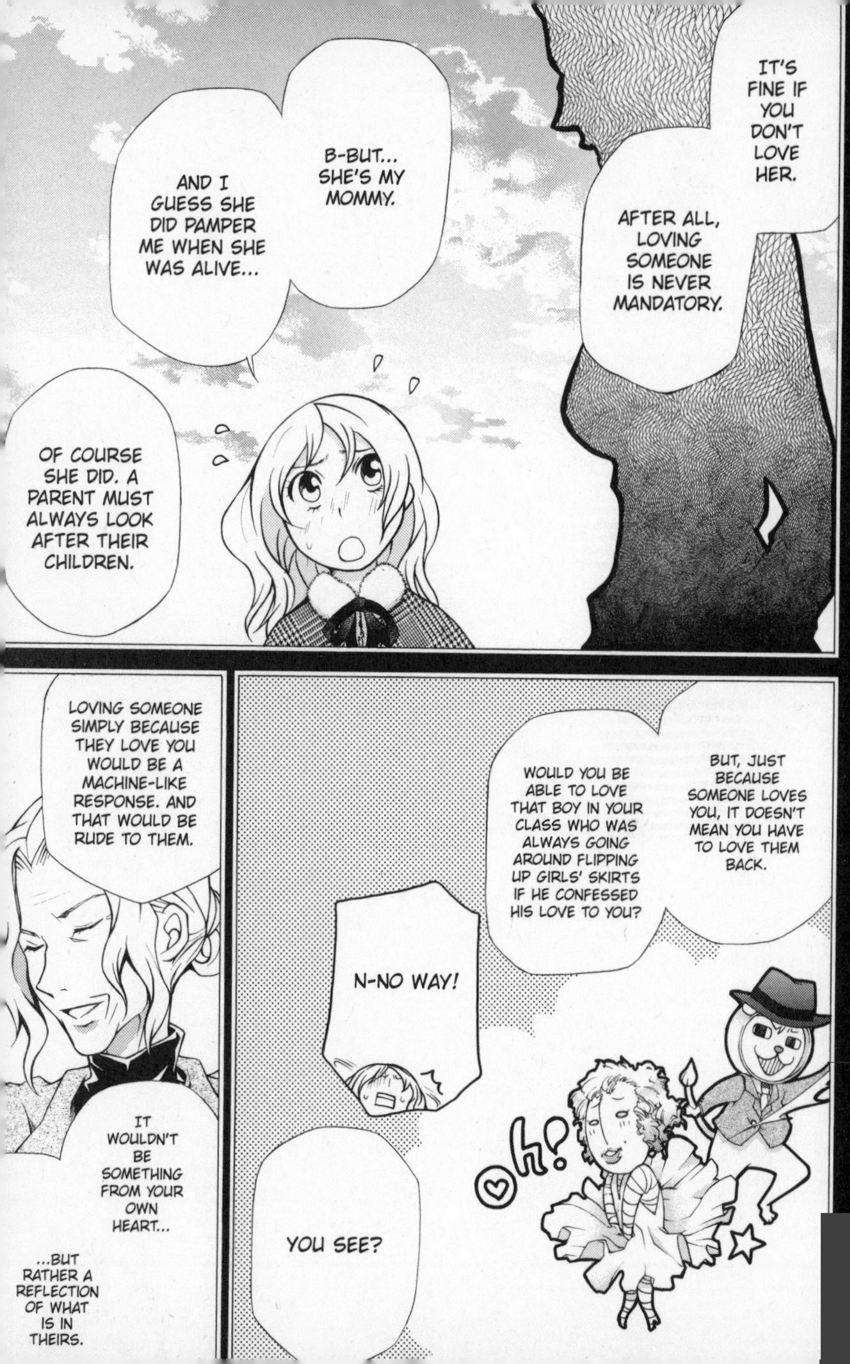
IT'S FINE IF YOU DON'T LOVE HER.
AFTER ALL, LOVING SOMEONE IS NEVER MANDATORY.
B-BUT... SHE'S MY MOMMY.
AND I GUESS SHE DID PAMPER ME WHEN SHE WAS ALIVE...
OF COURSE SHE DID. A PARENT MUST ALWAYS LOOK AFTER THEIR CHILDREN.
BUT, JUST BECAUSE SOMEONE LOVES YOU, IT DOESN'T MEAN YOU HAVE TO LOVE THEM BACK.
WOULD YOU BE ABLE TO LOVE THAT BOY IN YOUR CLASS WHO WAS ALWAYS GOING AROUND FLIPPING UP GIRLS' SKIRTS IF HE CONFESSED HIS LOVE TO YOU?
N-NO WAY!
oh!
YOU SEE?
LOVING SOMEONE SIMPLY BECAUSE THEY LOVE YOU WOULD BE A MACHINE-LIKE RESPONSE. AND THAT WOULD BE RUDE TO THEM.
IT WOULDN'T BE SOMETHING FROM YOUR OWN HEART...
...BUT RATHER A REFLECTION OF WHAT IS IN THEIRS.

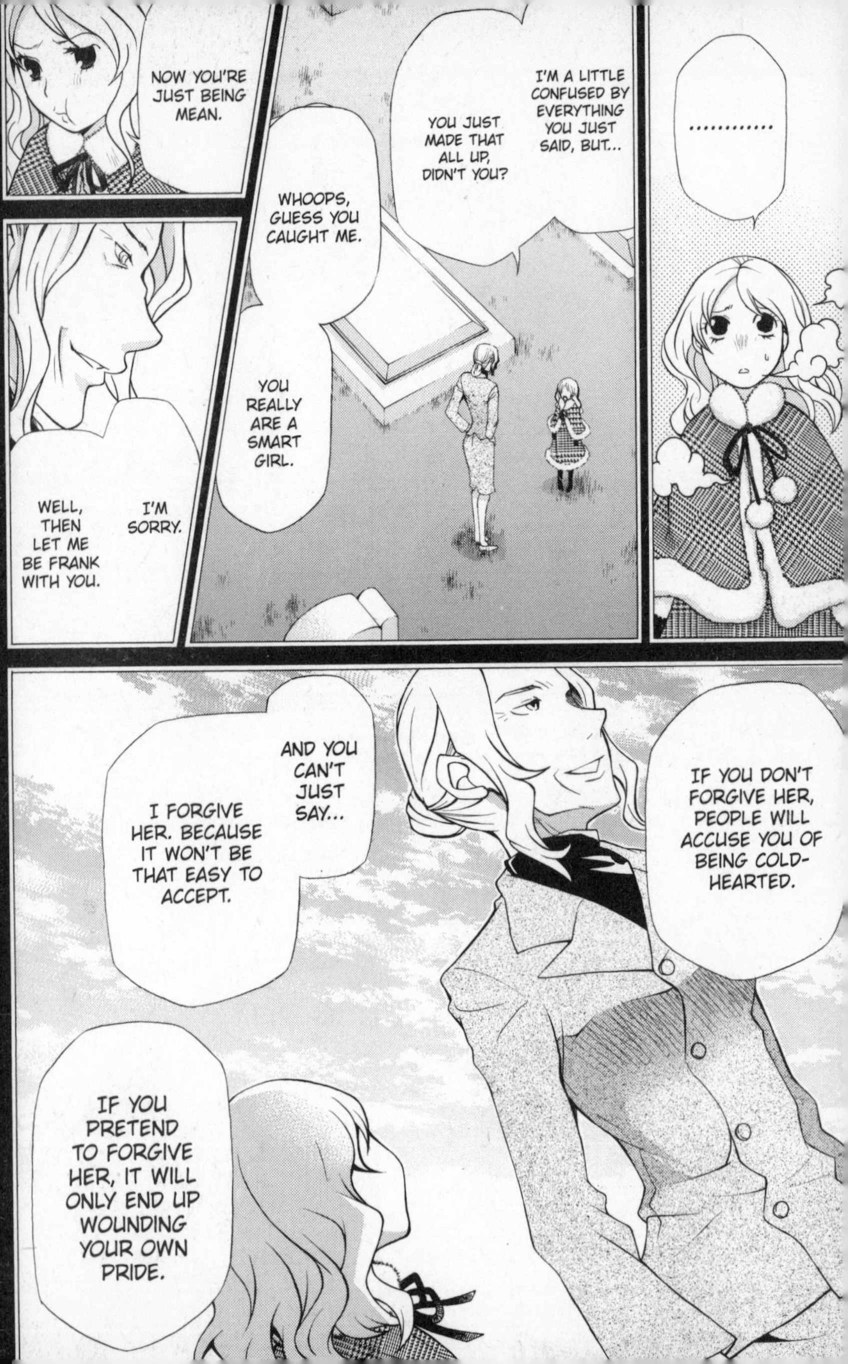
....
I'M A LITTLE CONFUSED BY EVERYTHING YOU JUST SAID, BUT...
YOU JUST MADE THAT ALL UP, DIDN'T YOU?
WHOOPS, GUESS YOU CAUGHT ME.
YOU REALLY ARE A SMART GIRL.
NOW YOU'RE JUST BEING MEAN.
I'M SORRY.
WELL, THEN LET ME BE FRANK WITH YOU.
IF YOU DON'T FORGIVE HER, PEOPLE WILL ACCUSE YOU OF BEING COLD-HEARTED.
AND YOU CAN'T JUST SAY...
I FORGIVE HER. BECAUSE IT WON'T BE THAT EASY TO ACCEPT.
IF YOU PRETEND TO FORGIVE HER, IT WILL ONLY END UP WOUNDING YOUR OWN PRIDE.

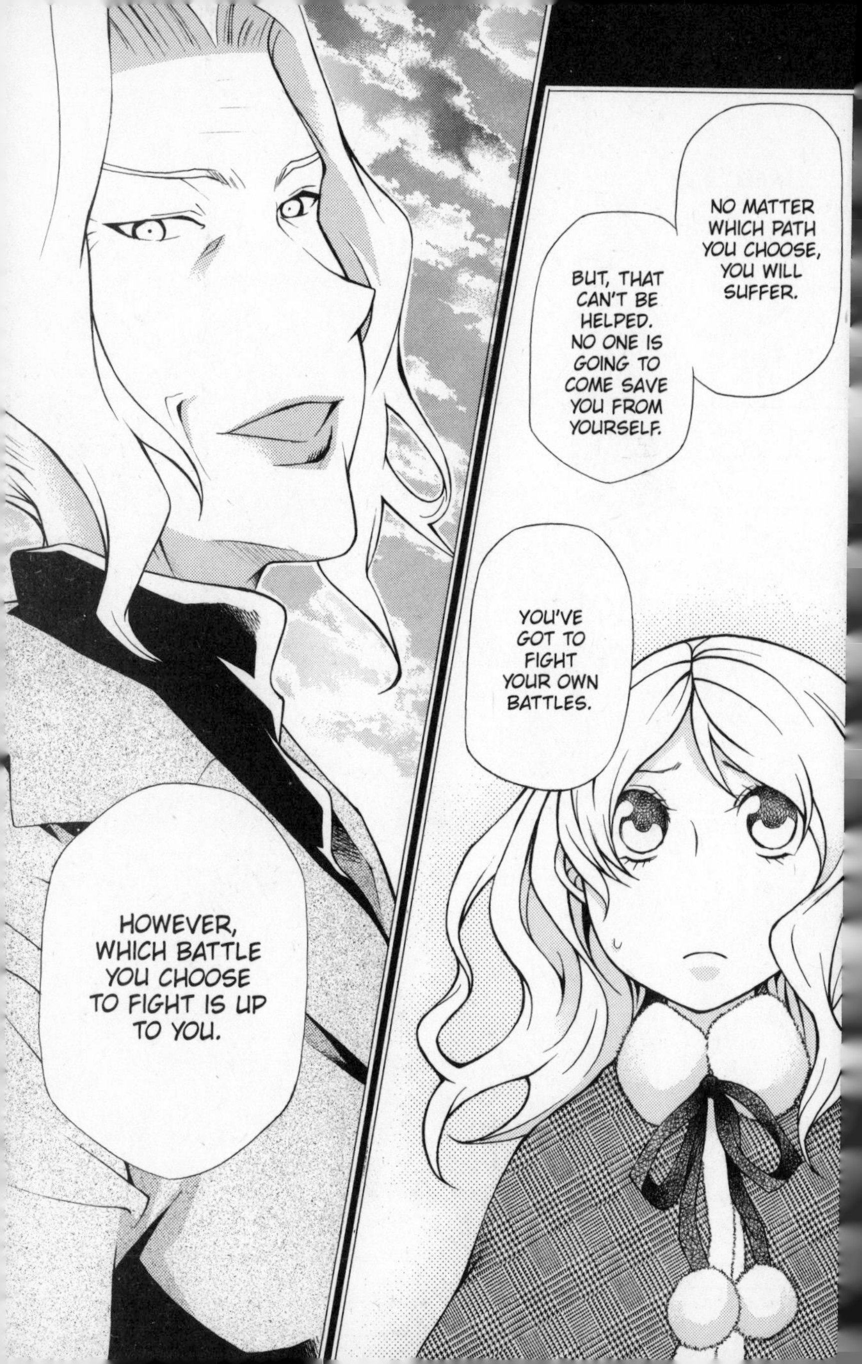
NO MATTER WHICH PATH YOU CHOOSE, YOU WILL SUFFER.
BUT, THAT CAN'T BE HELPED. NO ONE IS GOING TO COME SAVE YOU FROM YOURSELF.
YOU'VE GOT TO FIGHT YOUR OWN BATTLES.
HOWEVER, WHICH BATTLE YOU CHOOSE TO FIGHT IS UP TO YOU.

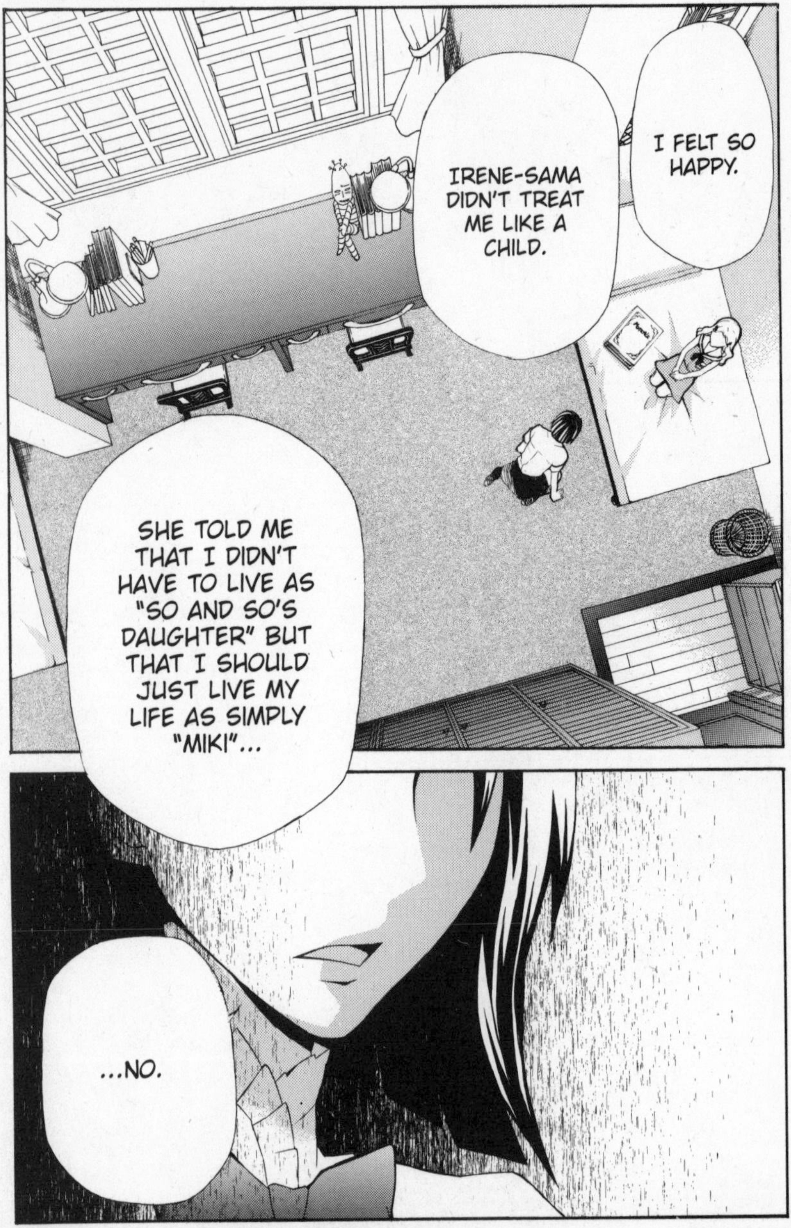
I FELT SO HAPPY.
IRENE-SAMA DIDN'T TREAT ME LIKE A CHILD.
SHE TOLD ME THAT I DIDN'T HAVE TO LIVE AS "SO AND SO'S DAUGHTER" BUT THAT I SHOULD JUST LIVE MY LIFE AS SIMPLY "MIKI"...
...NO.

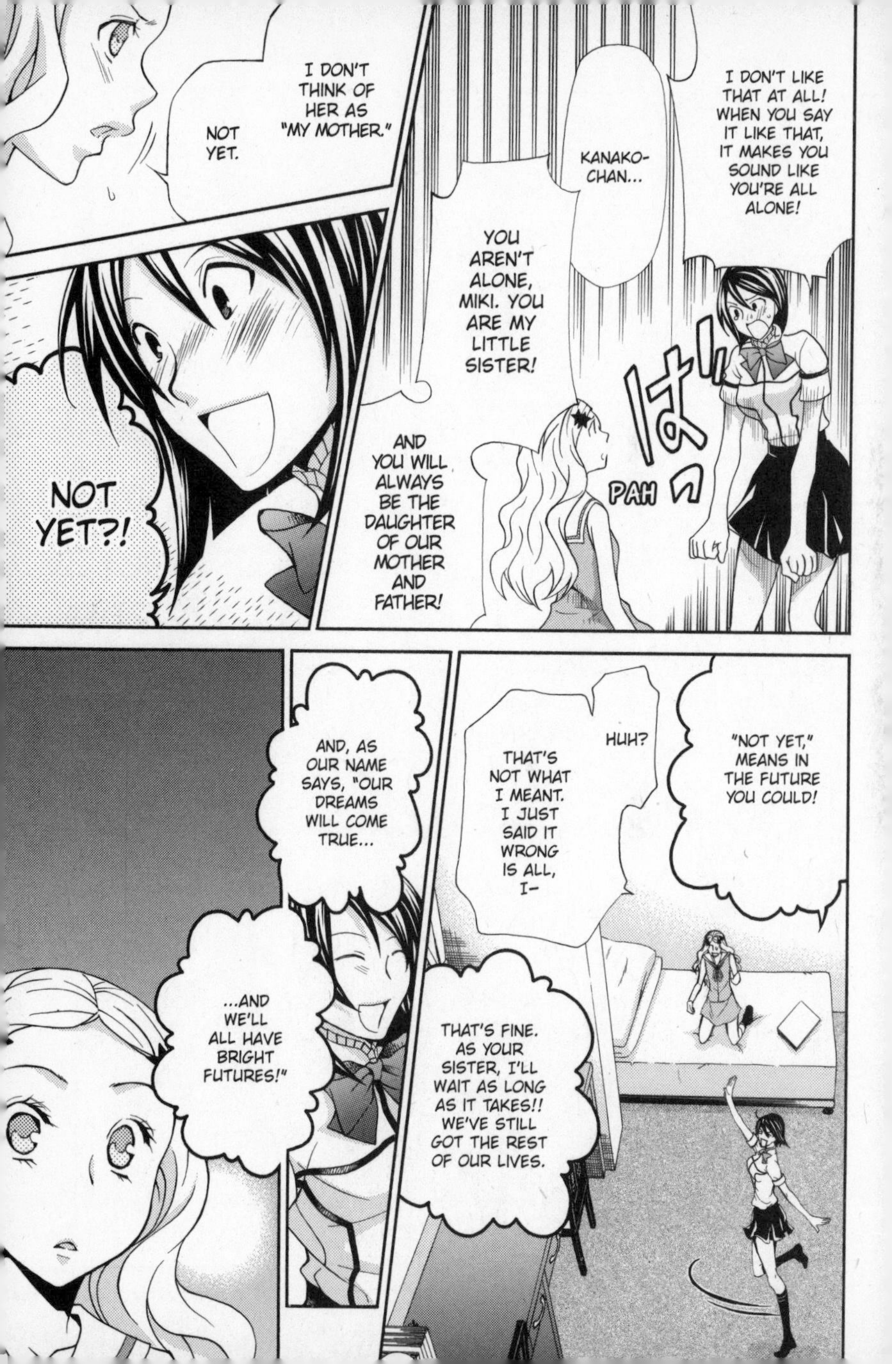
I DON'T LIKE THAT AT ALL! WHEN YOU SAY IT LIKE THAT, IT MAKES YOU SOUND LIKE YOU'RE ALL ALONE!
KANAKO-CHAN...
YOU AREN'T ALONE, MIKI. YOU ARE MY LITTLE SISTER!
AND YOU WILL ALWAYS BE THE DAUGHTER OF OUR MOTHER AND FATHER!
はっ
PAH
I DON'T THINK OF HER AS "MY MOTHER."
NOT YET.
NOT YET?!
"NOT YET," MEANS IN THE FUTURE YOU COULD!
HUH?
THAT'S NOT WHAT I MEANT. I JUST SAID IT WRONG IS ALL, I-
THAT'S FINE. AS YOUR SISTER, I'LL WAIT AS LONG AS IT TAKES!! WE'VE STILL GOT THE REST OF OUR LIVES.
AND, AS OUR NAME SAYS, "OUR DREAMS WILL COME TRUE...
...AND WE'LL ALL HAVE BRIGHT FUTURES!"

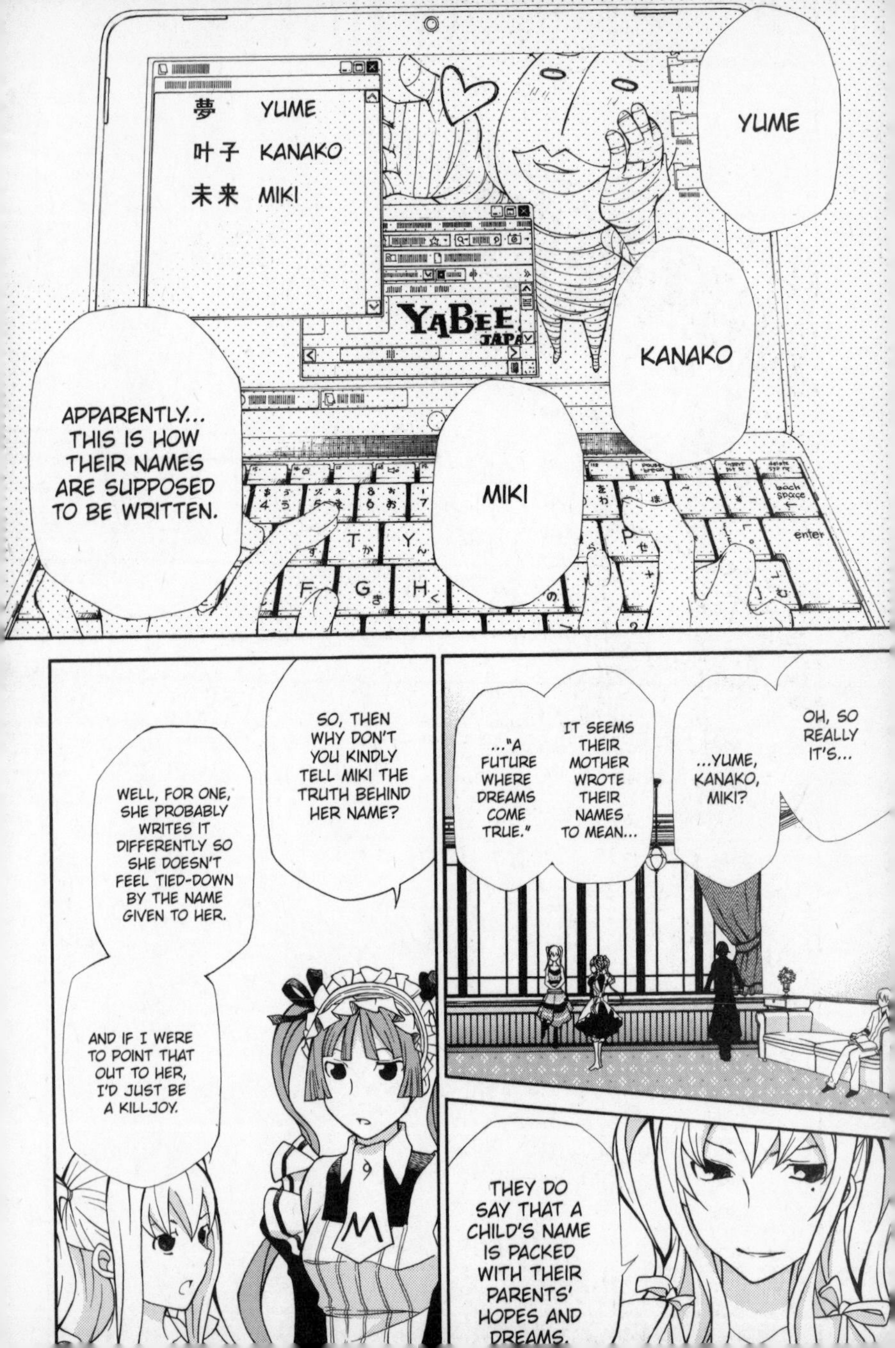

夢 YUME
叶子 KANAKO
未来 MIKI
YABEE JAPA
YUME
KANAKO
MIKI
APPARENTLY... THIS IS HOW THEIR NAMES ARE SUPPOSED TO BE WRITTEN.
OH, SO REALLY IT'S...
...YUME, KANAKO, MIKI?
IT SEEMS THEIR MOTHER WROTE THEIR NAMES TO MEAN...
..."A FUTURE WHERE DREAMS COME TRUE."
THEY DO SAY THAT A CHILD'S NAME IS PACKED WITH THEIR PARENTS' HOPES AND DREAMS.
SO, THEN WHY DON'T YOU KINDLY TELL MIKI THE TRUTH BEHIND HER NAME?
WELL, FOR ONE, SHE PROBABLY WRITES IT DIFFERENTLY SO SHE DOESN'T FEEL TIED-DOWN BY THE NAME GIVEN TO HER.
AND IF I WERE TO POINT THAT OUT TO HER, I'D JUST BE A KILLJOY.

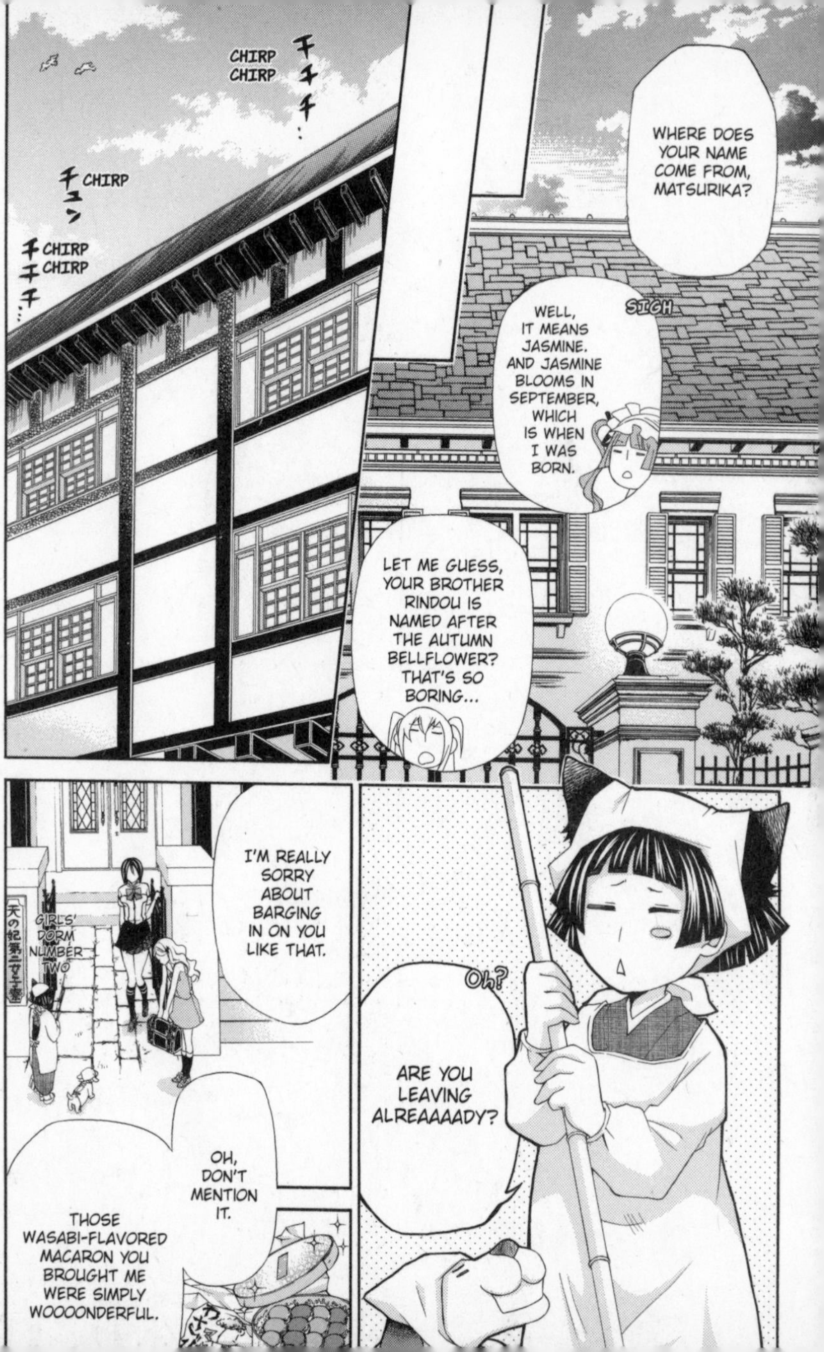
WHERE DOES YOUR NAME COME FROM, MATSURIKA?
SIGH
WELL, IT MEANS JASMINE. AND JASMINE BLOOMS IN SEPTEMBER, WHICH IS WHEN I WAS BORN.
LET ME GUESS, YOUR BROTHER RINDOU IS NAMED AFTER THE AUTUMN BELLFLOWER? THAT'S SO BORING...
チチチ…
CHIRP CHIRP
チュン
CHIRP
チチチ…
CHIRP CHIRP
Oh?
ARE YOU LEAVING ALREAAAADY?
I'M REALLY SORRY ABOUT BARGING IN ON YOU LIKE THAT.
GIRLS' DORM NUMBER TWO
OH, DON'T MENTION IT.
THOSE WASABI-FLAVORED MACARON YOU BROUGHT ME WERE SIMPLY WOOOONDERFUL.

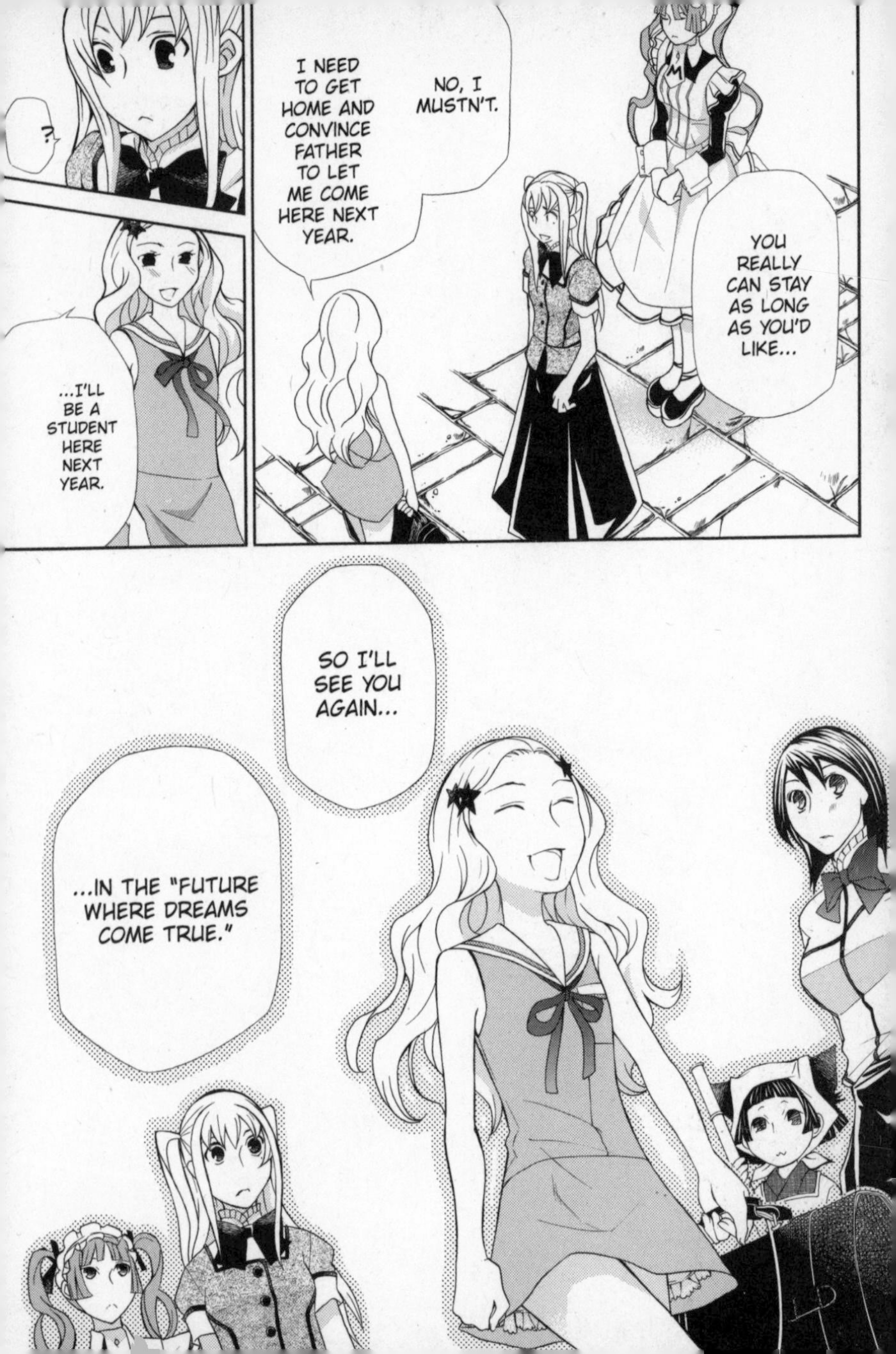
YOU REALLY CAN STAY AS LONG AS YOU'D LIKE...
NO, I MUSTN'T.
I NEED TO GET HOME AND CONVINCE FATHER TO LET ME COME HERE NEXT YEAR.
?
...I'LL BE A STUDENT HERE NEXT YEAR.
SO I'LL SEE YOU AGAIN...
...IN THE "FUTURE WHERE DREAMS COME TRUE."

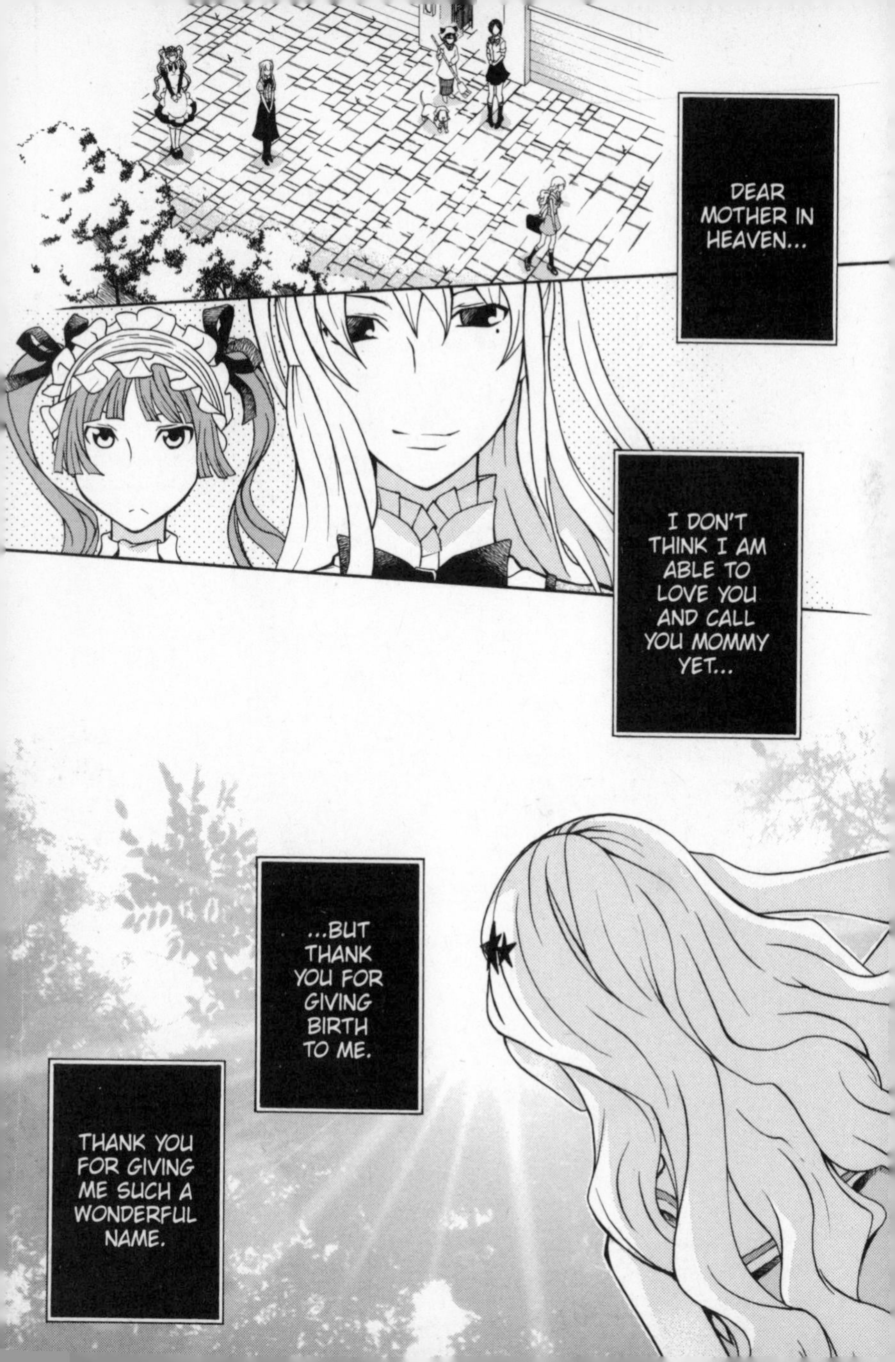
DEAR MOTHER IN HEAVEN...
I DON'T THINK I AM ABLE TO LOVE YOU AND CALL YOU MOMMY YET...
...BUT THANK YOU FOR GIVING BIRTH TO ME.
THANK YOU FOR GIVING ME SUCH A WONDERFUL NAME.

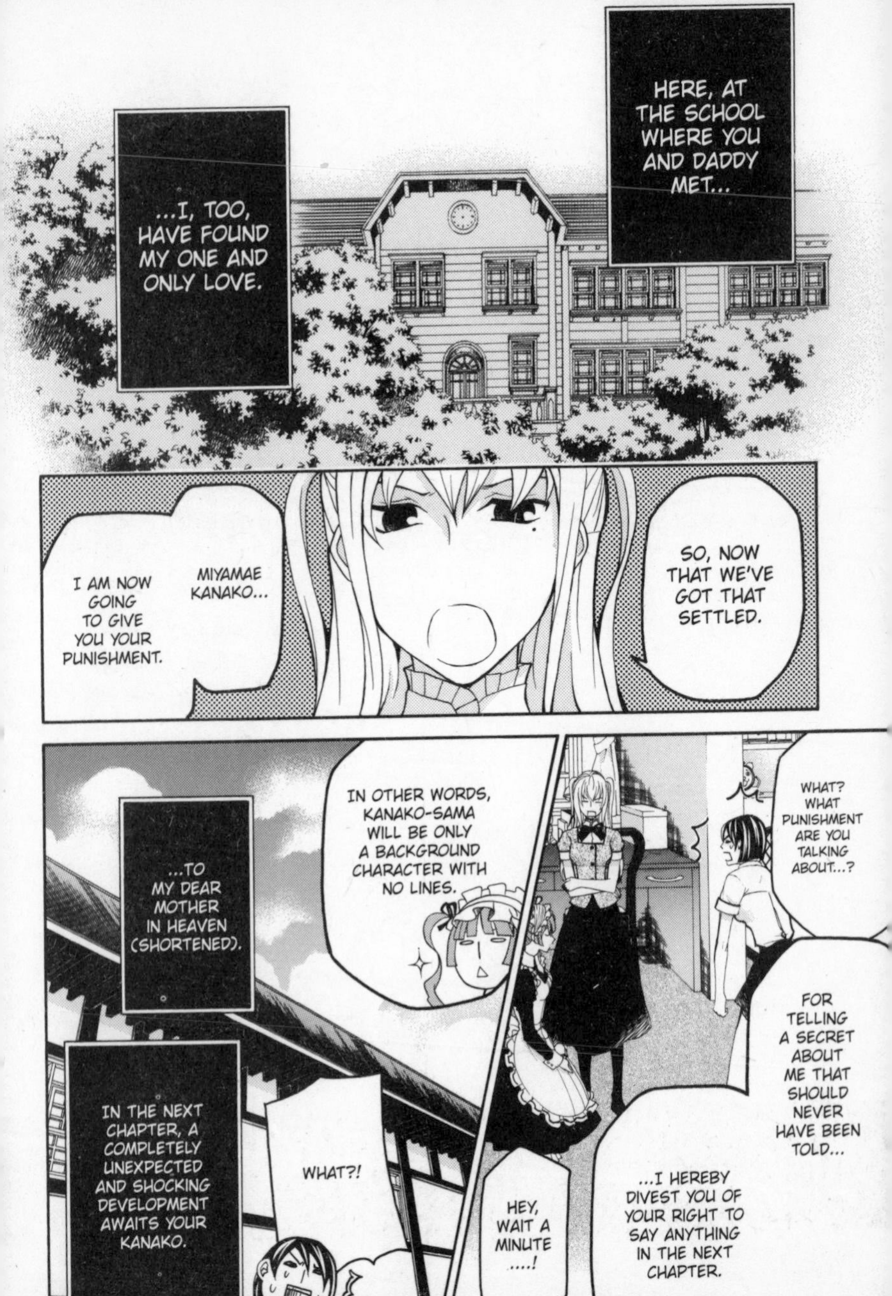
HERE, AT THE SCHOOL WHERE YOU AND DADDY MET...
...I, TOO, HAVE FOUND MY ONE AND ONLY LOVE.
SO, NOW THAT WE'VE GOT THAT SETTLED.
MIYAMAE KANAKO...
I AM NOW GOING TO GIVE YOU YOUR PUNISHMENT.
WHAT? WHAT PUNISHMENT ARE YOU TALKING ABOUT...?
FOR TELLING A SECRET ABOUT ME THAT SHOULD NEVER HAVE BEEN TOLD...
...I HEREBY DIVEST YOU OF YOUR RIGHT TO SAY ANYTHING IN THE NEXT CHAPTER.
HEY, WAIT A MINUTE .....!
IN OTHER WORDS, KANAKO-SAMA WILL BE ONLY A BACKGROUND CHARACTER WITH NO LINES.
...TO MY DEAR MOTHER IN HEAVEN (SHORTENED).
WHAT?!
IN THE NEXT CHAPTER, A COMPLETELY UNEXPECTED AND SHOCKING DEVELOPMENT AWAITS YOUR KANAKO.

M A R I A H O L I C

MARIA✝HOLIC

M A R I A H O L I C

MARIA†HOLIC

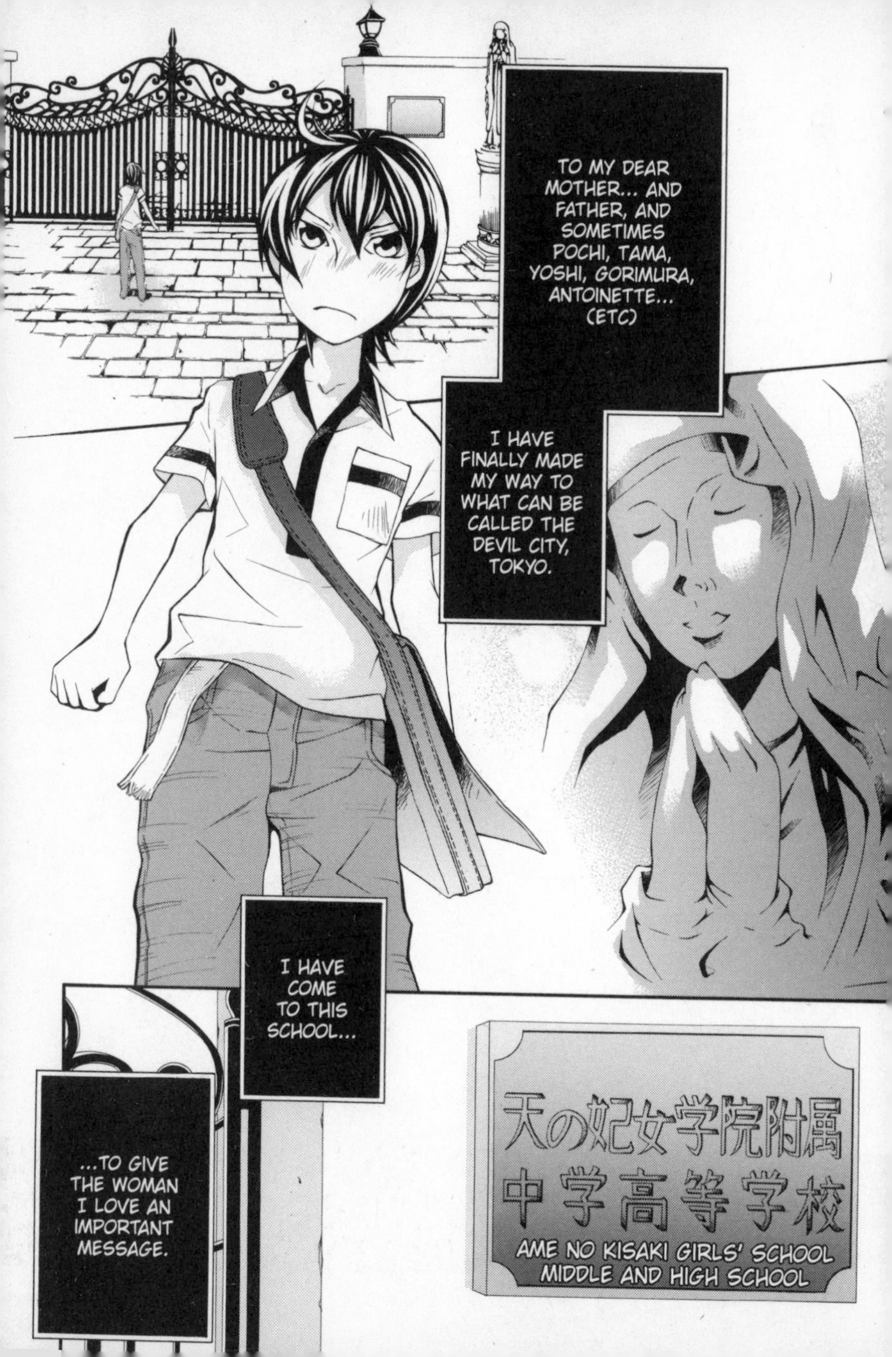
TO MY DEAR MOTHER... AND FATHER, AND SOMETIMES POCHI, TAMA, YOSHI, GORIMURA, ANTOINETTE... (ETC)
I HAVE FINALLY MADE MY WAY TO WHAT CAN BE CALLED THE DEVIL CITY, TOKYO.
I HAVE COME TO THIS SCHOOL...
天の妃女学院附属
中学高等学校
AME NO KISAKI GIRLS' SCHOOL MIDDLE AND HIGH SCHOOL
...TO GIVE THE WOMAN I LOVE AN IMPORTANT MESSAGE.

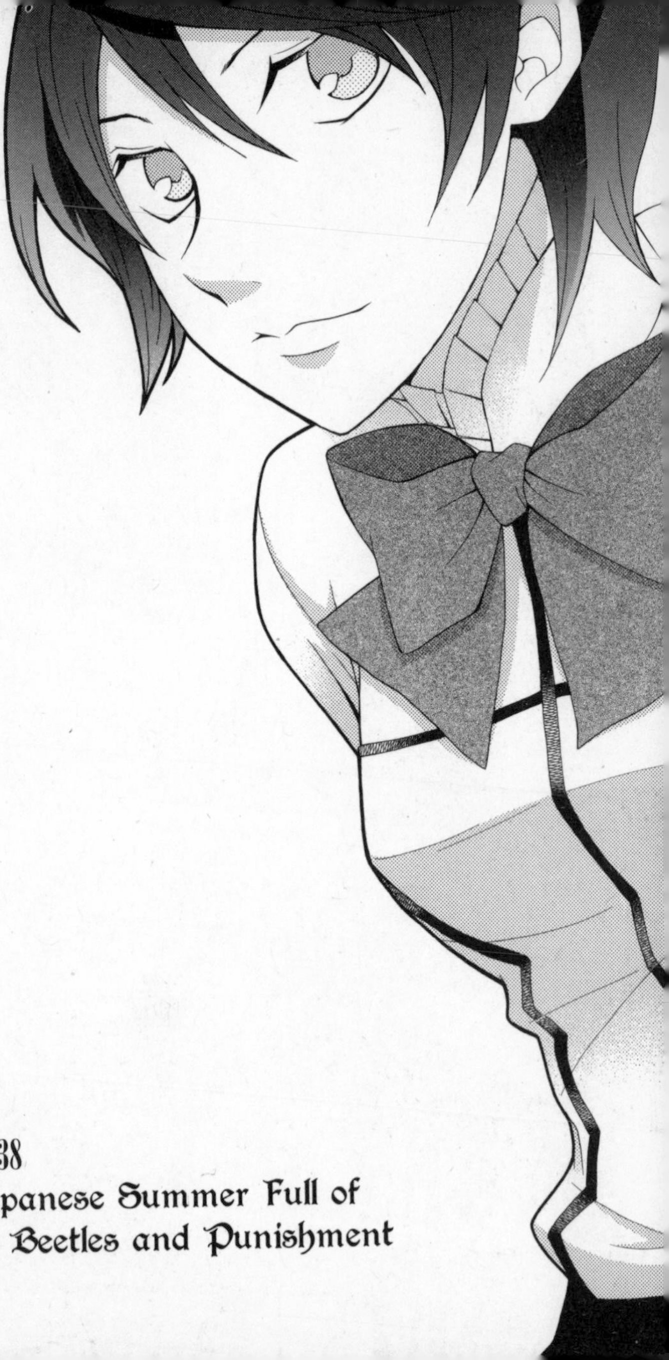

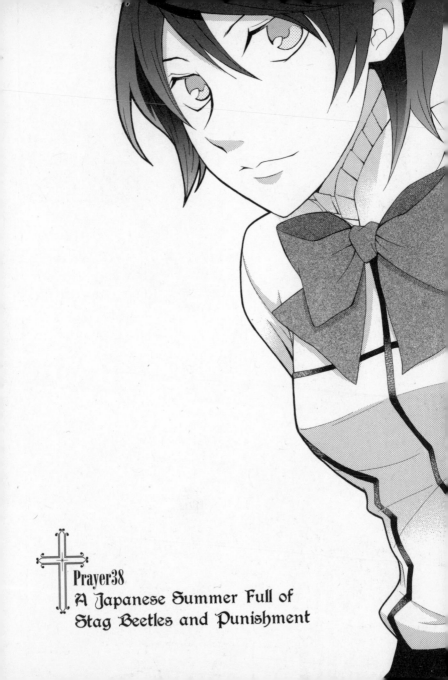

Prayer38
A Japanese Summer Full of Stag Beetles and Punishment

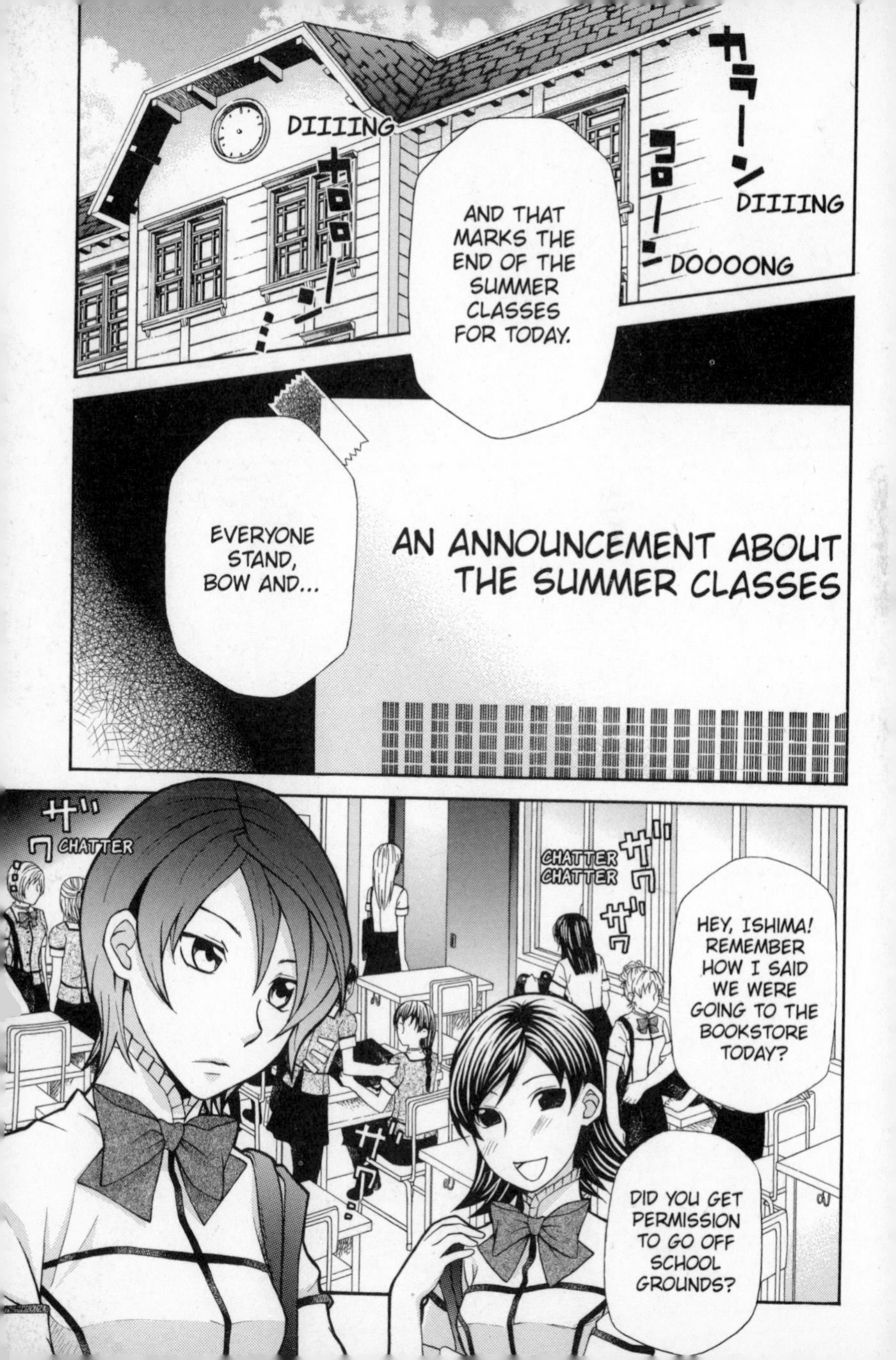
DIIIING
DOOOONG
DIIIING
AND THAT MARKS THE END OF THE SUMMER CLASSES FOR TODAY.
AN ANNOUNCEMENT ABOUT THE SUMMER CLASSES
EVERYONE STAND, BOW AND...
HEY, ISHIMA! REMEMBER HOW I SAID WE WERE GOING TO THE BOOKSTORE TODAY?
DID YOU GET PERMISSION TO GO OFF SCHOOL GROUNDS?
CHATTER CHATTER
CHATTER

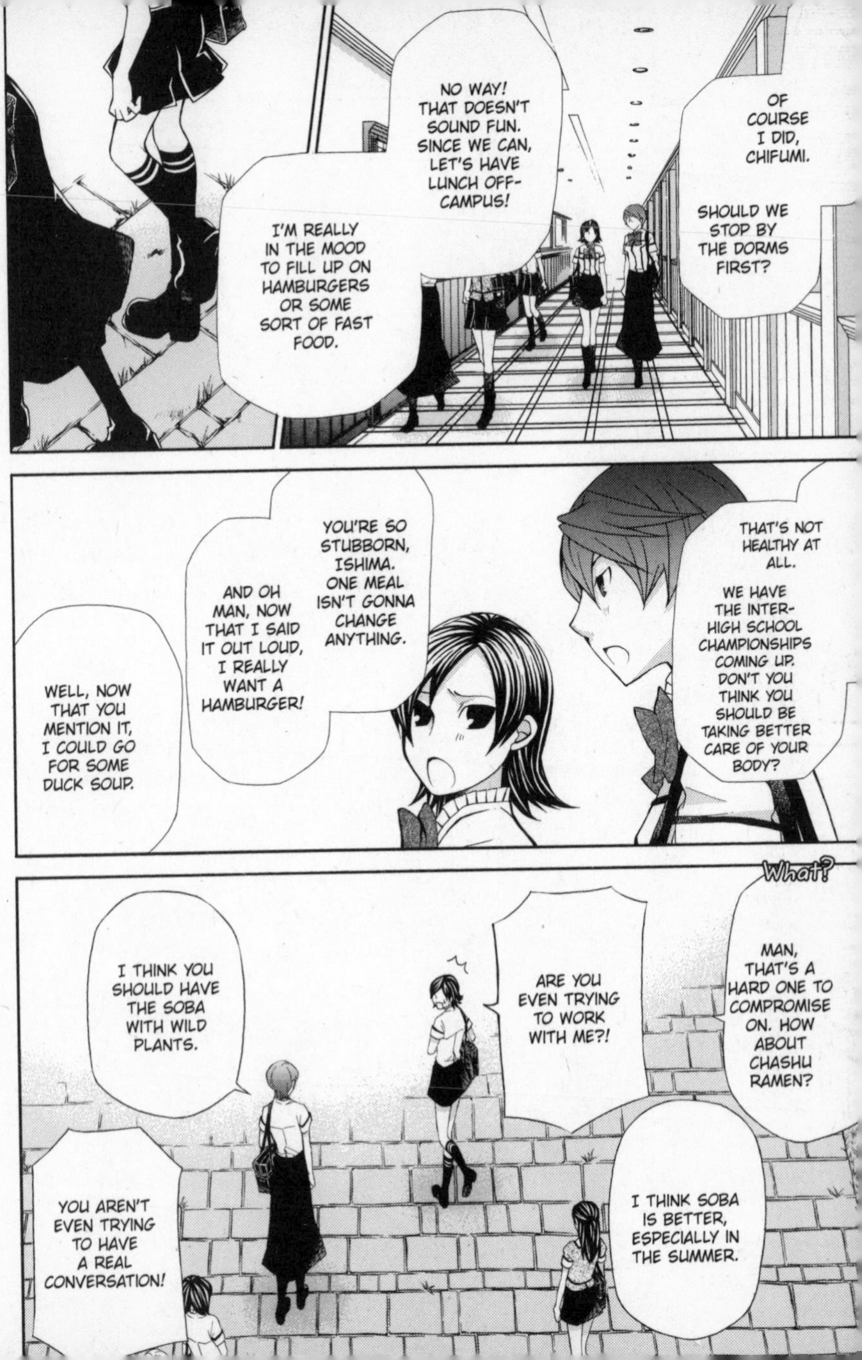
OF COURSE I DID, CHIFUMI.
SHOULD WE STOP BY THE DORMS FIRST?
NO WAY! THAT DOESN'T SOUND FUN. SINCE WE CAN, LET'S HAVE LUNCH OFF-CAMPUS!
I'M REALLY IN THE MOOD TO FILL UP ON HAMBURGERS OR SOME SORT OF FAST FOOD.
THAT'S NOT HEALTHY AT ALL.
WE HAVE THE INTER-HIGH SCHOOL CHAMPIONSHIPS COMING UP. DON'T YOU THINK YOU SHOULD BE TAKING BETTER CARE OF YOUR BODY?
YOU'RE SO STUBBORN, ISHIMA. ONE MEAL ISN'T GONNA CHANGE ANYTHING.
AND OH MAN, NOW THAT I SAID IT OUT LOUD, I REALLY WANT A HAMBURGER!
WELL, NOW THAT YOU MENTION IT, I COULD GO FOR SOME DUCK SOUP.
What?
MAN, THAT'S A HARD ONE TO COMPROMISE ON. HOW ABOUT CHASHU RAMEN?
ARE YOU EVEN TRYING TO WORK WITH ME?!
I THINK YOU SHOULD HAVE THE SOBA WITH WILD PLANTS.
I THINK SOBA IS BETTER, ESPECIALLY IN THE SUMMER.
YOU AREN'T EVEN TRYING TO HAVE A REAL CONVERSATION!

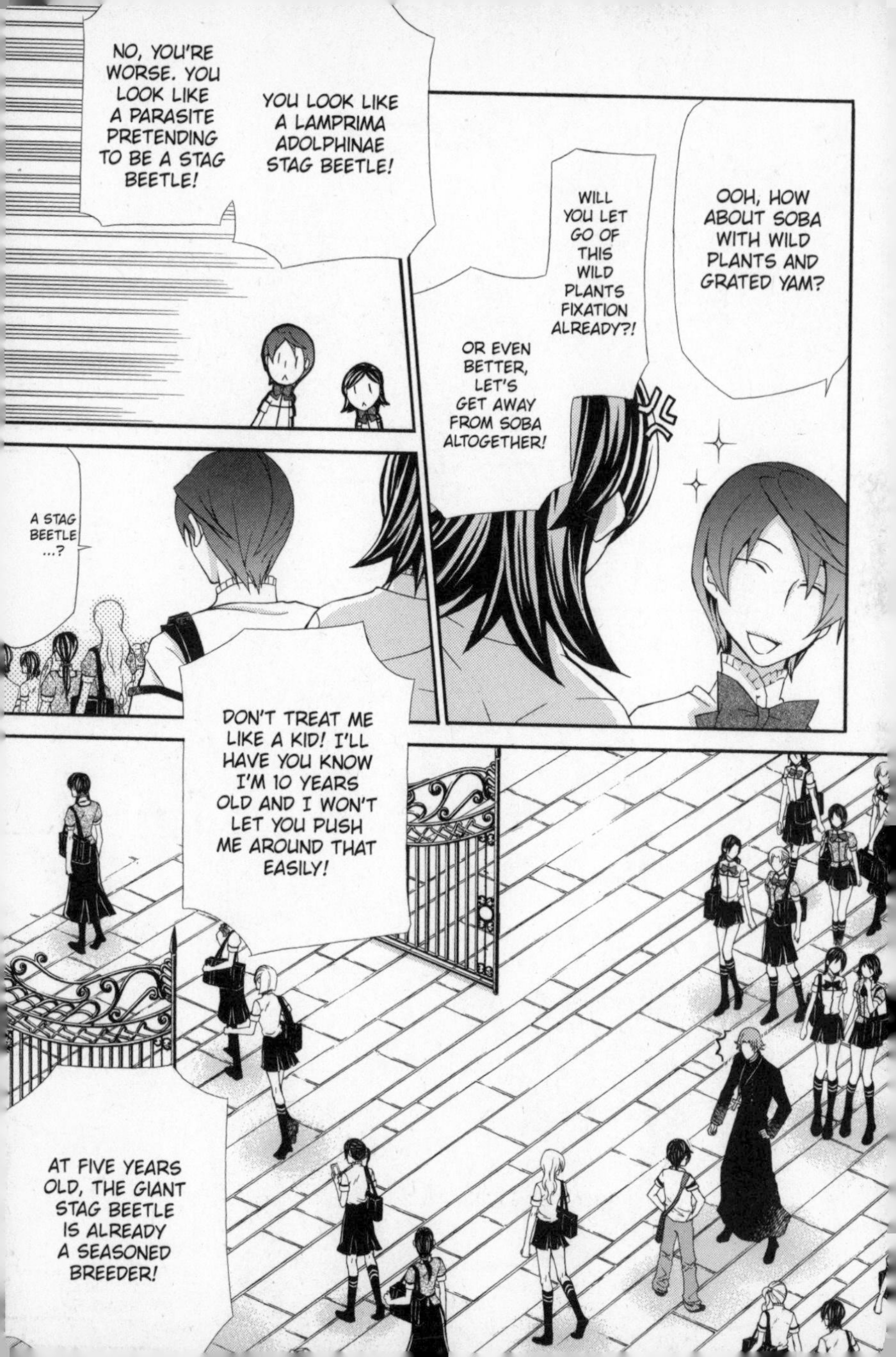
OOH, HOW ABOUT SOBA WITH WILD PLANTS AND GRATED YAM?
WILL YOU LET GO OF THIS WILD PLANTS FIXATION ALREADY?!
OR EVEN BETTER, LET'S GET AWAY FROM SOBA ALTOGETHER!
YOU LOOK LIKE A LAMPRIMA ADOLPHINAE STAG BEETLE!
NO, YOU'RE WORSE. YOU LOOK LIKE A PARASITE PRETENDING TO BE A STAG BEETLE!
A STAG BEETLE ...?
DON'T TREAT ME LIKE A KID! I'LL HAVE YOU KNOW I'M 10 YEARS OLD AND I WON'T LET YOU PUSH ME AROUND THAT EASILY!
AT FIVE YEARS OLD, THE GIANT STAG BEETLE IS ALREADY A SEASONED BREEDER!

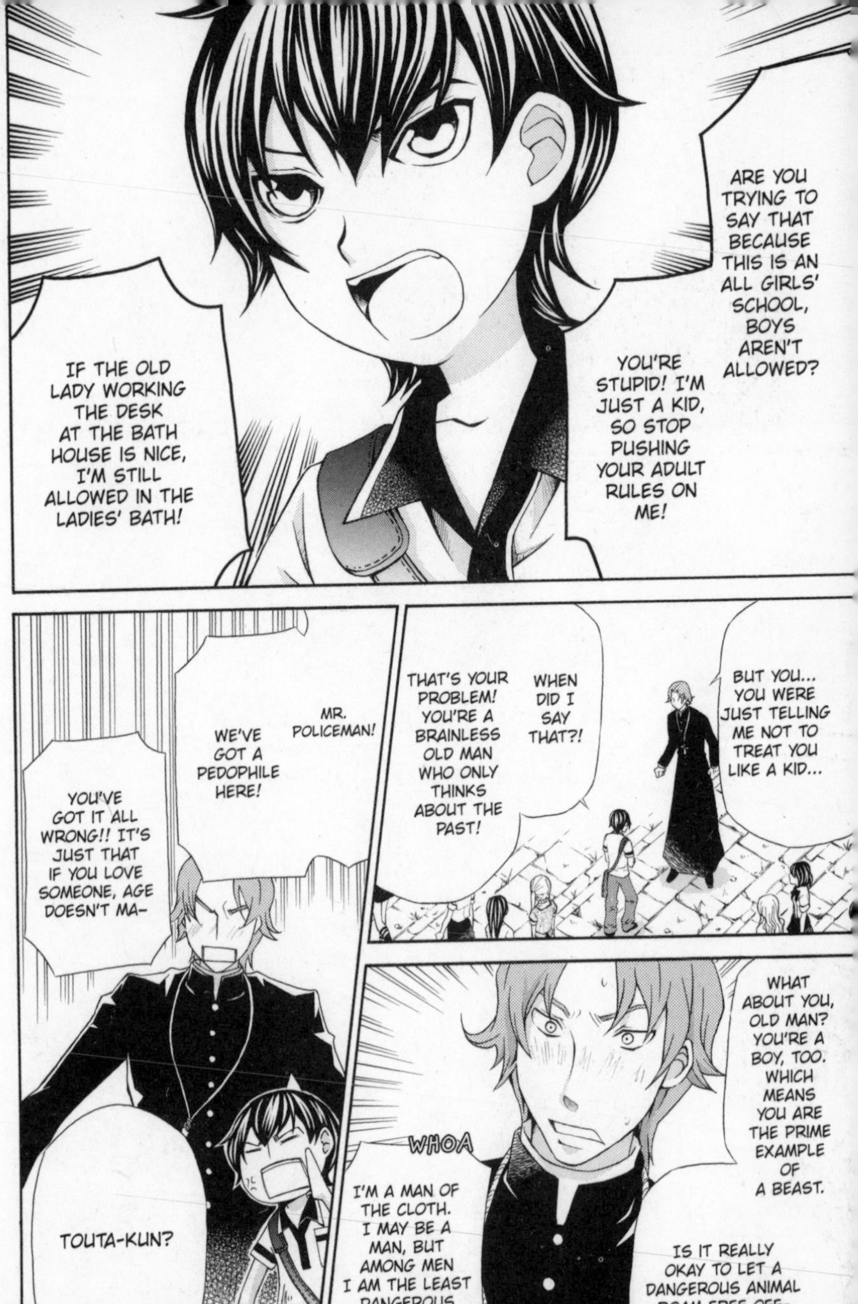
ARE YOU TRYING TO SAY THAT BECAUSE THIS IS AN ALL GIRLS' SCHOOL, BOYS AREN'T ALLOWED?
YOU'RE STUPID! I'M JUST A KID, SO STOP PUSHING YOUR ADULT RULES ON ME!
IF THE OLD LADY WORKING THE DESK AT THE BATH HOUSE IS NICE, I'M STILL ALLOWED IN THE LADIES' BATH!
BUT YOU... YOU WERE JUST TELLING ME NOT TO TREAT YOU LIKE A KID...
WHEN DID I SAY THAT?!
THAT'S YOUR PROBLEM! YOU'RE A BRAINLESS OLD MAN WHO ONLY THINKS ABOUT THE PAST!
WHAT ABOUT YOU, OLD MAN? YOU'RE A BOY, TOO. WHICH MEANS YOU ARE THE PRIME EXAMPLE OF A BEAST.
IS IT REALLY OKAY TO LET A DANGEROUS ANIMAL ROAM FREE OFF-LEASH LIKE THIS?!
WHOA
I'M A MAN OF THE CLOTH. I MAY BE A MAN, BUT AMONG MEN I AM THE LEAST DANGEROUS MAN YOU COULD EVER MEET!
MR. POLICEMAN!
WE'VE GOT A PEDOPHILE HERE!
YOU'VE GOT IT ALL WRONG!! IT'S JUST THAT IF YOU LOVE SOMEONE, AGE DOESN'T MA-
TOUTA-KUN?

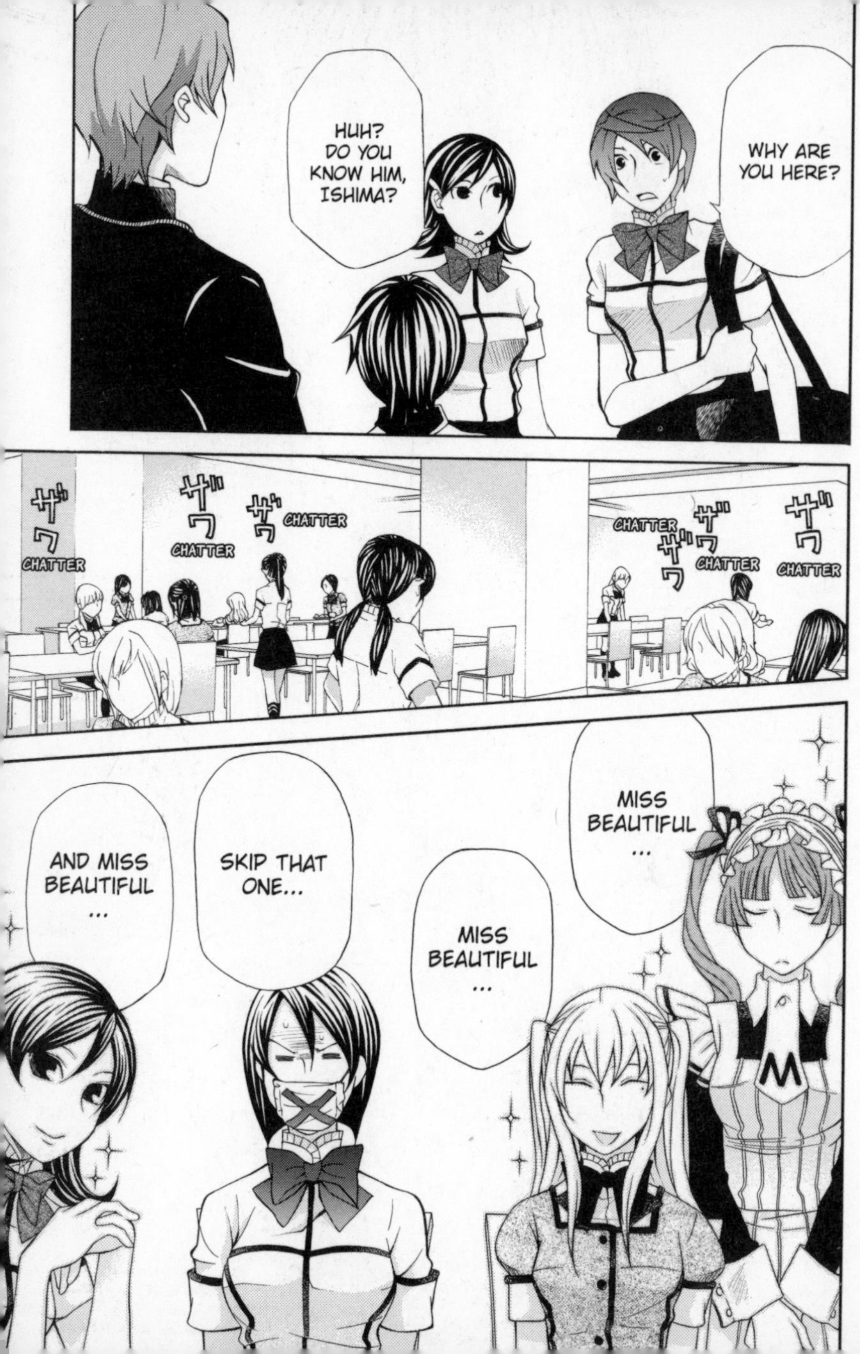
WHY ARE YOU HERE?
HUH? DO YOU KNOW HIM, ISHIMA?
ザワ
CHATTER
ザワ
CHATTER
ザワ
CHATTER
ザワ
CHATTER
ザワ
CHATTER
ザワ
CHATTER
MISS BEAUTIFUL ...
MISS BEAUTIFUL ...
SKIP THAT ONE...
AND MISS BEAUTIFUL ...

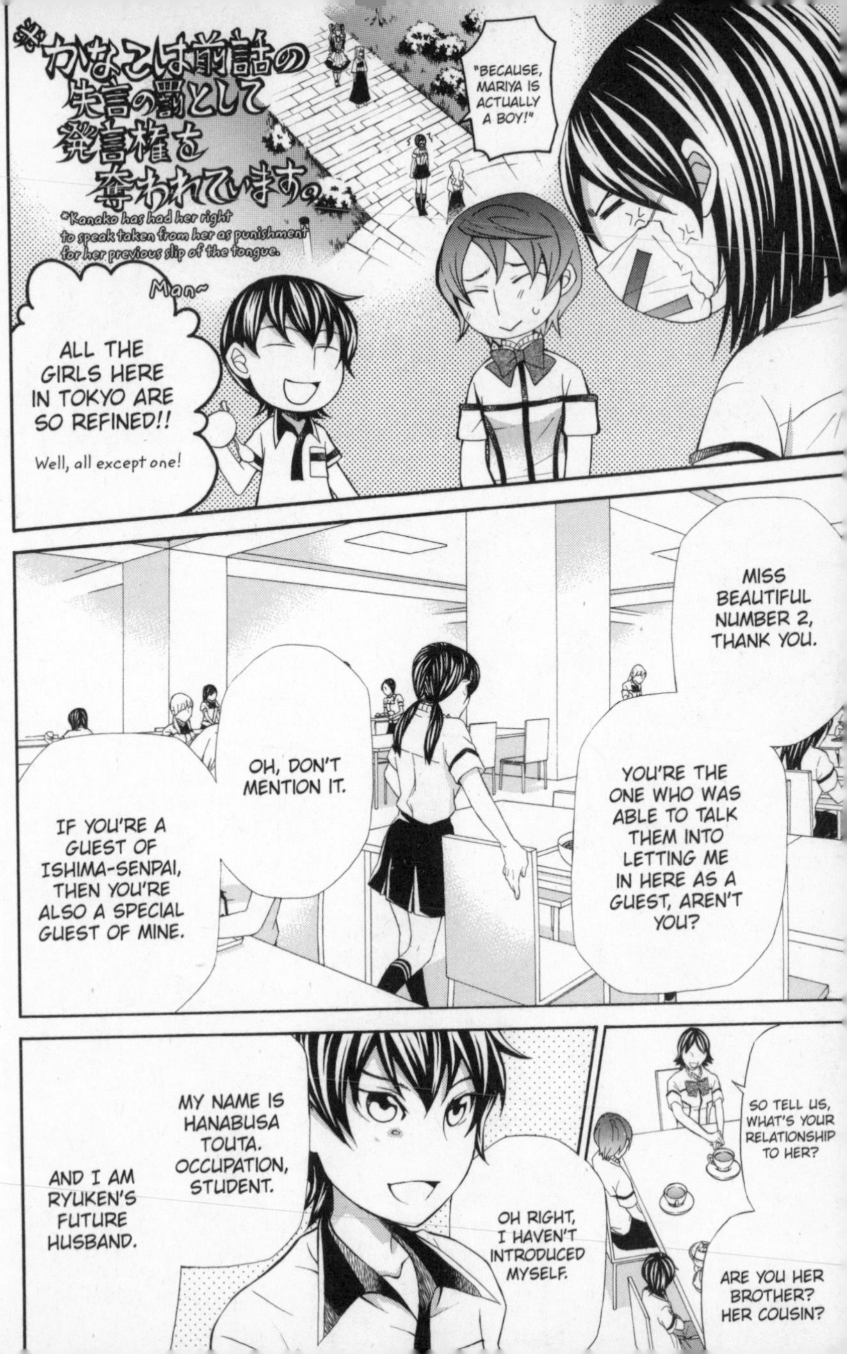
"BECAUSE, MARIYA IS ACTUALLY A BOY!"
※かなこは前話の失言の罰として発言権を奪われています。
*Kanako has had her right to speak taken from her as punishment for her previous slip of the tongue.
Man~
ALL THE GIRLS HERE IN TOKYO ARE SO REFINED!!
Well, all except one!
MISS BEAUTIFUL NUMBER 2, THANK YOU.
YOU'RE THE ONE WHO WAS ABLE TO TALK THEM INTO LETTING ME IN HERE AS A GUEST, AREN'T YOU?
OH, DON'T MENTION IT.
IF YOU'RE A GUEST OF ISHIMA-SENPAI, THEN YOU'RE ALSO A SPECIAL GUEST OF MINE.
SO TELL US, WHAT'S YOUR RELATIONSHIP TO HER?
ARE YOU HER BROTHER? HER COUSIN?
OH RIGHT, I HAVEN'T INTRODUCED MYSELF.
MY NAME IS HANABUSA TOUTA. OCCUPATION, STUDENT.
AND I AM RYUKEN'S FUTURE HUSBAND.

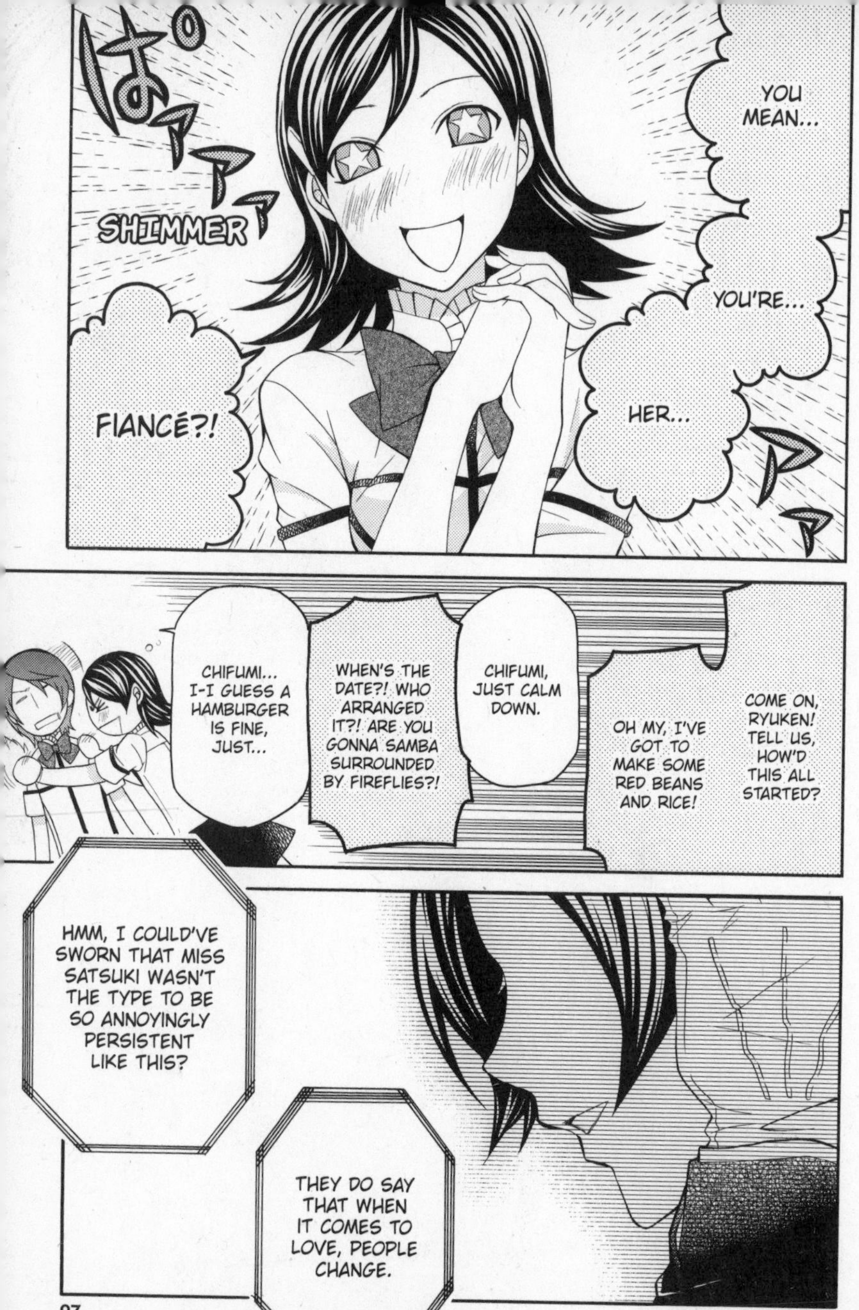
YOU MEAN...
YOU'RE...
HER...
FIANCÉ?!
SHIMMER
COME ON, RYUKEN! TELL US, HOW'D THIS ALL STARTED?
OH MY, I'VE GOT TO MAKE SOME RED BEANS AND RICE!
CHIFUMI, JUST CALM DOWN.
WHEN'S THE DATE?! WHO ARRANGED IT?! ARE YOU GONNA SAMBA SURROUNDED BY FIREFLIES?!
CHIFUMI... I-I GUESS A HAMBURGER IS FINE, JUST...
HMM, I COULD'VE SWORN THAT MISS SATSUKI WASN'T THE TYPE TO BE SO ANNOYINGLY PERSISTENT LIKE THIS?
THEY DO SAY THAT WHEN IT COMES TO LOVE, PEOPLE CHANGE.

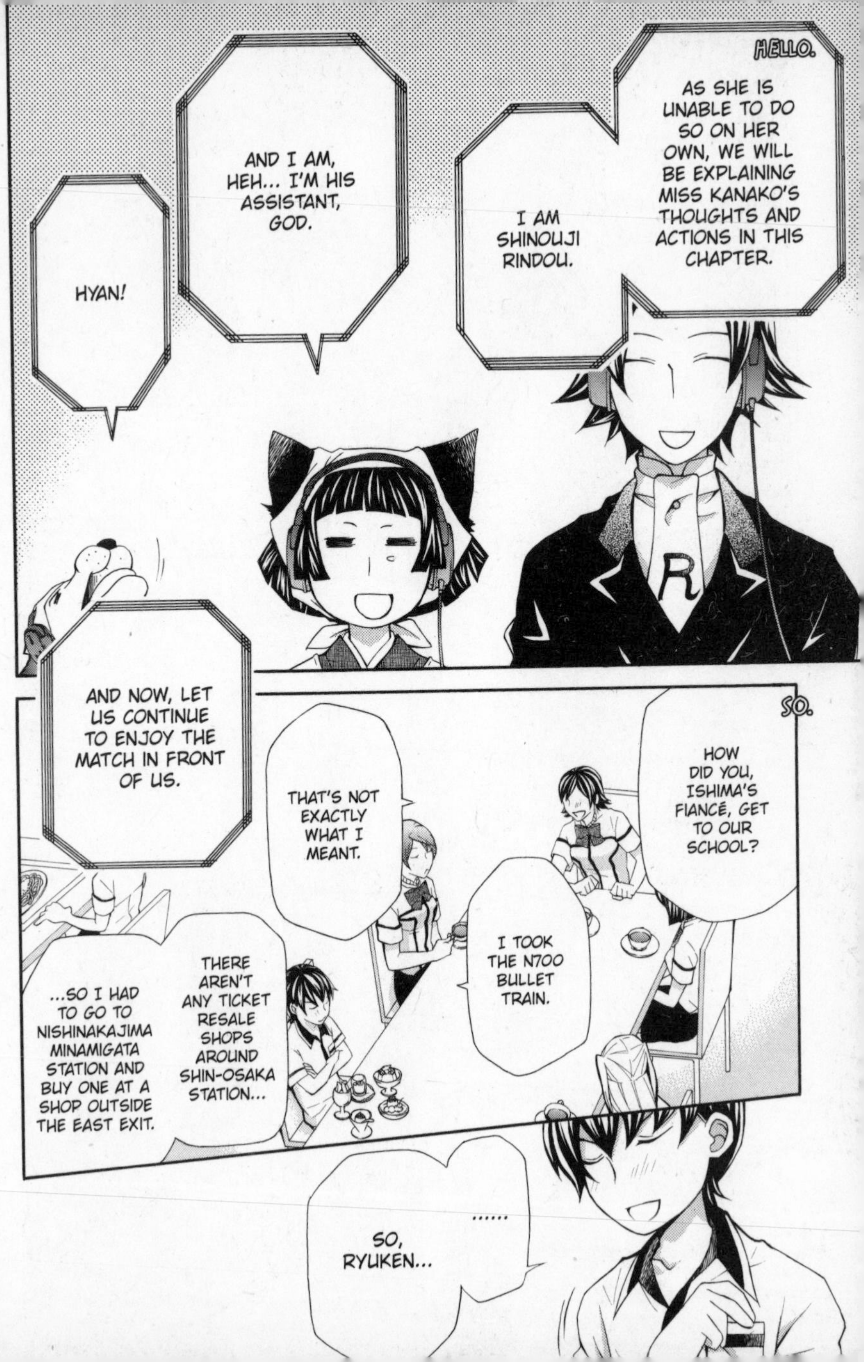
HELLO.
AS SHE IS UNABLE TO DO SO ON HER OWN, WE WILL BE EXPLAINING MISS KANAKO'S THOUGHTS AND ACTIONS IN THIS CHAPTER.
I AM SHINOUJI RINDOU.
AND I AM, HEH... I'M HIS ASSISTANT, GOD.
HYAN!
AND NOW, LET US CONTINUE TO ENJOY THE MATCH IN FRONT OF US.
SO.
HOW DID YOU, ISHIMA'S FIANCÉ, GET TO OUR SCHOOL?
I TOOK THE N700 BULLET TRAIN.
THAT'S NOT EXACTLY WHAT I MEANT.
THERE AREN'T ANY TICKET RESALE SHOPS AROUND SHIN-OSAKA STATION...
...SO I HAD TO GO TO NISHINAKAJIMA MINAMIGATA STATION AND BUY ONE AT A SHOP OUTSIDE THE EAST EXIT.
......
SO, RYUKEN...

COMMENTATOR RINDOU-SAN, DID YOU SEE MIYAMAE'S FACE JUST NOOOOOW?

THAT WAS MOST DEFINITELY A MENACE-FILLED GLARE.

INDEED.

THAT WAS THE LOOK I IMAGINE PEASANTS HAVING JUST BEFORE THEY STAGE A REVOLT.

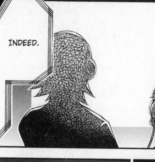

A REVOLT... SUCH A TERRIBLE THING, REEEEALLY...

HUNGRY PEASANTS STAND NO CHANCE AGAINST AN ARMY WITH FULL BELLIES.

JUST THE FACT THAT THEY HAVE NO WEAPONS AND USE WHATEVER THEY CAN FIND IS A FOOLISHLY BOLD MOVE.

YOU'RE RIGHT. AND SPEAKING OF THAT, THE VIETCONG USED STRATEGIES SUCH AS NIGHT ATTACKS AND BAMBOO TRAPS.

THEY PUT UP A VERY SKILLED FIGHT IN THAT REGARD.

AHH...

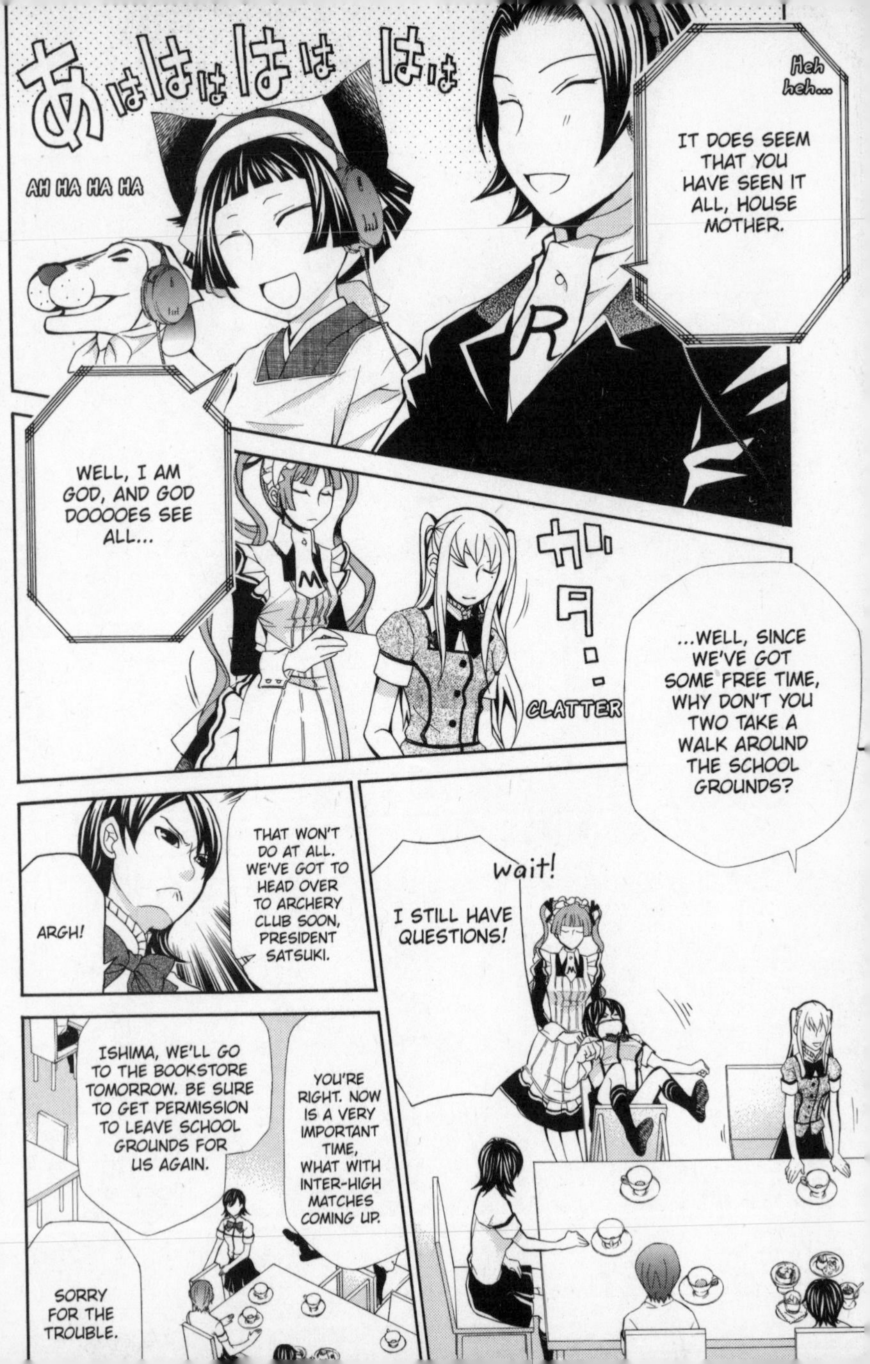
Heh heh...
IT DOES SEEM THAT YOU HAVE SEEN IT ALL, HOUSE MOTHER.
あははははははは
AH HA HA HA
WELL, I AM GOD, AND GOD DOOOOES SEE ALL...
カタ…
CLATTER
...WELL, SINCE WE'VE GOT SOME FREE TIME, WHY DON'T YOU TWO TAKE A WALK AROUND THE SCHOOL GROUNDS?
wait!
I STILL HAVE QUESTIONS!
THAT WON'T DO AT ALL. WE'VE GOT TO HEAD OVER TO ARCHERY CLUB SOON, PRESIDENT SATSUKI.
ARGH!
YOU'RE RIGHT. NOW IS A VERY IMPORTANT TIME, WHAT WITH INTER-HIGH MATCHES COMING UP.
ISHIMA, WE'LL GO TO THE BOOKSTORE TOMORROW. BE SURE TO GET PERMISSION TO LEAVE SCHOOL GROUNDS FOR US AGAIN.
SORRY FOR THE TROUBLE.

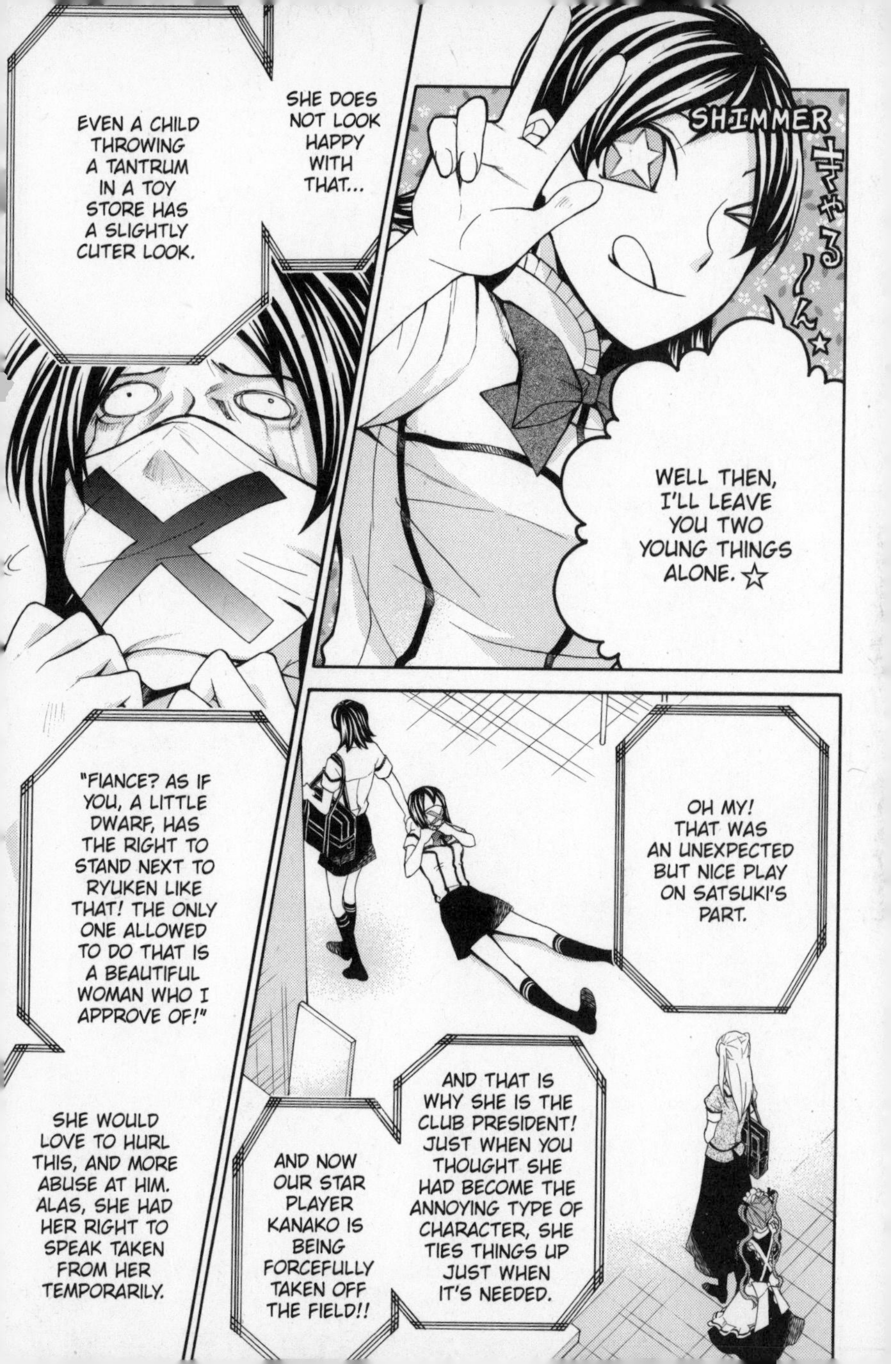
SHIMMER
きゃるーん☆
WELL THEN, I'LL LEAVE YOU TWO YOUNG THINGS ALONE. ☆
OH MY! THAT WAS AN UNEXPECTED BUT NICE PLAY ON SATSUKI'S PART.
AND THAT IS WHY SHE IS THE CLUB PRESIDENT! JUST WHEN YOU THOUGHT SHE HAD BECOME THE ANNOYING TYPE OF CHARACTER, SHE TIES THINGS UP JUST WHEN IT'S NEEDED.
AND NOW OUR STAR PLAYER KANAKO IS BEING FORCEFULLY TAKEN OFF THE FIELD!!
SHE DOES NOT LOOK HAPPY WITH THAT...
EVEN A CHILD THROWING A TANTRUM IN A TOY STORE HAS A SLIGHTLY CUTER LOOK.
"FIANCE? AS IF YOU, A LITTLE DWARF, HAS THE RIGHT TO STAND NEXT TO RYUKEN LIKE THAT! THE ONLY ONE ALLOWED TO DO THAT IS A BEAUTIFUL WOMAN WHO I APPROVE OF!"
SHE WOULD LOVE TO HURL THIS, AND MORE ABUSE AT HIM. ALAS, SHE HAD HER RIGHT TO SPEAK TAKEN FROM HER TEMPORARILY.

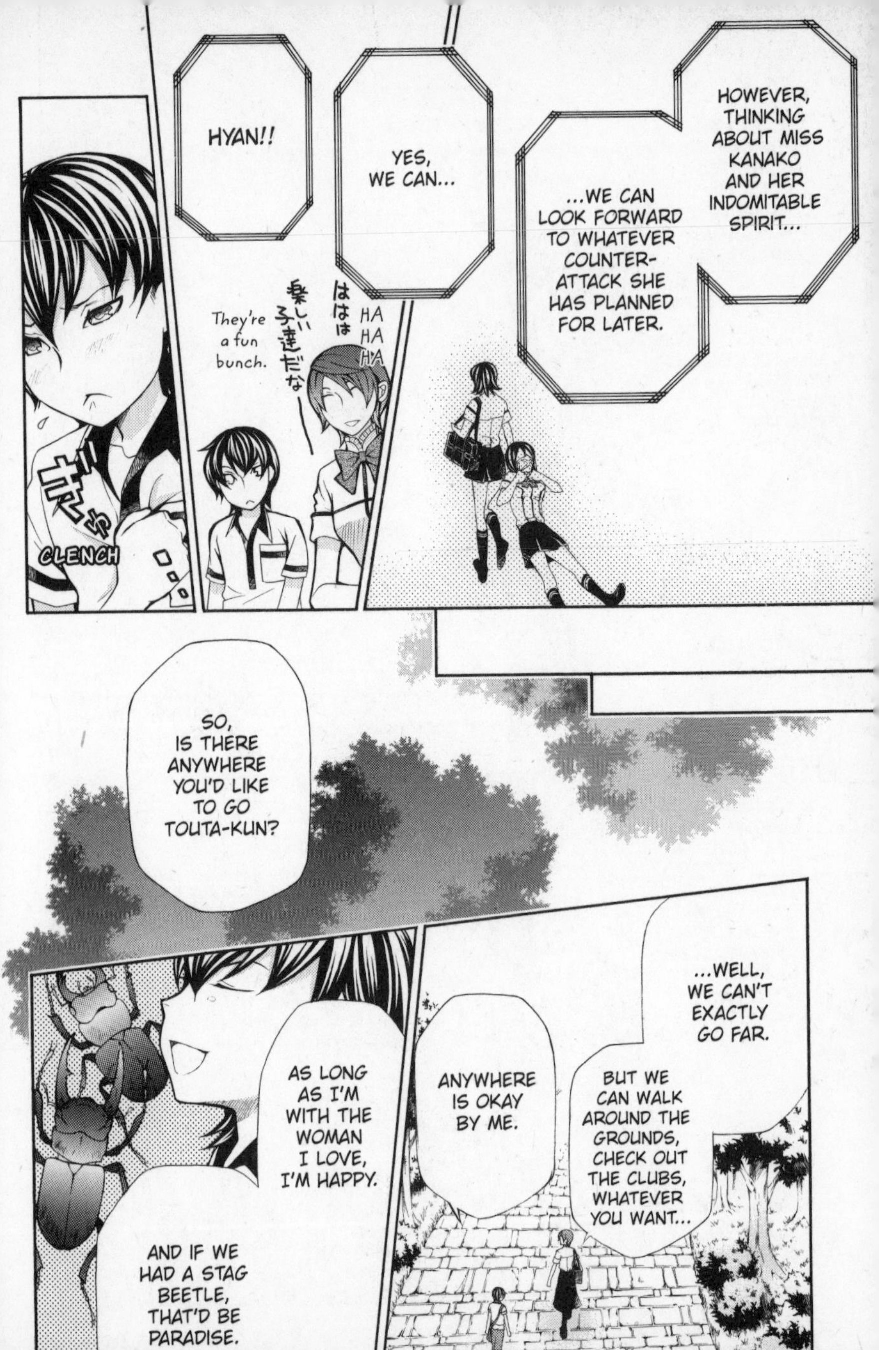
HOWEVER, THINKING ABOUT MISS KANAKO AND HER INDOMITABLE SPIRIT...
...WE CAN LOOK FORWARD TO WHATEVER COUNTER-ATTACK SHE HAS PLANNED FOR LATER.
YES, WE CAN...
HA HA HA
ははは
楽しい子達だな—
They're a fun bunch.
HYAN!!
ぎゅ
CLENCH
SO, IS THERE ANYWHERE YOU'D LIKE TO GO TOUTA-KUN?
...WELL, WE CAN'T EXACTLY GO FAR.
BUT WE CAN WALK AROUND THE GROUNDS, CHECK OUT THE CLUBS, WHATEVER YOU WANT...
ANYWHERE IS OKAY BY ME.
AS LONG AS I'M WITH THE WOMAN I LOVE, I'M HAPPY.
AND IF WE HAD A STAG BEETLE, THAT'D BE PARADISE.

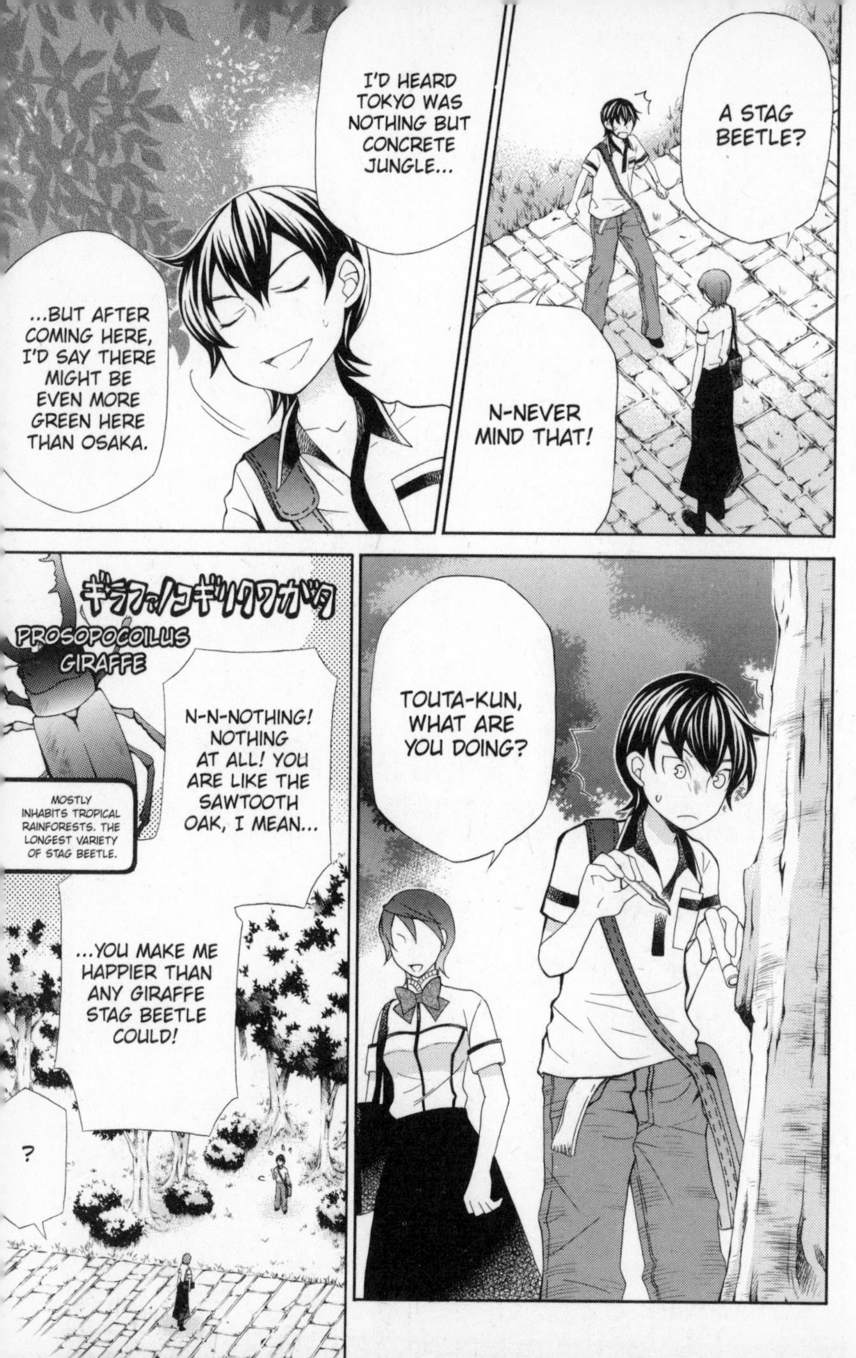
A STAG BEETLE?
N-NEVER MIND THAT!
I'D HEARD TOKYO WAS NOTHING BUT CONCRETE JUNGLE...
...BUT AFTER COMING HERE, I'D SAY THERE MIGHT BE EVEN MORE GREEN HERE THAN OSAKA.
TOUTA-KUN, WHAT ARE YOU DOING?
ギラファノコギリクワガタ
PROSOPOCOILUS GIRAFFE
MOSTLY INHABITS TROPICAL RAINFORESTS. THE LONGEST VARIETY OF STAG BEETLE.
N-N-NOTHING! NOTHING AT ALL! YOU ARE LIKE THE SAWTOOTH OAK, I MEAN...
...YOU MAKE ME HAPPIER THAN ANY GIRAFFE STAG BEETLE COULD!
?

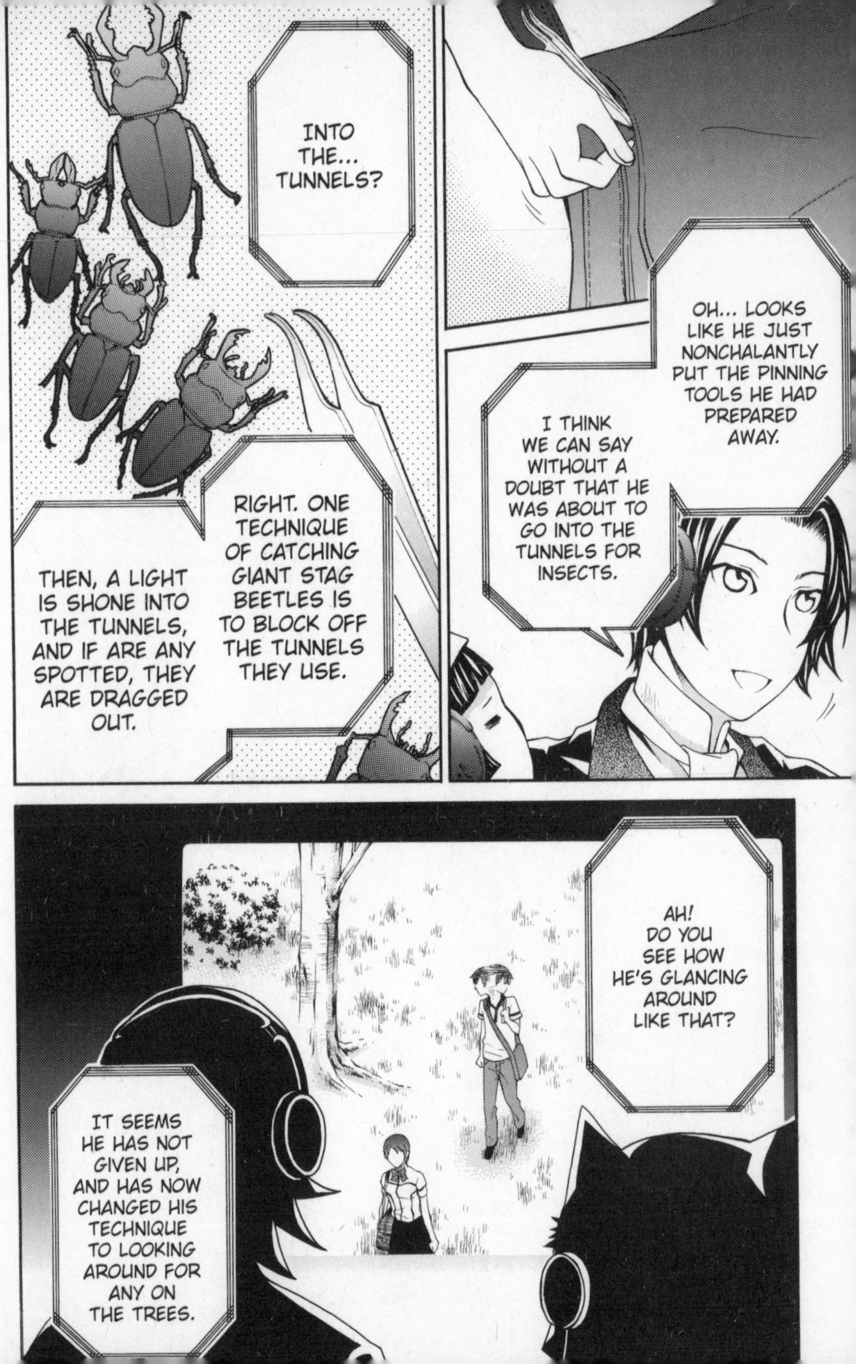
OH... LOOKS LIKE HE JUST NONCHALANTLY PUT THE PINNING TOOLS HE HAD PREPARED AWAY.
I THINK WE CAN SAY WITHOUT A DOUBT THAT HE WAS ABOUT TO GO INTO THE TUNNELS FOR INSECTS.
INTO THE... TUNNELS?
RIGHT. ONE TECHNIQUE OF CATCHING GIANT STAG BEETLES IS TO BLOCK OFF THE TUNNELS THEY USE.
THEN, A LIGHT IS SHONE INTO THE TUNNELS, AND IF ARE ANY SPOTTED, THEY ARE DRAGGED OUT.
AH! DO YOU SEE HOW HE'S GLANCING AROUND LIKE THAT?
IT SEEMS HE HAS NOT GIVEN UP, AND HAS NOW CHANGED HIS TECHNIQUE TO LOOKING AROUND FOR ANY ON THE TREES.

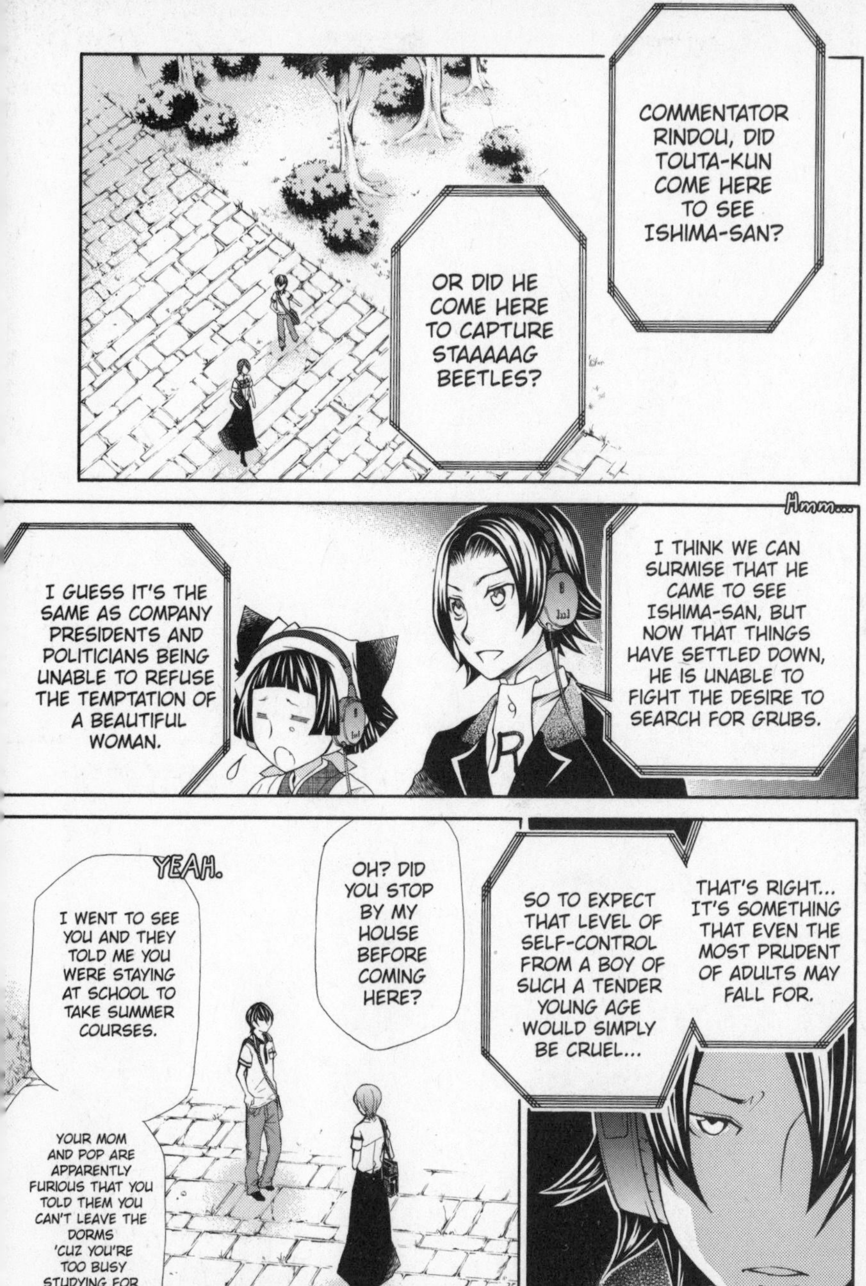
COMMENTATOR RINDOU, DID TOUTA-KUN COME HERE TO SEE ISHIMA-SAN?
OR DID HE COME HERE TO CAPTURE STAAAAAG BEETLES?
Hmm...
I THINK WE CAN SURMISE THAT HE CAME TO SEE ISHIMA-SAN, BUT NOW THAT THINGS HAVE SETTLED DOWN, HE IS UNABLE TO FIGHT THE DESIRE TO SEARCH FOR GRUBS.
I GUESS IT'S THE SAME AS COMPANY PRESIDENTS AND POLITICIANS BEING UNABLE TO REFUSE THE TEMPTATION OF A BEAUTIFUL WOMAN.
THAT'S RIGHT... IT'S SOMETHING THAT EVEN THE MOST PRUDENT OF ADULTS MAY FALL FOR.
SO TO EXPECT THAT LEVEL OF SELF-CONTROL FROM A BOY OF SUCH A TENDER YOUNG AGE WOULD SIMPLY BE CRUEL...
OH? DID YOU STOP BY MY HOUSE BEFORE COMING HERE?
YEAH.
I WENT TO SEE YOU AND THEY TOLD ME YOU WERE STAYING AT SCHOOL TO TAKE SUMMER COURSES.
YOUR MOM AND POP ARE APPARENTLY FURIOUS THAT YOU TOLD THEM YOU CAN'T LEAVE THE DORMS 'CUZ YOU'RE TOO BUSY STUDYING FOR EXAMS.

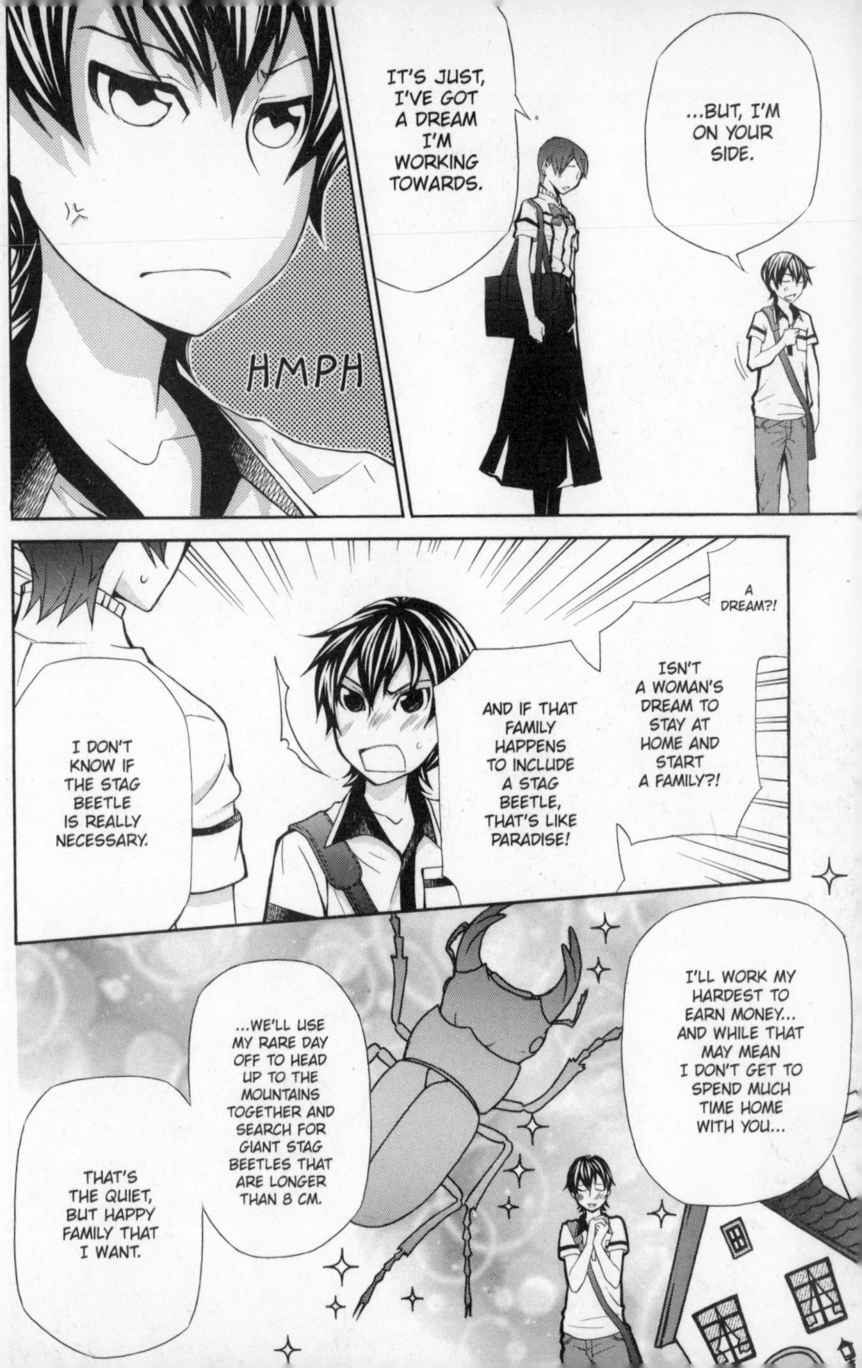
...BUT, I'M ON YOUR SIDE.
IT'S JUST, I'VE GOT A DREAM I'M WORKING TOWARDS.
HMPH
A DREAM?!
ISN'T A WOMAN'S DREAM TO STAY AT HOME AND START A FAMILY?!
AND IF THAT FAMILY HAPPENS TO INCLUDE A STAG BEETLE, THAT'S LIKE PARADISE!
I DON'T KNOW IF THE STAG BEETLE IS REALLY NECESSARY.
I'LL WORK MY HARDEST TO EARN MONEY... AND WHILE THAT MAY MEAN I DON'T GET TO SPEND MUCH TIME HOME WITH YOU...
...WE'LL USE MY RARE DAY OFF TO HEAD UP TO THE MOUNTAINS TOGETHER AND SEARCH FOR GIANT STAG BEETLES THAT ARE LONGER THAN 8 CM.
THAT'S THE QUIET, BUT HAPPY FAMILY THAT I WANT.

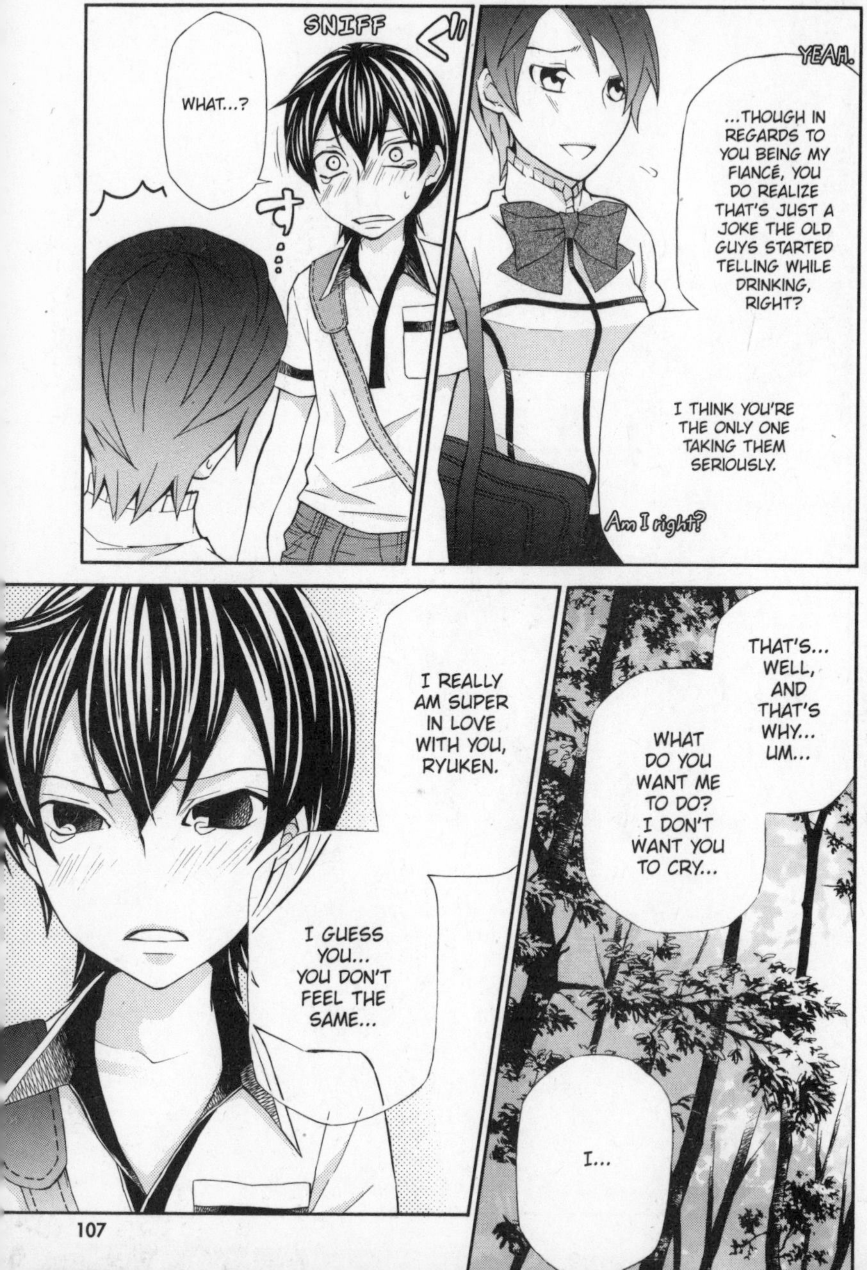
YEAH.
...THOUGH IN REGARDS TO YOU BEING MY FIANCÉ, YOU DO REALIZE THAT'S JUST A JOKE THE OLD GUYS STARTED TELLING WHILE DRINKING, RIGHT?
I THINK YOU'RE THE ONLY ONE TAKING THEM SERIOUSLY.
Am I right?
SNIFF
WHAT...?
THAT'S... WELL, AND THAT'S WHY... UM...
WHAT DO YOU WANT ME TO DO? I DON'T WANT YOU TO CRY...
I...
I REALLY AM SUPER IN LOVE WITH YOU, RYUKEN.
I GUESS YOU... YOU DON'T FEEL THE SAME...

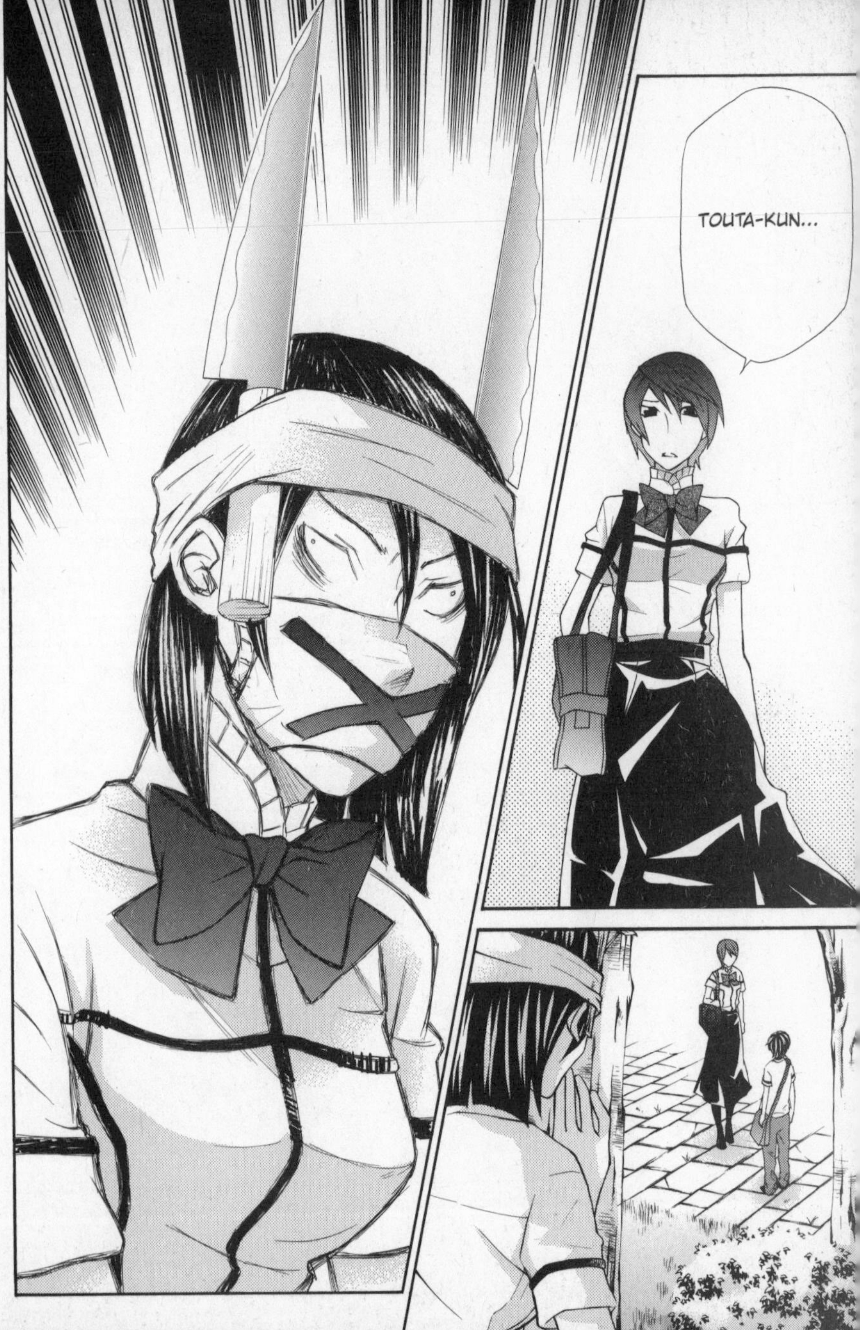
TOUTA-KUN...

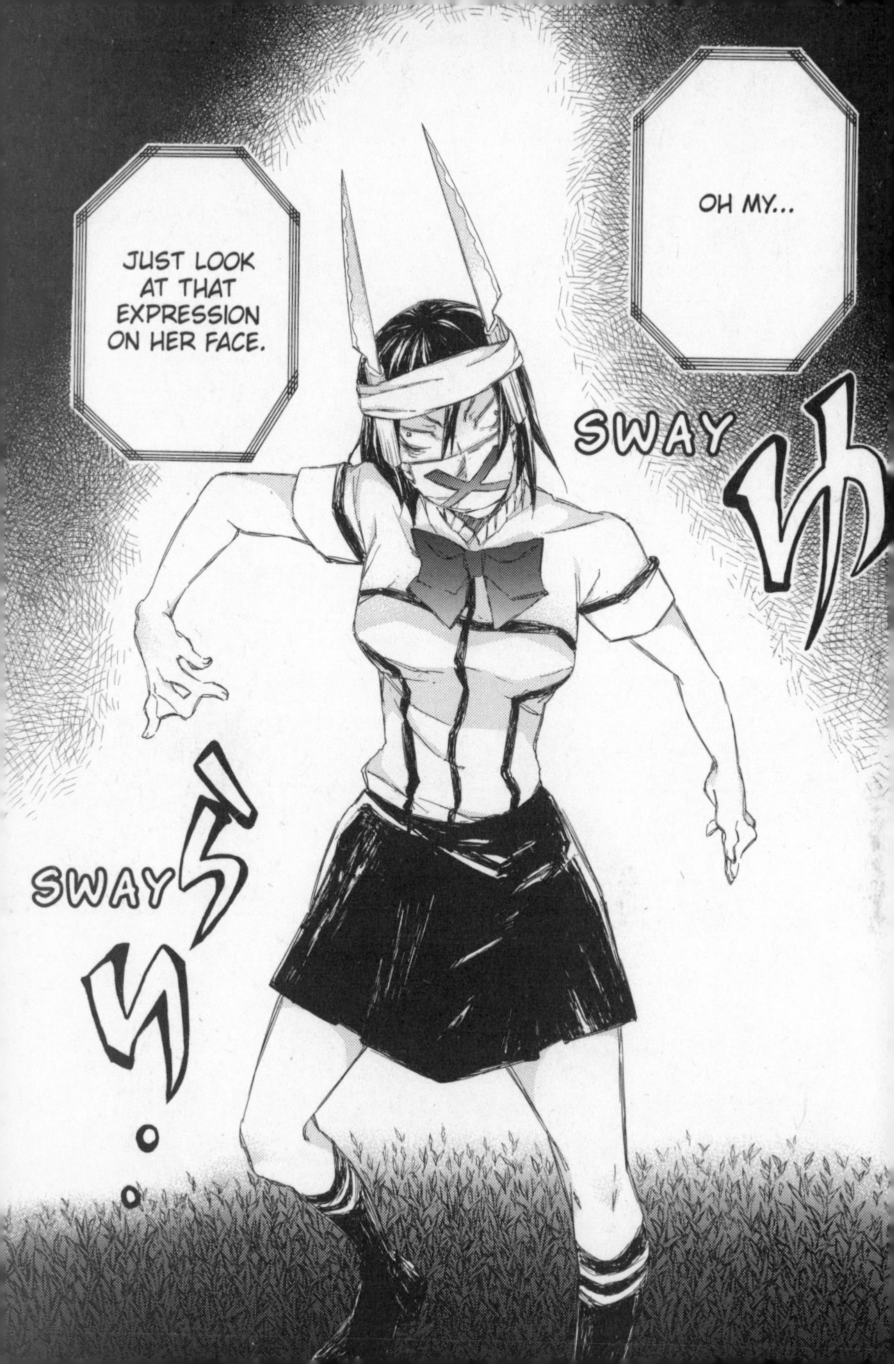
OH MY...
JUST LOOK AT THAT EXPRESSION ON HER FACE.
SWAY
SWAY

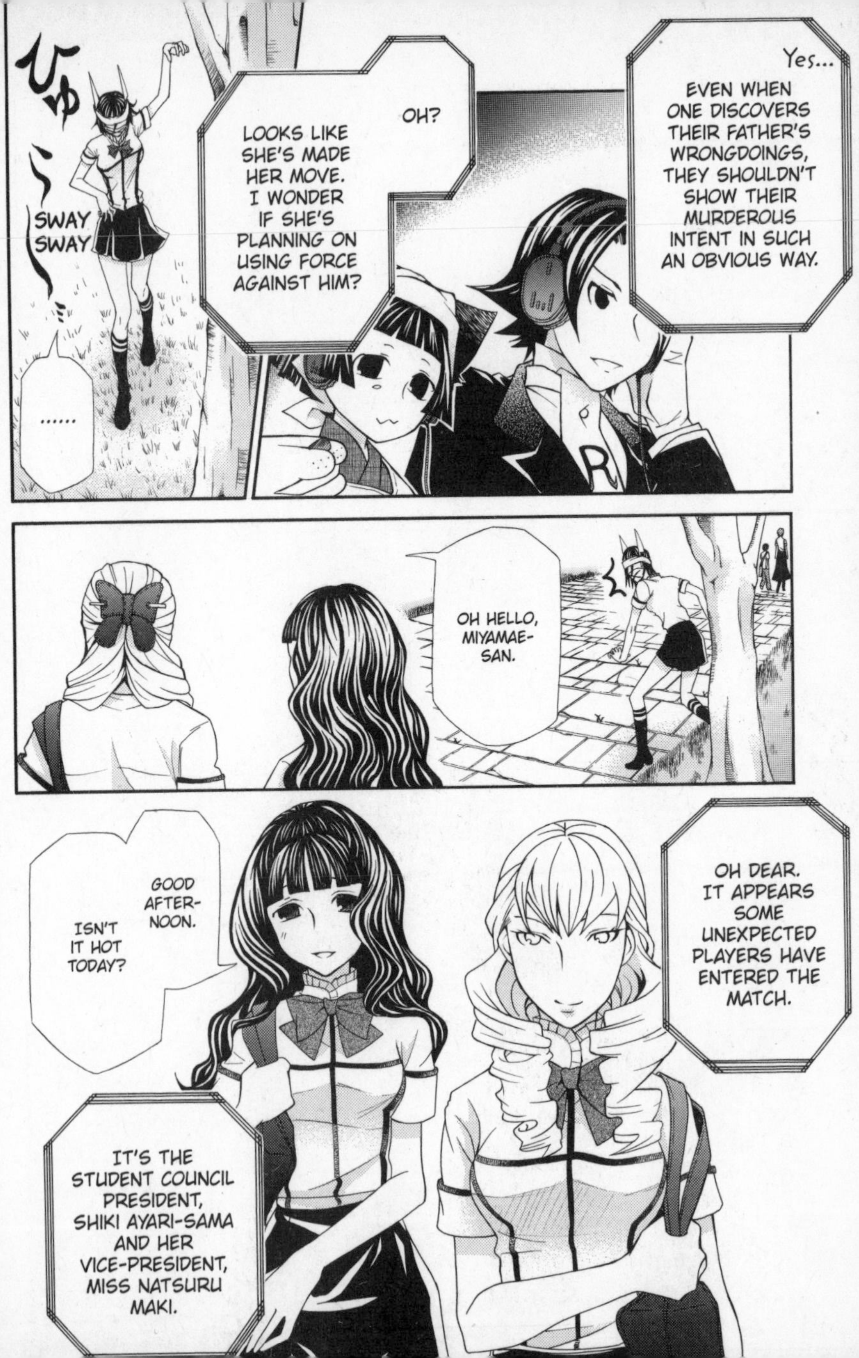
Yes...
EVEN WHEN ONE DISCOVERS THEIR FATHER'S WRONGDOINGS, THEY SHOULDN'T SHOW THEIR MURDEROUS INTENT IN SUCH AN OBVIOUS WAY.
OH?
LOOKS LIKE SHE'S MADE HER MOVE. I WONDER IF SHE'S PLANNING ON USING FORCE AGAINST HIM?
SWAY SWAY
......
OH HELLO, MIYAMAE-SAN.
OH DEAR. IT APPEARS SOME UNEXPECTED PLAYERS HAVE ENTERED THE MATCH.
GOOD AFTERNOON.
ISN'T IT HOT TODAY?
IT'S THE STUDENT COUNCIL PRESIDENT, SHIKI AYARI-SAMA AND HER VICE-PRESIDENT, MISS NATSURU MAKI.

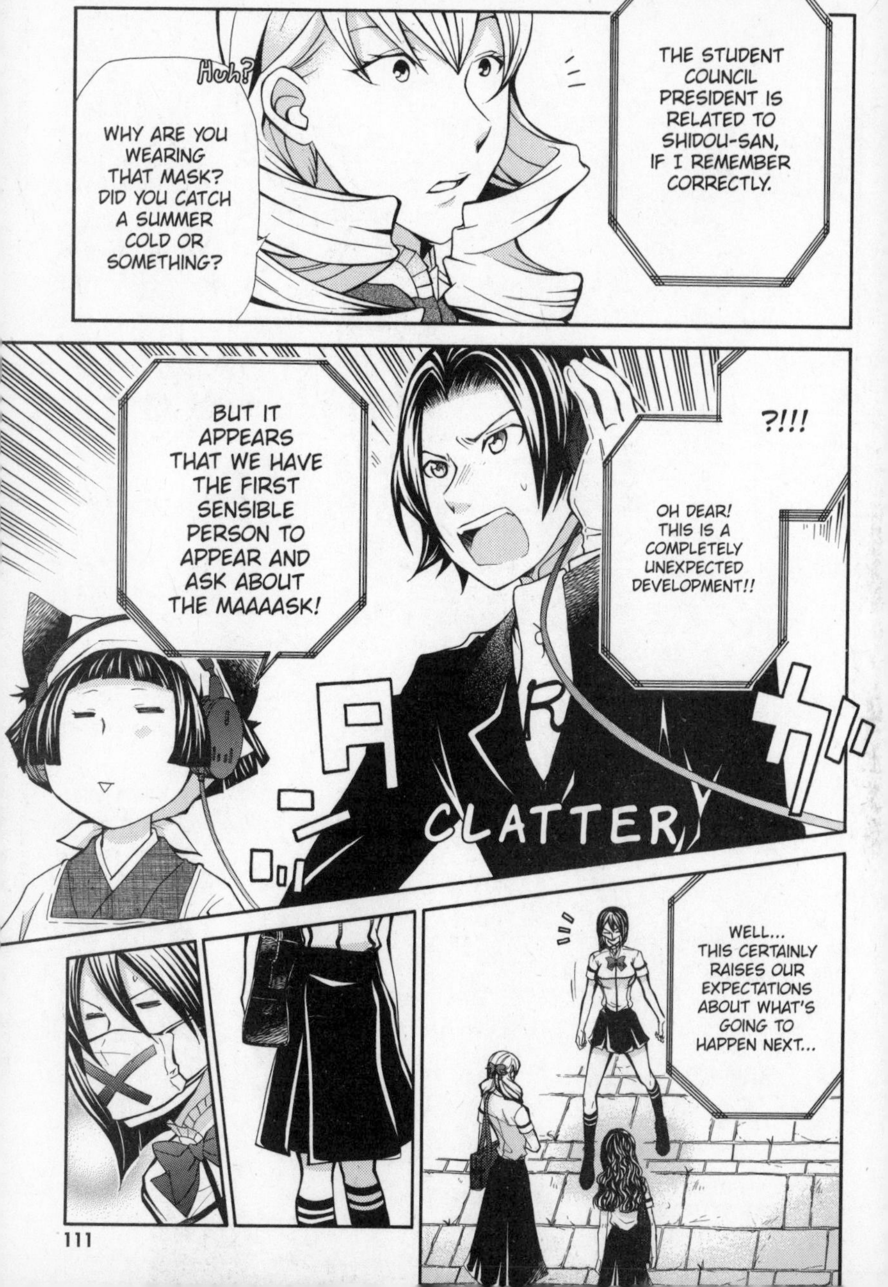
THE STUDENT COUNCIL PRESIDENT IS RELATED TO SHIDOU-SAN, IF I REMEMBER CORRECTLY.
Huh?
WHY ARE YOU WEARING THAT MASK? DID YOU CATCH A SUMMER COLD OR SOMETHING?
?!!!
OH DEAR! THIS IS A COMPLETELY UNEXPECTED DEVELOPMENT!!
BUT IT APPEARS THAT WE HAVE THE FIRST SENSIBLE PERSON TO APPEAR AND ASK ABOUT THE MAAAASK!
CLATTER
WELL... THIS CERTAINLY RAISES OUR EXPECTATIONS ABOUT WHAT'S GOING TO HAPPEN NEXT...

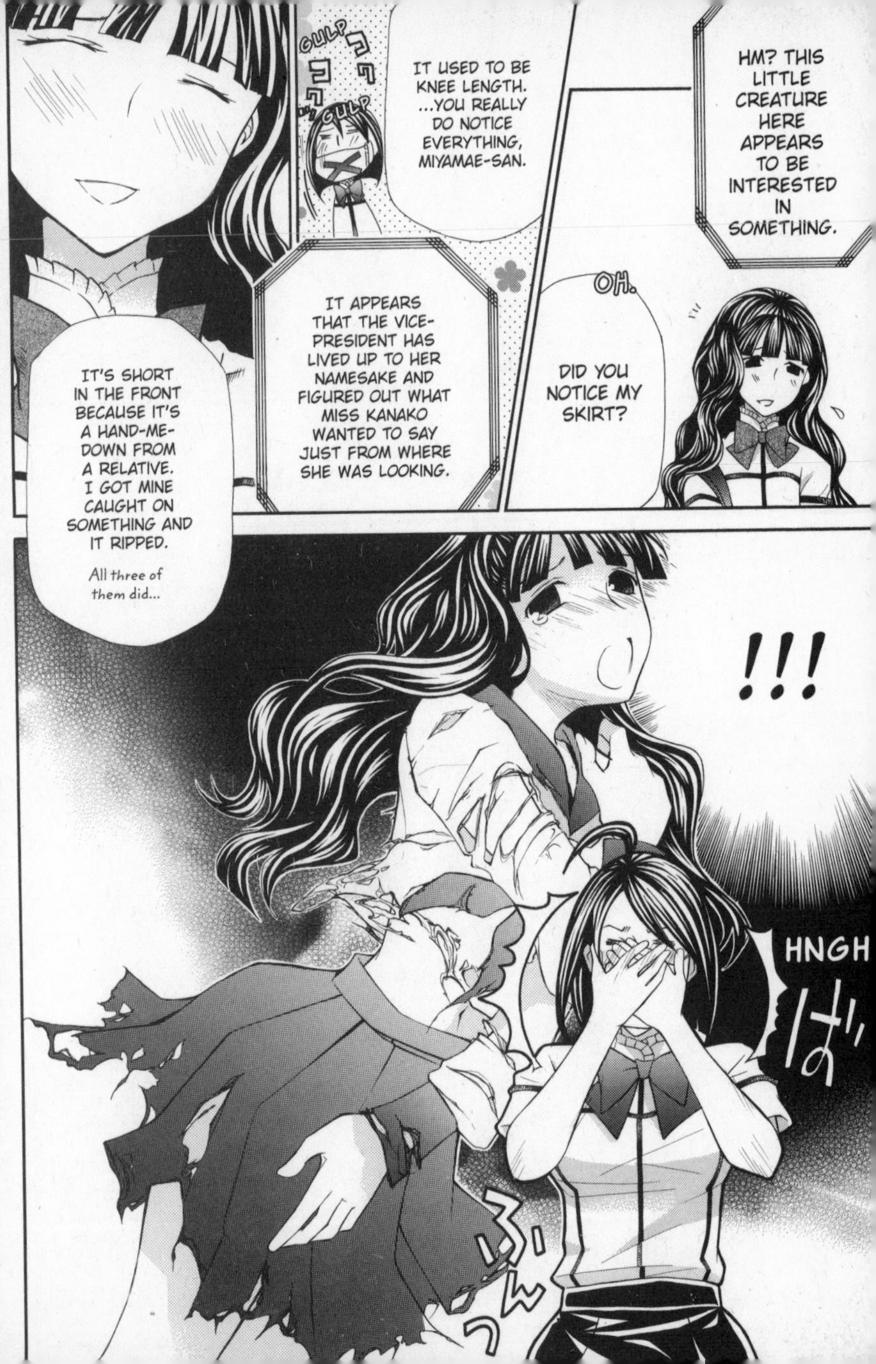
HM? THIS LITTLE CREATURE HERE APPEARS TO BE INTERESTED IN SOMETHING.
OH.
DID YOU NOTICE MY SKIRT?
IT USED TO BE KNEE LENGTH. ...YOU REALLY DO NOTICE EVERYTHING, MIYAMAE-SAN.
GULP
GULP
IT APPEARS THAT THE VICE-PRESIDENT HAS LIVED UP TO HER NAMESAKE AND FIGURED OUT WHAT MISS KANAKO WANTED TO SAY JUST FROM WHERE SHE WAS LOOKING.
IT'S SHORT IN THE FRONT BECAUSE IT'S A HAND-ME-DOWN FROM A RELATIVE. I GOT MINE CAUGHT ON SOMETHING AND IT RIPPED.
All three of them did...
!!!
HNGH

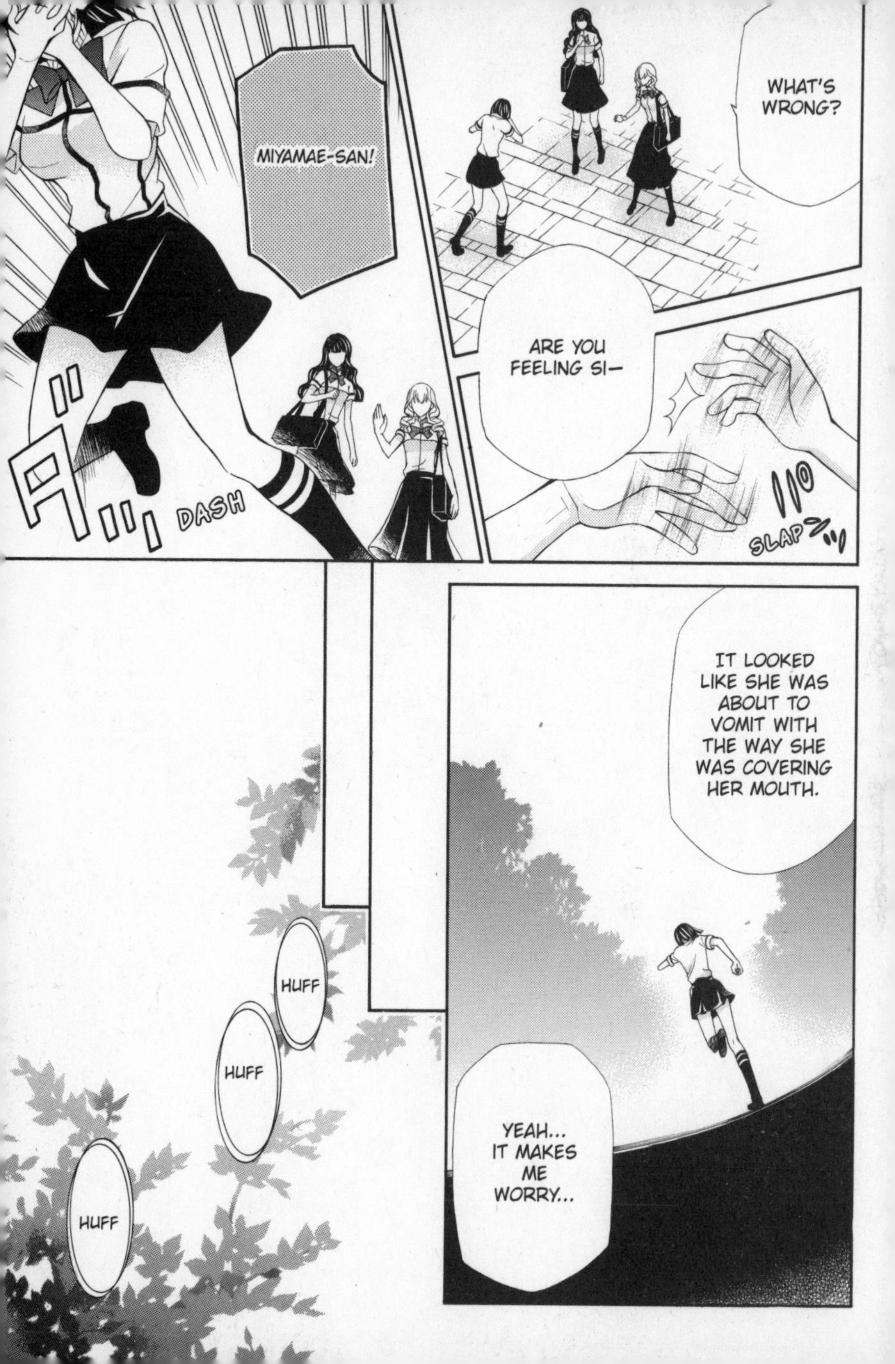
WHAT'S WRONG?
ARE YOU FEELING SI—
SLAP
MIYAMAE-SAN!
DASH
IT LOOKED LIKE SHE WAS ABOUT TO VOMIT WITH THE WAY SHE WAS COVERING HER MOUTH.
YEAH... IT MAKES ME WORRY...
HUFF
HUFF
HUFF

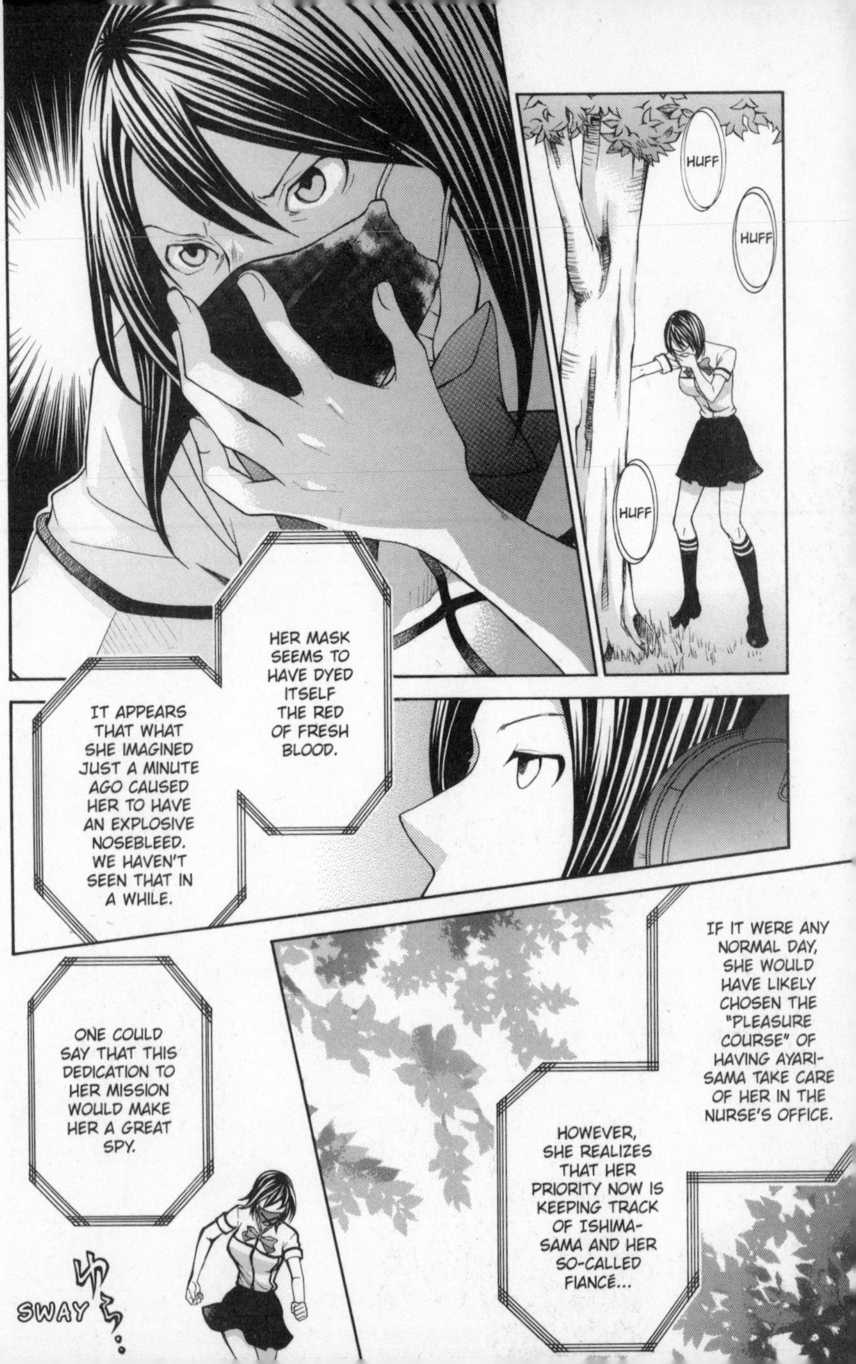
HUFF
HUFF
HUFF
HER MASK SEEMS TO HAVE DYED ITSELF THE RED OF FRESH BLOOD.
IT APPEARS THAT WHAT SHE IMAGINED JUST A MINUTE AGO CAUSED HER TO HAVE AN EXPLOSIVE NOSEBLEED. WE HAVEN'T SEEN THAT IN A WHILE.
IF IT WERE ANY NORMAL DAY, SHE WOULD HAVE LIKELY CHOSEN THE "PLEASURE COURSE" OF HAVING AYARI-SAMA TAKE CARE OF HER IN THE NURSE'S OFFICE.
HOWEVER, SHE REALIZES THAT HER PRIORITY NOW IS KEEPING TRACK OF ISHIMA-SAMA AND HER SO-CALLED FIANCÉ...
ONE COULD SAY THAT THIS DEDICATION TO HER MISSION WOULD MAKE HER A GREAT SPY.
ゆら
SWAY

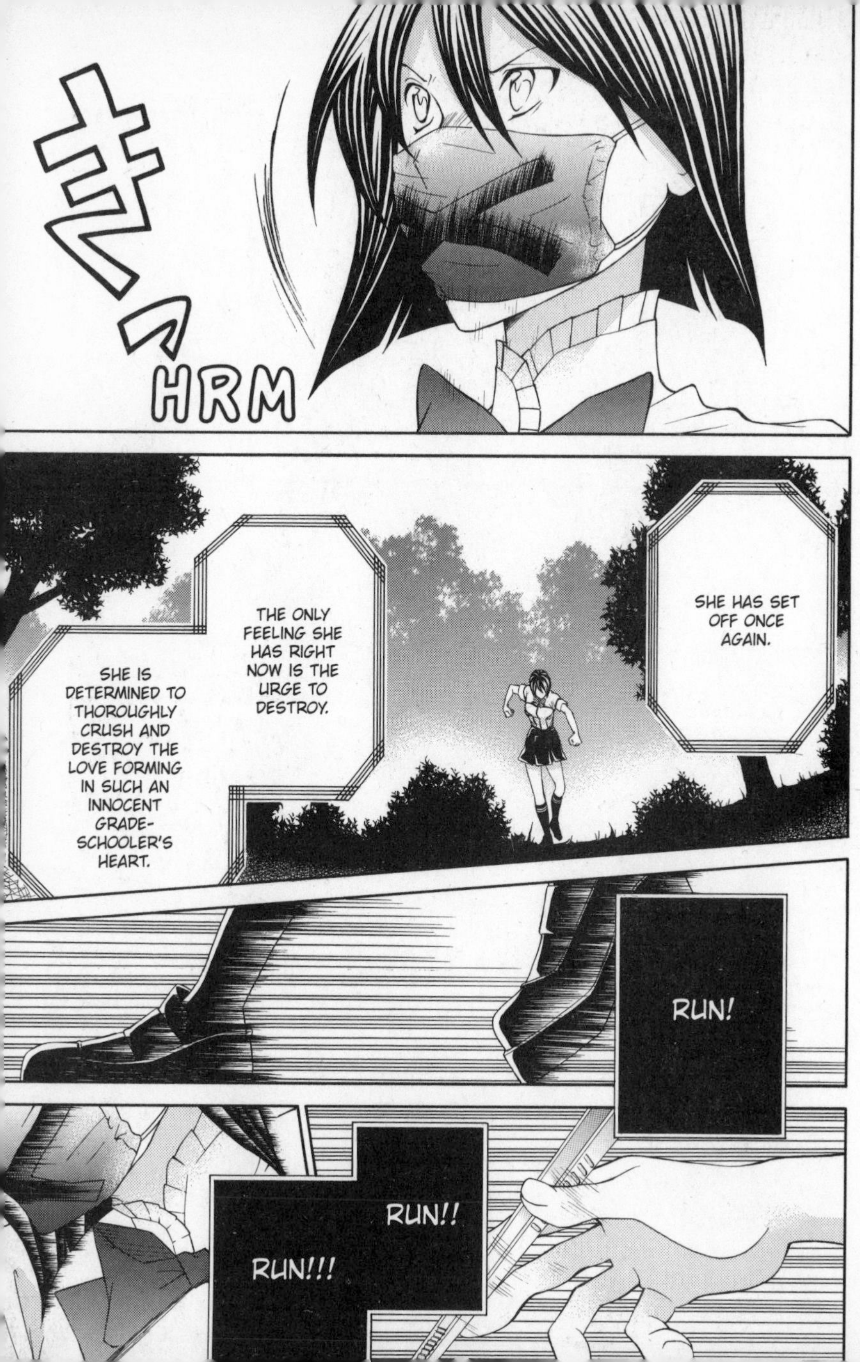

キッ
HRM
SHE HAS SET OFF ONCE AGAIN.
THE ONLY FEELING SHE HAS RIGHT NOW IS THE URGE TO DESTROY.
SHE IS DETERMINED TO THOROUGHLY CRUSH AND DESTROY THE LOVE FORMING IN SUCH AN INNOCENT GRADE-SCHOOLER'S HEART.
RUN!
RUN!!
RUN!!!

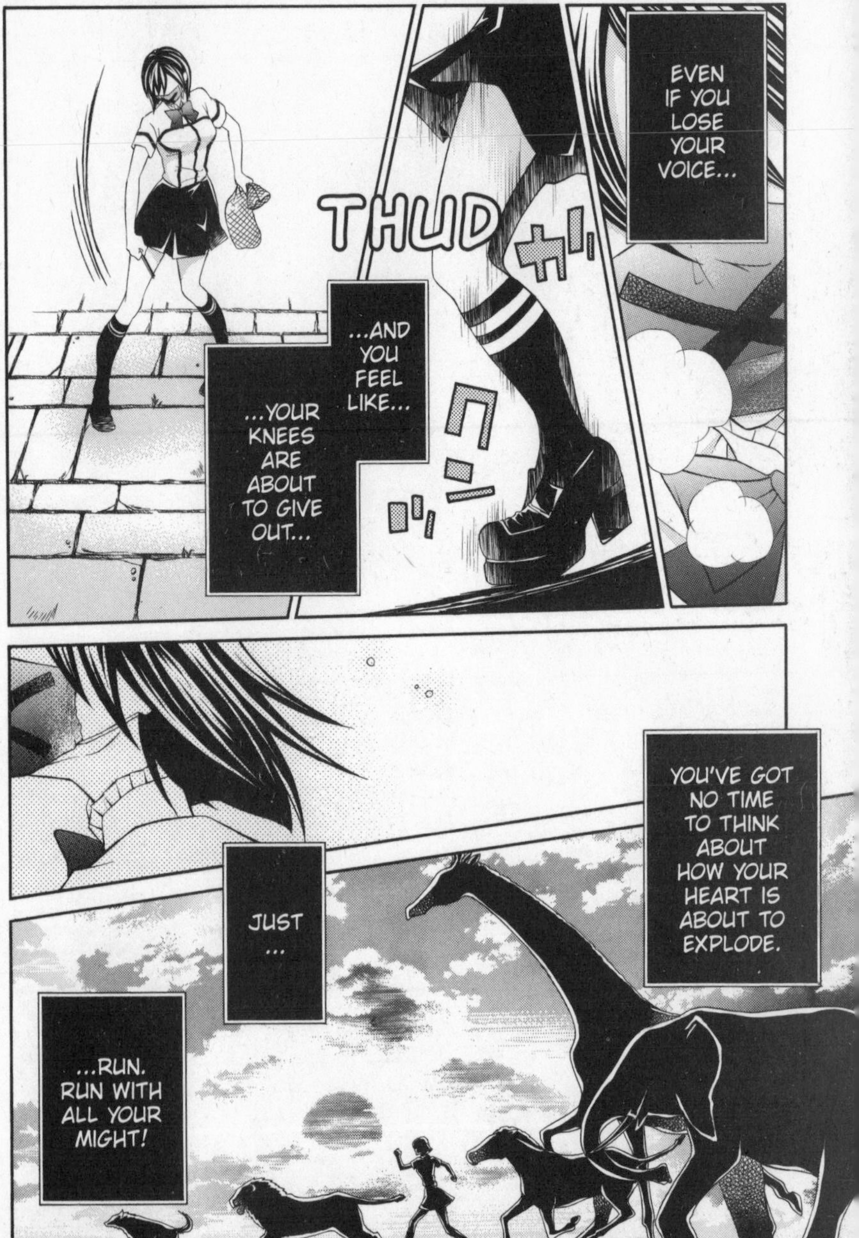
EVEN IF YOU LOSE YOUR VOICE...
THUD
...AND YOU FEEL LIKE...
...YOUR KNEES ARE ABOUT TO GIVE OUT...
YOU'VE GOT NO TIME TO THINK ABOUT HOW YOUR HEART IS ABOUT TO EXPLODE.
JUST ...
...RUN. RUN WITH ALL YOUR MIGHT!

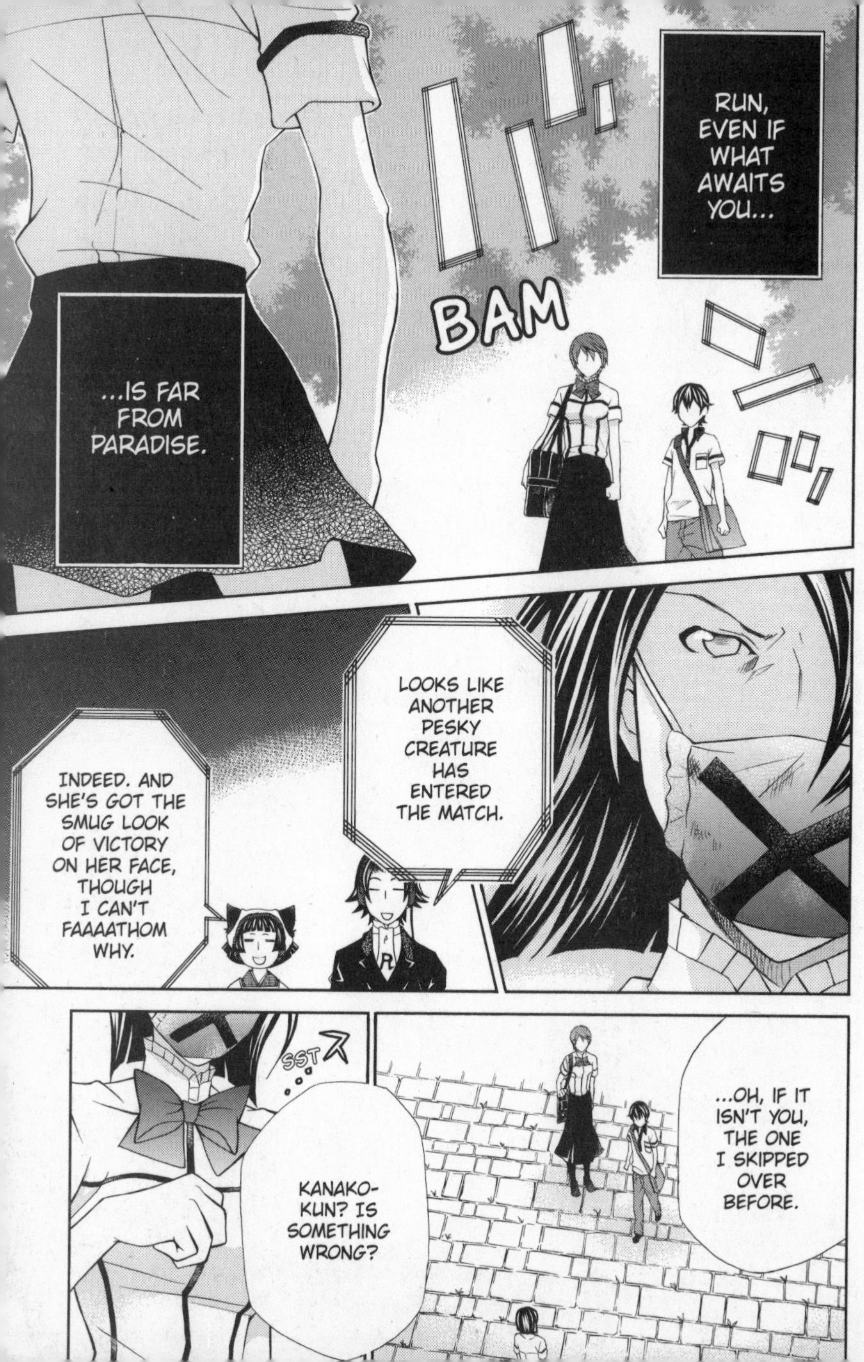
RUN, EVEN IF WHAT AWAITS YOU...
BAM
...IS FAR FROM PARADISE.
LOOKS LIKE ANOTHER PESKY CREATURE HAS ENTERED THE MATCH.
INDEED. AND SHE'S GOT THE SMUG LOOK OF VICTORY ON HER FACE, THOUGH I CAN'T FAAAATHOM WHY.
...OH, IF IT ISN'T YOU, THE ONE I SKIPPED OVER BEFORE.
SST ス
KANAKO-KUN? IS SOMETHING WRONG?

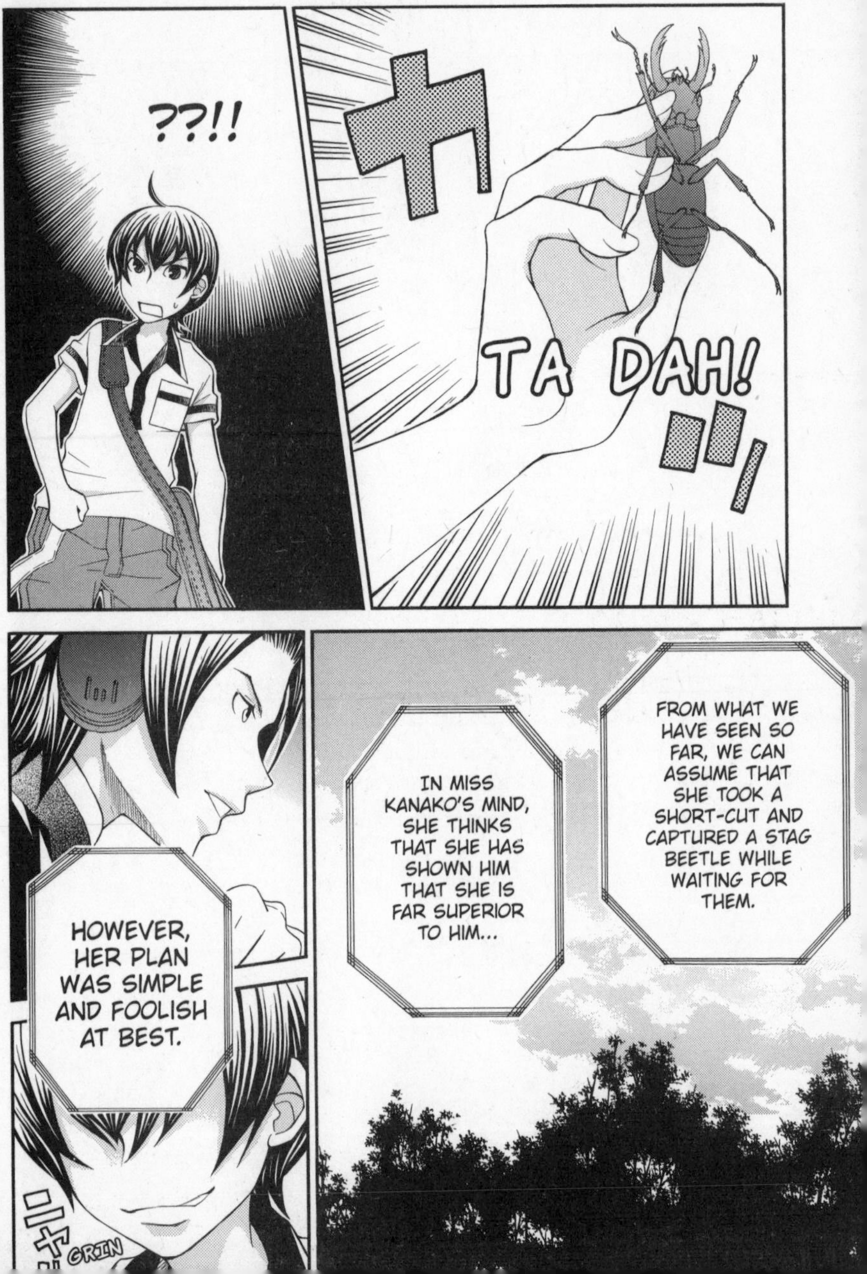
TA DAH!
??!!
FROM WHAT WE HAVE SEEN SO FAR, WE CAN ASSUME THAT SHE TOOK A SHORT-CUT AND CAPTURED A STAG BEETLE WHILE WAITING FOR THEM.
IN MISS KANAKO'S MIND, SHE THINKS THAT SHE HAS SHOWN HIM THAT SHE IS FAR SUPERIOR TO HIM...
HOWEVER, HER PLAN WAS SIMPLE AND FOOLISH AT BEST.
GRIN

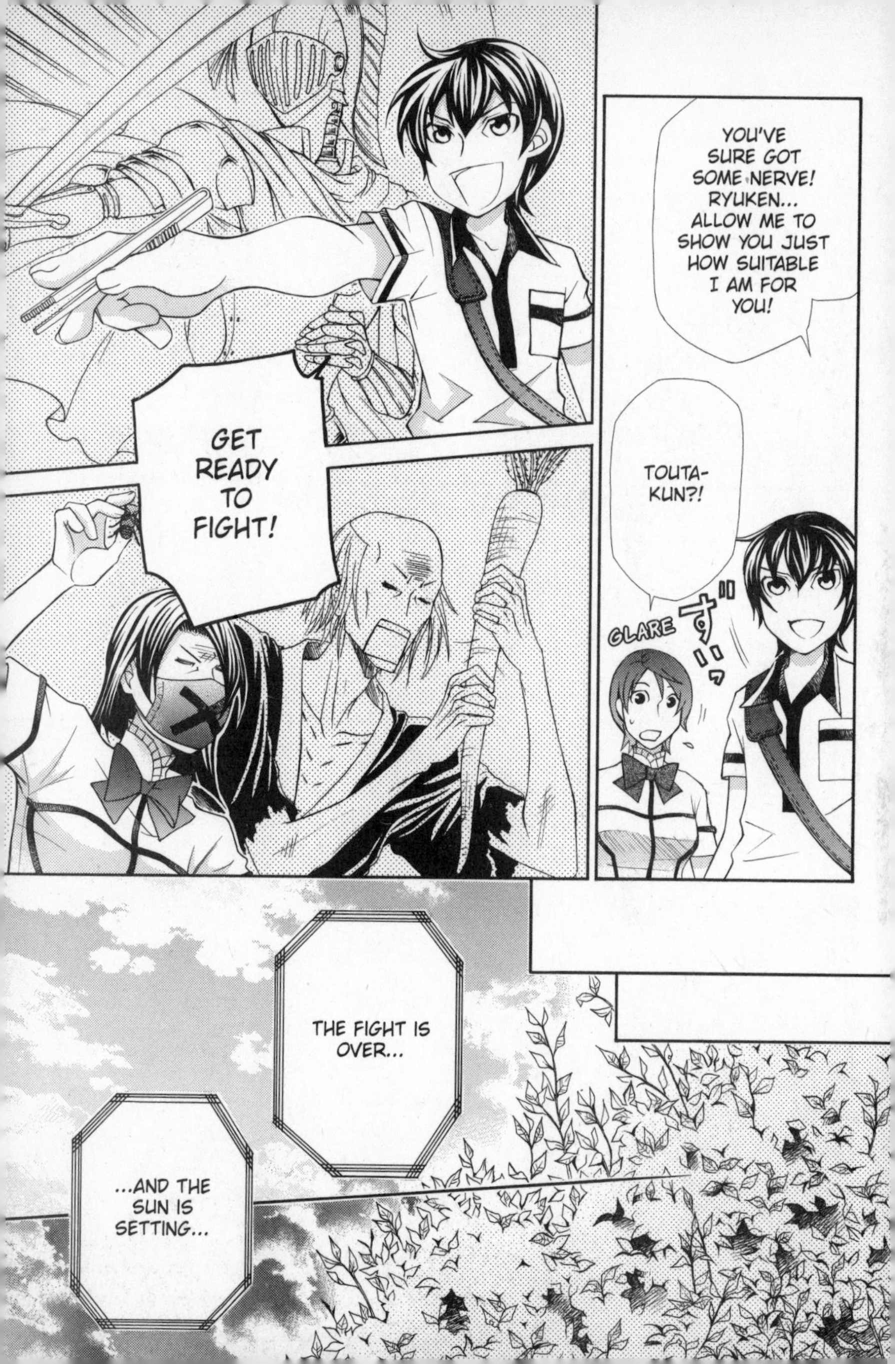

YOU'VE SURE GOT SOME NERVE! RYUKEN... ALLOW ME TO SHOW YOU JUST HOW SUITABLE I AM FOR YOU!
TOUTA-KUN?!
GLARE
GET READY TO FIGHT!
THE FIGHT IS OVER...
...AND THE SUN IS SETTING...

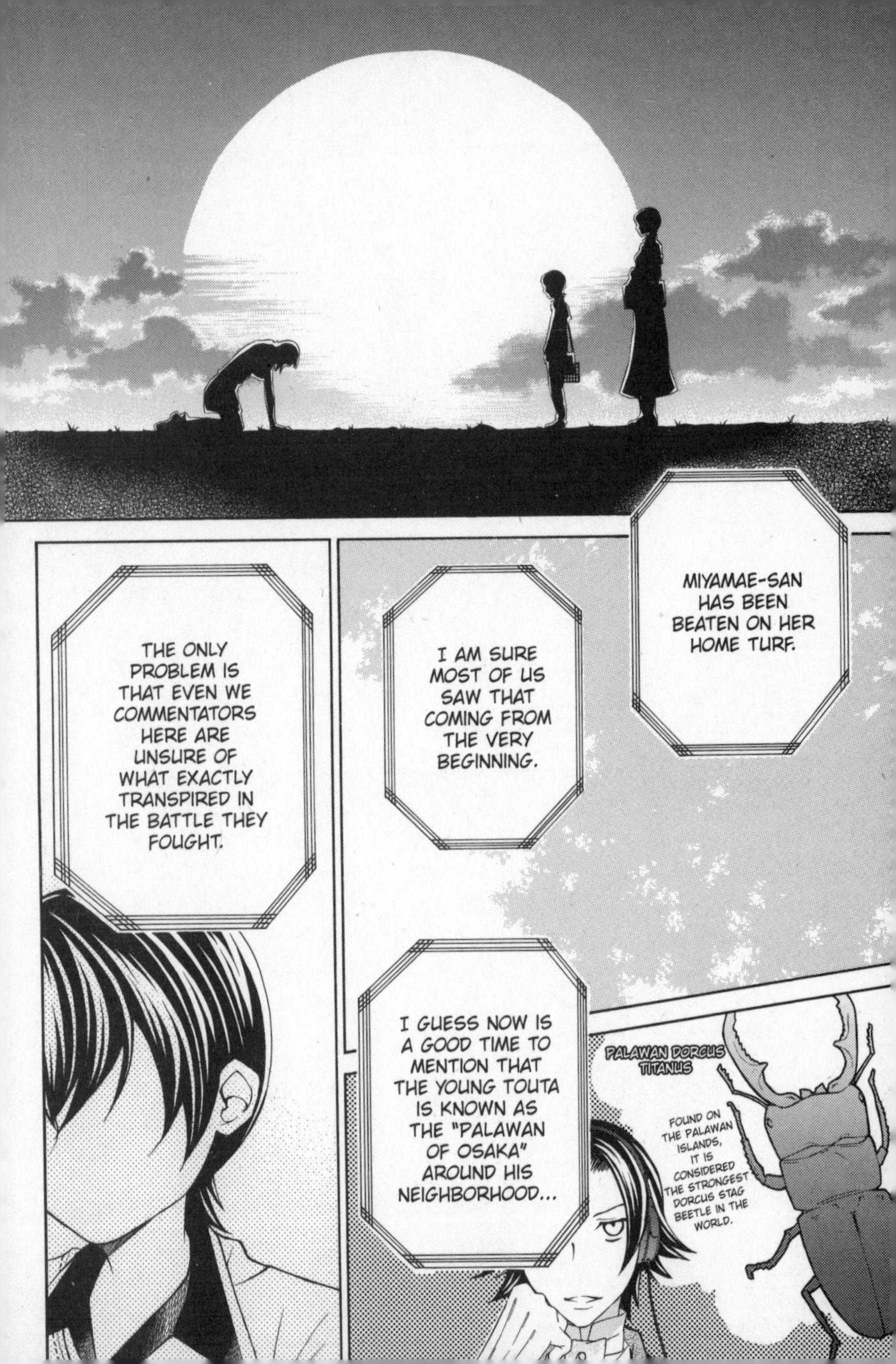
MIYAMAE-SAN HAS BEEN BEATEN ON HER HOME TURF.
I AM SURE MOST OF US SAW THAT COMING FROM THE VERY BEGINNING.
I GUESS NOW IS A GOOD TIME TO MENTION THAT THE YOUNG TOUTA IS KNOWN AS THE "PALAWAN OF OSAKA" AROUND HIS NEIGHBORHOOD...
PALAWAN DORCUS TITANUS
FOUND ON THE PALAWAN ISLANDS, IT IS CONSIDERED THE STRONGEST DORCUS STAG BEETLE IN THE WORLD.
THE ONLY PROBLEM IS THAT EVEN WE COMMENTATORS HERE ARE UNSURE OF WHAT EXACTLY TRANSPIRED IN THE BATTLE THEY FOUGHT.

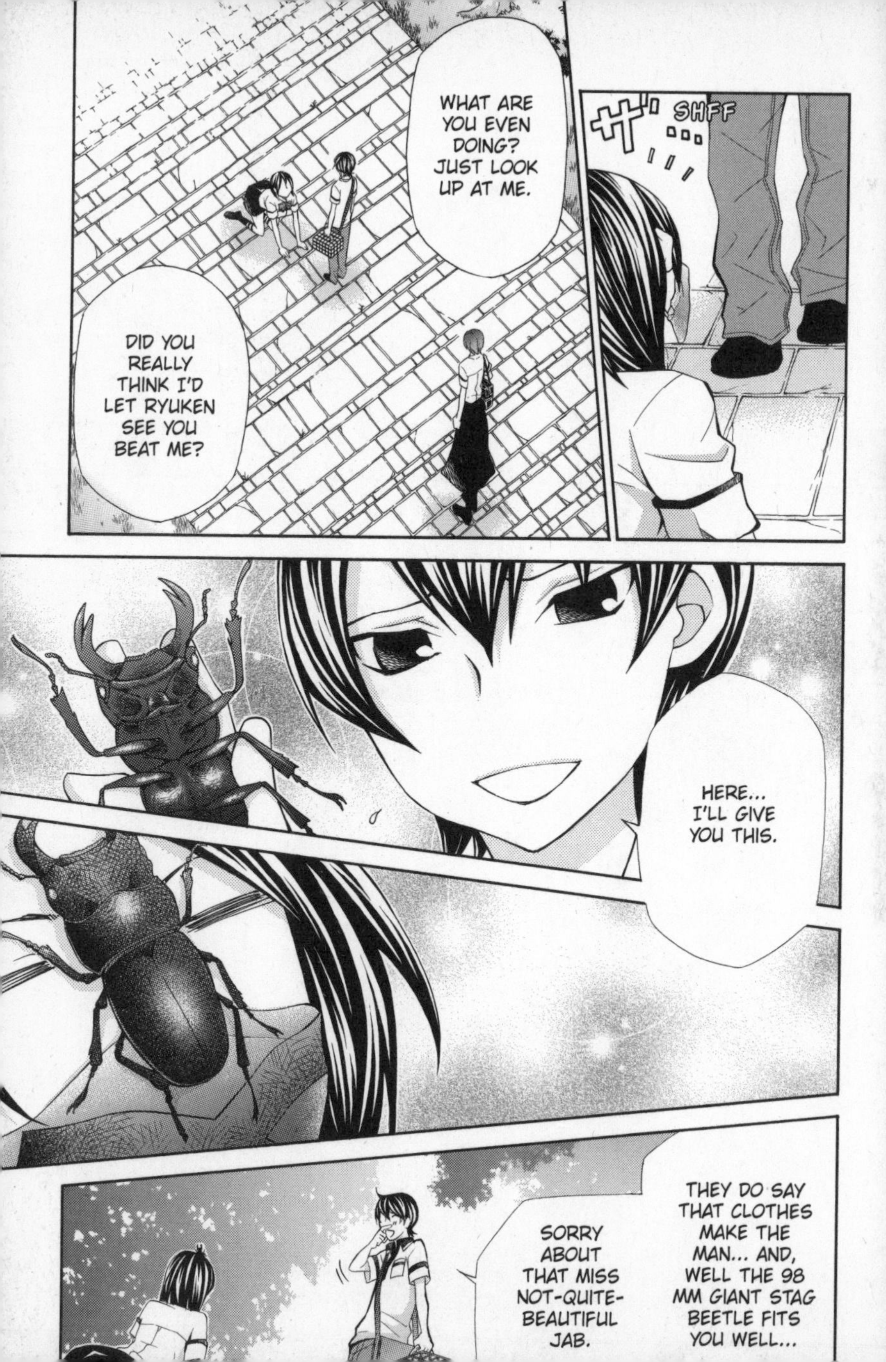
SHFF
WHAT ARE YOU EVEN DOING? JUST LOOK UP AT ME.
DID YOU REALLY THINK I'D LET RYUKEN SEE YOU BEAT ME?
HERE... I'LL GIVE YOU THIS.
THEY DO SAY THAT CLOTHES MAKE THE MAN... AND, WELL THE 98 MM GIANT STAG BEETLE FITS YOU WELL...
SORRY ABOUT THAT MISS NOT-QUITE-BEAUTIFUL JAB.

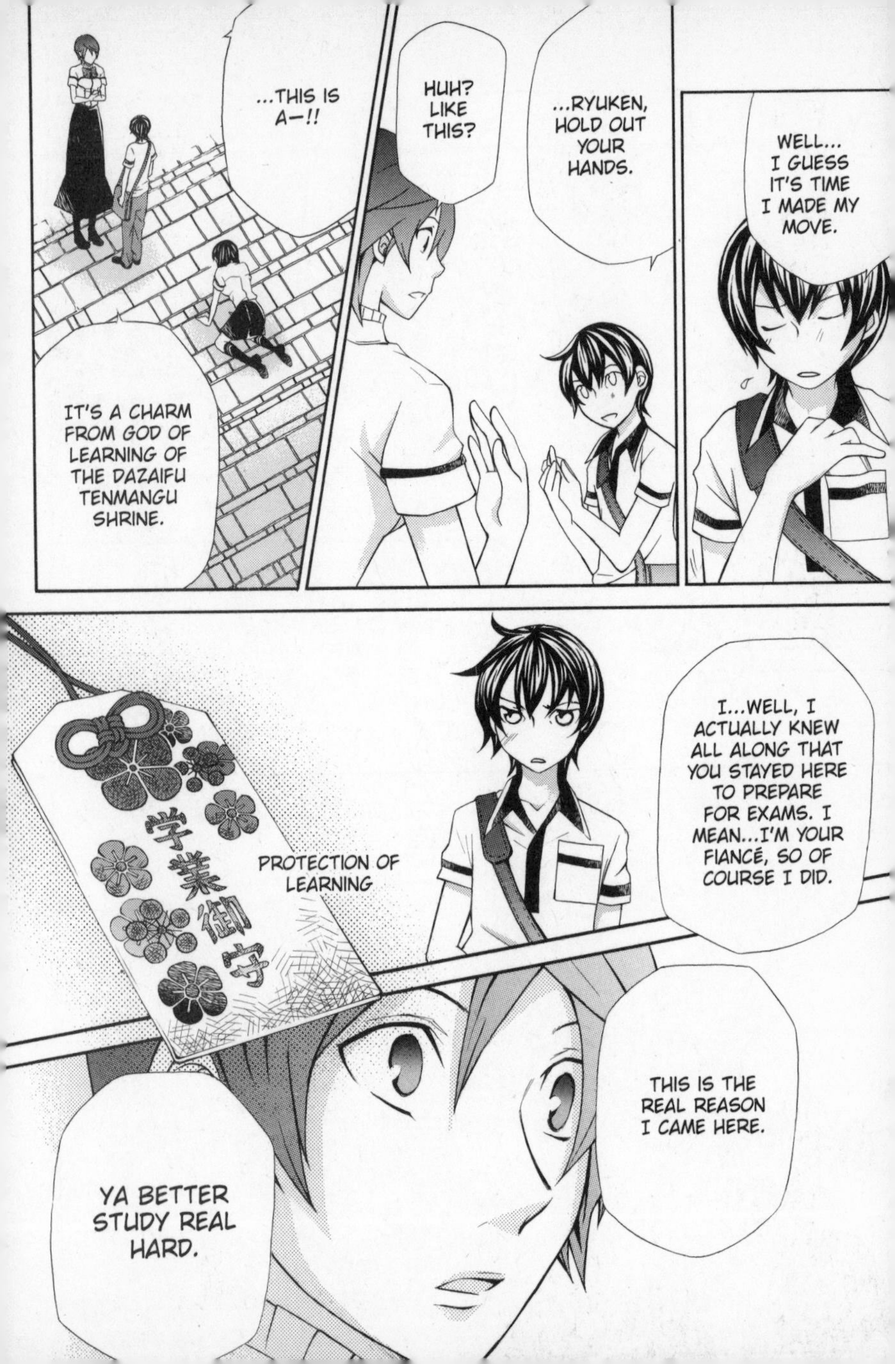
WELL... I GUESS IT'S TIME I MADE MY MOVE.
...RYUKEN, HOLD OUT YOUR HANDS.
HUH? LIKE THIS?
...THIS IS A—!!
IT'S A CHARM FROM GOD OF LEARNING OF THE DAZAIFU TENMANGU SHRINE.
I...WELL, I ACTUALLY KNEW ALL ALONG THAT YOU STAYED HERE TO PREPARE FOR EXAMS. I MEAN...I'M YOUR FIANCÉ, SO OF COURSE I DID.
学業御守
PROTECTION OF LEARNING
THIS IS THE REAL REASON I CAME HERE.
YA BETTER STUDY REAL HARD.

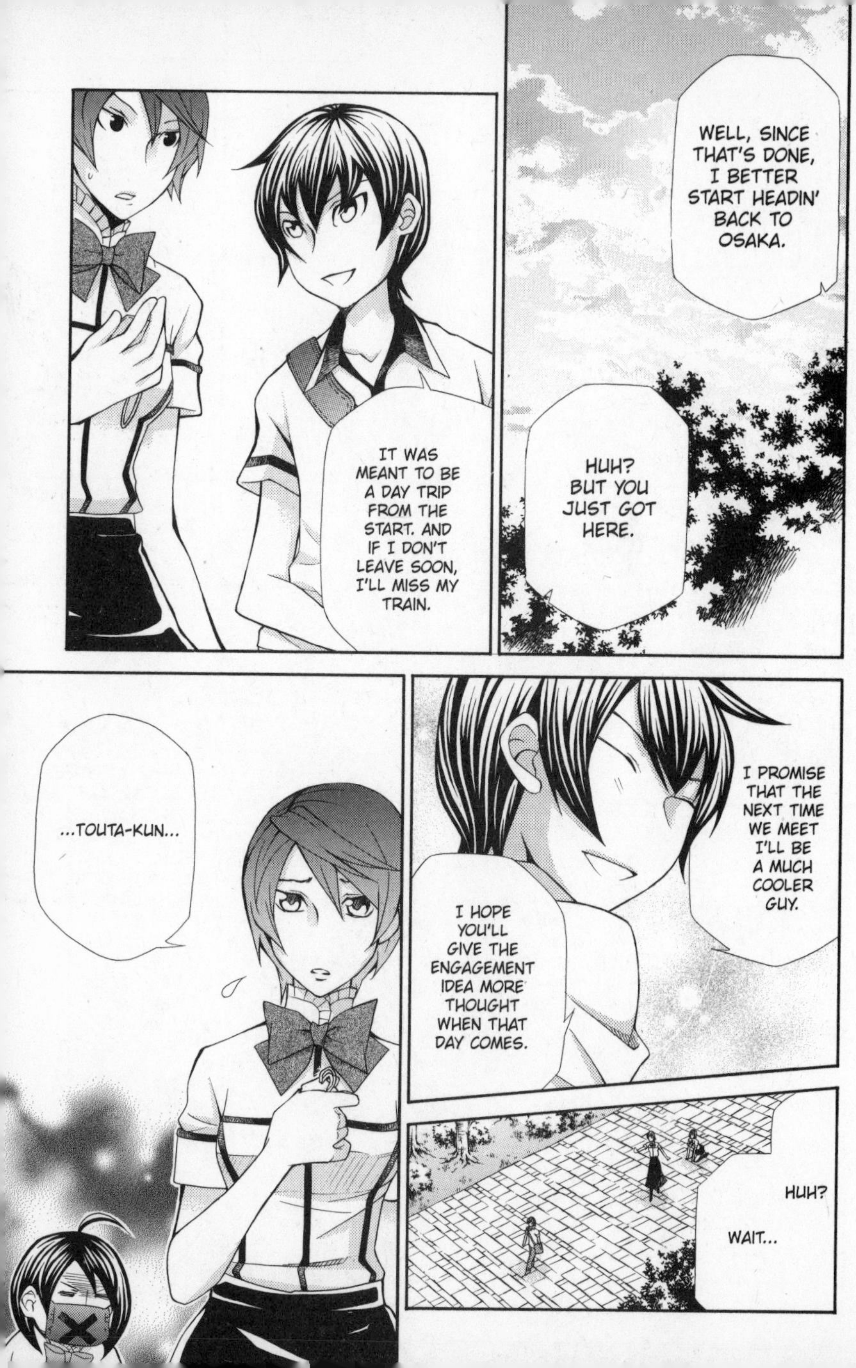
WELL, SINCE THAT'S DONE, I BETTER START HEADIN' BACK TO OSAKA.
HUH? BUT YOU JUST GOT HERE.
IT WAS MEANT TO BE A DAY TRIP FROM THE START. AND IF I DON'T LEAVE SOON, I'LL MISS MY TRAIN.
I PROMISE THAT THE NEXT TIME WE MEET I'LL BE A MUCH COOLER GUY.
I HOPE YOU'LL GIVE THE ENGAGEMENT IDEA MORE THOUGHT WHEN THAT DAY COMES.
HUH?
WAIT...
...TOUTA-KUN...

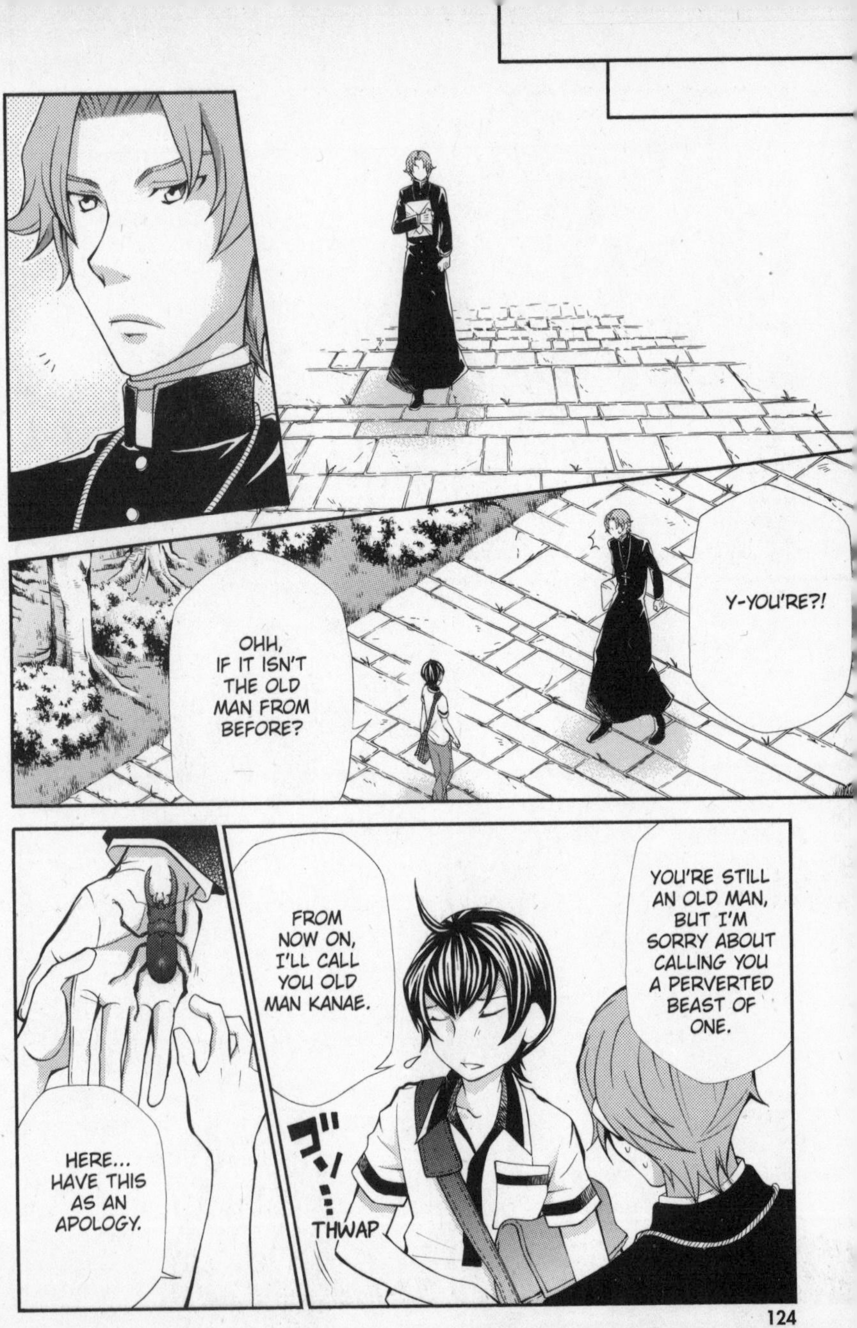
Y-YOU'RE?!
OHH, IF IT ISN'T THE OLD MAN FROM BEFORE?
YOU'RE STILL AN OLD MAN, BUT I'M SORRY ABOUT CALLING YOU A PERVERTED BEAST OF ONE.
FROM NOW ON, I'LL CALL YOU OLD MAN KANAE.
ゴッ
THWAP
HERE... HAVE THIS AS AN APOLOGY.

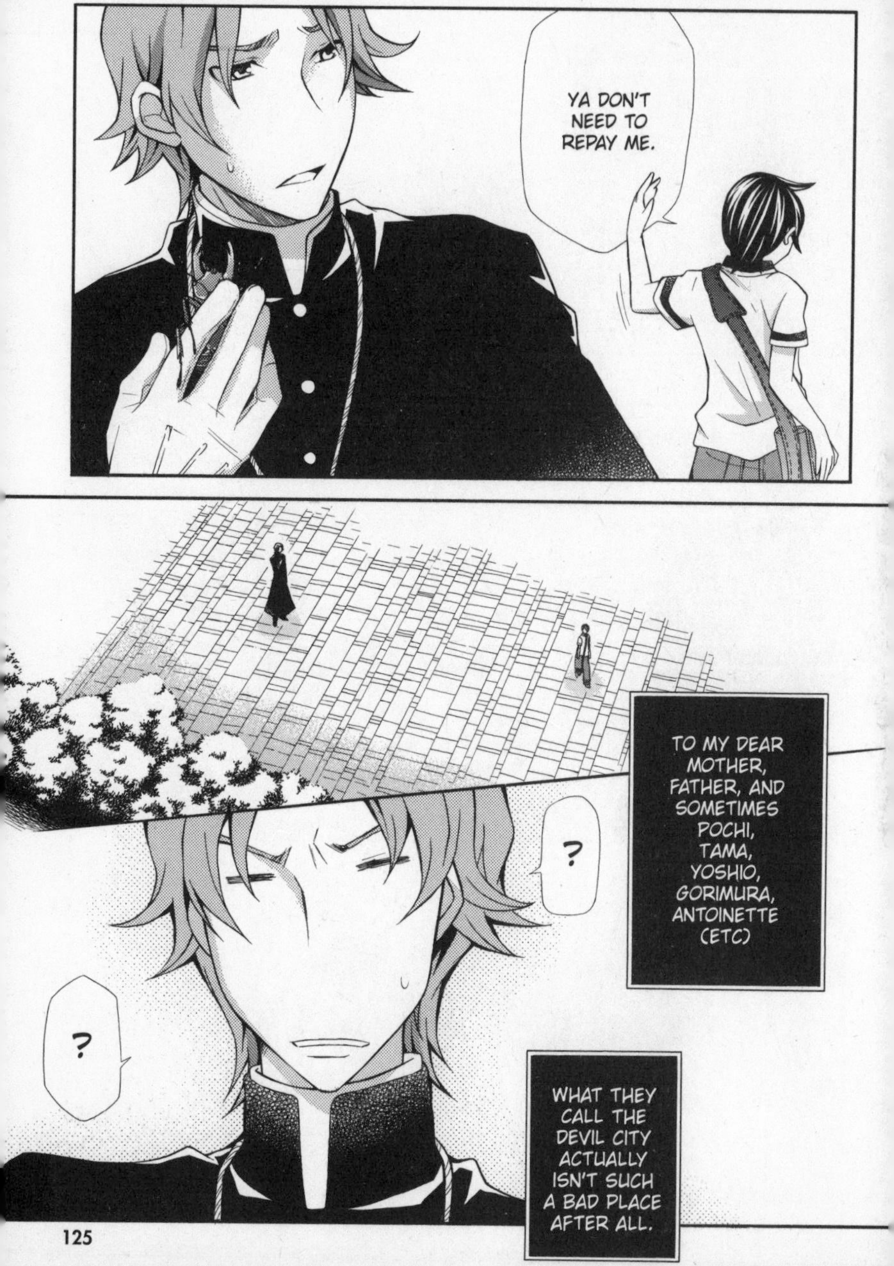
YA DON'T NEED TO REPAY ME.
TO MY DEAR MOTHER, FATHER, AND SOMETIMES POCHI, TAMA, YOSHIO, GORIMURA, ANTOINETTE (ETC)
?
?
WHAT THEY CALL THE DEVIL CITY ACTUALLY ISN'T SUCH A BAD PLACE AFTER ALL.

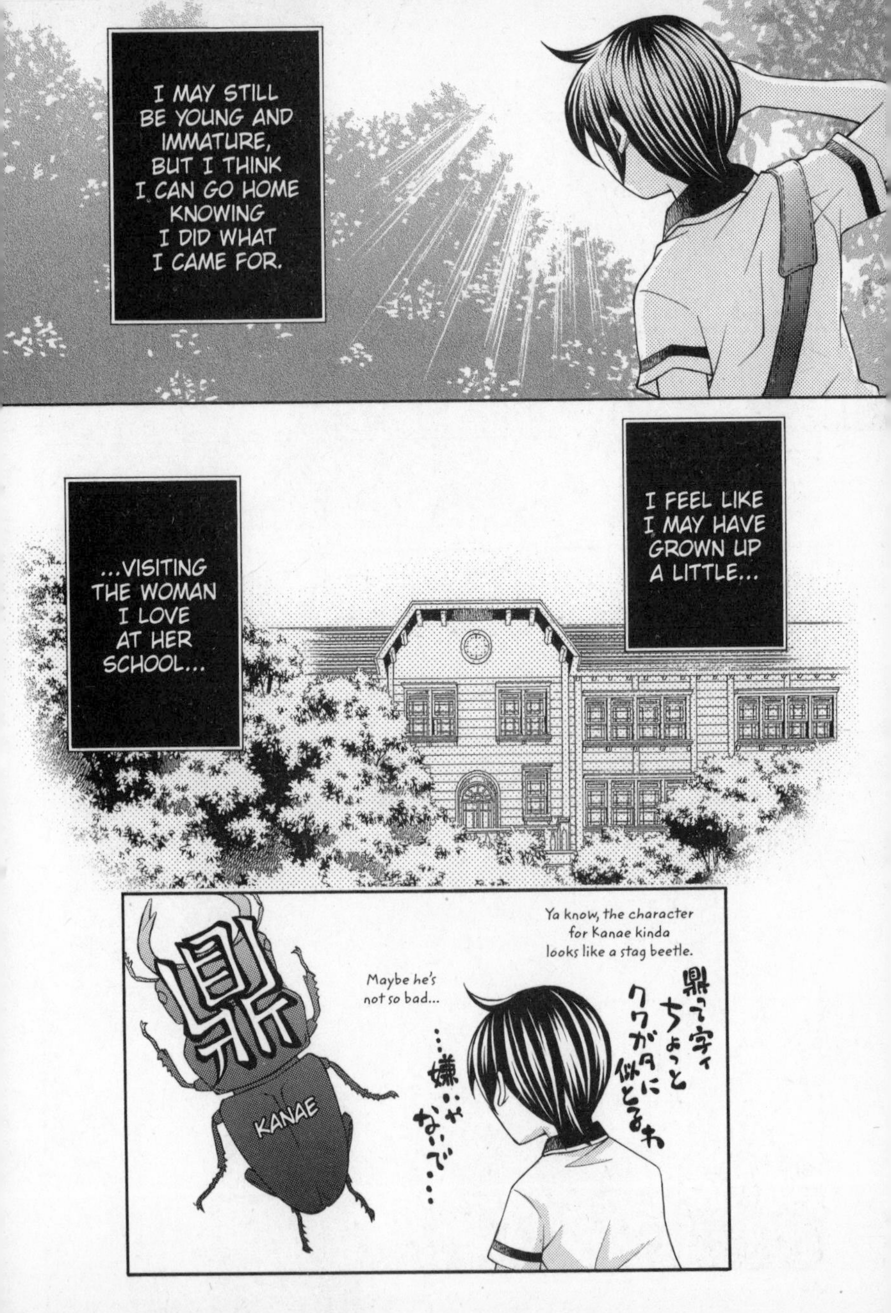
I MAY STILL BE YOUNG AND IMMATURE, BUT I THINK I CAN GO HOME KNOWING I DID WHAT I CAME FOR.
I FEEL LIKE I MAY HAVE GROWN UP A LITTLE...
...VISITING THE WOMAN I LOVE AT HER SCHOOL...
Ya know, the character for Kanae kinda looks like a stag beetle.
鼎って字ィちょっとクワガタに似とるわ
Maybe he's not so bad...
…嫌いやないで…
鼎
KANAE

Prayer 39

That Day of Summer Vacation That Was Filled With Acetic Acid

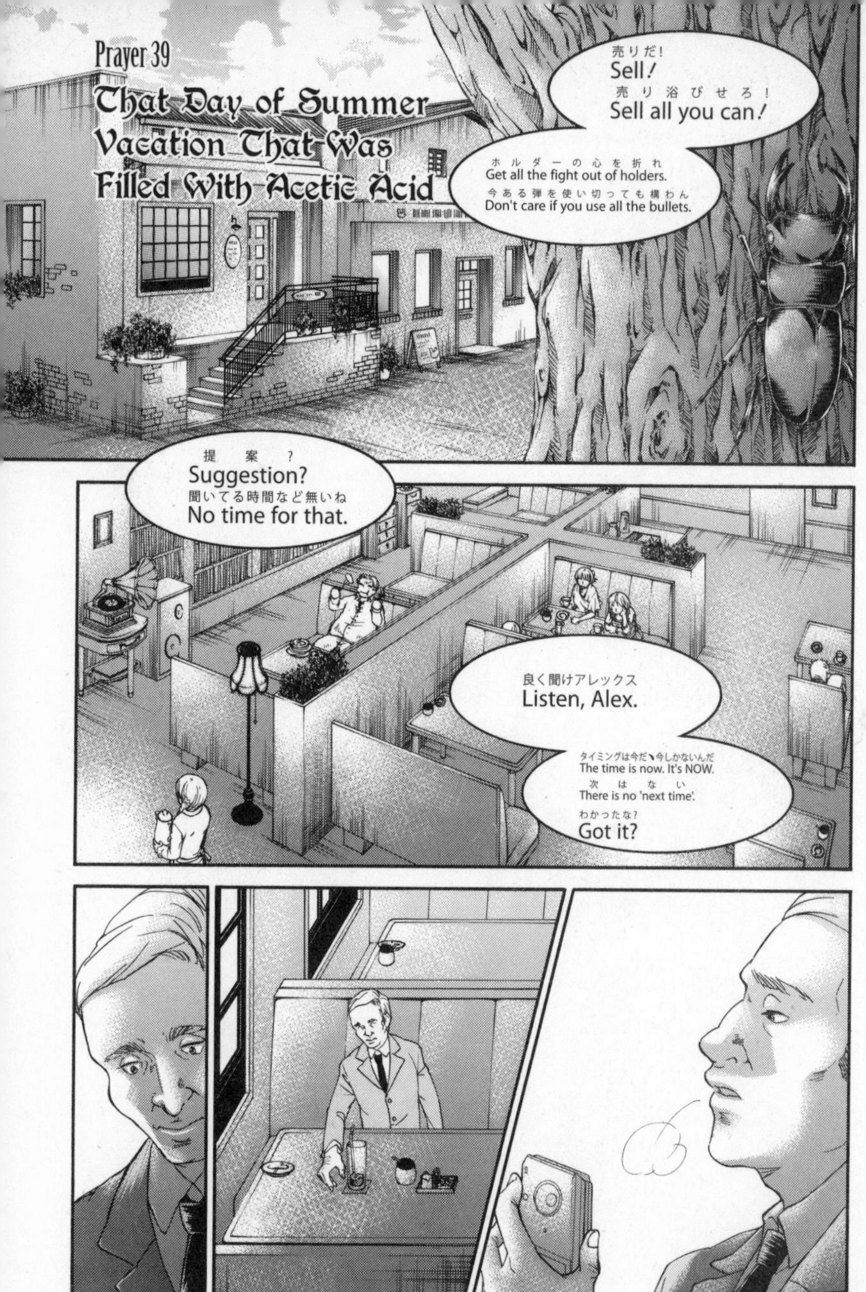

売りだ！
Sell!
売り浴びせろ！
Sell all you can!
ホルダーの心を折れ
Get all the fight out of holders.
今ある弾を使い切っても構わん
Don't care if you use all the bullets.
提案？
Suggestion?
聞いてる時間など無いね
No time for that.
良く聞けアレックス
Listen, Alex.
タイミングは今だ、今しかないんだ
The time is now. It's NOW.
次はない
There is no 'next time'.
わかったな？
Got it?

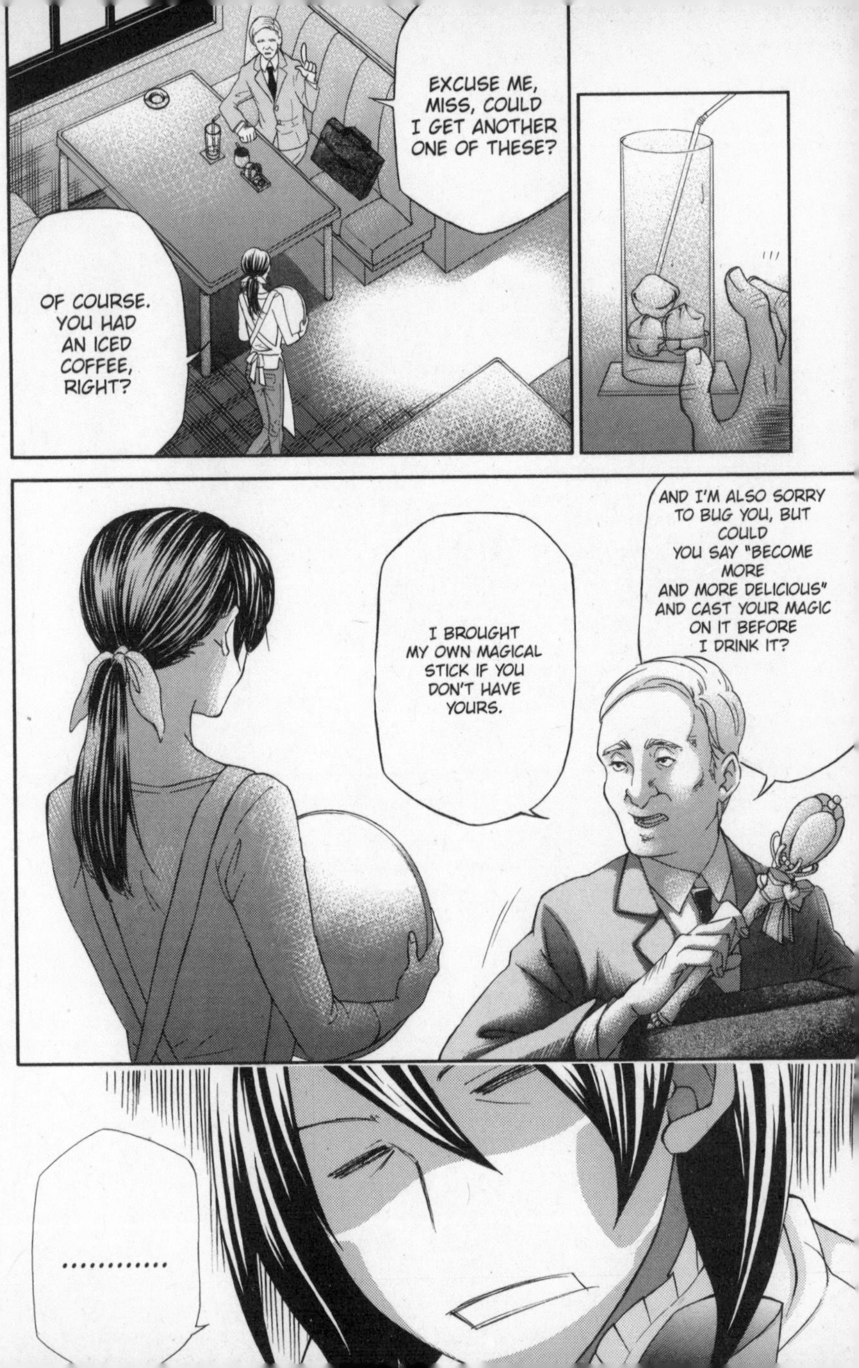
EXCUSE ME, MISS, COULD I GET ANOTHER ONE OF THESE?
OF COURSE. YOU HAD AN ICED COFFEE, RIGHT?
AND I'M ALSO SORRY TO BUG YOU, BUT COULD YOU SAY "BECOME MORE AND MORE DELICIOUS" AND CAST YOUR MAGIC ON IT BEFORE I DRINK IT?
I BROUGHT MY OWN MAGICAL STICK IF YOU DON'T HAVE YOURS.
....

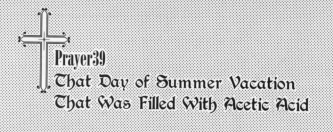

Prayer39

That Day of Summer Vacation That Was Filled With Acetic Acid

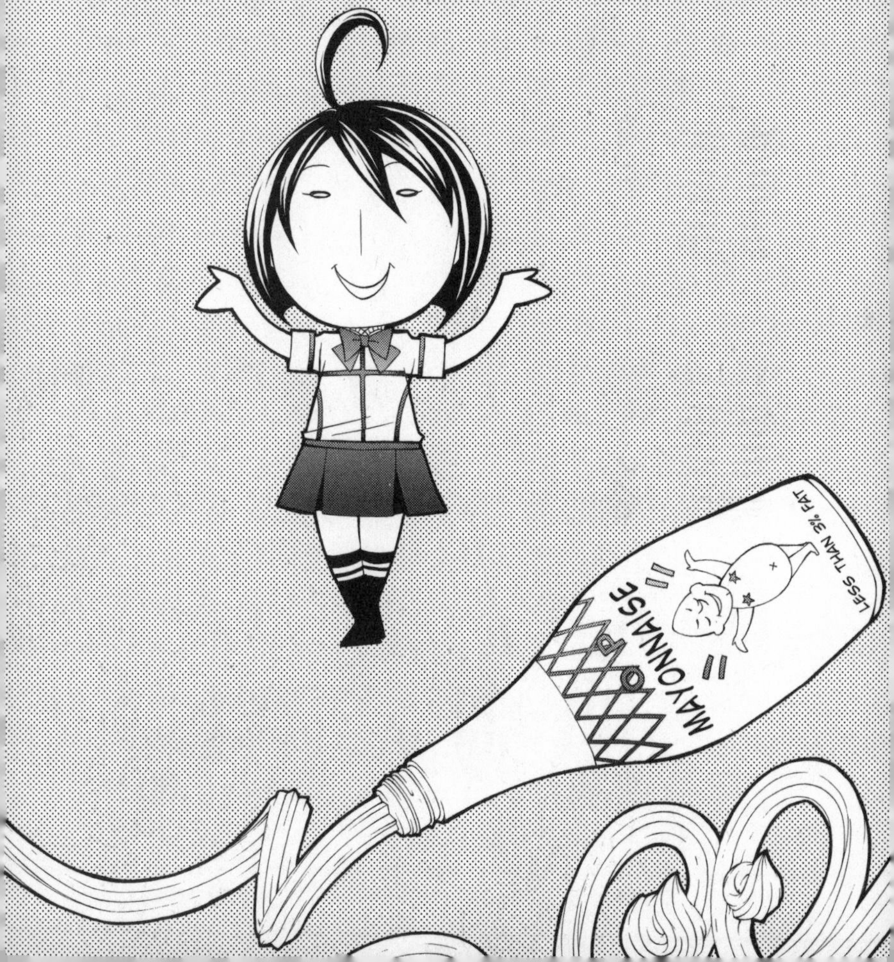
MAYONNAISE
LESS THAN 3% FAT

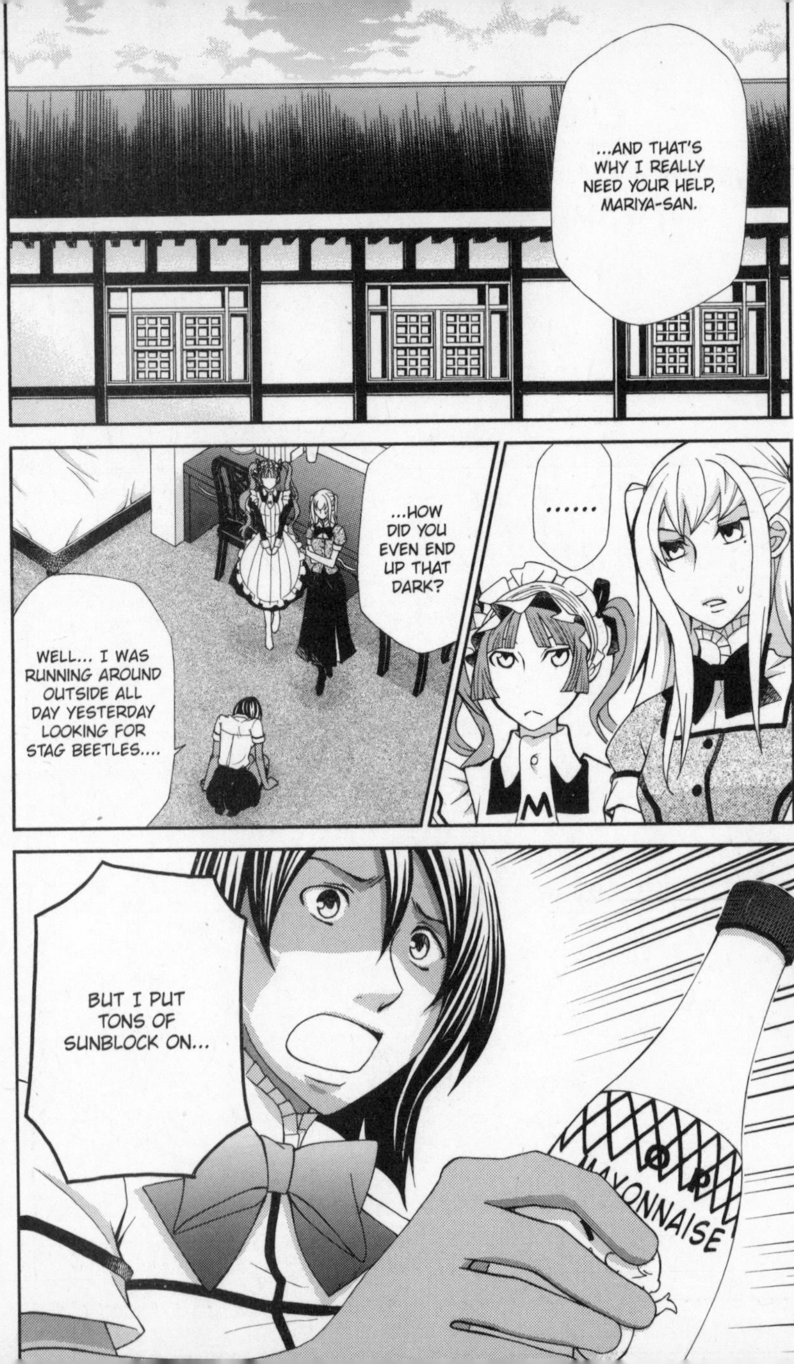
...AND THAT'S WHY I REALLY NEED YOUR HELP, MARIYA-SAN.
......
...HOW DID YOU EVEN END UP THAT DARK?
WELL... I WAS RUNNING AROUND OUTSIDE ALL DAY YESTERDAY LOOKING FOR STAG BEETLES....
BUT I PUT TONS OF SUNBLOCK ON...
MAYONNAISE

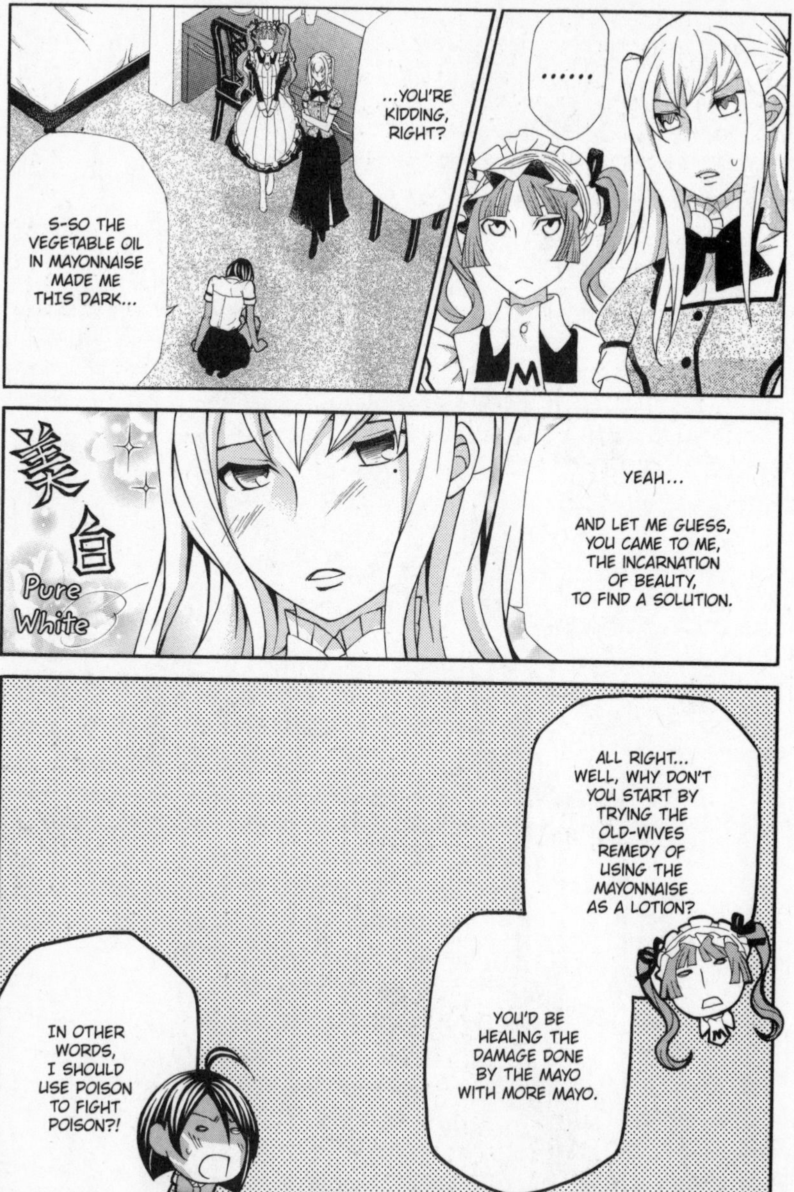
......
...YOU'RE KIDDING, RIGHT?
S-SO THE VEGETABLE OIL IN MAYONNAISE MADE ME THIS DARK...
YEAH...
AND LET ME GUESS, YOU CAME TO ME, THE INCARNATION OF BEAUTY, TO FIND A SOLUTION.
美白
Pure White
ALL RIGHT... WELL, WHY DON'T YOU START BY TRYING THE OLD-WIVES REMEDY OF USING THE MAYONNAISE AS A LOTION?
YOU'D BE HEALING THE DAMAGE DONE BY THE MAYO WITH MORE MAYO.
IN OTHER WORDS, I SHOULD USE POISON TO FIGHT POISON?!

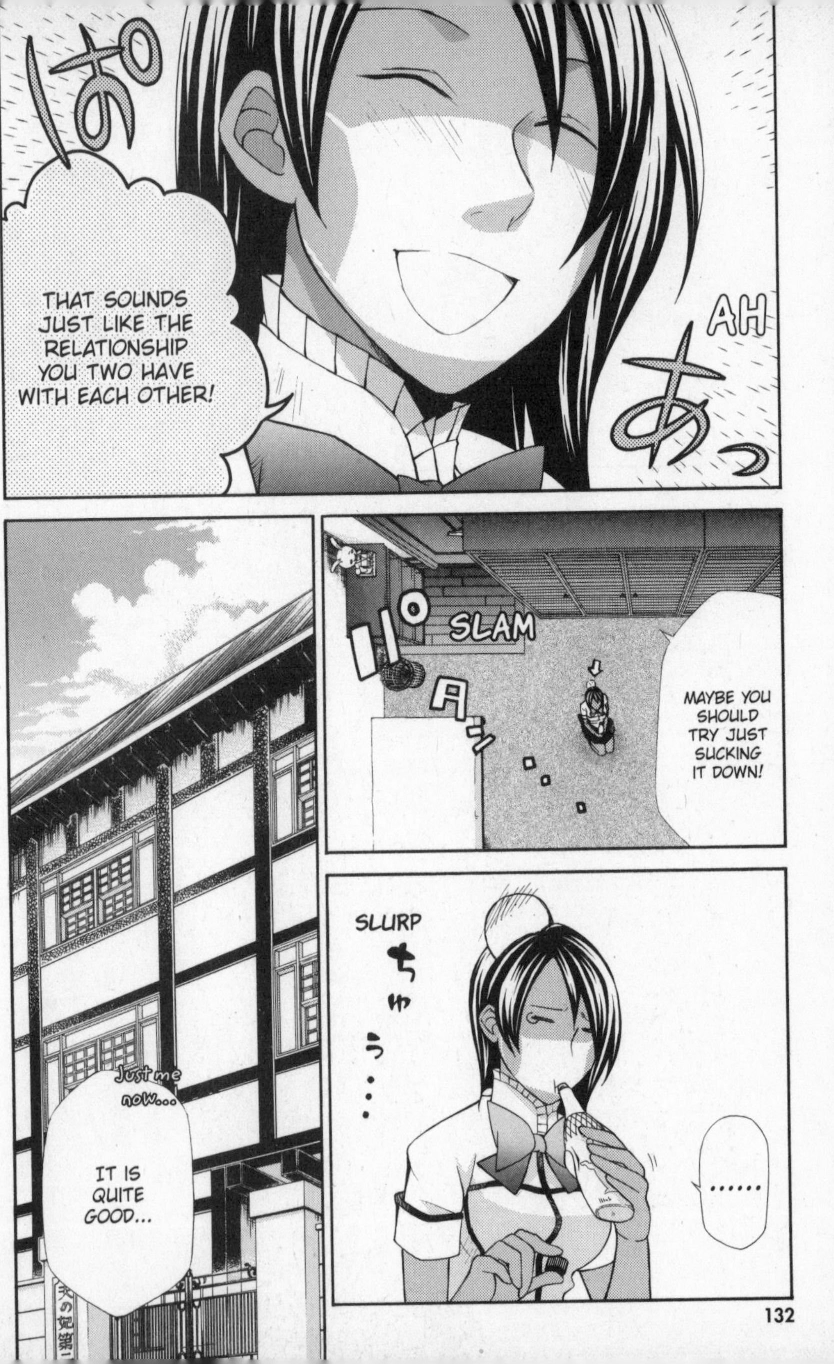
AH
あっ
THAT SOUNDS JUST LIKE THE RELATIONSHIP YOU TWO HAVE WITH EACH OTHER!
SLAM
MAYBE YOU SHOULD TRY JUST SUCKING IT DOWN!
SLURP
ちゅう…
……
Just me now…
IT IS QUITE GOOD…

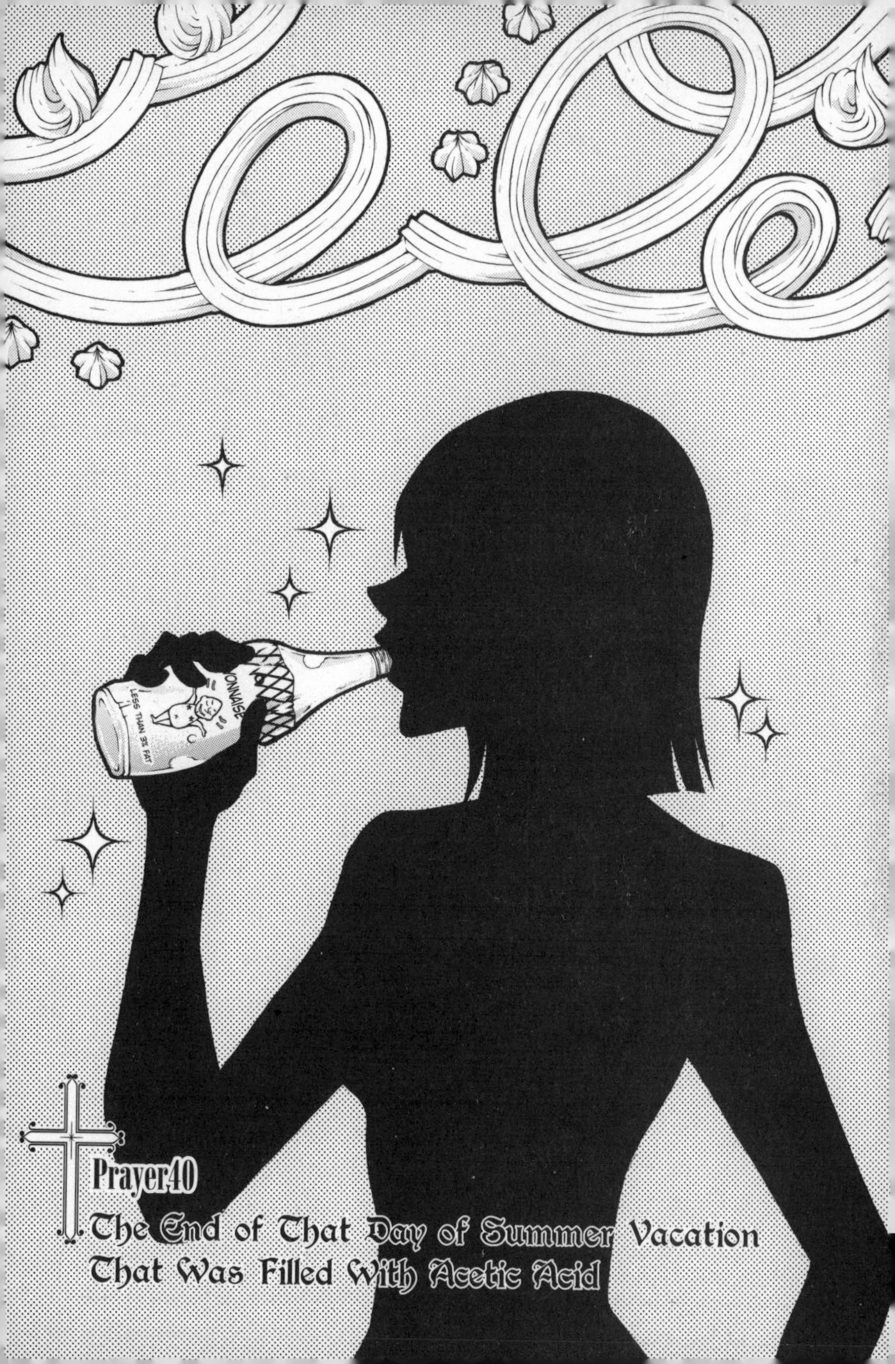
ONNAISE
LESS THAN 3% FAT
Prayer40
The End of That Day of Summer Vacation That Was Filled With Acetic Acid

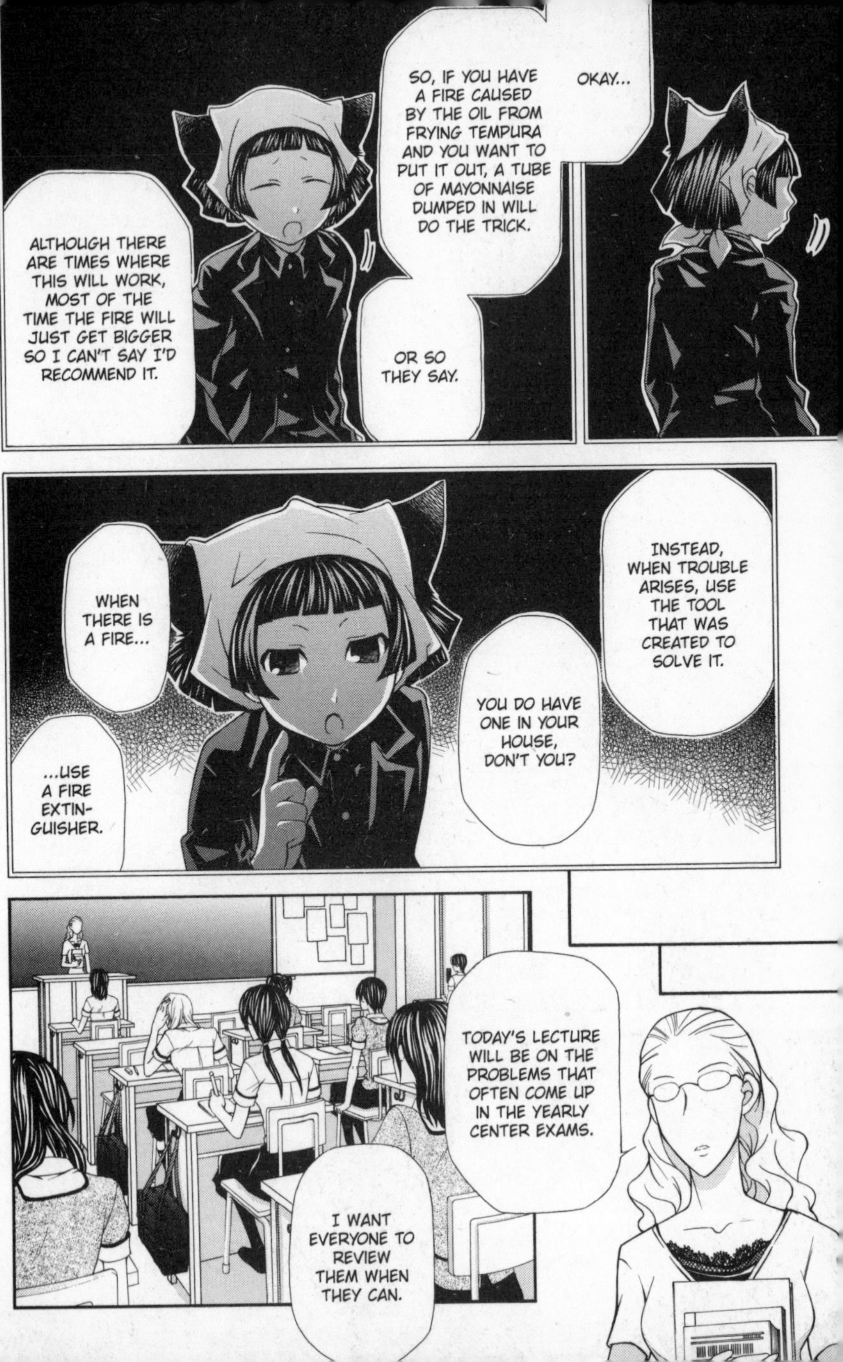

OKAY...
SO, IF YOU HAVE A FIRE CAUSED BY THE OIL FROM FRYING TEMPURA AND YOU WANT TO PUT IT OUT, A TUBE OF MAYONNAISE DUMPED IN WILL DO THE TRICK.
OR SO THEY SAY.
ALTHOUGH THERE ARE TIMES WHERE THIS WILL WORK, MOST OF THE TIME THE FIRE WILL JUST GET BIGGER SO I CAN'T SAY I'D RECOMMEND IT.
INSTEAD, WHEN TROUBLE ARISES, USE THE TOOL THAT WAS CREATED TO SOLVE IT.
WHEN THERE IS A FIRE...
YOU DO HAVE ONE IN YOUR HOUSE, DON'T YOU?
...USE A FIRE EXTIN-GUISHER.
TODAY'S LECTURE WILL BE ON THE PROBLEMS THAT OFTEN COME UP IN THE YEARLY CENTER EXAMS.
I WANT EVERYONE TO REVIEW THEM WHEN THEY CAN.

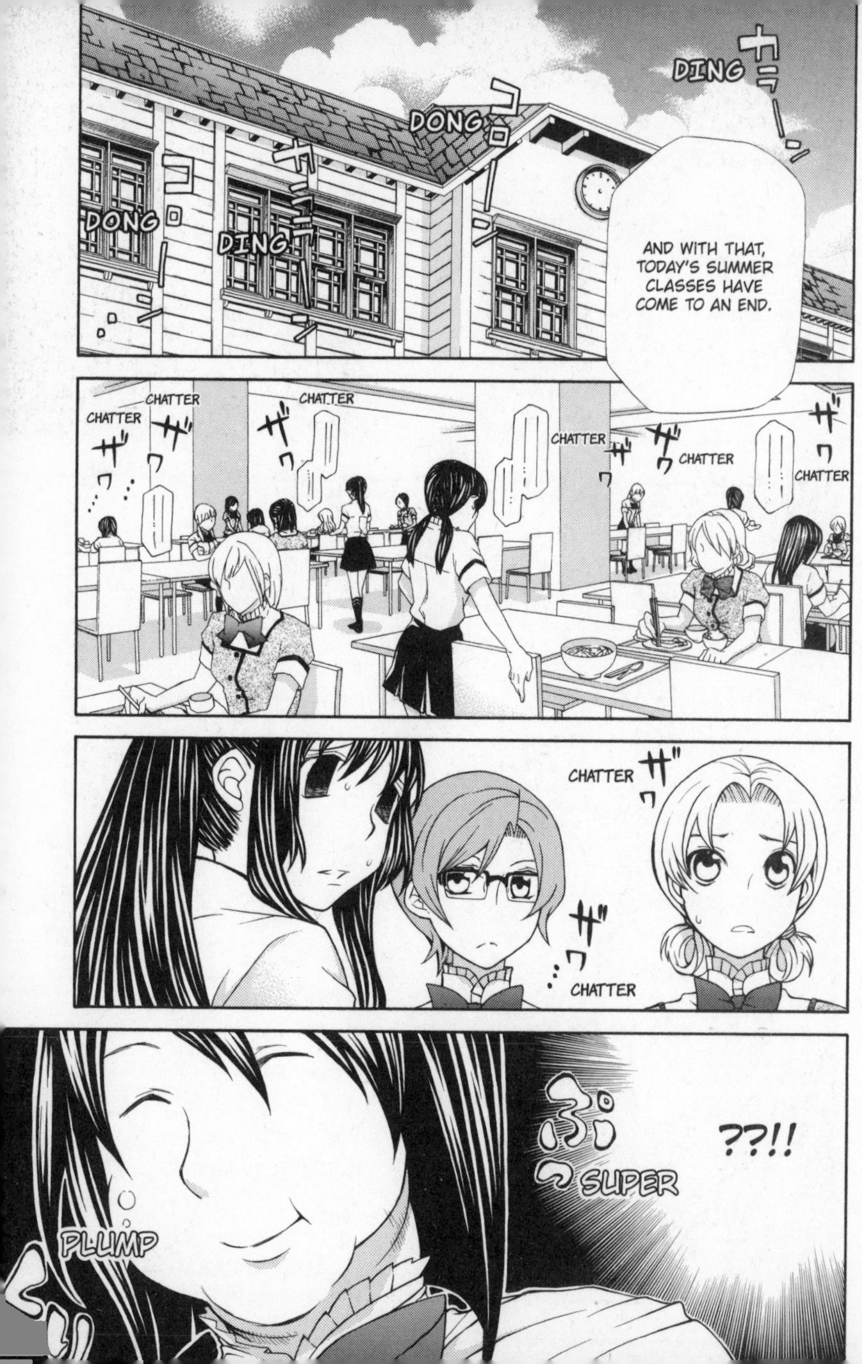
DING
AND WITH THAT, TODAY'S SUMMER CLASSES HAVE COME TO AN END.
DONG
DING
DONG
CHATTER
CHATTER
CHATTER
CHATTER
CHATTER
CHATTER
CHATTER
CHATTER
??!!
SUPER
PLUMP

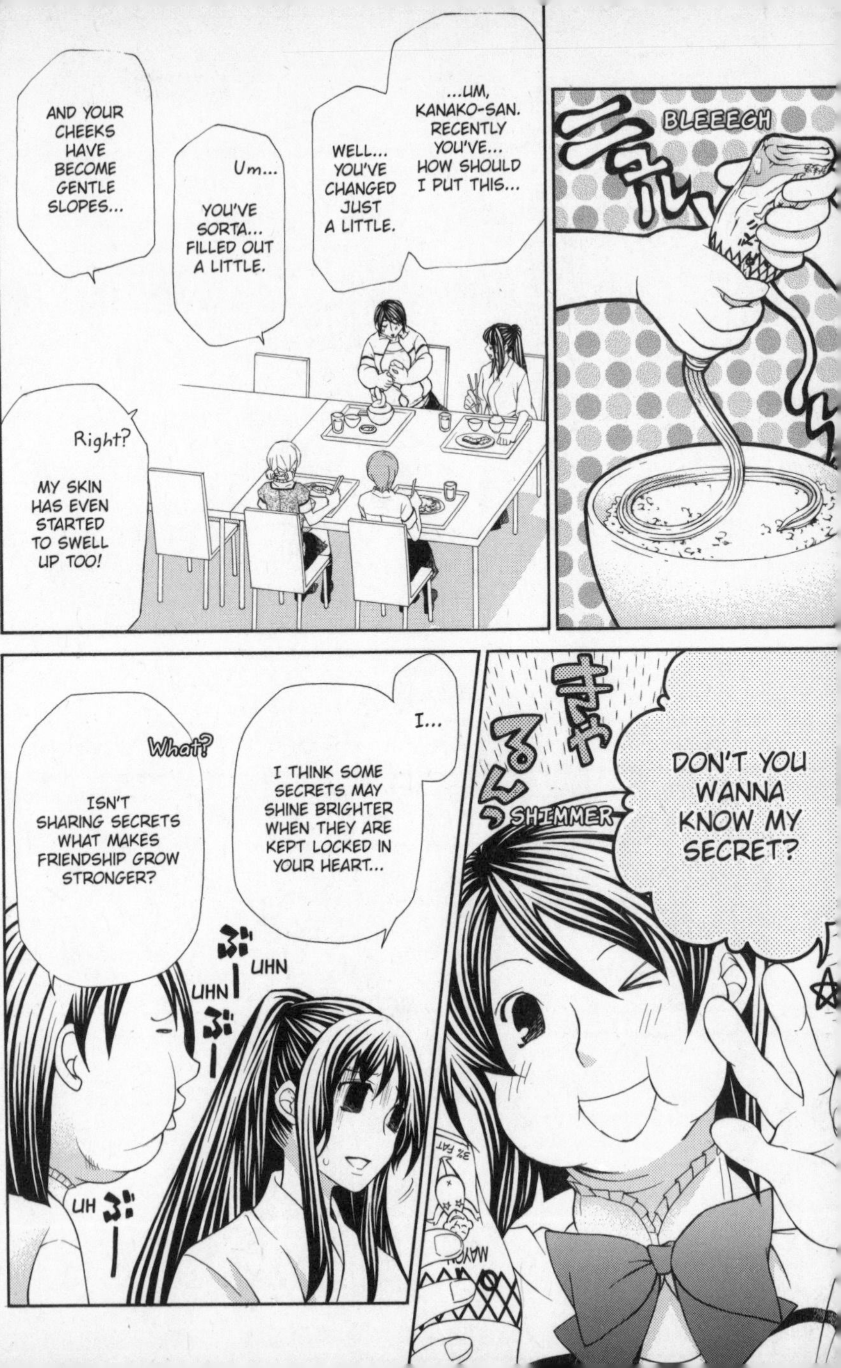
ニュル
BLEEEGH
...UM, KANAKO-SAN. RECENTLY YOU'VE... HOW SHOULD I PUT THIS...
WELL... YOU'VE CHANGED JUST A LITTLE.
Um... YOU'VE SORTA... FILLED OUT A LITTLE.
AND YOUR CHEEKS HAVE BECOME GENTLE SLOPES...
Right? MY SKIN HAS EVEN STARTED TO SWELL UP TOO!
きゃるん
SHIMMER
DON'T YOU WANNA KNOW MY SECRET?
3% FAT
MAYO
I...
I THINK SOME SECRETS MAY SHINE BRIGHTER WHEN THEY ARE KEPT LOCKED IN YOUR HEART...
What?
ISN'T SHARING SECRETS WHAT MAKES FRIENDSHIP GROW STRONGER?
ぶー
UHN
ぶー
UHN
ぶー
UH

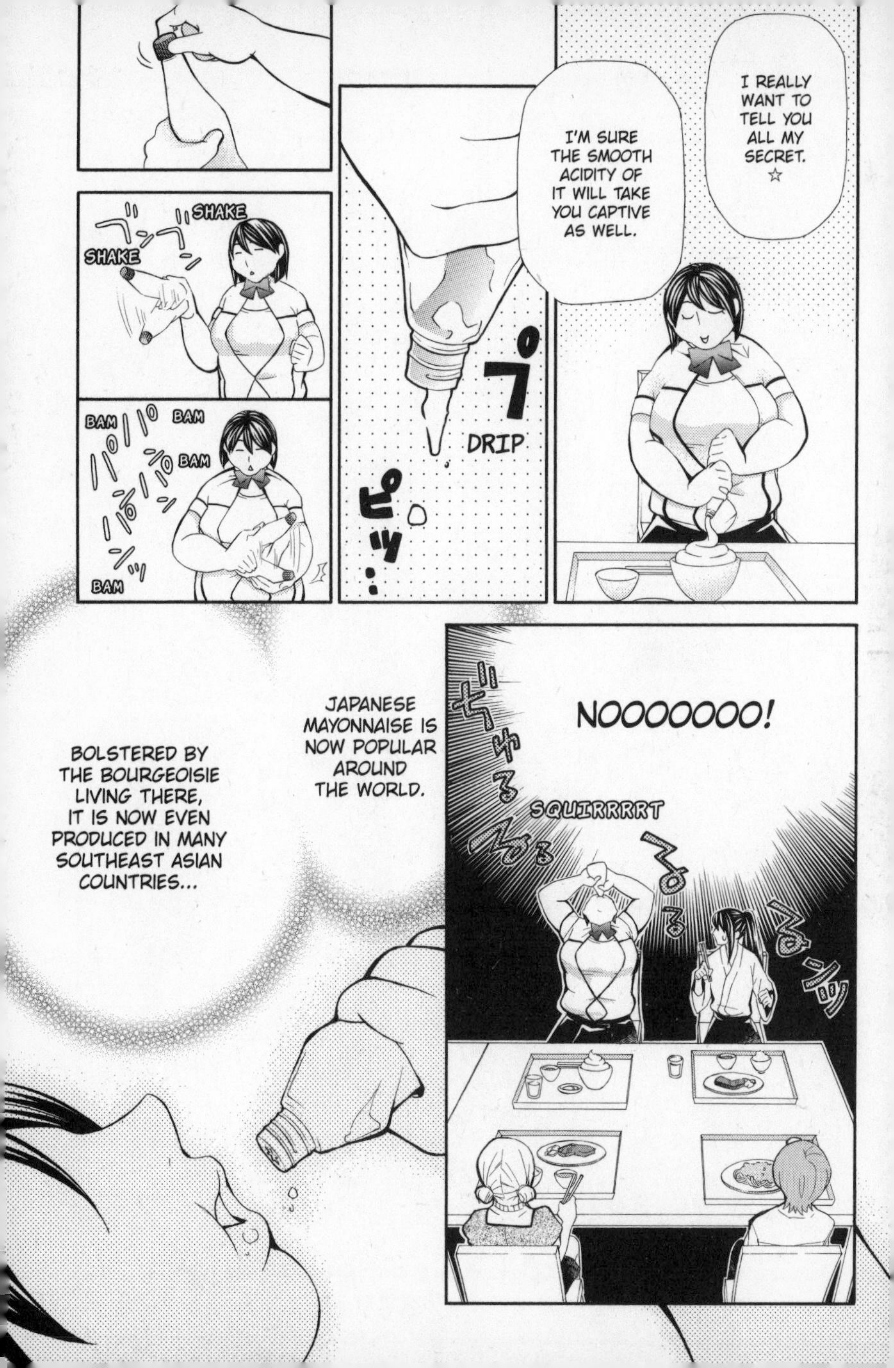

I REALLY WANT TO TELL YOU ALL MY SECRET. ☆
I'M SURE THE SMOOTH ACIDITY OF IT WILL TAKE YOU CAPTIVE AS WELL.
プ
DRIP
ピッ
SHAKE
SHAKE
BAM
BAM
BAM
BAM
NOOOOOOO!
SQUIRRRRT
JAPANESE MAYONNAISE IS NOW POPULAR AROUND THE WORLD.
BOLSTERED BY THE BOURGEOISIE LIVING THERE, IT IS NOW EVEN PRODUCED IN MANY SOUTHEAST ASIAN COUNTRIES...

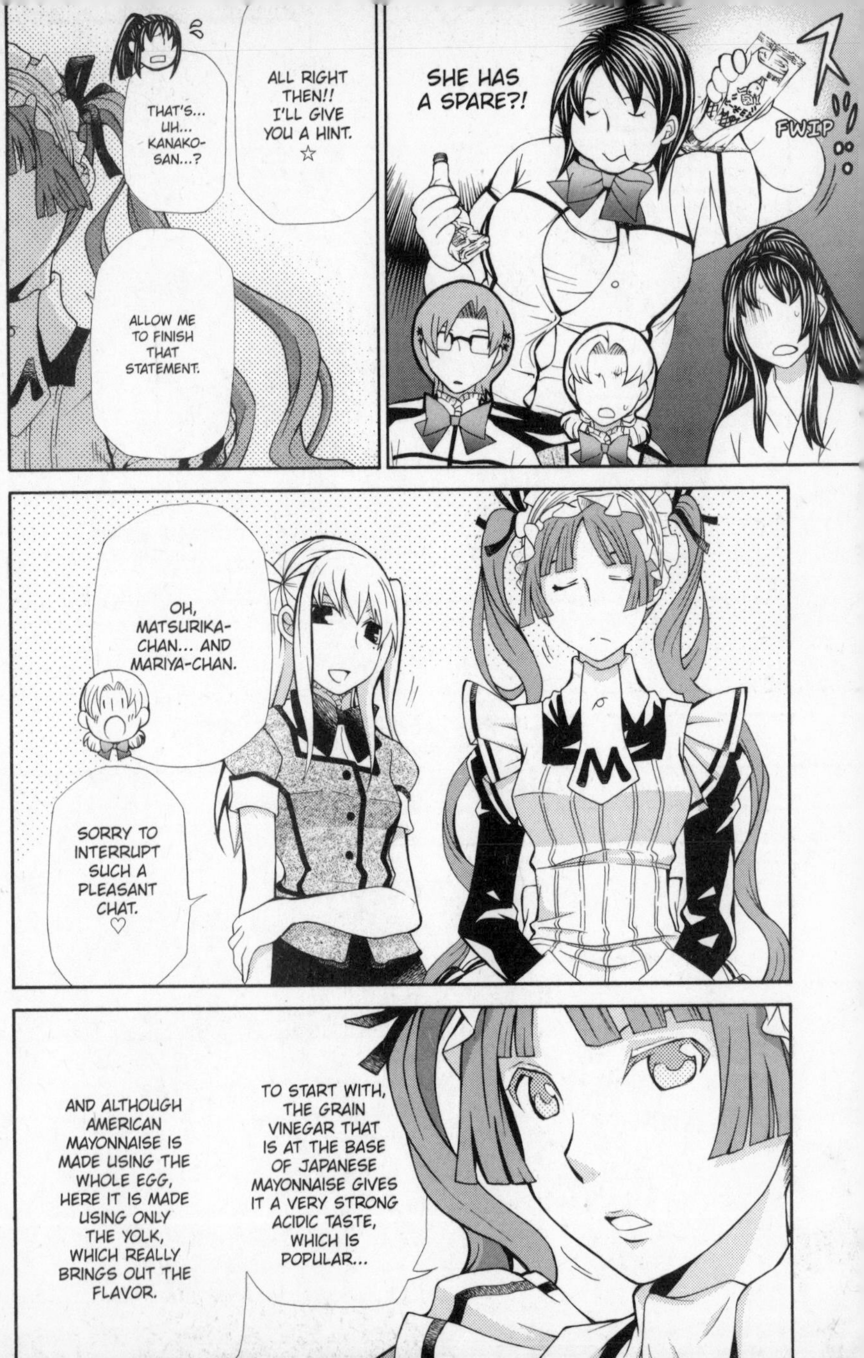
SHE HAS A SPARE?!
FWIP
ALL RIGHT THEN!! I'LL GIVE YOU A HINT. ☆
THAT'S... UH... KANAKO-SAN...?
ALLOW ME TO FINISH THAT STATEMENT.
OH, MATSURIKA-CHAN... AND MARIYA-CHAN.
SORRY TO INTERRUPT SUCH A PLEASANT CHAT. ♡
TO START WITH, THE GRAIN VINEGAR THAT IS AT THE BASE OF JAPANESE MAYONNAISE GIVES IT A VERY STRONG ACIDIC TASTE, WHICH IS POPULAR...
AND ALTHOUGH AMERICAN MAYONNAISE IS MADE USING THE WHOLE EGG, HERE IT IS MADE USING ONLY THE YOLK, WHICH REALLY BRINGS OUT THE FLAVOR.

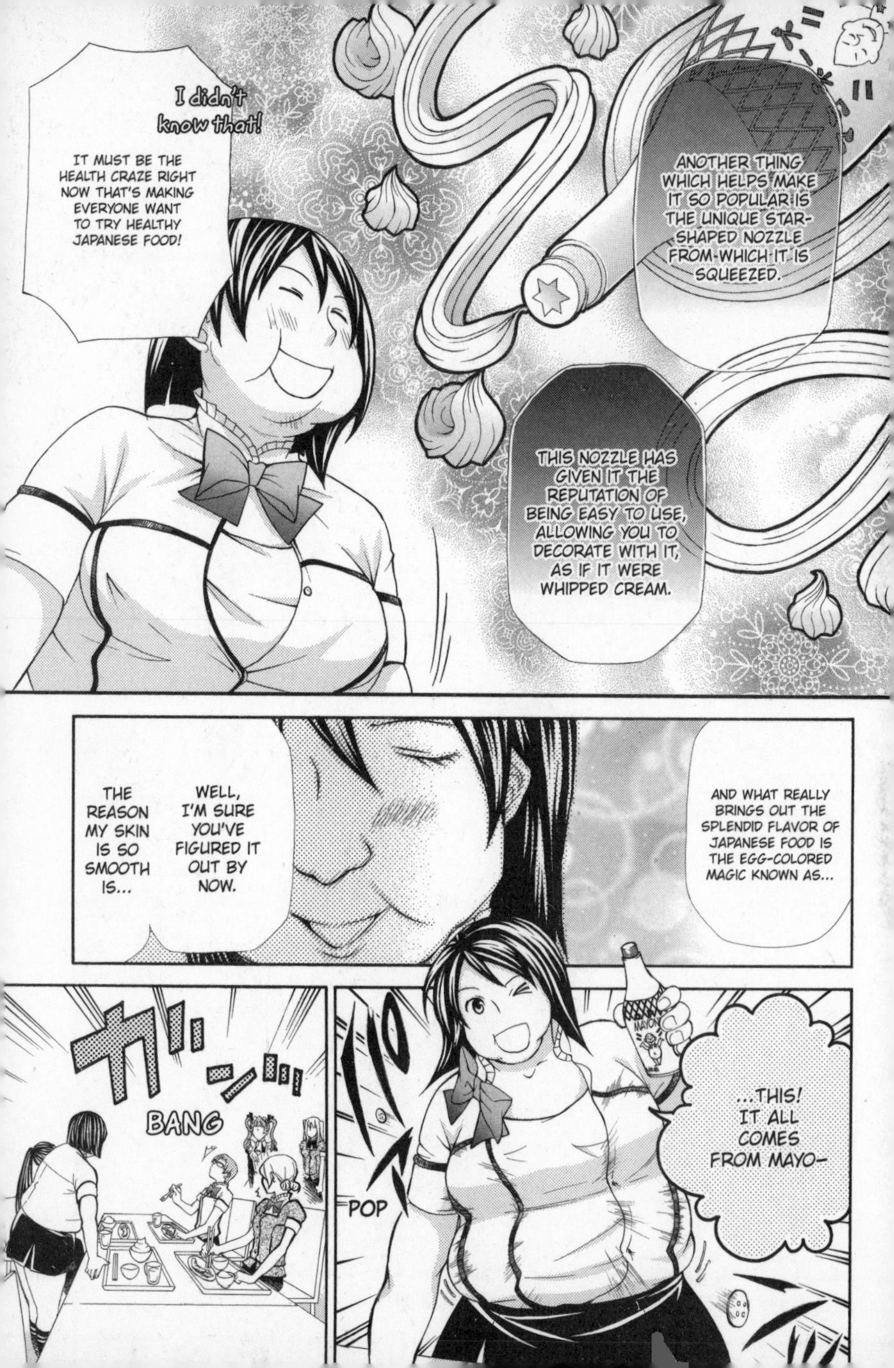

ANOTHER THING WHICH HELPS MAKE IT SO POPULAR IS THE UNIQUE STAR-SHAPED NOZZLE FROM WHICH IT IS SQUEEZED.
THIS NOZZLE HAS GIVEN IT THE REPUTATION OF BEING EASY TO USE, ALLOWING YOU TO DECORATE WITH IT, AS IF IT WERE WHIPPED CREAM.
I didn't know that!
IT MUST BE THE HEALTH CRAZE RIGHT NOW THAT'S MAKING EVERYONE WANT TO TRY HEALTHY JAPANESE FOOD!
WELL, I'M SURE YOU'VE FIGURED IT OUT BY NOW.
THE REASON MY SKIN IS SO SMOOTH IS...
AND WHAT REALLY BRINGS OUT THE SPLENDID FLAVOR OF JAPANESE FOOD IS THE EGG-COLORED MAGIC KNOWN AS...
...THIS! IT ALL COMES FROM MAYO-
MAYON
POP
BANG

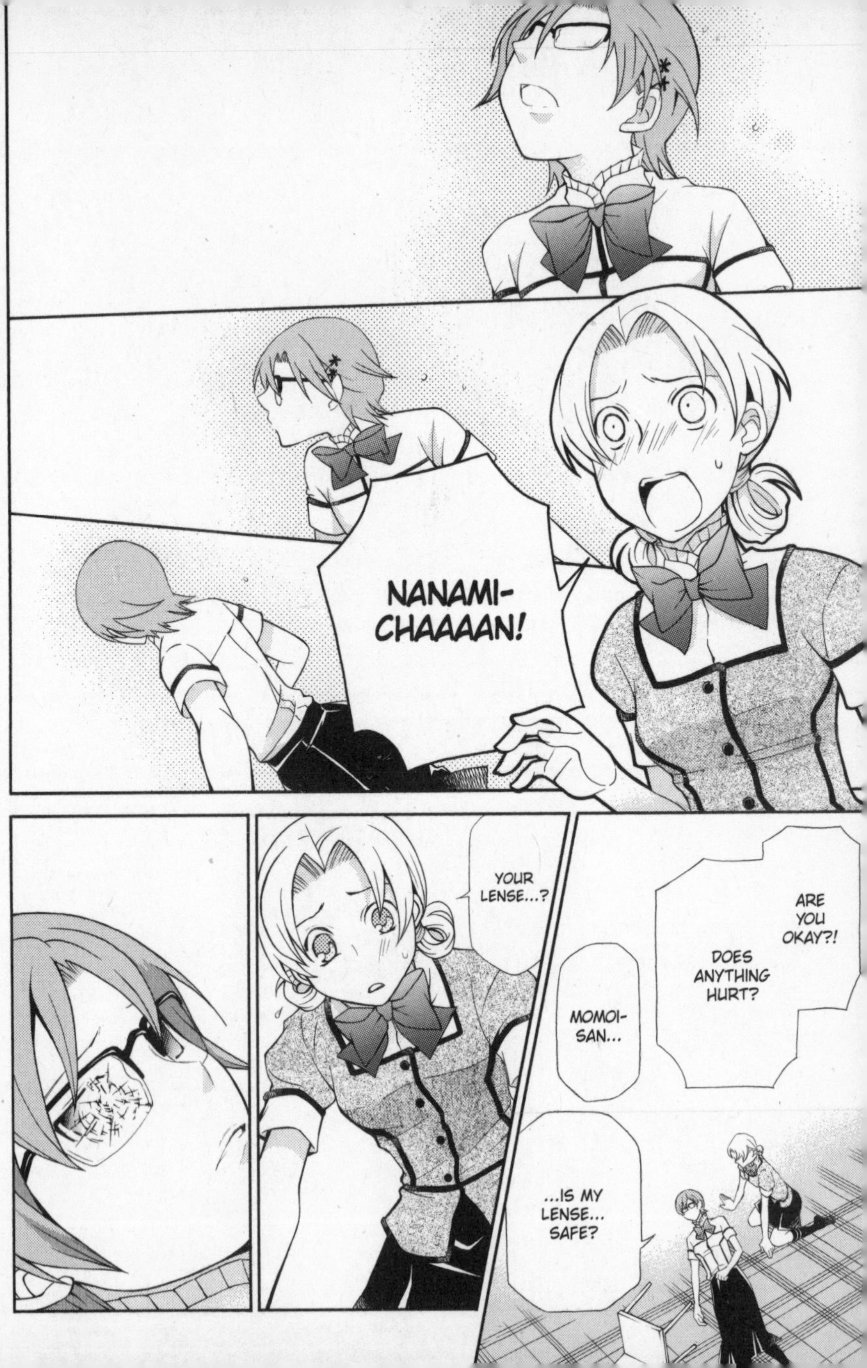
NANAMI-CHAAAAN!
ARE YOU OKAY?!
DOES ANYTHING HURT?
MOMOI-SAN...
...IS MY LENSE... SAFE?
YOUR LENSE...?

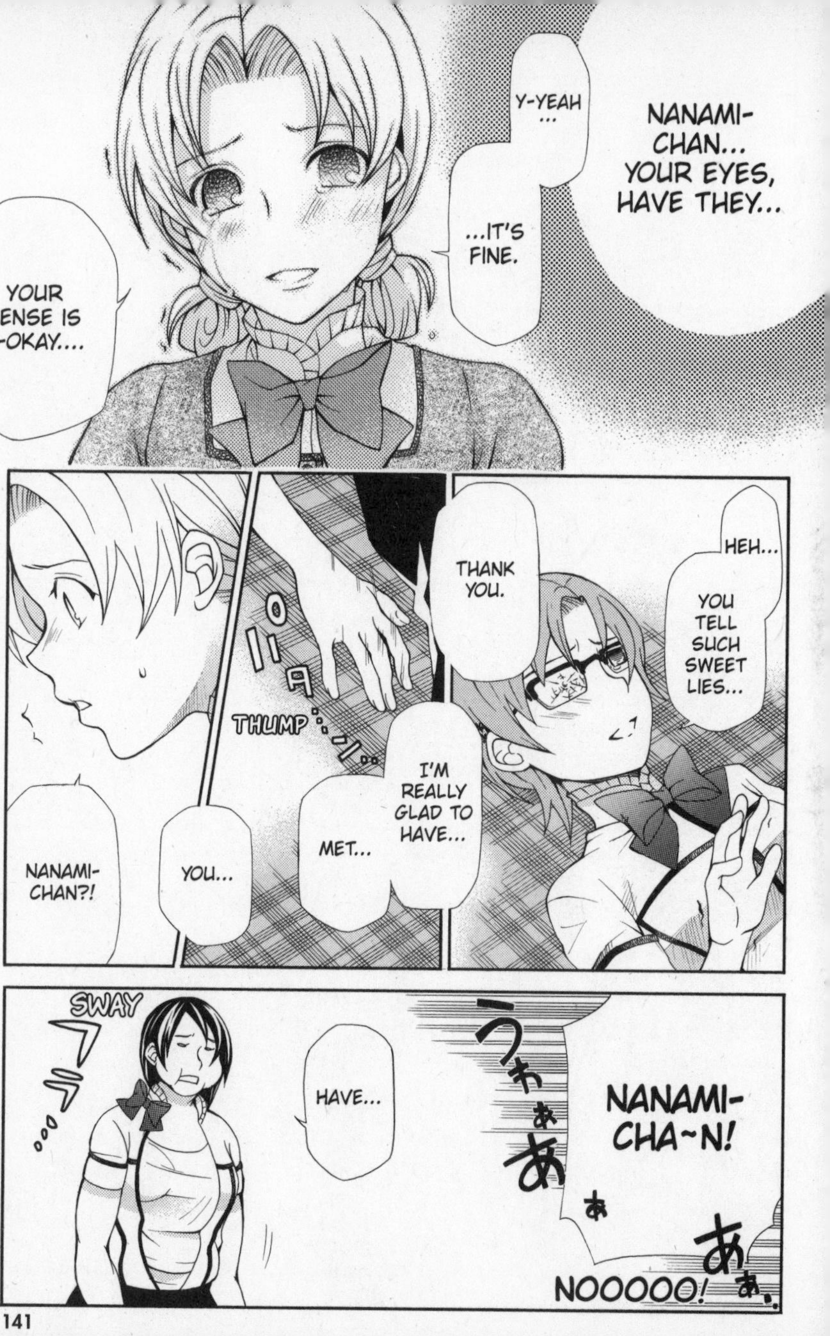
NANAMI-CHAN... YOUR EYES, HAVE THEY...
Y-YEAH ...
...IT'S FINE.
YOUR LENSE IS A-OKAY....
HEH...
YOU TELL SUCH SWEET LIES...
THANK YOU.
I'M REALLY GLAD TO HAVE...
MET...
YOU...
パタ...
THUMP
NANAMI-CHAN?!
うわぁあぁあぁ
NANAMI-CHA~N!
NOOOOO!
HAVE...
フラ...
SWAY

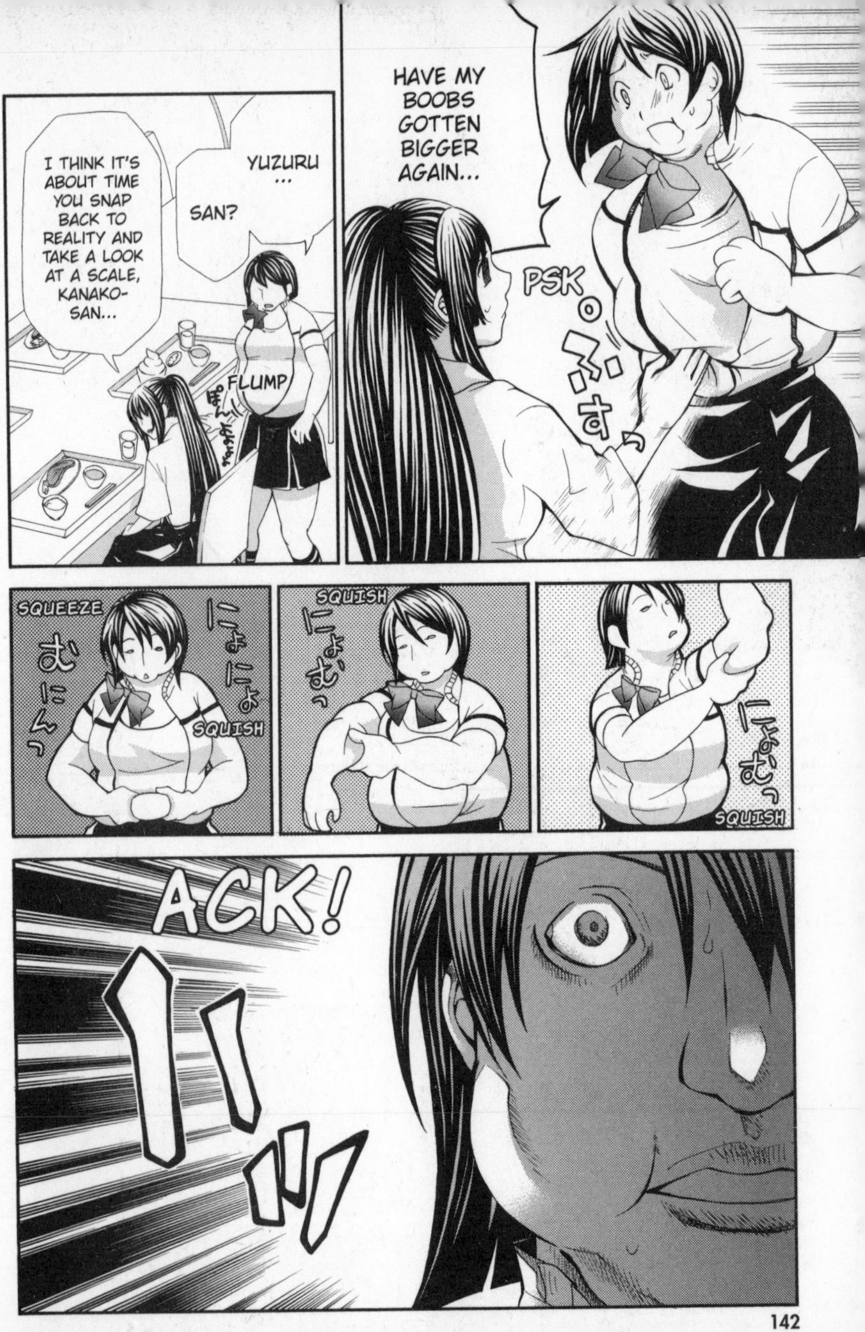
HAVE MY BOOBS GOTTEN BIGGER AGAIN...
PSK
ふすっ
YUZURU ...
SAN?
I THINK IT'S ABOUT TIME YOU SNAP BACK TO REALITY AND TAKE A LOOK AT A SCALE, KANAKO-SAN...
FLUMP
にょむっ
SQUISH
SQUISH
にょむっ
SQUEEZE
にょにょ
SQUISH
むにんっ
ACK!

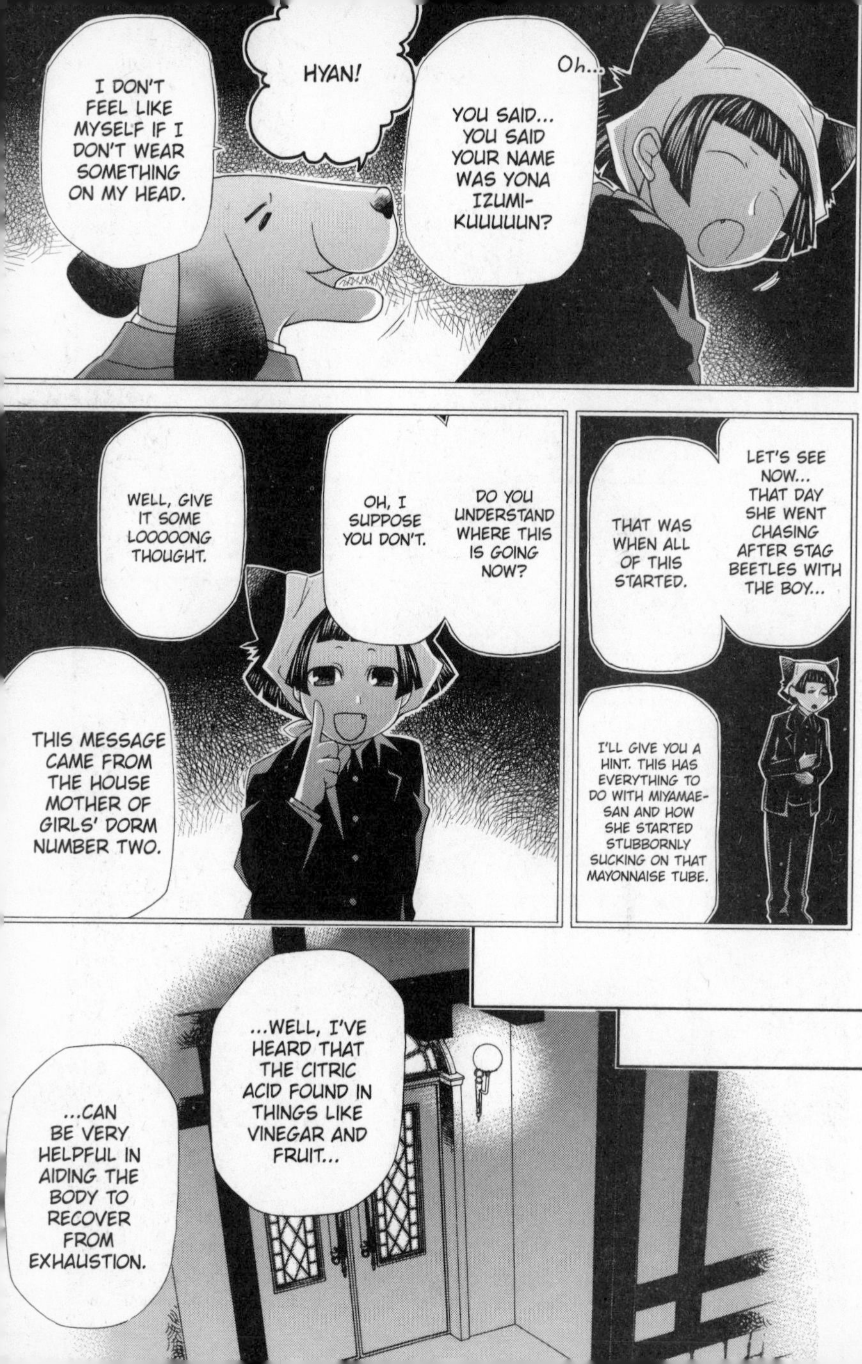
Oh...
YOU SAID... YOU SAID YOUR NAME WAS YONA IZUMI-KUUUUUN?
HYAN!
I DON'T FEEL LIKE MYSELF IF I DON'T WEAR SOMETHING ON MY HEAD.
LET'S SEE NOW... THAT DAY SHE WENT CHASING AFTER STAG BEETLES WITH THE BOY...
THAT WAS WHEN ALL OF THIS STARTED.
I'LL GIVE YOU A HINT. THIS HAS EVERYTHING TO DO WITH MIYAMAE-SAN AND HOW SHE STARTED STUBBORNLY SUCKING ON THAT MAYONNAISE TUBE.
DO YOU UNDERSTAND WHERE THIS IS GOING NOW?
OH, I SUPPOSE YOU DON'T.
WELL, GIVE IT SOME LOOOOONG THOUGHT.
THIS MESSAGE CAME FROM THE HOUSE MOTHER OF GIRLS' DORM NUMBER TWO.
...WELL, I'VE HEARD THAT THE CITRIC ACID FOUND IN THINGS LIKE VINEGAR AND FRUIT...
...CAN BE VERY HELPFUL IN AIDING THE BODY TO RECOVER FROM EXHAUSTION.

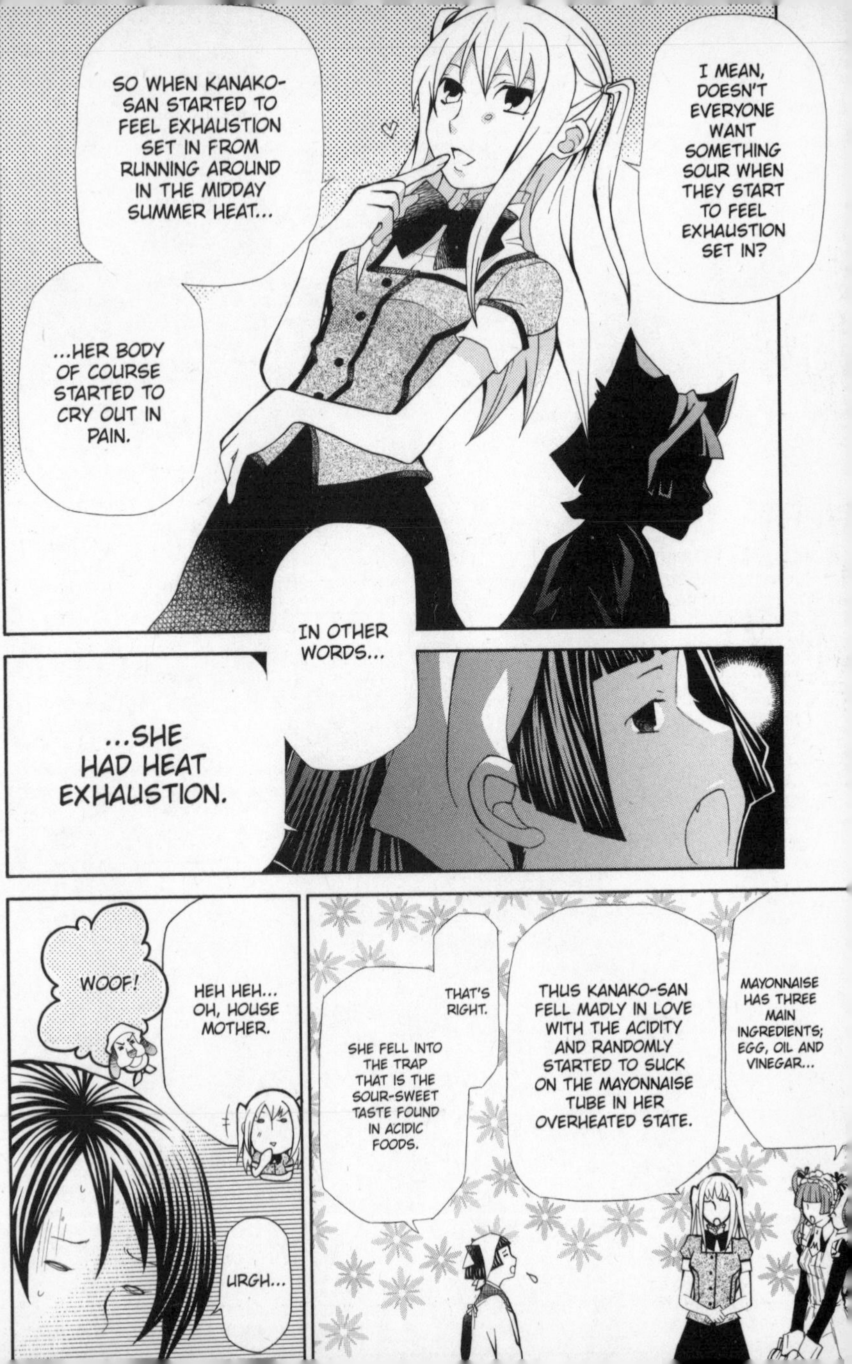
I MEAN, DOESN'T EVERYONE WANT SOMETHING SOUR WHEN THEY START TO FEEL EXHAUSTION SET IN?
SO WHEN KANAKO-SAN STARTED TO FEEL EXHAUSTION SET IN FROM RUNNING AROUND IN THE MIDDAY SUMMER HEAT...
...HER BODY OF COURSE STARTED TO CRY OUT IN PAIN.
IN OTHER WORDS...
...SHE HAD HEAT EXHAUSTION.
MAYONNAISE HAS THREE MAIN INGREDIENTS; EGG, OIL AND VINEGAR...
THUS KANAKO-SAN FELL MADLY IN LOVE WITH THE ACIDITY AND RANDOMLY STARTED TO SUCK ON THE MAYONNAISE TUBE IN HER OVERHEATED STATE.
THAT'S RIGHT.
SHE FELL INTO THE TRAP THAT IS THE SOUR-SWEET TASTE FOUND IN ACIDIC FOODS.
HEH HEH... OH, HOUSE MOTHER.
WOOF!
URGH...

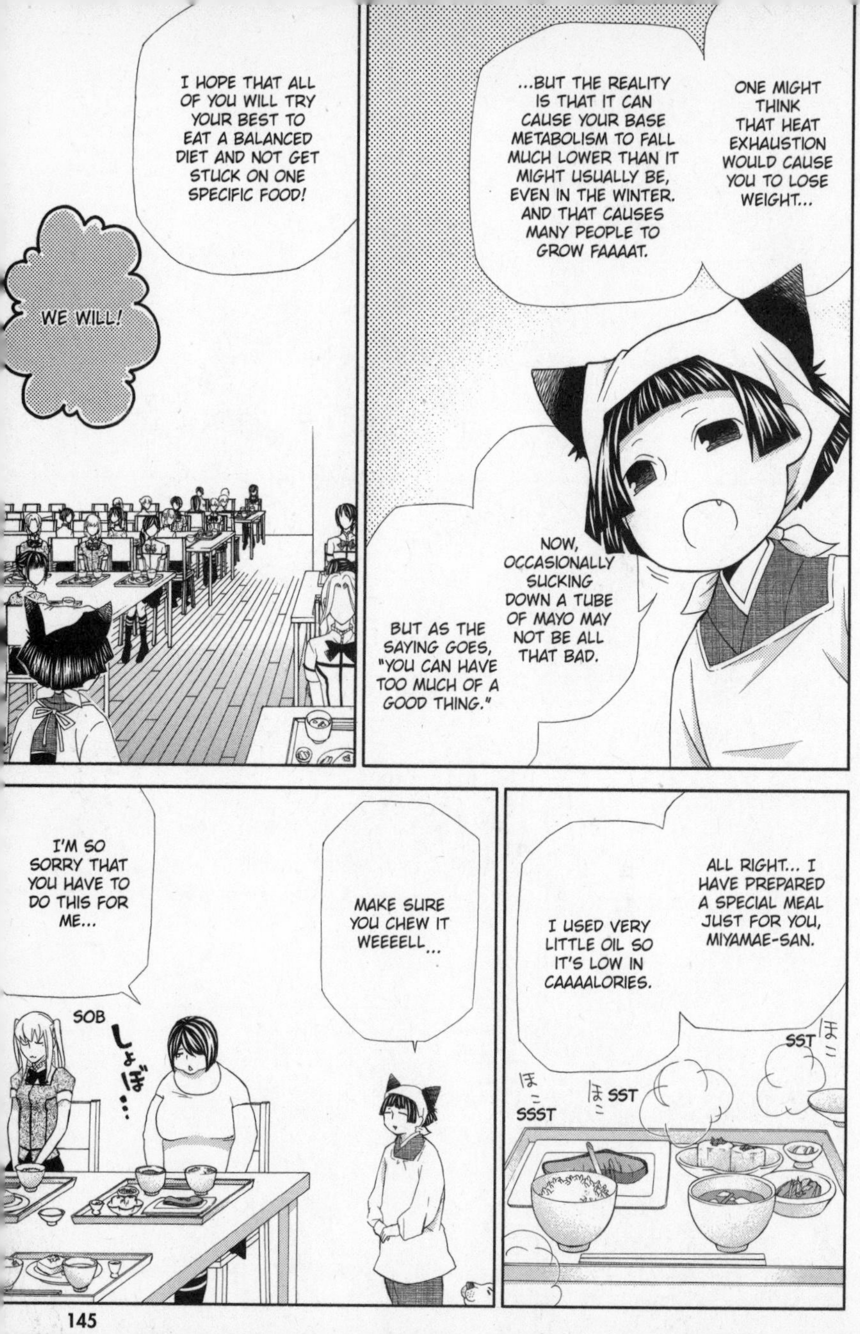
ONE MIGHT THINK THAT HEAT EXHAUSTION WOULD CAUSE YOU TO LOSE WEIGHT...
...BUT THE REALITY IS THAT IT CAN CAUSE YOUR BASE METABOLISM TO FALL MUCH LOWER THAN IT MIGHT USUALLY BE, EVEN IN THE WINTER. AND THAT CAUSES MANY PEOPLE TO GROW FAAAAT.
NOW, OCCASIONALLY SUCKING DOWN A TUBE OF MAYO MAY NOT BE ALL THAT BAD.
BUT AS THE SAYING GOES, "YOU CAN HAVE TOO MUCH OF A GOOD THING."
I HOPE THAT ALL OF YOU WILL TRY YOUR BEST TO EAT A BALANCED DIET AND NOT GET STUCK ON ONE SPECIFIC FOOD!
WE WILL!
ALL RIGHT... I HAVE PREPARED A SPECIAL MEAL JUST FOR YOU, MIYAMAE-SAN.
I USED VERY LITTLE OIL SO IT'S LOW IN CAAAALORIES.
SST ほこ
ほこ SST
ほこ SSST
MAKE SURE YOU CHEW IT WEEEELL...
I'M SO SORRY THAT YOU HAVE TO DO THIS FOR ME...
SOB
しょぼ...

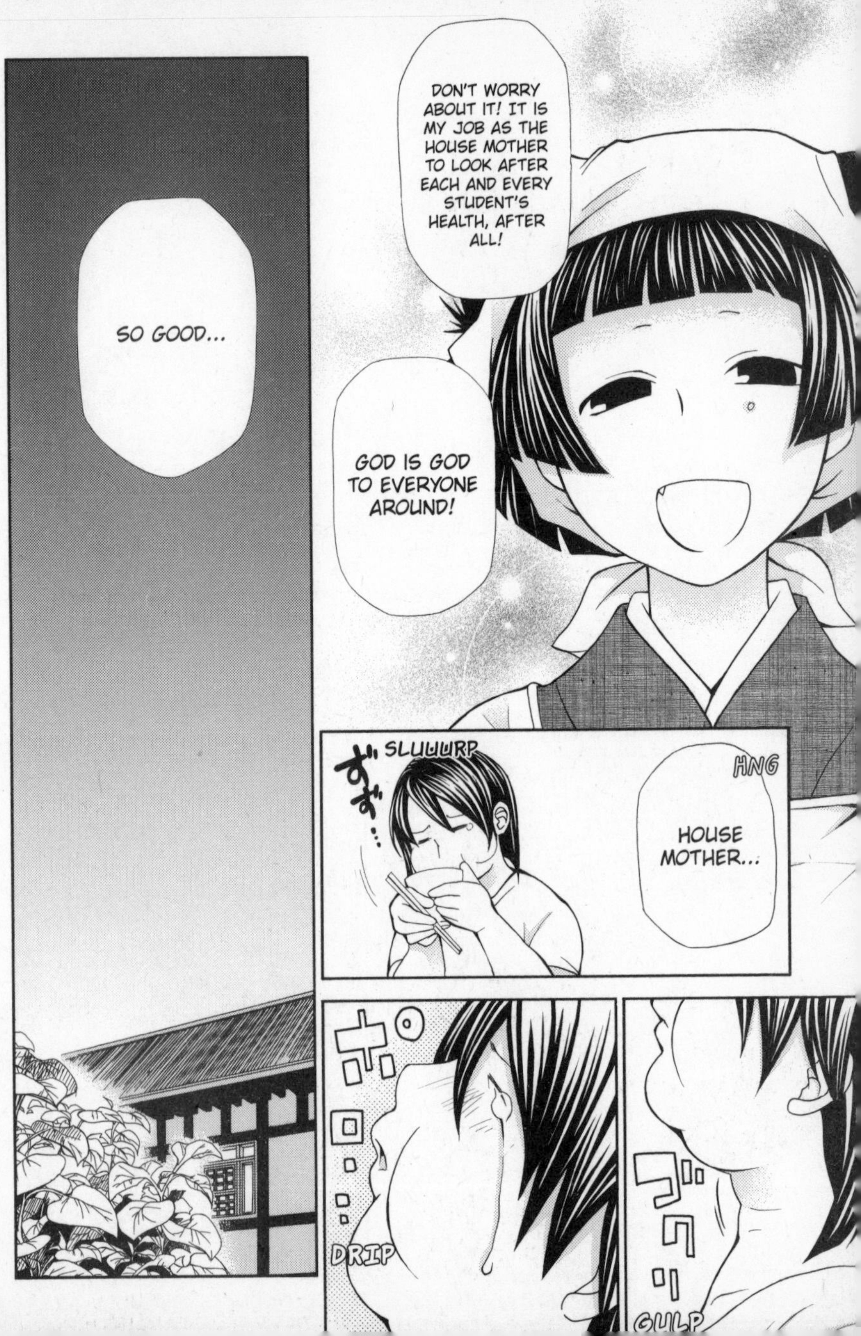
DON'T WORRY ABOUT IT! IT IS MY JOB AS THE HOUSE MOTHER TO LOOK AFTER EACH AND EVERY STUDENT'S HEALTH, AFTER ALL!
GOD IS GOD TO EVERYONE AROUND!
HNG
HOUSE MOTHER...
SLUUURP
ずず…
ゴクッ
GULP
ポロ…
DRIP
SO GOOD...

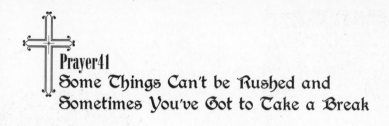

Prayer41
Some Things Can't be Rushed and Sometimes You've Got to Take a Break

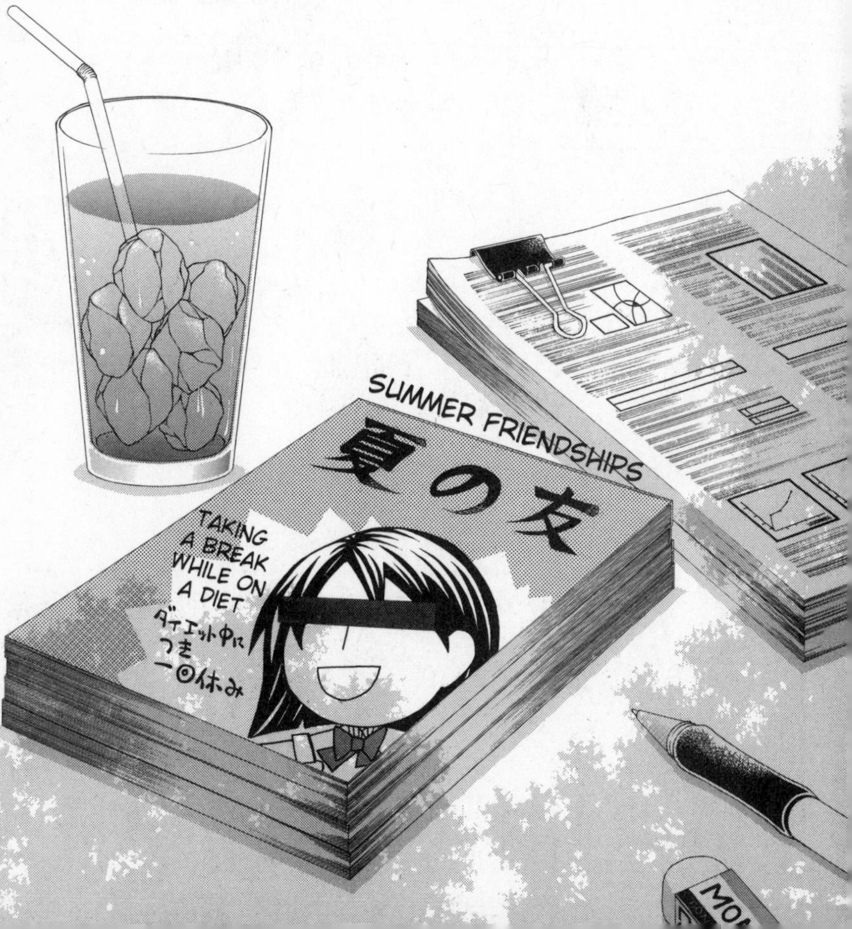
SUMMER FRIENDSHIPS
夏の友
TAKING A BREAK WHILE ON A DIET
ダイエット中につき一回休み

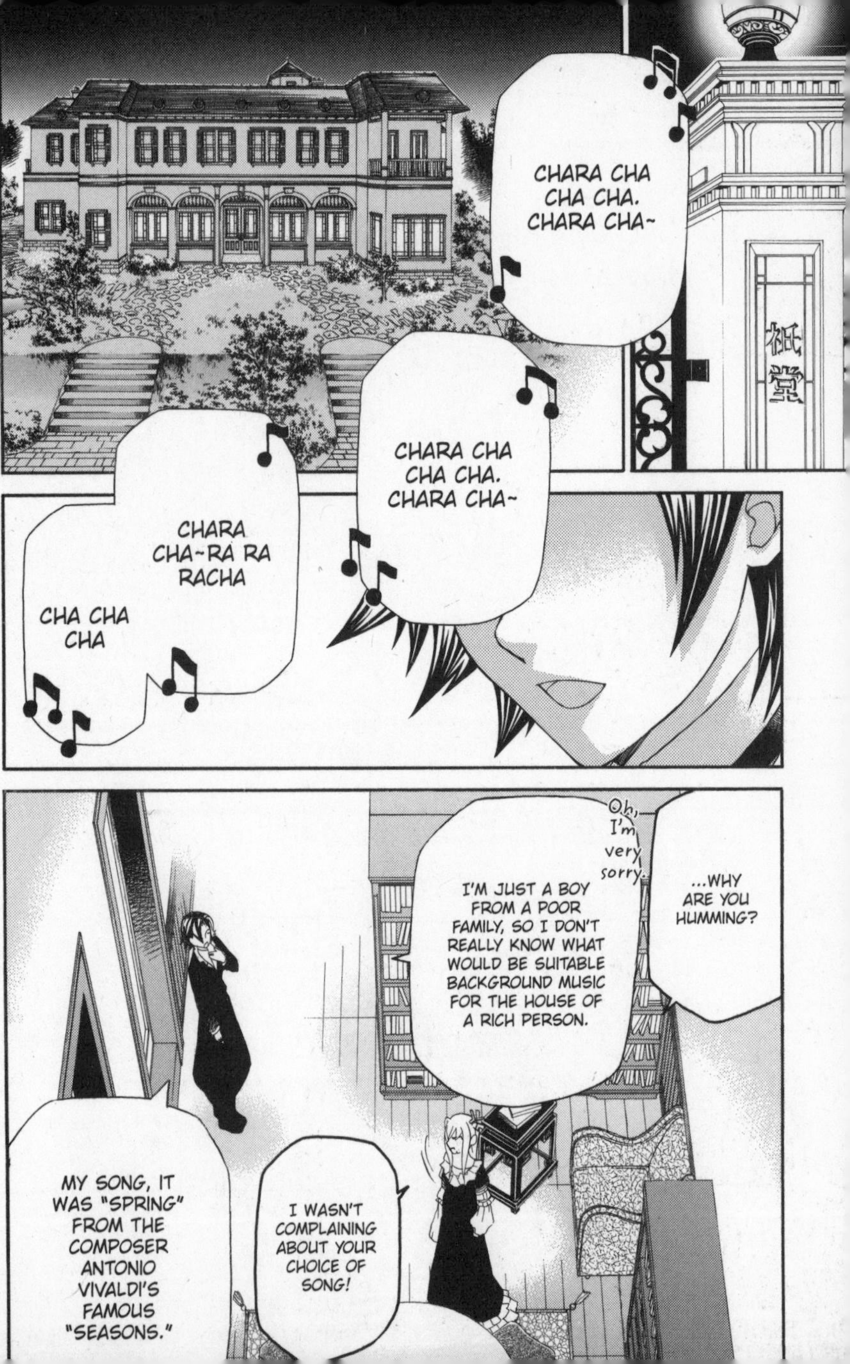
CHARA CHA CHA CHA. CHARA CHA~
CHARA CHA CHA CHA. CHARA CHA~
CHARA CHA~RA RA RACHA
CHA CHA CHA
...WHY ARE YOU HUMMING?
Oh, I'm very sorry.
I'M JUST A BOY FROM A POOR FAMILY, SO I DON'T REALLY KNOW WHAT WOULD BE SUITABLE BACKGROUND MUSIC FOR THE HOUSE OF A RICH PERSON.
I WASN'T COMPLAINING ABOUT YOUR CHOICE OF SONG!
MY SONG, IT WAS "SPRING" FROM THE COMPOSER ANTONIO VIVALDI'S FAMOUS "SEASONS."

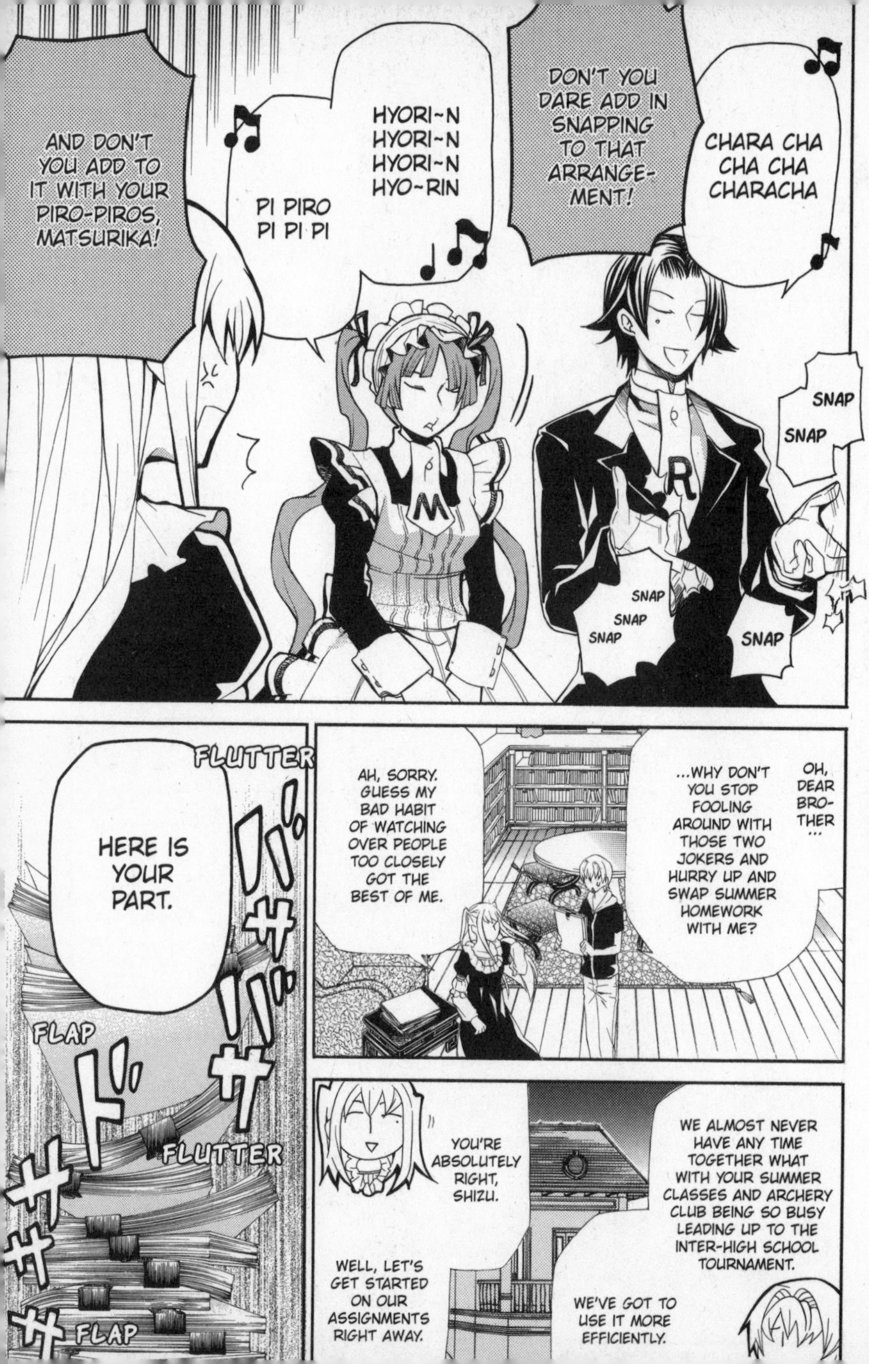
CHARA CHA CHA CHA CHARACHA
DON'T YOU DARE ADD IN SNAPPING TO THAT ARRANGE-MENT!
SNAP
SNAP
HYORI~N HYORI~N HYORI~N HYO~RIN
PI PIRO PI PI PI
AND DON'T YOU ADD TO IT WITH YOUR PIRO-PIROS, MATSURIKA!
SNAP
SNAP
SNAP
SNAP
OH, DEAR BROTHER...
...WHY DON'T YOU STOP FOOLING AROUND WITH THOSE TWO JOKERS AND HURRY UP AND SWAP SUMMER HOMEWORK WITH ME?
AH, SORRY. GUESS MY BAD HABIT OF WATCHING OVER PEOPLE TOO CLOSELY GOT THE BEST OF ME.
WE ALMOST NEVER HAVE ANY TIME TOGETHER WHAT WITH YOUR SUMMER CLASSES AND ARCHERY CLUB BEING SO BUSY LEADING UP TO THE INTER-HIGH SCHOOL TOURNAMENT.
WE'VE GOT TO USE IT MORE EFFICIENTLY.
YOU'RE ABSOLUTELY RIGHT, SHIZU.
WELL, LET'S GET STARTED ON OUR ASSIGNMENTS RIGHT AWAY.
FLUTTER
HERE IS YOUR PART.
FLAP
FLUTTER
FLAP

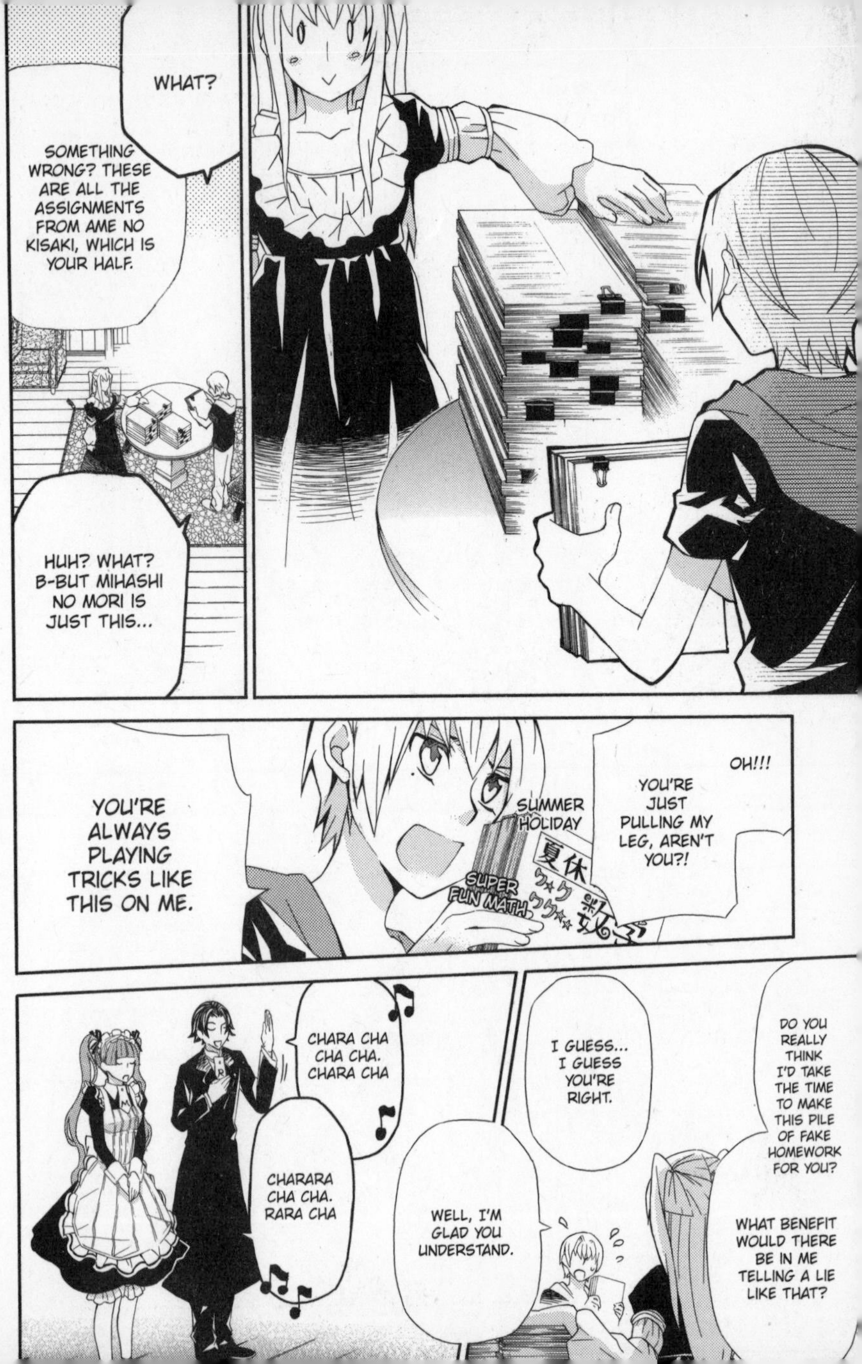
WHAT?
SOMETHING WRONG? THESE ARE ALL THE ASSIGNMENTS FROM AME NO KISAKI, WHICH IS YOUR HALF.
HUH? WHAT? B-BUT MIHASHI NO MORI IS JUST THIS...
OH!!!
YOU'RE JUST PULLING MY LEG, AREN'T YOU?!
SUMMER HOLIDAY
夏休
SUPER FUN MATH
YOU'RE ALWAYS PLAYING TRICKS LIKE THIS ON ME.
DO YOU REALLY THINK I'D TAKE THE TIME TO MAKE THIS PILE OF FAKE HOMEWORK FOR YOU?
WHAT BENEFIT WOULD THERE BE IN ME TELLING A LIE LIKE THAT?
I GUESS... I GUESS YOU'RE RIGHT.
WELL, I'M GLAD YOU UNDERSTAND.
CHARA CHA CHA CHA. CHARA CHA
CHARARA CHA CHA. RARA CHA

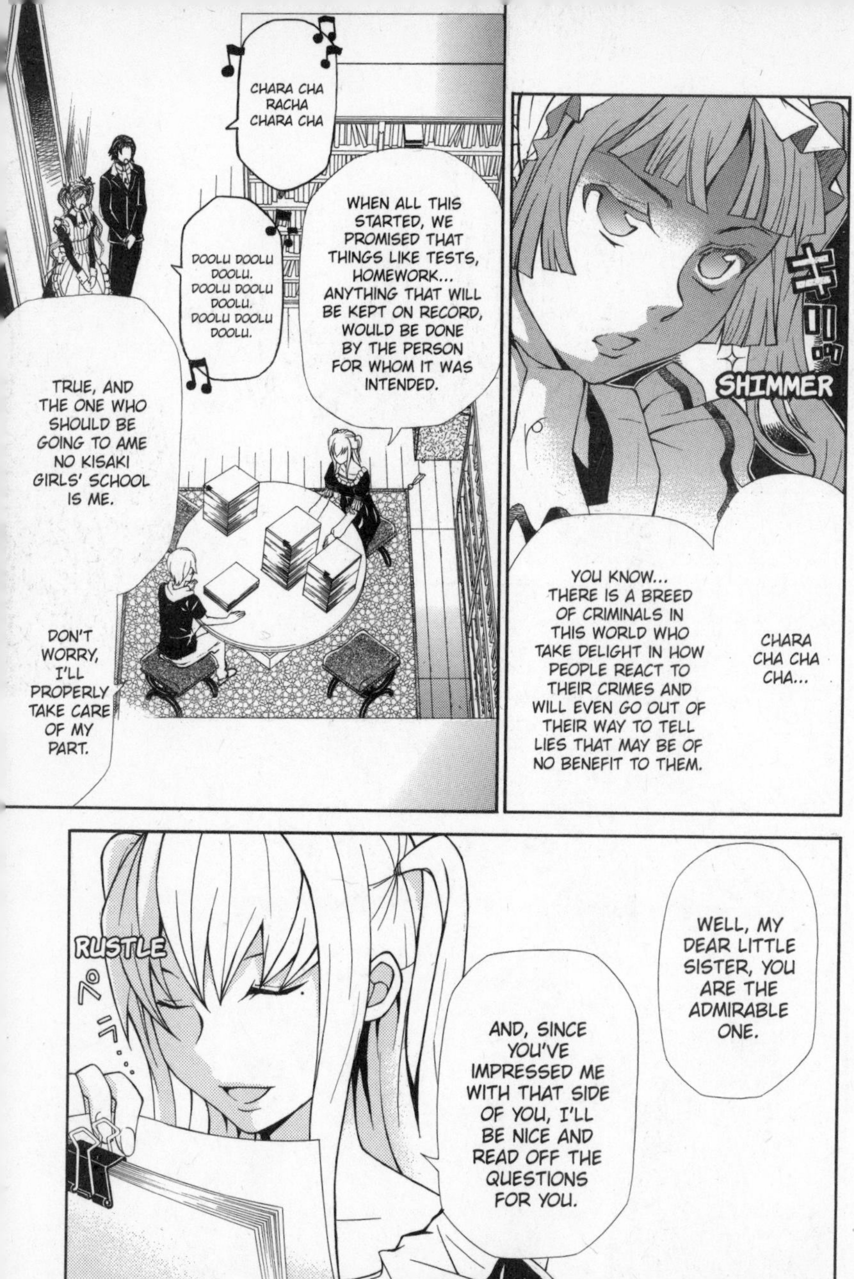

SHIMMER
YOU KNOW... THERE IS A BREED OF CRIMINALS IN THIS WORLD WHO TAKE DELIGHT IN HOW PEOPLE REACT TO THEIR CRIMES AND WILL EVEN GO OUT OF THEIR WAY TO TELL LIES THAT MAY BE OF NO BENEFIT TO THEM.
CHARA CHA CHA CHA...
CHARA CHA RACHA CHARA CHA
WHEN ALL THIS STARTED, WE PROMISED THAT THINGS LIKE TESTS, HOMEWORK... ANYTHING THAT WILL BE KEPT ON RECORD, WOULD BE DONE BY THE PERSON FOR WHOM IT WAS INTENDED.
DOOLU DOOLU DOOLU. DOOLU DOOLU DOOLU. DOOLU DOOLU DOOLU.
TRUE, AND THE ONE WHO SHOULD BE GOING TO AME NO KISAKI GIRLS' SCHOOL IS ME.
DON'T WORRY, I'LL PROPERLY TAKE CARE OF MY PART.
WELL, MY DEAR LITTLE SISTER, YOU ARE THE ADMIRABLE ONE.
AND, SINCE YOU'VE IMPRESSED ME WITH THAT SIDE OF YOU, I'LL BE NICE AND READ OFF THE QUESTIONS FOR YOU.
RUSTLE

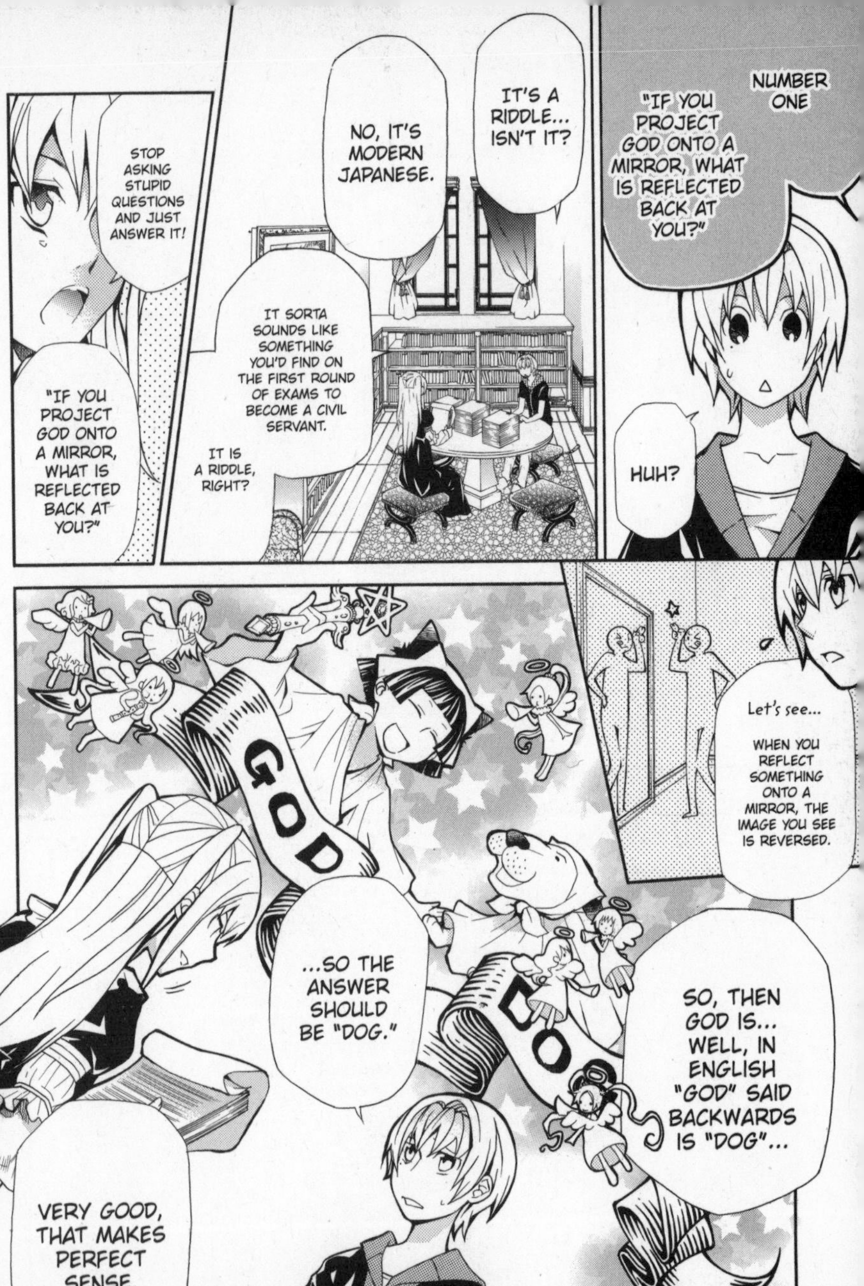
NUMBER ONE
"IF YOU PROJECT GOD ONTO A MIRROR, WHAT IS REFLECTED BACK AT YOU?"
HUH?
IT'S A RIDDLE... ISN'T IT?
NO, IT'S MODERN JAPANESE.
IT SORTA SOUNDS LIKE SOMETHING YOU'D FIND ON THE FIRST ROUND OF EXAMS TO BECOME A CIVIL SERVANT.
IT IS A RIDDLE, RIGHT?
STOP ASKING STUPID QUESTIONS AND JUST ANSWER IT!
"IF YOU PROJECT GOD ONTO A MIRROR, WHAT IS REFLECTED BACK AT YOU?"
Let's see...
WHEN YOU REFLECT SOMETHING ONTO A MIRROR, THE IMAGE YOU SEE IS REVERSED.
SO, THEN GOD IS... WELL, IN ENGLISH "GOD" SAID BACKWARDS IS "DOG"...
GOD
DOG
...SO THE ANSWER SHOULD BE "DOG."
VERY GOOD, THAT MAKES PERFECT SENSE.

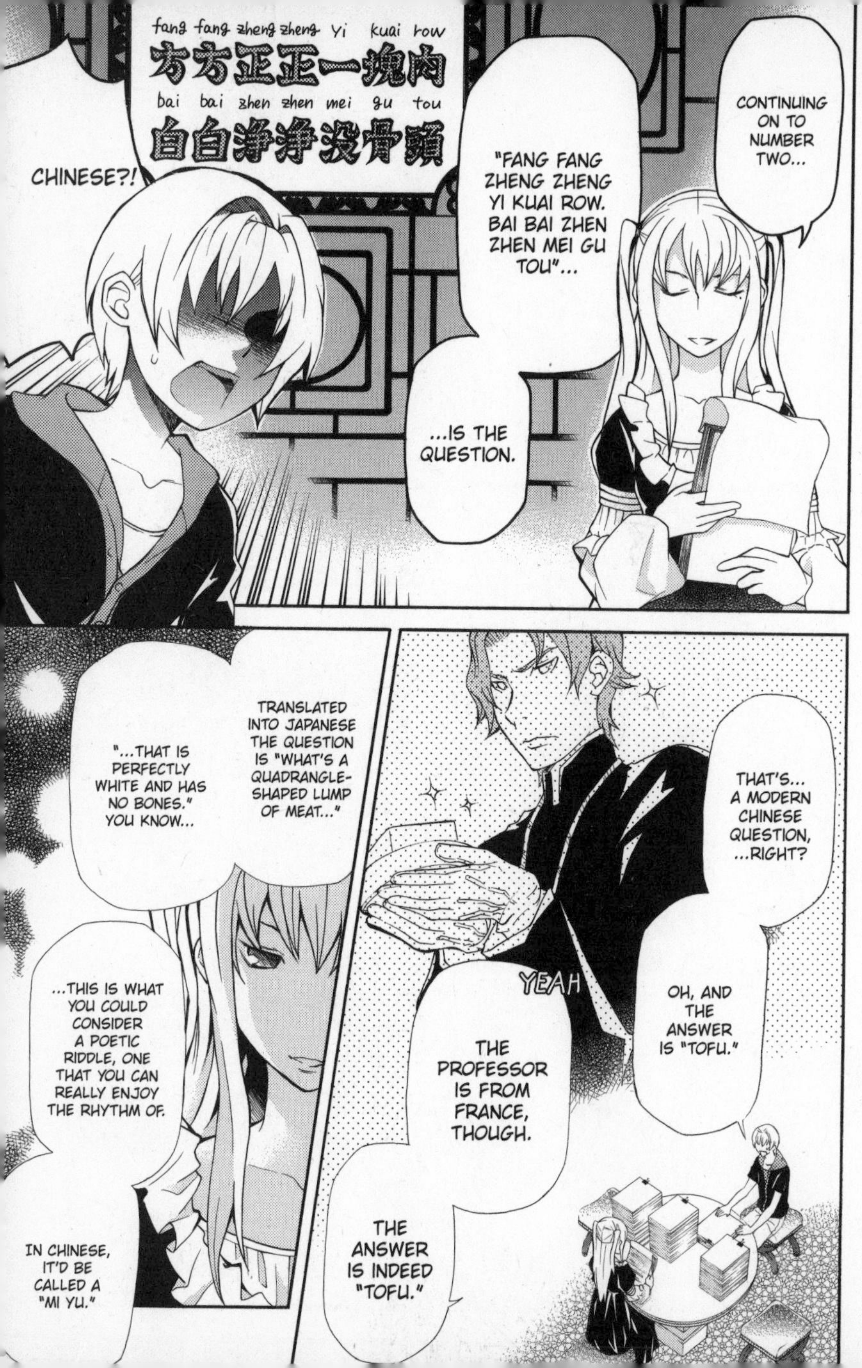
CONTINUING ON TO NUMBER TWO...
"FANG FANG ZHENG ZHENG YI KUAI ROW. BAI BAI ZHEN ZHEN MEI GU TOU"...
...IS THE QUESTION.
fang fang zheng zheng yi kuai row
方方正正一塊肉
bai bai zhen zhen mei gu tou
白白浄浄没骨頭
CHINESE?!
THAT'S... A MODERN CHINESE QUESTION, ...RIGHT?
TRANSLATED INTO JAPANESE THE QUESTION IS "WHAT'S A QUADRANGLE-SHAPED LUMP OF MEAT..."
"...THAT IS PERFECTLY WHITE AND HAS NO BONES." YOU KNOW...
...THIS IS WHAT YOU COULD CONSIDER A POETIC RIDDLE, ONE THAT YOU CAN REALLY ENJOY THE RHYTHM OF.
IN CHINESE, IT'D BE CALLED A "MI YU."
OH, AND THE ANSWER IS "TOFU."
YEAH
THE PROFESSOR IS FROM FRANCE, THOUGH.
THE ANSWER IS INDEED "TOFU."

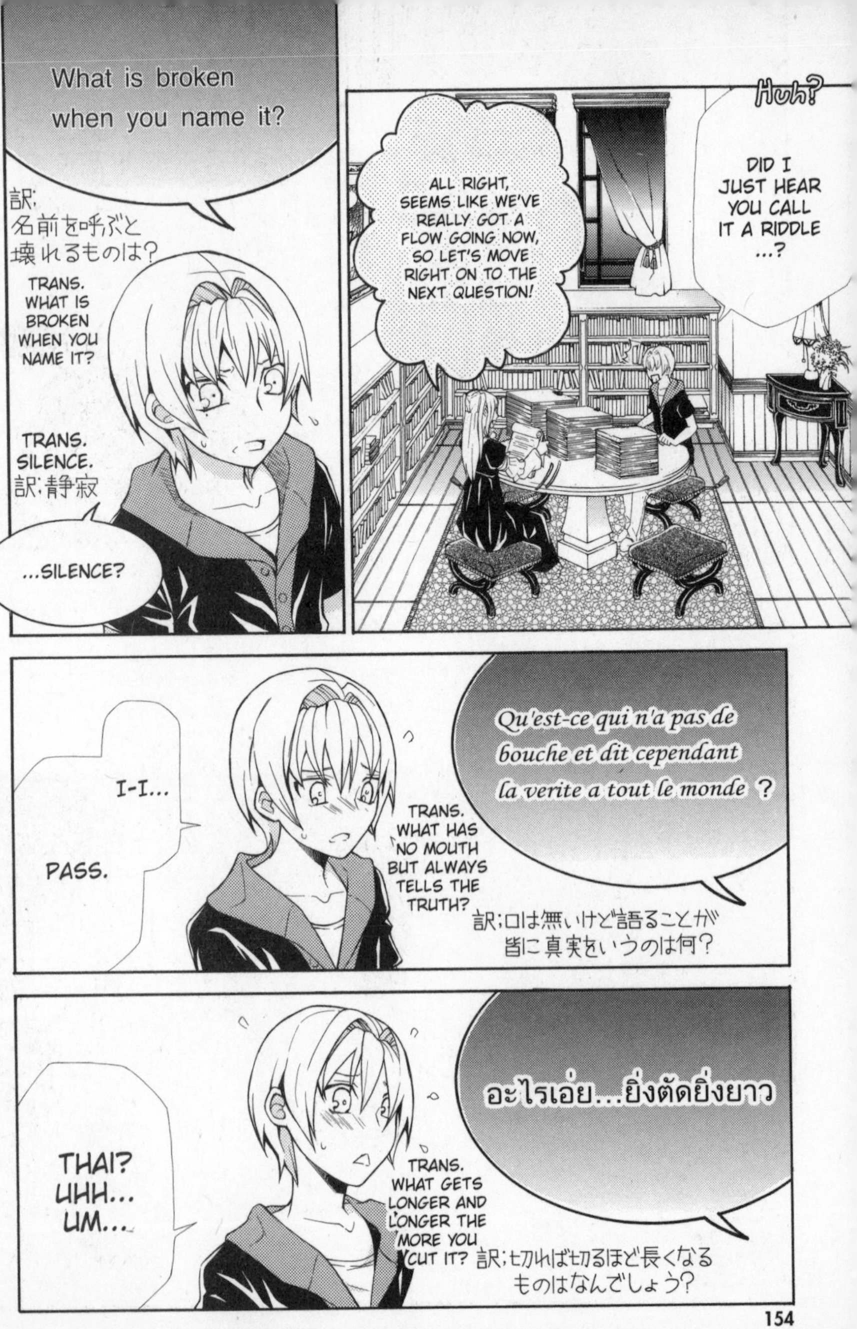
Huh?
DID I JUST HEAR YOU CALL IT A RIDDLE ...?
ALL RIGHT, SEEMS LIKE WE'VE REALLY GOT A FLOW GOING NOW, SO LET'S MOVE RIGHT ON TO THE NEXT QUESTION!
What is broken when you name it?
訳;名前を呼ぶと壊れるものは?
TRANS. WHAT IS BROKEN WHEN YOU NAME IT?
TRANS. SILENCE.
訳;静寂
...SILENCE?
Qu'est-ce qui n'a pas de bouche et dit cependant la verite a tout le monde ?
TRANS. WHAT HAS NO MOUTH BUT ALWAYS TELLS THE TRUTH?
訳;口は無いけど語ることが皆に真実をいうのは何?
I-I...
PASS.
อะไรเอ่ย...ยิ่งตัดยิ่งยาว
TRANS. WHAT GETS LONGER AND LONGER THE MORE YOU CUT IT?
訳;切れば切るほど長くなるものはなんでしょう?
THAI? UHH... UM...

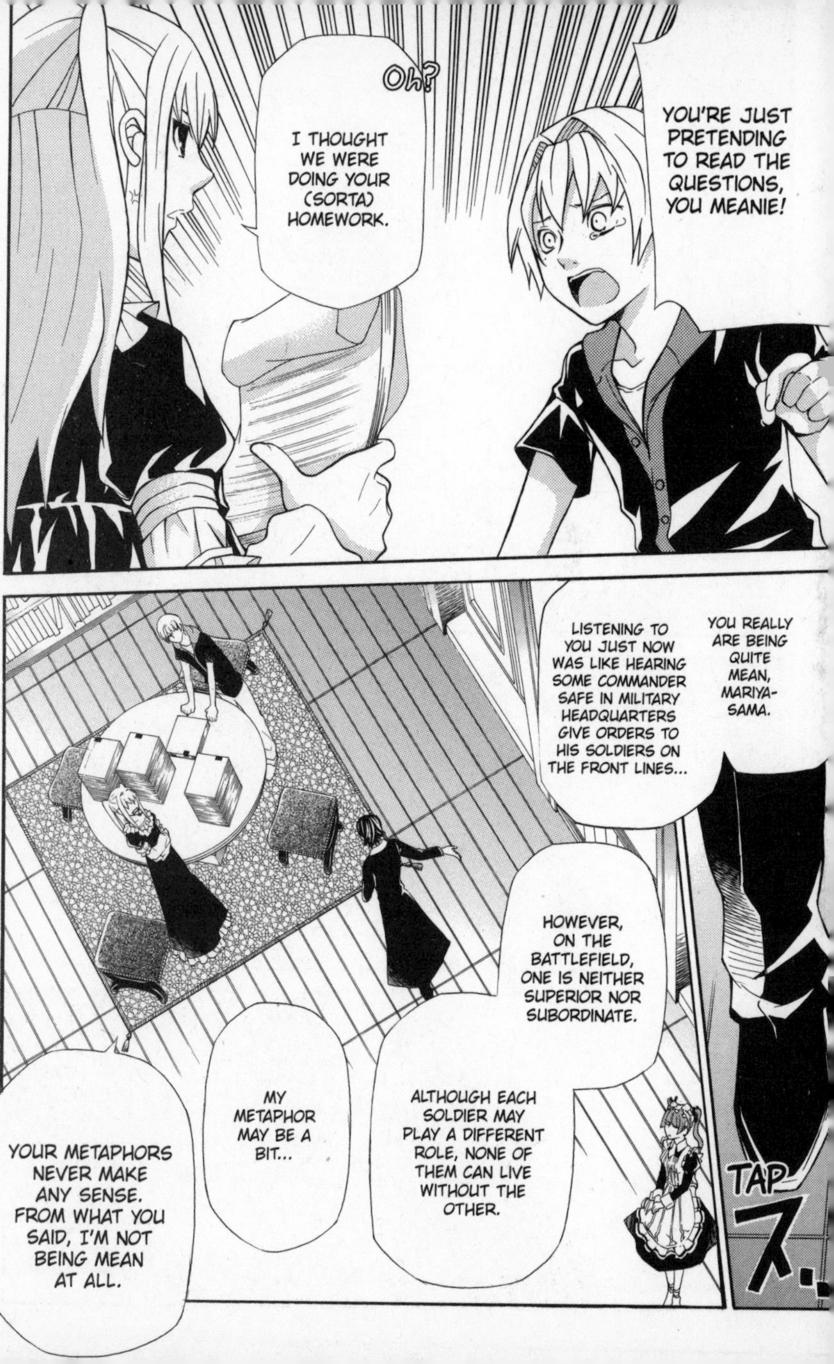
YOU'RE JUST PRETENDING TO READ THE QUESTIONS, YOU MEANIE!
Oh?
I THOUGHT WE WERE DOING YOUR (SORTA) HOMEWORK.
YOU REALLY ARE BEING QUITE MEAN, MARIYA-SAMA.
LISTENING TO YOU JUST NOW WAS LIKE HEARING SOME COMMANDER SAFE IN MILITARY HEADQUARTERS GIVE ORDERS TO HIS SOLDIERS ON THE FRONT LINES...
HOWEVER, ON THE BATTLEFIELD, ONE IS NEITHER SUPERIOR NOR SUBORDINATE.
TAP
ALTHOUGH EACH SOLDIER MAY PLAY A DIFFERENT ROLE, NONE OF THEM CAN LIVE WITHOUT THE OTHER.
MY METAPHOR MAY BE A BIT...
YOUR METAPHORS NEVER MAKE ANY SENSE. FROM WHAT YOU SAID, I'M NOT BEING MEAN AT ALL.

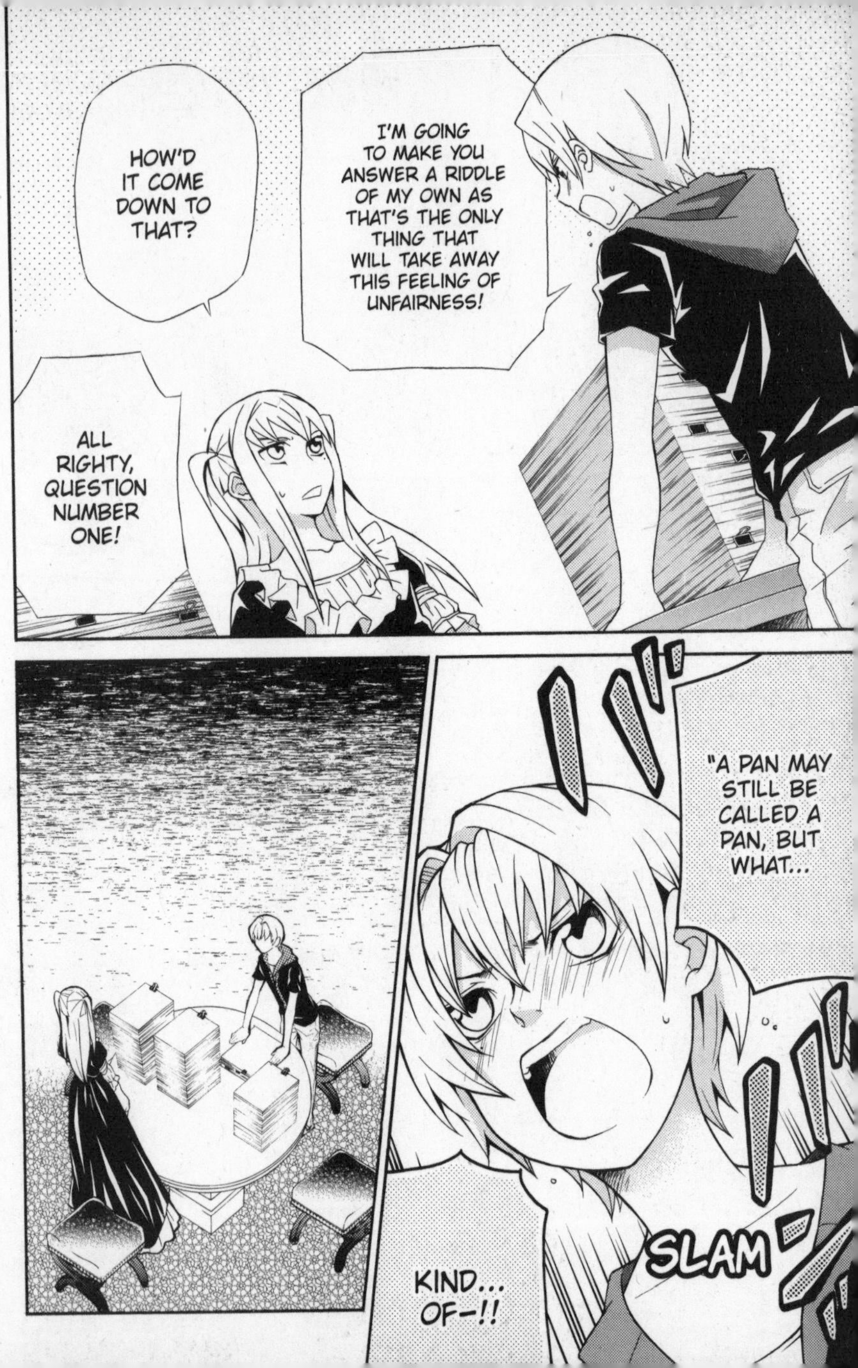
I'M GOING TO MAKE YOU ANSWER A RIDDLE OF MY OWN AS THAT'S THE ONLY THING THAT WILL TAKE AWAY THIS FEELING OF UNFAIRNESS!
HOW'D IT COME DOWN TO THAT?
ALL RIGHTY, QUESTION NUMBER ONE!
"A PAN MAY STILL BE CALLED A PAN, BUT WHAT...
SLAM
KIND... OF-!!

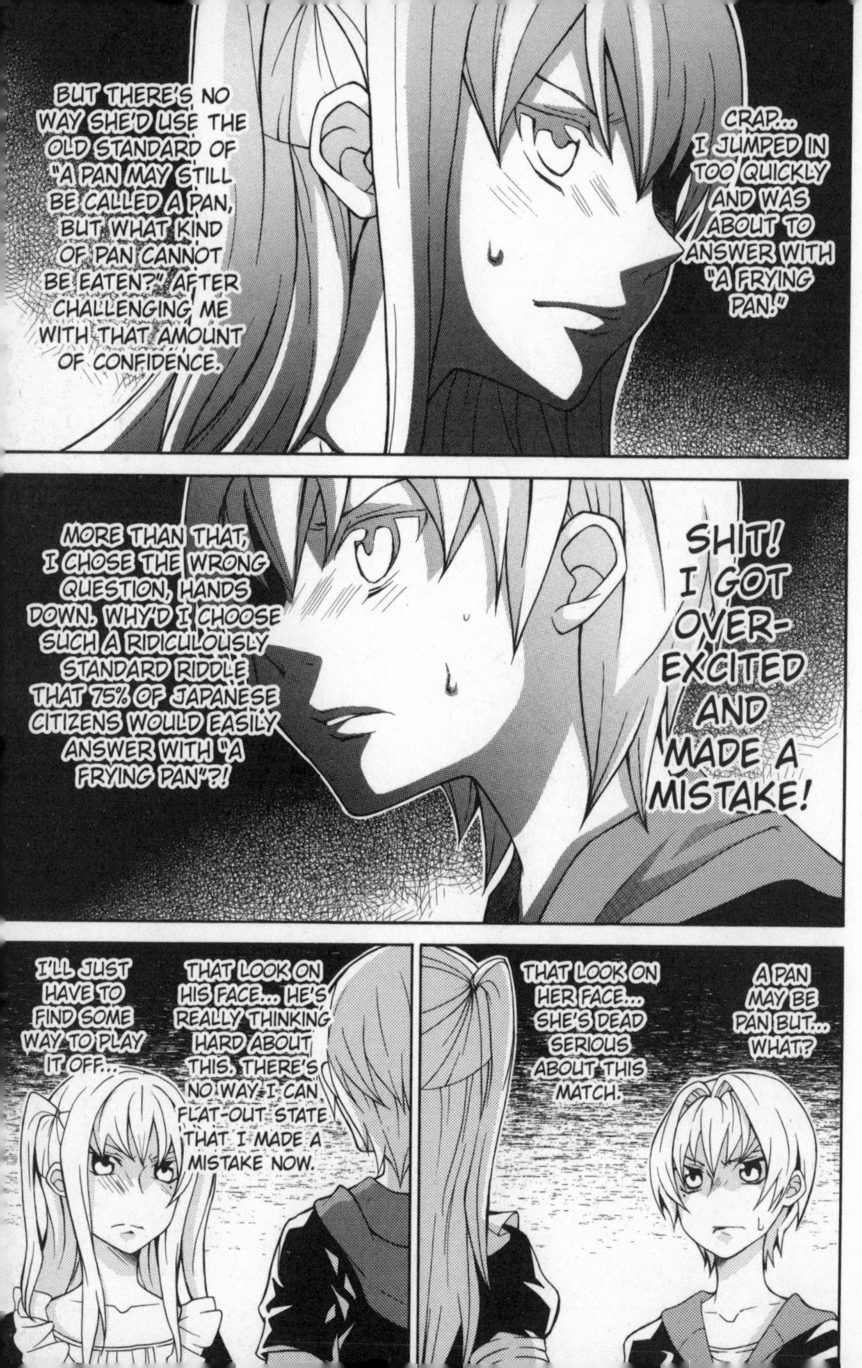
CRAP... I JUMPED IN TOO QUICKLY AND WAS ABOUT TO ANSWER WITH "A FRYING PAN."
BUT THERE'S NO WAY SHE'D USE THE OLD STANDARD OF "A PAN MAY STILL BE CALLED A PAN, BUT WHAT KIND OF PAN CANNOT BE EATEN?" AFTER CHALLENGING ME WITH THAT AMOUNT OF CONFIDENCE.
SHIT! I GOT OVER-EXCITED AND MADE A MISTAKE!
MORE THAN THAT, I CHOSE THE WRONG QUESTION, HANDS DOWN. WHY'D I CHOOSE SUCH A RIDICULOUSLY STANDARD RIDDLE THAT 75% OF JAPANESE CITIZENS WOULD EASILY ANSWER WITH "A FRYING PAN"?!
A PAN MAY BE PAN BUT... WHAT?
THAT LOOK ON HER FACE... SHE'S DEAD SERIOUS ABOUT THIS MATCH.
THAT LOOK ON HIS FACE... HE'S REALLY THINKING HARD ABOUT THIS. THERE'S NO WAY I CAN FLAT-OUT STATE THAT I MADE A MISTAKE NOW.
I'LL JUST HAVE TO FIND SOME WAY TO PLAY IT OFF...

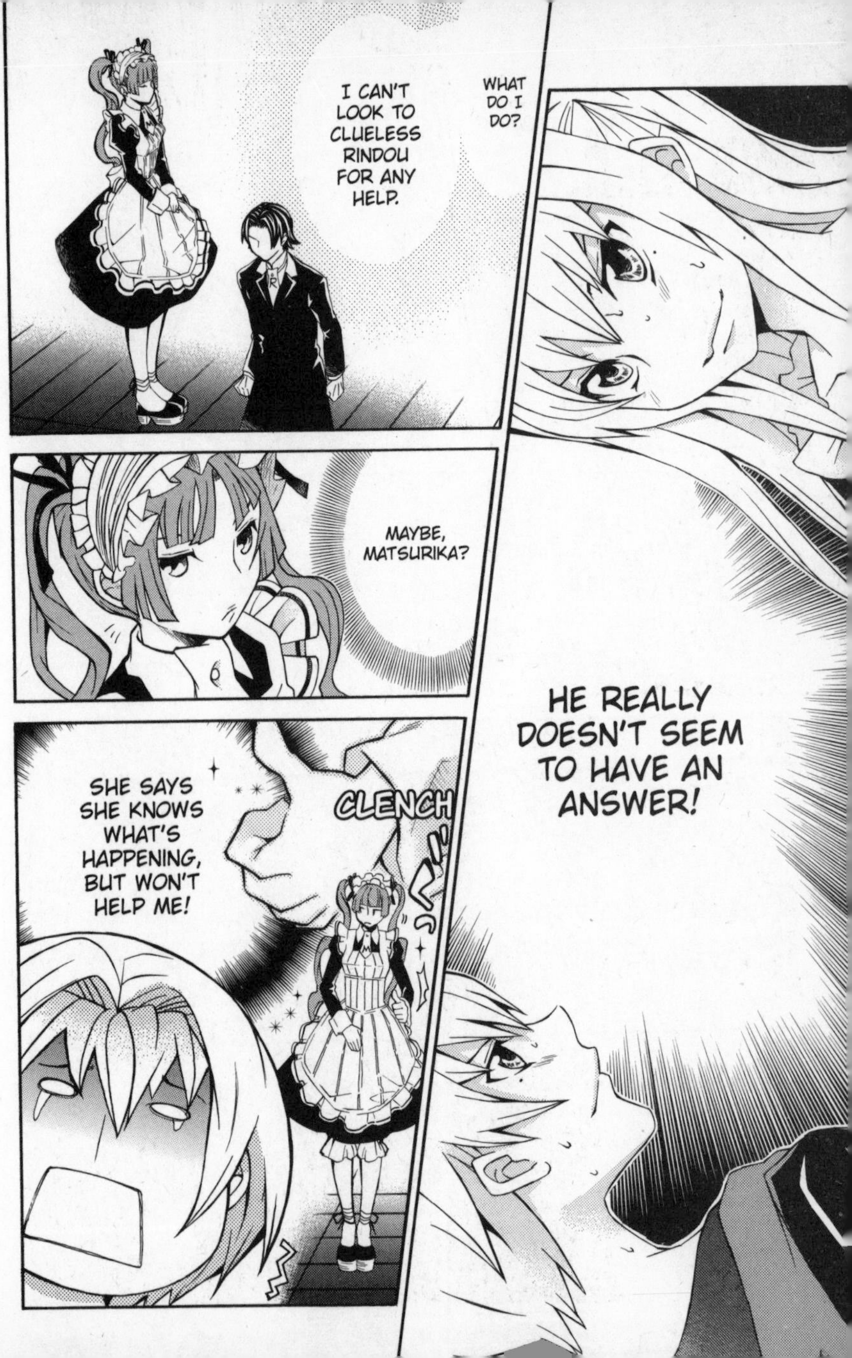
WHAT DO I DO?
I CAN'T LOOK TO CLUELESS RINDOU FOR ANY HELP.
HE REALLY DOESN'T SEEM TO HAVE AN ANSWER!
MAYBE, MATSURIKA?
CLENCH
SHE SAYS SHE KNOWS WHAT'S HAPPENING, BUT WON'T HELP ME!

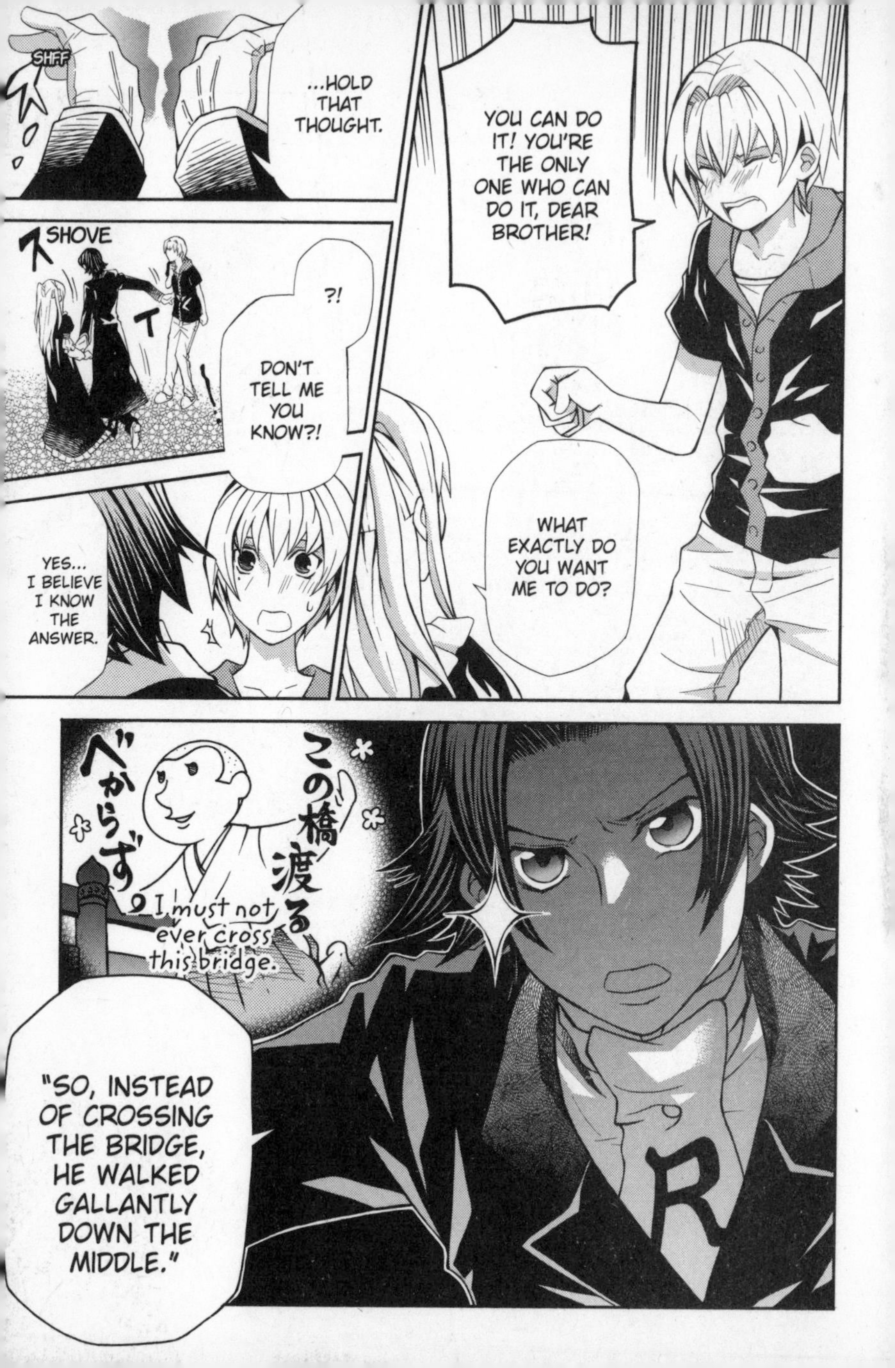

YOU CAN DO IT! YOU'RE THE ONLY ONE WHO CAN DO IT, DEAR BROTHER!
WHAT EXACTLY DO YOU WANT ME TO DO?
SHFF
...HOLD THAT THOUGHT.
SHOVE
?!
DON'T TELL ME YOU KNOW?!
YES... I BELIEVE I KNOW THE ANSWER.
この橋渡るべからず
I must not ever cross this bridge.
"SO, INSTEAD OF CROSSING THE BRIDGE, HE WALKED GALLANTLY DOWN THE MIDDLE."

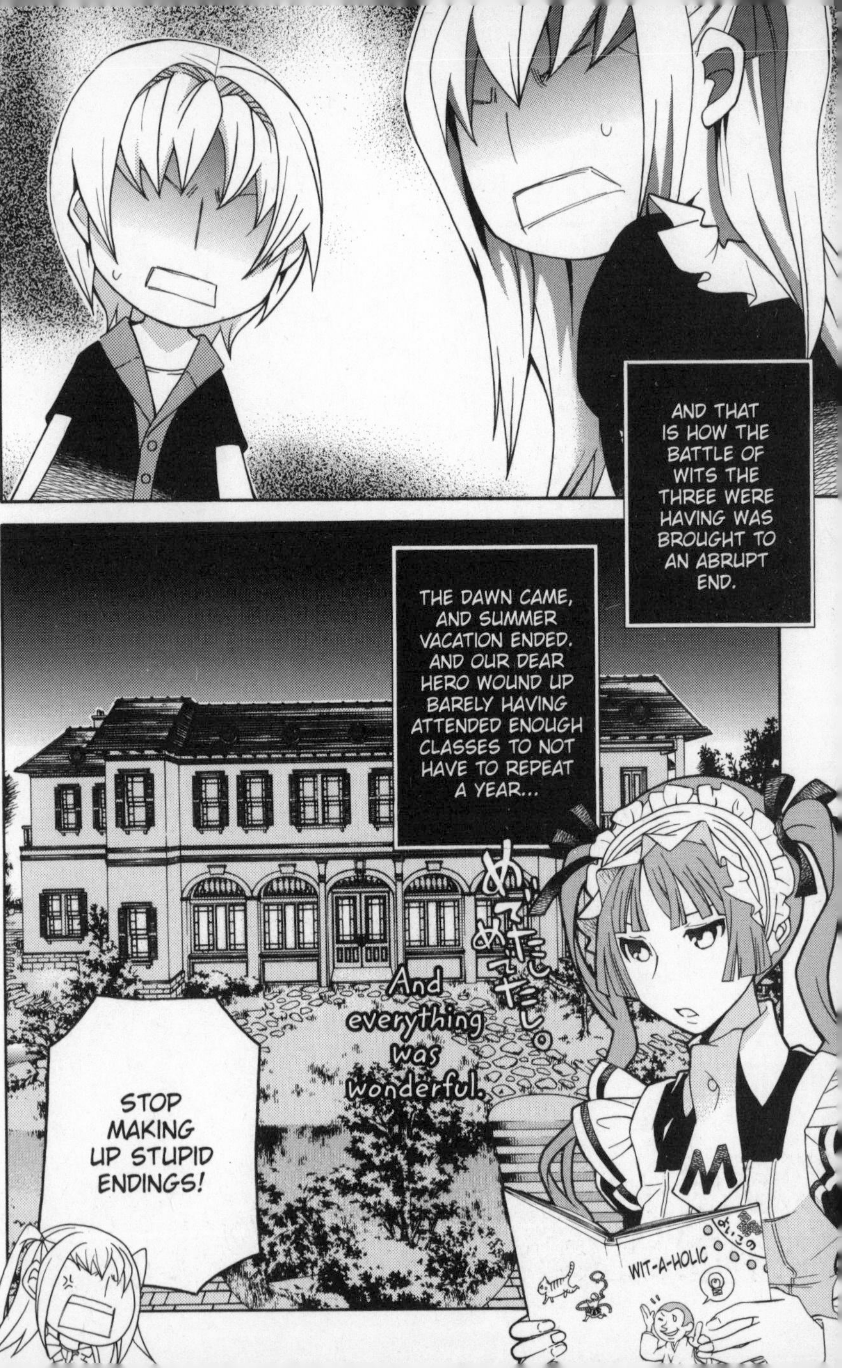
AND THAT IS HOW THE BATTLE OF WITS THE THREE WERE HAVING WAS BROUGHT TO AN ABRUPT END.
THE DAWN CAME, AND SUMMER VACATION ENDED. AND OUR DEAR HERO WOUND UP BARELY HAVING ATTENDED ENOUGH CLASSES TO NOT HAVE TO REPEAT A YEAR...
めでたしめでたし。
And everything was wonderful.
STOP MAKING UP STUPID ENDINGS!
WIT-A-HOLIC

M A R I A H O L I C

MARIA HOLIC

Maria Holic Volume 7

© Minari Endou 2012
First published by KADOKAWA CORPORATION in 2012 in Japan.
English translation rights arranged by One Peace Books
under the license from KADOKAWA CORPORATION,Japan.

ISBN 978-1-944937-01-0

Written and illustrated by Minari Endou
English Edition Published by One Peace Books 2016

Printed in Canada

1 2 3 4 5 6 7 8 9 10

One Peace Books
43-32 22nd Street STE 204 Long Island City New York 11101
www.onepeacebooks.com